F·E·M·I·N·I·Z·I·N·G T·H·E F·E·T·I·S·H

Feminizing the Fetish

Psychoanalysis and Narrative Obsession in Turn-of-the-Century France

EMILY APTER

Cornell University Press

ITHACA AND LONDON

Open access edition funded by the National Endowment for the Humanities/ Andrew W. Mellon Foundation Humanities Open Book Program.

Copyright © 1991 by Cornell University

All rights reserved. Except for brief quotations in a review, this book, or parts thereof, must not be reproduced in any form without permission in writing from the publisher. For information, address Cornell University Press, Sage House, 512 East State Street, Ithaca, New York 14850, or visit our website at cornellpress.cornell.edu.

First published 1991 by Cornell University Press

Library of Congress Cataloging-in-Publication Data
Apter, Emily S.
    Feminizing the fetish : psychoanalysis and narrative obsession in turn-of-the-century France / Emily Apter.
        p. cm.
    Includes bibliographical references and index.
    ISBN-13: 978-0-8014-2653-7 (cloth) — ISBN-13: 978-0-8014-9952-4 (pbk.)
    1. French fiction—19th century—History and criticism. 2. French fiction—20th century—History and criticism. 3. Obsessive-compulsive disorder in literature. 4. Femininity (Psychology) in literature. 7. Narration (Rhetoric). 8. Women in literature. I. Title.
PQ653 .A77   1991
843'.809353—dc20   91-55067

An open access (OA) ebook edition of this title is available under the following Creative Commons license: Attribution-NonCommercial-NoDerivatives 4.0 International (CC BY-NC-ND 4.0): https://creativecommons.org/licenses/by-nc-nd/4.0/. For more information about Cornell University Press's OA program or to download our OA titles, visit cornellopen.org.

Jacket illustration: Advertisement in Vogue, 1909.

For Eleanor and David Apter

Contents

	Preface	ix
1	Fetishism in Theory: Marx, Freud, Baudrillard	1
2	The Epistemology of Perversion: From Pathology to Pathography	15
3	Cabinet Secrets: Peep Shows, Prostitution, and Bric-a-bracomania in the Fin-de-siècle Interior	39
4	Unmasking the Masquerade: Fetishism and Femininity from the Goncourt Brothers to Joan Riviere	65
5	Splitting Hairs: Female Fetishism and Postpartum Sentimentality in Maupassant's Fiction	99
6	Mystical Pathography: A Case of Maso-fetishism in the Goncourts' *Madame Gervaisais*	124
7	Hysterical Vision: The Scopophilic Garden from Monet to Mirbeau	147
8	Master Narratives/Servant Texts: Representing the Maid from Flaubert to Freud	176
9	*Stigma Indelebile*: Zola, Gide, and the Deviant Detail	210
	Conclusion	244
	Selected Bibliography	250
	Index	267

· Preface

· The interdisciplinary approaches that I employ to look at the topic of fetishism in this book—narratological, New Historical, hermeneutical, feminist, and psychoanalytical—have often proved difficult to reconcile. I began with an interest in that fin-de-siècle ethos of morbid sexual obsession permeating realist narrative and the early history of psychiatry alike, and ended with a constellation of abstract analytical and political concerns: the poetics of reification and specularity, the relation between theories of the gaze and the textual representation of scopophilia ("love of looking"), the gendering of perversion, the question of how to critique the history of feminist social constructionism without relinquishing the subtleties of masquerade, travesty, and mystification. Though in certain respects this interweaving of critical theory with historically grounded nineteenth-century French studies became unavoidably anachronistic, I purposely wanted to blur traditional chronological perimeters in an effort to bring the questions of contemporary psychoanalysis, literary interpretation, and feminism into fruitful confrontation with their formative past.

There remains, however, a definite historical consistency in the book's concentration on the turn of the century. As distinct from "fin de siècle" or "early modernism," each of which suggests a clear demarcation on either side of the 1900 divide, the turn of the century evokes a revolving door, allowing for quintessential nineteenth-century genres and styles—realism, naturalism, decadence, symbolism— to be seen surviving into the early twentieth century. Though they clearly atrophy over time (overshadowed by the brilliance of formal experiment in the early avant-garde), it is precisely what happens to these genres as they endure that is of particular interest to me. Contaminated by psychoanalysis, criminology, socioanthropology, trade books on collecting, fashion, and social etiquette, Catholic primers, and mass-market journalism, realist-naturalist-decadent works, from those of the Goncourt brothers to Octave Mirbeau, offer a rich parallel to contemporary genres of prose fiction that plunder the tabloids, the police file, and the psychiatric archive.

Fetishism to most people connotes a monothematic if "kinky" or unorthodox subject. Examples of fixations on shoes, velvet, fur, hair, gloves, underwear, umbrellas, and cigars that are not just cigars are readily volunteered whenever the term is introduced. Though I am intrigued by the aesthetics of erotic symbolism, displacement, substitution, and the cutting or splitting of anatomical totalities (*le corps morcelé*) implicit in localized fixations, I never intended to write a book organized around variety-show fetishes. What interested me more than a catalog of motifs was the sensibility infusing historic bourgeois phantasms, subterranean longings, and gender performances. The logic of psychoanalytical fetishism presumes castration anxiety, penis fixation, or, in the case of women, penis envy. I have sought to emphasize a broader, less gender-restricted conception of partial object substitutionism in sexuality, thereby culturally and historically relativizing those all-purpose referents, the surrogate male phallus and the phallic mother.

It also seemed to me that the museological manias informing fin-de-siècle popular culture corresponded in unexpected ways to our present-day preoccupation with lost aura, sublimation, and ironic peek-a-boo eroticism. Late nineteenth-century bric-a-bracomania, with its domestic altars of eroticized things, brought Freud and Marx into collusion, and this connection, in turn, helped to explain the prevalent and subtly disquieting present-day consumerist practices of collecting, hoarding, displaying, desiring, fondling, possessing, and continually looking.

At its core, this study of fetishism also involves an inquiry into a common reading disposition—the practice of seizing and worrying literary details, which is second nature to close readers. Close reading is analogous to the conquest of Madame de Rênal's arm in Stendhal's *Le Rouge et le noir*. Recounted as a mock-Napoleonic conquest, Julien Sorel's seduction of his benefactress is an allegory of synecdoche unbound. Sorel stakes out his territorial claim on

Madame de Rênal's anatomy, forcing its surrender piece by piece, fingers to shoulder. This episode mirrors the inherently fetishistic process of what Naomi Schor has called "reading in detail": that incremental fragment cathexis whereby individual parts eventually crowd together and usurp the original whole. The detail has just this tendency to prick consciousness, to encroach on the terrain of inner feelings, to expand to the point of obsession. Like Barthes's *punctum* or Lacan's *point tichique*, the superfluous, perplexing, derailing detail operates as the object of one's love, apprehension, hunger, or repulsion. It is the detail that affords a point of entry into the aesthetics of textual appropriation, an aperture or rent proceeding from a small, fixed image. Spots, tattoos, bloodstains, stigmas, scars, abrasions, hairy patches, stained clothing, worn keepsakes, fingered relics—these emerge as those details that stand out as dark symbolic concentrates in the visual field of fetishistic description.

I have anchored my "reading of the fetishism of reading" in analyses of authors who share a stylistic propensity for what has been referred to as nosological realism. "Cliniciens ès lettres" (to borrow the title of Victor Segalen's 1902 thesis on medicalized literariness), the Goncourt brothers, Emile Zola, Guy de Maupassant, Octave Mirbeau, and their epigones and offspring Remy de Gourmont, Georges Rodenbach, Rachilde, Léo Taxil, Augustin Cabanès, Octave Uzanne, Cazalis, Paul Bourget each at some level fused the medical *observation* with the literary chronicle of behavioral aberration. Little studied, their critical legacies often weighed down with platitudes regarding their use of grotesque details, social panoramas high and low, moralized urban landscape, gender stereotypes, the darker side of desire, they have each in their idiosyncratic ways helped to spawn a genre of fetishistic fiction that I have called, borrowing from Freud, *pathography*—a genre fusing biography, cliography (or the historical biographies of legendary men and women), and the clinical case history of exemplary "perverts."

Pathology and pathography have, of course, a particular relevance for the present moment. Ironically, at the very moment when critics may be most inclined to throw out epistemological divisions between normal and deviant, or to criticize them within the history of masculinities, femininities, homosexualities, and so on, the mass media seem to rely more than ever on pathographic sensationalism, from the trials of serial killers and child abusers to, on a more mundane level, the fatal flaws of larger-than-life politicians and stars. The nineteenth-century legacy of hereditary taints, characterological and criminological physiognomical signs, mimetic transfers of behavior from class to class, or transmissible diseases of the body and the psyche seems eerily still in place within our own "fin-de-sièclisms." My interest in nosological or clinical realism (a genre anchored in the art of describing the morbid symptoms of the body) may be interpreted as a reminder that psychoanalytical discourse can always be remedicalized when the threat of disease becomes more real.

And of course the threat of disease has become more real, and, accordingly, there has been a resurgence of medical dystopias in the spheres of art and literature. Though parallels between the nineteenth century's obsession with syphilis and the twentieth century's focus on the AIDS tragedy must be treated warily, there are certainly specific reasons why a turn-of-the-century novel such as Léon Daudet's *Les Morticoles* (1894)—which describes an island of "degenerates" managed exclusively by doctors—seems worth reading with an eye to present-day stigmatizations of the sick. Similarly, when Robert Nye re-asks the nineteenth-century question posed by Gaston Danville, "Is love a pathological condition?" it takes on chilling resonances in the context of more immediate homophobic responses to the AIDS crisis.

In its provocation of the reader's prurient curiosity, the pathographic genre also leads to a revised look at the visual dimension of repression and its subversive overturning. It is well known that Freud emphasized verbal denial (*Verdrängung, Verleugnung*) over visual occlusion (*scotomisation*) in his theory of repression. Excavating the French psychiatric record up to and including Freud, I have attempted to redress this privileging of oral *dénégation* or denial (so crucial to the talking cure) by rehabilitating the French emphasis on hysterical vision from Charcot to Lacan. The debate over scotomization (from the Greek *skotos*, "darkness," a term used by ophthalmologists to mean distorted, partial, or peripheral vision) between Freud and his Alsatian disciple René Laforgue takes place allusively in Freud's seminal 1927 essay on fetishism. It is probably no accident that this particular essay provided the place for that encounter. "Fetishism," read in tandem with Freud's writings on the "psychogenic disturbance of vision," may provide the grounds for a theory of optical repression and points, more generally, to the *oculocentric* bias within French psychoanalytic culture.

Throughout this investigation, I have exploited the lack of fixed boundaries between the perversions in order to associate fetishism with a blocking and fixating function synonymous with the repression of the scopic drive. Though Laura Mulvey has argued that fetishism is inherently antiscopic insofar as the deflected gaze of the fetishist represents a refusal to see and know what is inside Pandora's box (the voyeur, by contrast, is characterized by his lack of resistance to an overriding curiosity), one might want to soften this rigid distinction between fetishist and voyeur by saying that the fetishist does indeed refuse to look, but in refusing to look, he stares. It is a "not looking" sustained paradoxically through visual fixation on the substitute phallus.

My aim in reemphasizing the scopic (though it breathes new life into Charcot's French school, with its antifeminist and anti-Semitic history) has been to highlight the force of visual desire as it targets sexual and commercial objects within a nineteenth-century consumer culture. While Freud's 1927 essay illuminates the importance of strenuous, ambivalent denial in the gestation of a fetish object, his quarrel with Laforgue over the appropriateness of the term scotomization limited the opportunities for applying his sexual definition in a Marxist sense, that is, to explain the cultural pulsion toward appropriating material embodiments of value, or "congealed capital." While I do not really have a coherent theory of how erotic and materialistic desire mutually augment each other (producing a "surinvestment" in the object of desire), I do think that a greater understanding of how they commingle might be achieved by giving further credence to scopophilia's role in motivating the social gaze.

Investigating the relay between this social gaze of desire and its psychoanalytical equivalent has been another major thrust of this work. Here the examination of narrative ocularization has proved to be crucial. In his *Nouveau discours du récit* (1983), Gérard Genette employed the term ocularization to distinguish the restricted field of vision belonging to the subjective eye of the narrator. Indications of this gaze, filmically literary, include an exaggeration of foreground (the decor of a room through a peephole); foot-level perspective (as in the training of descriptive movement from below to above); hyperfocalization on a part of the body; peripheral vision, or the shadow recording of the viewer's presence—the sly materialization of his or her image in a literary representation of the sighting device (descriptions of cameras, binoculars, dioramas, or photo albums are especially telltale in this regard). Unlike the umbrella term *focalization* (from *focal personnage*, "omniscient narrator"), ocularization implies a particular emphasis on the techniques and tropes that psychologize the gaze, privatize the stolen glance, rivet the obsessive regard.

My chapters are roughly diachronic and may be linked to one another through their common treatment of a resurgent narrative paradigm stemming directly from the literary psychodynamics of vision: the conceit of concatenated case histories exhibited to a lay public. This frame technique invariably has the effect of simultaneously shaping and shielding the curiosity-riddled looking characteristic of scopic fetishism. It heightens erotic atmosphere by placing the reader-viewer at a distance (the suspense of image-suspension) or situating him or her at some transgressively hidden vantage point. The reader is a lonely voyeur, hunched over a keyhole, and the space that separates him or her from the spectacle correlates to the temporality of lingering on the way to a sexual aim—what Freud called perversion, and what Peter Brooks (glossing Freud) has described as the protracted forepleasure of narrative "clock-teasing."

Stereoscopic, akin to the *roman à tiroir*, this display-case narrative artifice predominates in fictions of interiority, structurally aligning *topoi* as diverse as the confessional box, the bordello, the socialite's dressing room, the medical cabinet, the museum, or the library. Barthes's expostulation in *Fragments d'un discours amoureux*, "I am not in the picture," belied by his self-insertion into the theoretical frame, captures the position of the narrator-critic intrusively spying on scenes of nineteenth-century domestic ritual and its attendant erotic fixations.

In a passage in his *Introductory Lectures*, Freud elided the ocular and the textual when he fashioned a processual carnival of each so-called perversion. Comparing the gamut of perversions to the monsters of Breughel or the succession of vanished gods described by Flaubert in *La Tentation de Saint Antoine*, Freud marched them by his audience in deliberate order: led by homosexuals, coprophiliacs, fetishists, necrophiliacs—all those, that is, in whom the sexual object had undergone some change—his grotesque cortège was completed by exhibitionists, sadists, and their counterparts, the masochists—those in whom the sexual aim had been altered. But the marching order seems less important than the frieze itself as a sign of the power of the visual in Freud's method.

Of course, as Freud emphasized, each perversion has its own distinct ontology of paranormality, its own character types, its own vast literature. In this book, however, fetishism has been treated as the perversion that regulates all the rest, not because I think of it as a "master" anomaly informing the others, but because it does seem to perform a significant mediating function between exhibitionism and voyeurism on the one hand and masochism and sadism on the other. The initial and concluding chapters seek to define the distinctive genre of pathography and its stylistic corollary, nosological or grotesque realism. Fetishism as exhibitionism is the focus of my chapters on "cabinet secrets" and Mirbeau's "garden of scopic perversion." I examine the display of prostitutes in the peep-show interior of the bordello in the former and chart the exhibition of spectacles of cruelty in the latter. Discussion of the hunger of the gaze prompted by these narrative viewing frames is also carried over in the section on the maternal collectomania of the female fetishist. Gradually fetishism emerges as a test case for the fixing of gender typology in the early history of psychoanalysis. In this fixing of gender a predominantly male-authored naturalist literature replete with images of female religious hysteria and erotic criminality (the Goncourts' *Madame Gervaisais*) is considered to be of crucial importance.

In the fin de siècle, we find a curious predilection on the part of male authors for writing femininity, that is, masquerading as a woman's consciousness. From Flaubert's putative exclamation "Madame Bovary, c'est moi!" to Zola's fetishism of women's garments in *Au bonheur des dames*, Baron Octave Uzanne's sighs of ecstasy over the fashion system, and Mallarmé's adopted pseudonym "Miss Satin" in *La Dernière Mode*, a cross-dressed narrative voice insistently echoes. I explore this issue further in a critique of fetishism, femininity, and the sartorial superego. Fetishism as the "third term," negotiating between sadism and masochism (or master narratives and servant texts), informs my examination of novels focusing on the female domestic. I also consider the relationship between homoeroticism and fetishism, posed by Freud as alternate strategies of castration repudiation, in my treatment of Gide's displacements of the realist stigma. Unifying the chapters is a New Historical consideration of the connection between literary medicalization and psychiatric literariness discernible throughout French turn-of-the-century culture.

Beyond the oblique analogies to contemporary issues of daily life this study of fetishism is also intended to address broader concerns pertaining to the "disciplines," especially as their fusions and separations have evolved within French studies. Feminist scholarship, often anchored in Annales school methodologies, has pointed the way to an examination of documents that formerly had no literary or historical status, thus helping to reveal the hidden places where gender typologies have germinated and been stored. Domesticity; the spatial eroticism of the interior; the history of clothing; anonymous case histories of feminine neurosis found in medical and criminological archives; the bourgeois private rituals of sentimentality, prayer, or letter writing; the prostitute's quotidian struggles; the conditions of life for working-class women; the banal racisms and sexisms of everyday life; the imagery of ethnographic imperialism—these New Historical concerns (which have received careful attention from French scholars such as Michelle Perrot, Alain Corbin, and Anne Martin-Fugier) were always part of a culture that formed the backdrop of high literature. Now they seem to constitute the basis for critical narratives in their own right.

But how to write that narrative? For a generation reared on deconstruction there is something exhilarating about archival work, but it nonetheless remains virtually impossible to return to an unproblematic definition of the real, the factual, or, for that matter, the nontextual. This book has been an experiment in how to read literature with history in a late deconstructionist period. Following Carlo Ginzburg's lead, I have made detection and decipherment heuristic devices as well as transparent themes. I have asked how applications of techniques of reading (and by reading I imply some measure of ironic distance from accounts of the material or the real) differ from New Historians to literary critics. I have thought about where to draw the parameters of "text," "writer," and "subject of history" and whether or not the "new cultural history" argues for or against the return of a unitary subject (a particularly important issue for feminist debates). I have also asked to what extent practices of reading "otherwise" have required and produced new genres of critical interpretation, as in the case of what Nancy K. Miller has called "personal criticism." There seems to be a new respect for the first-person inflection, for the personal stake, for the de-repressed articulation of the ethnic, gender, and cultural status of the speaker. There also seems to be a backlash against them, a dismissal of such narrative strategies as overly self-indulgent. Although this book contains no definitive pronouncements on the contemporary politics of self-situationism, it does engage implicitly in the project of defining a critical voice.

Oscillating rather self-consciously between psychoanalysis and feminism, history and theory, canonical and noncanonical texts, the first-person voice of "I am in the picture!" and the omniscient, academicizing tone of an overarching critical agenda, this study of fetishism has doubled as an investigation into how to write "new literary history" in the context of turn-of-the-century cultural studies.

I gratefully acknowledge a grant from the American Council of Learned Societies, summer funding from the National Endowment for the Humanities, and sabbatical leaves from Williams College in 1985–86 and 1989–90. A Mellon Fellowship at the University of Pennsylvania during the year 1989–90 enabled me to complete the writing and revisions of the manuscript. Generous research funds from the Williams College Humanities Division allowed for successive summers of research at the Bibliothèque Nationale.

Innumerable friends and colleagues have been essential to this project. I would like to express special thanks to John Reichert, Dean of Faculty at Williams, and Lawrence Graver, who invited me to present material on "household fetishes and literary taboos" in the Faculty Lecture Series. Many of the ideas in this book were initially sketched in a Williams Humanities and Social Science Center seminar, "The Social Construction of Sexuality," in 1988–89. For their stimulating collaboration on various fetishism projects, I thank William Pietz and Michael Taussig.

This book also benefited a great deal from opportunities I had to present draft chapters in a variety of institutional and intellectual contexts. Lynn Hunt, Frances Restuccia, Seyla Benhabib, Michael Riffaterre, Sara Whiting, and Pierre Saint-Amand made these opportunities possible. Gerald Prince and Carroll Smith-Rosenberg each led thought-provoking faculty seminars at the University of Pennsylvania which helped me to refine my arguments. I also thank Charles Bernheimer, Victor Brombert, Kevin Brownlee, François George, K. Michael Hays, Paul Holdengräber, Jean Piel, Laurence Porter, Richard Terdiman, and Georges Teyssot for their help at various stages.

Special recognition must be conveyed to a number of women whose ideas have served as continual points of reference and whose friendship has proved invaluable. I am grateful to Naomi Schor for her incisive, ground-breaking work on female fetishism; to Susan Suleiman for her exemplary syntheses of politics, history, and narrative theory; to Nancy K. Miller for her knowledge of feminist cabinets and masquerades; to Rosalind Krauss and Linda Nochlin for their inspiring work on visual culture; to Lynn Hunt and Monique Eleb-Vidal for their intriguing historical investigations of private life in France; to Jann Matlock for her archival tips; to Parveen Adams and Joan Copjec for their inimitable articulations of psychoanalysis; and to my mother, Eleanor Apter, whose critical insights have so often set me off on a train of reflection. Anthony Vidler has been my interlocutor at every stage.

Portions of this book have already appeared in a variety of journals and collective volumes. I thank the editors for permission to use this material in revised form. All translations, unless otherwise noted, are my own.

"Cabinet Secrets: Peep Shows, Prostitution, and Bric-a-bracomania in the Fin-de-siècle Interior" appeared virtually in its entirety in *Assemblage* 9 (Spring 1989).

A version of "Splitting Hairs: Female Fetishism and Postpartum Sentimentality in Maupassant's Fiction" has been published in *Eroticism and the Body Politic*, ed. Lynn Hunt (Baltimore: Johns Hopkins University Press, 1990).

Material on Luce Irigaray included in "Mystical Pathography: A Case of Maso-fetishism in the Goncourts' *Madame Gervaisais*" was published in *The National Women's Studies Association Journal* 2 (Spring 1990).

"Hysterical Vision: The Scopophilic Garden from Monet to Mirbeau" was published in *October* 47 (Winter 1988).

A French translation of "Master Narratives/Servant Texts: Representing the Maid from Flaubert to Freud" appeared in *Poétique* 70 (April 1987).

Portions of "*Stigma indelebile*: Zola, Gide, and the Deviant Detail" were published in *Romanic Review* 4 (Fall 1989) and *Modern Language Notes* 101 (September 1986).

EMILY APTER

Oakland, California

F·E·M·I·N·I·Z·I·N·G T·H·E F·E·T·I·S·H

CHAPTER 1

· Fetishism in Theory:
Marx, Freud, Baudrillard

· In his discussion of commodity fetishism, Karl Marx spoke of an object's hidden value—its fetish character—as a "secret": "Value, therefore, does not stalk about with a label describing what it is. It is value, rather, that converts every product into a social hieroglyphic. Later on, we try to decipher the hieroglyphic, to get behind the secret of our own social products; for to stamp an object of utility as a value, is just as much a social product as language."[1] Marx's conception of the fetish as socioeconomic hieroglyphic and opaque verbal sign emerged, in the course of my writing, as curiously compatible with Freud's sense of the strangeness of fetish consciousness: a state of mind divided between the reality of noncastration and the fear of it all the same. Both enigmas, in turn, seemed to arrange themselves around a "third term." Michel Leiris (distilling his impressions of Giacometti's neoprimitivist sculptural artifacts) identified his own embattled, Eurocentric fetishism—that mimetic "objectivized form of our desire"—with an ethnopsychiatric condition of "affective ambivalence":

· I love Giacometti's sculpture because everything he makes is like the petrification of one of these crises, the intensity of a chance event swiftly caught and immediately frozen, the stone stele telling its tale. And there's nothing deathlike about this sculpture; on the contrary, like the

---

1. Karl Marx, *Capital: A Critique of Political Economy*, trans. Samuel Moore and Edward Aveling, ed. Frederick Engels (New York: Modern Library, 1906), p. 85. Further references to this work will be abbreviated *C*.

real fetishes we idolize (real fetishes, meaning those that resemble us and are objectivized forms of our desire) everything here is prodigiously alive—graciously living and strongly shaded with humor, nicely expressing that affective ambivalence, that tender sphinx we nourish, more or less secretly, at our core.[2]

Where the "secret" joins the "strange," and the "strange" encounters that "affective ambivalence, that tender sphinx we nourish, more or less secretly, at our core," is precisely the nonlocatable spot where these investigations theoretically and methodologically situate themselves.

In his chapter on fetishism and ideology in *For a Critique of the Political Economy of the Sign*, Jean Baudrillard characterized the term *fetishism* as almost having "a life of its own." "Instead of functioning as a metalanguage for the magical thinking of others," he argued, "it turns against those who use it, and surreptitiously exposes their own magical thinking."[3] Baudrillard here identifies the uncanny retroactivity of fetishism as a theory, noting its strange ability to hex the user through the haunting inevitability of a "deconstructive turn."

Neither Marx nor Freud managed to escape the return of the repressed fetish. Freud endowed the fetish of the (castrated) maternal phallus with an animus when he wrote: "It seems rather that when the fetish comes to life, so to speak, some process has been suddenly interrupted—it reminds one of the abrupt halt made by memory in traumatic amnesias."[4] Marx, endeavoring in *Capital* to define the commodity fetish, lures the reader into a labyrinth of discomfiting allusions. "A commodity appears, at first sight, a very trivial thing, and easily understood," he began, only to retract: "Its analysis shows that it is, in reality, a very queer thing, abounding in metaphysical subtleties and theological niceties" (*C* 81). The same paragraph ends on an even more "fantastic" note, when an ordinary table, transformed into a commodity, "evolves out of its wooden brain grotesque ideas, far more wonderful than 'table-turning'" (*C* 82). If here the metaphor is table-turning, later the mysterious value of the fetish commodity floats before the eye like

2. Michel Leiris, "Alberto Giacometti," *Documents* 1, no. 4 (1929): 209; trans. James Clifford in *Sulfer*, no. 15 (1986): 39.
3. Jean Baudrillard, *For a Critique of the Political Economy of the Sign*, trans. Charles Levin (St. Louis: Telos Press, 1981), p. 90.
4. Sigmund Freud, "Fetishism" (1927), in *Standard Edition* 21:149. Further references to this work will be abbreviated "F."

an apparition. After constructing an optical analogy for the relation between man and commodity, Marx advises "recourse to the mist-enveloped regions of the religious world" (*C* 83). Alternately confusing and conflating appearance and reality, *Eidos* and materialism; alienation and belief, Marx, according to W. J. T. Mitchell, "disabled" his discourse through the very master tropes that gave his arguments the power to imprint themselves on the political unconscious.[5] The *camera obscura* was his preferred figure for ideology, and fetishism his preferred figure for commodities, but the two terms were frequently "crossed," for as Mitchell points out, both signify false images, with the former connoting an "idol of the mind" and the latter, in Francis Bacon's wording, an "idol of the marketplace." At some level, these idols become indistinguishable, rendering commodities dangerously interchangeable with the "true" currency of ideas. Mirroring each other as "icons" of illusion, both tropes, according to Mitchell, ultimately subvert their author's attempt at demystification. "Ideology and fetishism," he ascertains, "have taken a sort of revenge on Marxist criticism, insofar as it has made a fetish out of the concept of fetishism, and treated 'ideology' as an occasion for the elaboration of a new idealism."[6]

Now even if we disagree with Mitchell's conclusion that Marxist criticism has reified the elements of its own theory or allowed fetishism to masquerade as demystification, it does seem true that within contemporary discourse a kind of fetishism of fetishism is in the air. And this hypertrophic character is hardly confined to Marxist usage; it seems, as Baudrillard suggests, endemic to fetishism's history as a metaphysical construct.

In what follows, I want to examine briefly the history of fetishism as a theory, emphasizing (1) its simultaneous critique of and implication in the very sociosymbolic phenomena that it seeks to unveil (from commodification to castration anxiety), (2) its importance as a specular meeting point for psychoanalytic and materialist discourses, and (3) its implications for a radical theoretical praxis in the domain of contemporary aesthetic production.

In the course of its etymological life from its Chaucerian prehistory to its post-Enlightenment usage in the twentieth century, the word *fetisso* and its phonological cognates have provoked a chain of

---

5. W. J. T. Mitchell, *Iconology: Image, Text, Ideology* (Chicago: University of Chicago Press, 1986), p. 163 in particular, but in general the entire chapter titled "The Rhetoric of Iconoclasm: Marxism, Ideology, and Fetishism," pp. 160–208.

6. Ibid., p. 163.

divergent interpretations, all generated according to the codes of a romance linguistics forced to accept the untranslatable Other into its thoroughly Western genealogy. Used in the eighteenth century by Charles de Brosses (dubbed "the little fetish" for his pains by Voltaire) to describe the idolatrous worship of material objects in "primitive" societies, the term was traced to *fatum*, signifying both fate and charm. A century later the British ethnologist Edward Tylor derived the term from a different though related root (*factitius*), comprising both the "magic arts" and the "work of art."[7] The Italian philosopher Giorgio Agamben, following Marx (fetishism of commodities as false consciousness) and Freud (the fetish as spurious, surrogate object of desire), deduced from the Latin *facere* neither charm nor beauty but rather the degraded simulacrum or false representation of things sacred, beautiful, or enchanting.[8]

Though a semantic disjunction clearly emerges each time the word *fetishism* is displaced from language to language, discipline to discipline, and culture to culture, it is precisely this process of creative mistranslation that endows the term with its value as currency of literary exchange, as verbal token. Thus the word *charme*, a favored key word of Mallarmé and Valéry commonly used to denote the incantatory power of music (*carmen*: psalm, oracle, sacred song), was seen as the carrier of an authenticated neoprimitivism, a sign linking symbolism to an exotic repertory of votive objects including the *gri-gri*, the *juju* or the *phiphob*. Like a good-luck charm or native artifact offered to the European traveler, the verbal fetish, surrounded by an aura of otherness, was aestheticized by the French poets of the turn of the century from Stéphane Mallarmé to Victor Segalen and Guillaume Apollinaire. As *fetys*, "well-made, beautiful," the fetish emerged as a catalyst of symbolist artifice; as *fatum*, or fateful chance, it recalled the master narratives of shipwreck, solitude, and confrontation between civilized and "savage mind" from *Robinson Crusoe* to "Un coup de dés"; and as "Christs of another form, another belief, inferior Christs of obscure wishes" in Apollinaire's poem "Zone" (1912), it became a protosurrealist icon, mediating between urban anomie and a "phantom Africa."[9]

The literary history of fetishism may reveal a discursive pattern

---

7. Edward Tylor, *Primitive Culture*, 2 vols. (New York: Brentano's, 1924), 2: 143–59.
8. Giorgio Agamben, *Stanze*, trans. Yves Hersant (Paris: Christian Bourgois, 1981), pp. 69–71. See also part 2, chaps. 1, 2, 3, and 5, for discussion of fetishism in Marx and Baudelaire.
9. See Michel Leiris, *L'Afrique fantôme* (Paris: Gallimard, 1981).

of difference, but its philosophical history deconstructs in the form of a rhetorical chiasmus. William Pietz has given us the most historically nuanced account of the philosophical fetish, which, he argues, points to the "emerging articulation of a theoretical materialism quite incompatible and in conflict with the philosophical tradition."[10] Following his scheme, one sees that from Kant (fetishism as a degraded sublime, a "trifle") and Hegel (fetishism as a "factitious universal," an unmediated particular) to Whitehead ("a fallacy of misplaced concreteness") and Heidegger (an *Ereigenes*, an Appropriation), fetishism has been portrayed as theoretically worthless.[11] As a word, it was not even admitted into the French language by the Académie Française until 1835. But it is just this quantity of negative value that ultimately enables fetishism to undermine monolithic belief structures from Christianity and Enlightenment philosophy to the "rational" laws of capitalist exchange. For example, the Portuguese trading word *fetisso* stood not just for the native idol but also for the "small wares" or trinkets that European merchants used for barter or upon which they would swear an oath to honor a commercial transaction. According to William Pietz, these trading rituals inevitably led to "a perversion of the natural processes of economic negotiation and legal contact. Desiring a clean economic interaction, seventeenth-century merchants unhappily found themselves entering into social relations and quasi-religious ceremonies that should have been irrelevant to the conduct of trade."[12] Pietz implies that Africa perverted Western capitalism (forcing it to adopt the superstitious worship of material objects) just as European capitalists perverted indigenous economics through exploitation. One may further deduce from this historico-philosophical chiasmus two central consequences: first, that the "civilized" mimesis of "primitive" object worship was only the explicit acting out of Europe's own (masked) commodity fetishism; and second, that almost as a result of Europe's initial contempt for "tribal" artifacts, the exotic fetish "returned" to Continental shores,

10. William Pietz, "The Problem of the Fetish, I," *Res* 9 (Spring 1985): 6. I am deeply indebted to William Pietz's brilliant work on fetishism. Our discussions have nourished and influenced many of the arguments put forward in this book. This and its companion piece, "The Problem of the Fetish, II," *Res* 13 (Spring 1987): 23–45, offer an invaluable synthesis of fetishism's etymological ambiguities as well as its inner contradictions as a cross-disciplinary critical discourse. See also "The Problem of the Fetish IIIa," *Res* 16 (Autumn 1988): 105–23.
11. See Pietz, "The Problem of the Fetish, I," pp. 6–9, 14.
12. Pietz, "The Problem of the Fetish, II," p. 45.

where it was henceforth recommodified as art. Developing these points, and insisting on the irrecuperably "savage" nature of the African *feitiço*, V. Y. Mudimbe has seen the history of the aestheticization of the fetish from its "culturally neutral" origins as a curio collected by the trader-observer in the fifteenth and sixteenth centuries, to its gradual mystification as "strange and ugly artifact," as an unregenerate example of Europe's notion of African art.[13]

Pierre Loti's *Le Roman d'un spahi* (The novel of a colonial conscript; 1881) provides an exemplary illustration of Mudimbe's argument in its coded framing of Europe's racist, exoticist construction of the African fetish. The novel recounts the story of a French soldier posted in Senegal who, having "gone native" (donning the Muslim fez, living with a black concubine), is rudely recalled to his European origins when his mistress secretly sells his watch in exchange for "worthless" *pacotille* (shoddy goods). Described as a crude silver watch to which he was as attached as Fatou was to her amulets, the spahi's paternal heirloom is guarded in a "boîte aux fétiches" (fetish box), thus emphasizing the cross-cultural transference of fetishisms that has occurred. But the lesson of this episode rides on its revelation that such transferences are nothing other than a concession to barbarism. Black fetishes, in a picturesque market scene, are presented as profanations of Western sacred objects:

> Marchandes de poisson salé, marchandes de pipes, marchandes de tout;—marchandes de vieux bijoux, de vieux pagnes crasseux et pouilleux, sentant le cadavre;—de beurre de Galam pour l'entretien crépu de la chevelure;—de vieilles petites queues, coupées ou arrachées sur des têtes de négresses mortes, et pouvant resservir telles quelles, toutes tressées et gommées, toutes prêtes.
> Marchandes de grigris, d'amulettes, de vieux fusils, de crottes de gazelles, de vieux *corans* annotés par les pieux marabouts du désert;—de musc, de flûtes, de vieux poignards à manche d'argent, de vieux couteaux de fer ayant ouvert des ventres,—de tam-tams, de cornes de girafes et de vieilles guitares.

> Sellers of salted fish, sellers of pipes, sellers of everything;—sellers of old jewelry, of filthy, louse-ridden loin-cloths, reeking of corpses;—of Galam butter for keeping hair kinky;—of little old tresses, cut or torn

---

13. V. Y. Mudimbe, *The Invention of Africa: Gnosis, Philosophy, and the Order of Knowledge* (Bloomington: Indiana University Press, 1988), pp. 10–11.

from the heads of dead Negro women, ready for recycling as is, all plaited and glued together.

Sellers of gri-gris, amulets, old rifles, gazelle turd, old Korans annotated by pious marabouts of the desert;—of musk, flutes, old daggers with silver handles, old iron blades used to open up stomachs,—tamtams, giraffe horns, and old guitars.[14]

This excremental mound of otherness, these "strange and ugly artifacts" pilfered from rotting corpses, confirm the age-old posture of horrified voyeurism habitually adopted by the Western tourist.

Mudimbe's caveat against the entrenched nature of Europe's racist vision of African fetishism notwithstanding, one can argue that a more "enlightened" representation of black commodities and votive objects could be found in what James Clifford has characterized as "ethnographic surrealism" (itself in part a reaction against the fin-de-siècle exoticist clichés of authors such as Loti): "For the Paris avant-garde, Africa (and to a lesser degree, Oceania and America) provided a reservoir of other forms and other beliefs. This suggests a second element of the ethnographic surrealist attitude, a belief that the Other (whether accessible in dreams, fetishes, or Lévy-Bruhl's *mentalité primitive*) was a crucial object of modern research."[15] Clifford enumerates the ways in which Africa was decoded and recoded in Europe, a process effected, to a great extent, through an "artsy" appropriation of the display techniques employed in the ethnographic museum. Walter Benjamin, citing Hippolyte Taine ("L'Europe s'est déplacé pour voir des marchandises [The whole of Europe displaced itself in order to view the goods]"), has provided the most poetic evocations of these fanciful world exhibitions. A "profane glow," he observed, "bathed" the commodity, eclectically arrayed in the marketplace, arcade, or *vitrine*.[16] It

14. Pierre Loti, *Le Roman d'un spahi*, in *Pierre Loti* (Paris: Presses de la Cité, 1989), p. 334.
15. James Clifford, "On Ethnographic Surrealism," *Comparative Studies in Society and History* 23 (Oct. 1981): 542.
16. Walter Benjamin, section entitled "Taste" in addendum to "The Paris of the Second Empire in Baudelaire," in *Charles Baudelaire: A Lyric Poet in the Era of High Capitalism*, trans. Harry Zohn (London: New Left Books, 1973), p. 105. Benjamin writes: "Mass production, which aims at turning out inexpensive commodities, must be bent upon disguising bad quality.... The more industry progresses, the more perfect are the imitations which it throws on the market. The commodity is bathed in a profane glow." In another section on fashion, "Grandville or the World Exhibitions," Benjamin associates fetishism with prostitution and a kind of pornog-

was, of course, against such a view that Theodor Adorno, returning to a stricter Marxist interpretation of the fetish in commodity culture, would criticize Benjamin's arcades project. For Adorno, the concept of fetishism remained dialectical only so long as it was understood that, as he wrote in a celebrated letter to Benjamin, "the fetish character of the commodity is not a fact of consciousness; rather, it is dialectical, in the eminent sense that it produces consciousness."[17] Benjamin, in formulating the dialectical image as a "dream" of collective consciousness, had, according to Adorno, both removed its potential magic and deprived it of its essential materialism. Adorno was scornful of what he called "the replica realism" of Benjamin's method, preferring to retain the fetish as a value before psychology.[18]

Benjamin's concept of the phantasmagoria has, however, retained its importance for critical representations of the consumerist imagination. Thus, the contemporary artist Judith Barry, whose work revolves around the visual dynamics of shopping, refers us back to the Greco-Roman tradition of exhibiting the spoils of war.[19] Her question "who possesses whom?" the conquered object or the conquered spectator/subject? is clearly relevant to the analysis of the ethnographic collection, but it is also implicit in surrealist montage. In the famous surrealist journal *Documents*, Clifford sees:

> the order of an unfinished collage rather than of a unified organism. Its images, in their equalizing gloss and distancing effect, present in the same plane a Châtelet show advertisement, a Hollywood movie clip, a

---

raphy of death: "Fashion prescribed the ritual by which the fetish Commodity wished to be worshipped, and Grandville extended the sway of fashion over the objects of daily use as much as over the cosmos. In pursuing it to its extremes, he revealed its nature. It stands in opposition to the organic. It prostitutes the living body to the inorganic world. In relation to the living it represents the rights of the corpse. Fetishism, which succumbs to the sex-appeal of the commodity recruits this to its service" (p. 166).

17. Theodor Adorno, in *Aesthetics and Politics* (London: Verso, 1977), p. 111.

18. Theodor Adorno, "Fetish Character in Music and Regression of Listening," in *The Essential Frankfurt School Reader*, ed. Andrew Arato and Eike Gebhardt (New York: Continuum, 1988), pp. 278–79. Adorno argues: "The concept of musical fetishism cannot be psychologically derived. That 'values' are consumed and draw feelings to themselves without their specific consciousness being reached by the consciousness of the consumer, is a *later* expression of their commodity character" (278–79; my emphasis).

19. Judith Barry, "Dissenting Spaces," in *Damaged Goods: Desire and the Economy of the Object* (exhibition catalog) (New York: New Museum of Contemporary Art, 1986), p. 49.

Picasso, a Giacometti, a documentary photo from colonial New Caledonia, a newspaper clip, an Eskimo mask, an old master, a musical instrument— the world's iconography and cultural forms presented as evidence, or data. Evidence of what? Evidence, one can only say, of surprising, declassified cultural orders and of an expanded range of human artistic invention. This odd museum merely documents, juxtaposes, relativizes—a perverse collection.[20]

Though, in its display of heterogeneous objects, *Documents* (like its successor *Minotaure*) clearly perverted the classificatory codes of the museological discourse, its order of things was not necessarily as arbitrary, as purely "semiotic," as Clifford seems to imply in this context. Picasso's paintings of African masks or Giacometti's "primitive" sculptural cages also appear (as Clifford is the first to point out) as self-conscious simulations of exotica rather than, simply, naive destabilizations of taxonomy and its institutional mystifications. Commodification, with its cynical rites of replication and reproduceability, would seem to have installed itself at the very inception of surrealism.

In a catalog essay for a show of contemporary art entitled "Damaged Goods," Hal Foster encourages us to see the scattered masks and cult figurines of avant-garde art and surrealism not as arbitrary signifiers but rather as "magical commodities" containing the repressed promise of a utopian cathexis between the work of art and society, between the artist and the viewer-consumer. "Was the (primitive object's) attraction," he queries, "not, in part, its suggestiveness that (1) modern art might (re)claim a ritual function or cult value, and (2) the modern artist, made marginal in the bureaucratic world of late capitalism, might (re)gain a shamanistic centrality to society?" Asserting that "(dis)agreeable objects," from the mask to the Duchampian readymade, "demonstrated allegorically that the work of art in capitalist society cannot escape the status of the commodity," Foster, one may infer, wants to preclude the possibility of salvaging fetishism as a modern aesthetic.[21] But without falling into the trap of mystically reauthenticating "fallen," alienated neoprimitivism, we do perhaps find a place for modern fetishism in its artistic and theoretical definition of an ironic simulacrum. According to this line of reasoning, the fetish, in its relays between Africa and Europe, has escaped becoming altogether

20. Clifford, "On Ethnographic Surrealism," p. 552.
21. Hal Foster, "(Dis)agreeable Objects," in *Damaged Goods*, p. 13.

ossified, reified, or as Foster has put it, "fetishized"—its "difference disavowed."

In the twentieth century, I suggest, the concept of fetishism (despite "damaging" criticism) has gone from being negatively to positively valorized in a number of ways. If Kant, Marx, and Freud gave it infelicitous ascriptions, then Georges Bataille and fellow members of the Collège de Sociologie, intent on shattering the complacencies of bourgeois civilization, recuperated fetishism as a form of transgressive idolatry. Strengthening its status as a perversion (more than the surrealists ever dared) Bataille and Michel Leiris transformed fetishism, along with a host of other de-repressed pathologies, into a "good" theoretical praxis. Leiris, who according to Clifford renewed the Real by seeing "'facts' as performances, tropic productions, or heightened cut-out elements (fetishes)," fabricated what he called "true fetishism" out of a kind of self-reflexive, narcissistic "thingification": "In the domain of art we seldom find any object (paintings or sculptures) able in some measure to respond to the needs of this true fetishism, which is really the *loving* love of ourselves projected from the inside out and clothed in a solid carapace, thus trapping it within the bounds of a precise thing and situating it, rather like a piece of furniture for our use, in the vast foreign room called space."[22] Leiris's turn of phrase, "the *loving* love of ourselves," itself placed, like a freestanding object in an uncannily "foreign" space of the subject, denotes the schizoid, liminal eroticism of this "cut-out, true fetishism." Bataille would generate a comparable sense of the profane with the ironic invention of a spectator-fetishist whose look is displaced or implicated within a phobic narrative. In his *Histoire de l'oeil* (*Story of the Eye*) he anticipated a number of postmodern narrators all perversely "scopic": Michel Tournier's *The Fetishist*, Patrick Süsskind's *Perfume*, Julian Barnes's *Flaubert's Parrot*, Paul West's *Rat Man of Paris*, and Bruce Chatwin's *Utz*, to mention just a few. In each of these novels, fetishism is generated through the quest for trophies, themselves ironically exposed as magical commodities.

Let us take as our most extended example Tournier's fetishist, depicted in the short story of the same title. Like a bloodhound, he tracks, expropriates, and triumphantly worries his spoils—a lady's handkerchief, a bra, or best of all, a garter belt: "I had my

22. James Clifford, "The Tropological Realism of Michel Leiris," in *Sulfur*, no. 15 (1986): 11; Leiris, "Alberto Giacometti," p. 38.

trophy.... I brandished my garter belt like a red Indian flaunting his paleface's scalp."[23] On the surface, one fetish object is as good as another, but upon closer inspection we learn that these feminine undergarments function symbolically as mystical "icons" of capital. As *une femme chiffrée* ("a numbered woman") appraised with all her measurements—bust, waist, hips—the Fetishist's wife, through a series of subtle permutations, is transformed into her masculine counterpart as money value: "I was burning old, torn, dirty, mutilated bills—but the most important thing about them was that they had been softened" (T 203).[24] Here, the gender conversion from female to male fetish object parallels the conversion of sexual into commodity fetishes. If the Fetishist performs a traditional Freudian substitution when he "deceives" his wife with another woman's bra ("Yes, all right, I *was* being unfaithful to her with Francine, with a bra as proxy" [T 208]), he, in effect, deceives the bra, with a host of commodity idols: "The slips, the panty hose, the stockings, the panties, the chemisettes... I bought, and bought, and in less than two hours we didn't have a sou left" (T 208). Finally, the Fetishist's orgy of spending simulates the libidinal expenditure psychoanalytically associated with phallic substitution and points to paradigms of "economimesis" and "metafetishism," or fetishism *en abyme*, within Tournier's short story.[25]

Throughout Tournier's fiction, sexual desire is collapsed into the erotic *frisson* provoked by the commodity. In his novel *La Goutte d'or*, a title that refers to the Algerian quarter of Paris north of the Boulevard Montmartre, the attraction to material items subsumes the attraction to a real-life object of desire. After a young Maghrebian named Idriss sells a polyethylene cast of his body to the Parisian department store Chez Tati, he is urged by one of the salesmen to simulate himself as a commodity.

---

23. Michel Tournier, "The Fetishist," in *The Fetishist*, trans. Barbara Wright (Garden City, N.Y.: Doubleday, 1984), p. 209. Further references to this work will be abbreviated T.

24. Tournier inadvertently raises the question of fetishism and gender when his fetishist classifies his objects of obsession according to criteria of sexual difference: "Women are delicate, soft, perfumed lingerie. Men are a wallet swollen with secret things and silky, sweetsmelling bills" (T 205).

25. Jacques Derrida, "Economimesis," in *Mimesis des articulations*, ed. Jacques Derrida et al. (Paris: Flammarion, 1975). Derrida evokes a mimetic and infinitely specular chain of representations that refer in themselves to a libidinal economy of representation. See, in particular, pp. 66–71.

12 · Feminizing the Fetish

> Et dans un mois une vingtaine d'Idriss, qui se ressembleront comme des frères jumeaux, vont peupler mes vitrines et mes étalages intérieurs. Alors, à ce propos, j'ai une idée que je voudrais vous soumettre. Voilà: supposez que vous appreniez à faire l'automate? On vous habille comme les autres mannequins, vos frères jumeaux. On vous maquille pour que votre visage, vos cheveux, vos mains aient l'air faux, si vous voyez ce que je veux dire. Et vous, raide comme un piquet dans la vitrine, vous accomplissez quelques gestes anguleux et saccadés. Ça c'est déjà fait, notez-le bien. Le succès est assuré. Matin et soir, c'est l'attroupement devant la vitrine.

> And in a month's time, twenty Idrisses, each resembling the other like twin brothers, will populate my shop windows and display cases. And now, on this subject, I have an idea that I'd like to try out on you. It goes like this: suppose you learn how to do the automaton number? We'll dress you up like the other mannequins, your twin brothers. We'll make you up so that your face, your hair, and your hands will seem fake, if you see what I mean. And you, stiff as a rail in the window, you'll perform a few angular, spasmodic gestures. It's been done before, mind you. A guaranteed success. From morning to night, it's a mob scene in front of the store window.[26]

Transmogrified into a capitalist lure that magnetizes the rapacious look of the potential customer, Idriss personifies the famous Marxist chiasmus of double alienation, by which "people and things exchange semblances: social relations take on the character of object relations, and commodities assume the active agency of people."[27]

Tournier's agents of commodification—ogres, tourists, admen, and filmmakers—certainly discredit fetishism as a culturally constructed perversion and seem to follow the received interpretation of fetishism as a negative effect of commodification. But if we take the description of Idriss at one step removed, that is, as an illustration of the ironic play of simulacra, we might begin to define a kind of critical fetishism, an aesthetic of fetishization that reflexively exposes the commodity as an impostor value. In the mirror reflection of a thousand, identical department-store mannequins, one can extract a political critique of the alienated, colonized, North African self. In this sense, fetishism "buys back" its political redemption. Though Idriss may be prostituted, frozen, and reified, his dead stare (Medusa's head) gives back to consumer society the

---

26. Michel Tournier, *La Goutte d'or* (Paris: Gallimard, 1985), pp. 219–20.
27. Marx as paraphrased by Foster, "(Dis)agreeable Objects," p. 13.

very alienation that consumer society has inflicted on him. This form of doubled fetishization clearly has implications for contemporary aesthetic production. What creates the inherently doubled status of the fetish, to go back to Freudian theory, is the original paradigm of the ersatz phallus. Thus Freud writes in his 1927 essay on fetishism:

> . When I now disclose that the fetish is a penis-substitute I shall certainly arouse disappointment; so I hasten to add that it is not a substitute for any chance penis, but for a particular quite special penis that has been extremely important in early childhood but was afterwards lost. That is to say: it should normally have been given up, but the purpose of the fetish precisely is to preserve it from being lost. To put it plainly: the fetish is a substitute for the woman's (mother's) phallus which the little boy once believed in and does not wish to forego—we know why. ("F" 203)

Freud's formulation employs, interestingly enough, a language of undecidability, as if by way of reinforcing the attitude of avowal and disavowal that he wishes to emphasize in his characterization of the fetishist. Caught between specular absences, Freud's fetishist seems to operate entirely in the realm of the simulacrum, generating a copy or surrogate phallus for an original that never was there in the first place. The Lacanian reformulation of this paradigm pictures the fetishist-subject caught between "having" and "being" a maternal phallus that he or she can ultimately never possess, thus vacillating between illusory mastery on the one hand, and phantasms of lack or the permanently barred subject position on the other.

What emerges as particularly relevant here for an aesthetic critique is the uneasy mixture of credulity and disbelief that typifies the fetishist's attitude to the object-simulacrum. Repressing the (hypothetically posited) existence of the maternal penis, he deflects his gaze to the nearest, most convenient substitute, as in the classic scenario of boy and mother: "Thus the foot or shoe owes its attraction as a fetish, or part of it, to the circumstance that the inquisitive boy used to peer up the woman's legs toward her genitals. Velvet and fur reproduce—as has long been suspected—the sight of the pubic hair which ought to have revealed the longed-for penis; the underlinen so often adopted as a fetish reproduces the scene of undressing; the last moment in which the woman could still be regarded as phallic" ("F" 201). Expressions such as "ought to have revealed the longed-for penis," or "the last moment in which the woman could still be regarded as phallic," inject a subtle note of sympathy on the part of the analyst for the boy's suspension of disbelief. Freud's rhetoric, in other words, encourages us to believe with the boy in the existence of an original phallic woman, and in the viability of the fetish as a substitute for the female phallus that has been lost. But such mistaken perceptions are only partially allowed to subsist. "It is not true that the child emerges from his experience of seeing the female parts with an unchanged belief in the woman having a phallus," Freud writes. "He retains this belief but he also gives it up" ("F" 200). In other words, though he knows that feet, underwear, and velvet constitute nothing but a false or simulated phallus, the Freudian fetishist continues to regard them as real *nonetheless*: in the words of Octave Mannoni, "je sais bien, mais quand même [I know, but nonetheless]."[28] With true psychic ingenuity, or perhaps through the assistance of "magical thinking," the fetishist manages to hold the simulated original in a state of ironic suspension adjacent to the real and the facsimile. As Freud would have it, this hexed state of mind is a "compromise": "during the conflict between the deadweight of the unwelcome perception and the force of the opposite wish, a compromise is constructed" ("F" 200). In this way, fetishism emerges as an ever-shifting form of specular mimesis, an ambiguous state that demystifies and falsifies at the same time, or that reveals its own techniques of masquerade while putting into doubt any fixed referent.

28. The title of Octave Mannoni's seminal essay illustrates the Freudian paradigm of *dénégation*, or negative affirmation, whereby "I do not deny" qualifies as the repressed version of "I affirm"; see "Je sais bien, mais quand même," in *Clefs pour l'Imaginaire* (Paris: Seuil, 1969), pp. 9–33.

CHAPTER 2

· The Epistemology of Perversion: From Pathology to Pathography

· The perpetually unstable nature of the fetish in theoretical discourse has been mirrored by a continuing debate on the place of fetishism within the larger realm of perversion. In an article published in 1933 in the surrealist journal *Minotaure*, Maurice Heine (known for his diagnoses of the Marquis de Sade) included an illustration captioned *"L' Arbre des perversions."*[1] This "perversion tree" is used to demonstrate several points: its roots, forming a bolus beneath the soil and wrapped in the classificatory label *bisexualisme*, show irrepressible homosexual tendencies gaining ascendancy over heterosexualism as they travel upward on a phallic stalk. Each side of the trunk sports the banner *parésthésies*—a term proposed by Heine to abolish "ethico-religious" distinctions between the born *perverse* and the socialized *perverti*. On the side of *parésethésies psychologiques* we find passions qualified as perverse on account of their objects—narcissism, zoophilia, gerontophilia, necrophilia, pedophilia. These strains are distinguished from *parésthésies physiologiques* only insofar as repressed homosexuality plays a less significant role in their gestation. Situated on the physiological side, fetishism merits a leaf of its own sandwiched between exhibitionism and sadomasochism. What is significant about Heine's perversion tree is not the persuasiveness of its categorizations but, rather, its emphasis on the structural similarities binding each perversion to

---

1. Maurice Heine, "Notes sur un classement psycho-biologique des parésthésies sexuelles," *Minotaure*, no. 3–4 (Dec. 1933): 36.

its mirror opposite, pairing and cross-referencing them within an epistemological matrix. The tree also anticipates current controversies over sexual difference, for each perversion is shown originating in an unresolved sexual difference that, as it evolves, bypasses the orthodox gender differentiations of "normal" masculinity and femininity.

In attempting to frame the epistemological field of perversion, Foucault directs us to an earlier phase of psychoanalysis, to that period in the 1870s and 1880s during which "perverse pleasure" was, in his words, subject to "psychiatrization."[2] Of all the perversions classified and "entomologized" in this era, fetishism emerges as Foucault's "model perversion... which, from at least as early as 1877, served as the guiding thread for analyzing all the other deviations" (HS 1:154). Why did Foucault place fetishism so high up in the epistemological hierarchy of deviant sexuality? Was there something about this perversion in and of itself that attracted the heuristic skills of the early psychoanalysts? Did its kinship ties with the eighteenth-century legacy of libertinage render fetishism in an age of bourgeois moralism a return ticket to the decadent past? Did the blasphemous adjacency of object fixation to "primitive idolatry" (a degenerate cultural atavism within modern Christian civilization in the Eurocentric mind) cause fetishism to become the imperative target of social repression and correction? Or were its regressive, infantile characteristics (touching, gazing, fondling) an affront to the ideology of progressive maturation and psychosexual development historically deriving from fin-de-siècle *sélectionnisme* and social Darwinism?

It may have been the fundamentally harmless, gratuitous nature of fetishism that endowed it with the quality of a threatening enigma. Police reports recording that scissor assaults of fetishists on plaits of hair or patches of velvet skirt reveal how rarely physical harm was done to the (invariably female) victims.[3] The motive for such peccadillos remained as elusive to law enforcers as the infa-

2. Michel Foucault, *The History of Sexuality*, vol. 1: *An Introduction*, trans. Robert Hurley (New York: Vintage, 1980), p. 43. Further references to this work will be abbreviated HS.

3. See Gustave Macé's *La Police parisienne: Un joli monde* (The Parisian Police: A Pretty World) (Paris: Charpentier, 1887), in which he hierarchically organized fetishists into categories defined according to stereotypical behavior: "les peloteurs" (those who stroke), "les frotteurs" (those who rub), "les éperviers" (experts at tracking their prey), "les destructeurs" (destroyers—a particular menace to dresses and coats), "les coupeurs de cheveux" (cutters of hair—of whom Macé wrote: "In this sentimental category of memory harvesters, I question an individual who would approach young girls of ten to twelve years whose hair fell straight down or in braids

mous *acte gratuit* (gratuitous act) of the Gidean *sotie*. Unlike Gide's brazen adolescents, however, fetishistic marauders were typically mild-mannered, pitiable, petit bourgeois who lacked the hereditary stigmata normally used to construe evidence of moral atrophication and criminal character. The "portrait of the fetishist as a young man" was modeled on the stereotype of the shy, foppish, "feminized" male whose taste for collecting betrayed an overly developed epicureanism and an attraction to the sampling of "bizarraries" (fetishists, ever since Jean-Martin Charcot and Valentin Magnan's groundbreaking article on "genital inversion" [1882] were suspected of being latent homosexuals).[4] The typical fetishist was susceptible to manic passions, from bric-a-bracomania to erotomania. Though far less sinister than the sadist or masochist whose sexual appetites and proclivities, luridly cataloged in Krafft-Ebing's *Psychopathia Sexualis* (1886), could be satisfied only through violence, the fetishist shared with the sadomasochist a socially reprehensible propensity to "linger" (Freud's term) in the realm of foreplay.[5] Digressing on the path to coital consummation, foiling civilization's righteous aim to propagate the species, he was guilty of an exemplary dalliance in *gratuitous* sex.[6]

---

on their shoulders. Armed with scissors, he would mutilate their silky hair by cutting half of it off" [p. 268]), and "les collectionneurs de mouchoirs" (collectors of handkerchiefs—"When one of these individuals has just picked up a handkerchief, he passes it over his lips in a passionate gesture, he breathes in the perfume and wanders off staggering like a drunkard" [p. 269]).

4. Jean-Martin Charcot and Valentin Magnan, "Inversion du sens génital et autres perversions sexuelles," *Archives de Neurologie* 3 (Jan.–Feb. 1882): 53–60, and 4 (July 1882): 296–322.

5. In the section "The Sexual Aberrations" in the *Three Essays on the Theory of Sexuality, Standard Edition* 7, Freud placed the burden of perversity on this rather elusive notion of "lingering": "Perversions are sexual activities which either (a) extend, in an anatomical sense, beyond the regions of the body that are designed for sexual union, or (b) linger over the intermediate relations to the sexual object which should normally be traversed rapidly on the path towards the final sexual aim" (p. 150). Freud introduces an interesting notion here of normative temporality within sexual conduct. How long does it take, we are tempted to ask, before foreplay deteriorates into perverse "lingering"?

6. In his fastidious classification of perverse practices entitled *Fétichistes et érotomanes* (Paris: Vigot Frères, 1905), Paul Laurent offered a stereotypical portrayal of the fetishist featuring his "timid" nature and the "absurd" quality of his predilections: "The sexually perverted fetishist is therefore not a *monstrum per excessem* (monster by excess), like the masochist or the sadist, but rather a *monstrum per defectum* (monster by default). In effect, he spends himself genitally, and by a kind of amorous ectopy (transport), in an illogical, bizarre and absurd ritual, that could be considered as a sort of psychic onanism. Far from being excited sexually by venereal pleasures, he is on the contrary timid in matters of love, impotent and uninterested in the union of the sexes; genitally he sins much more often by default than by excess" (p. 7).

In constructing the genealogy of these fetishist character types the pre-Freudian doctors relied not only on a collection of endlessly repeated and elaborated case studies but also on the weighty evidence provided by literature of the fetishist's continuous presence in history. *La Revue Thérapeutique des Alcaloïdes* (which featured a regular column on famous neurotics of the past), *La Chronique Médicale* (under the direction of Dr. Augustin Cabanès), and *Aesculape* (a glossy, well-illustrated compendium of anomaly including articles ranging from the photographic materialization of ghosts to hypertrichoses, or hairiness, in women) were among the many therapeutical journals containing studies of local or exotic strains of fetishistic obsession.

In the field of medical speculation on literary examples, the eighteenth century, widely regarded as the last age of true libertinage, held a privileged place.[7] Jean-Jacques Rousseau, Rétif de la Bretonne, and later the Marquis de Sade consistently surfaced as the prototypes for nineteenth- and early-twentieth-century sexology. From Alfred Binet's interpretation of Rousseau's masochistic tendencies in his article "Le Fétichisme dans l'amour" (1887) to the reflections of the doctors Avalon and Charpentier in "Rétif de la Bretonne fétichiste" (1912), through to Havelock Ellis's discussions of "rétifisme" qua foot fetishism in his famous *Studies on the Psychology of Sex* (1936) and Maurice Heine's analyses of de Sade's newly discovered oeuvre, readings of eighteenth-century literary texts were legion.[8] We may infer from them a consistent hermeneutic

---

7. The medicalization of the eighteenth century by the nineteenth century took place on two levels: the first involved reconceiving libertine sexual practices (adultery, libertinage, anal eroticism, etc.) as perversions ("morbidity," "erotic madness," "genital inversion," etc.). The writing of Jean-Martin Charcot and Valentin Magnan, A. Moll, Benjamin Ball, Paul Laurent, Charles Féré and Paul Garnier, and the Goncourt brothers contributed to this sociomedical reconstruction. The second level was fostered primarily by Dr. Augustin Cabanès, who wrote on "the secret cabinet of history peeped into by a doctor" (1897). He was particularly well known for his psychophysiological diagnoses of Rousseau, Marie Antoinette, and Citizen Marat.

8. According to the Baron Octave Uzanne, a period of "Restifomania" began in 1883 and developed into a debate over foot fetishism (which would last well into the 1930s) after Binet's article appeared. Doctor Louis fixed the terms of the controversy in his analysis of *Le Pied de Fanchette* and *Le Joli Pied* ("Un Romancier fétichiste: Restif de la Bretonne," *La Chronique Médicale*, June 1904). Refusing to accept the characterization of Rétif as a foot fetishist, John Grand-Carteret (an eminent critic of caricature) accused Dr. Louis of being among the "déboulonneurs de grands hommes" (debunkers of great men) in his preface to an abridged edition of *Monsieur Nicolas* (1911). Dr. J. Avalon resumed the debate in *Aesculape*, Apr. 1912, pp. 89–93, and Doctor Louis Barras devoted an entire thesis to the subject: *Restif de la Bretonne: Fut-il fétichiste?* (Montpellier, 1912), in which he argued, according to Havelock Ellis,

strategy toward the definition and interpretation of fetishism that mediates between historical periods and literary genres.

Alfred Binet's seminal essay "Le Fétichisme dans l'amour" was the first study to transpose the concept from religion (as in Charles de Brosses's *Du Culte des dieux fétiches, ou Parallèle de l'ancienne Religion de l' Egypte avec la Religion actuelle de Nigritie* of 1760) and economics (Marx's *Capital*, 1867) to psychology. Binet is known primarily for his invention of the modern intelligence test; his work on fetishism, some fifteen years prior to his research on craniometry, seems to belong to a separate career.[9] Though informed, like the work of Cesare Lombroso (taxonomist of the physiognomical traits of "born prostitutes" and criminals) and Alphonse Bertillon (inventor of the identity card and fingerprint test), by a concern with descriptive measurement, the article eschews a narrow statistical approach. Binet invented a fetishism indebted to Enlightenment theories of classification and comparative religion, but modern in its psychosexual application.

This modern aspect, the fin-de-siècle circumstances under which his article was written, has been traced to a debate with Richard von Krafft-Ebing over the origins and causes of perversion. Krafft-Ebing had subscribed to the conventional "heredito-degenerescence" theory, believing perversion to be essentially innate or socially induced. Binet, taking issue with the blind belief in external causation, proposed a more purely psychological explanation, attributing the eclectic choice of fetish objects to some traumatic early sexual impression.[10]

Opening his essay, Binet offered a synopsis of fetishism's etymological origins that would become a kind of stock point of departure for future writers on the subject.[11] *Fetisso*, the pidgin version,

---

that Rétif's fetishism was a general condition (Havelock Ellis, *From Rousseau to Proust* [London: Constable, 1936], pp. 149–50, 172–75).

9. For a precis of Binet's career as the father of the modern intelligence test, see Stephen Jay Gould, *The Mismeasure of Man* (New York: Norton, 1981), pp. 146–55. Like many doctors of the period, Binet also dabbled in literature, collaborating with André de Latour de Lorde on a number of melodramas featuring the domestic havoc caused by hereditary madness (see *L'Obsession* [1905], *L'Horrible Expérience* [1909], *L'Homme mystérieux* [1910], *Les Invisibles* [1912], and *Un Crime dans une maison des fous* [1915].

10. See Elisabeth Roudinesco, *Histoire de la psychanalyse en France*, vol. 1: 1885–1939 (Paris: Seuil, 1986), pp. 235–38.

11. Dr. Paul Laurent, for example, began his *Fétichistes et érotomanes* (1904) with the same linguistic derivation from the Portuguese trading term *feitiço*, or native charm.

referred, as Binet pointed out, to the idea of an "enchanted object" that mysteriously held sway over individual destiny (from *fatum*). Borrowing Max Müller's pejorative allusion to the role of cult artifacts within pagan ritual and superstitious belief, Binet ascribed the term to a specific form of erotomania. Focusing on the role of the "object of obsession" in the stimulation of desire, he replaced Stendhal's celebrated *crystallization* with his own more shamanistic *divinization*, thus reinforcing a theoretically novel analogy between erotomania and cult worship: "The term *fetishism*, it seems to us, is rather appropriate for this genre of sexual perversion. The adoration these patients exhibit toward inert objects such as the nightcap or the bootnail resembles on every level the adoration exhibited by the savage or Negro toward fish-bones or shiny pebbles, with this single important difference that, in the cult of our patients, religious adoration is replaced by sexual appetite."[12] Binet thus emphasized the fractal, metonymic nature of the fetish, religious or sexual. Whether inanimate (the night cap, the apron, the nail of the shoe) or alive (red lips, an alluring curl of hair, an eye or mouth), the fetish was *partial*; a detached spot of intense visual cathexis. Foreshadowing Freud (though offering nothing as sophisticated as Freud's causal link between castration anxiety and phallic substitution), Binet placed the fetish in a signifying chain of synecdoches marking the displacement of genital desire to objects and hearkening back etiologically to a moment of sexual prehistory when the erotic idée fixe was indelibly scored on the psyche.

Inadvertently throwing into relief the dangerous ease with which passional devotion could give way to erotic interest (thereby exposing the fragile epistemological grounds dividing religion from sexuality, or "normal" from perverse desire), Binet went on to analyze the operations of fetishism in the writings of Jean-Jacques Rousseau. Rousseau's compulsive lying, strange erotic tastes, and erratic volleys of abuse toward the love object rendered him an

---

12. Alfred Binet, "Le Fétichisme dans l'amour," *Revue Philosophique* (1887): 144. Further references to this essay will be abbreviated B. Binet's identification of fetishism at the heart of religious worship continued to be endorsed by a subsequent generation of sexologists, including Freud and Magnus Hirschfeld, who wrote: "The transposition of sexual impulses into religious impulses, their mutual substitution, is only possible by virtue of a certain kinship existing between religious and sexual ecstasy. Just as the lover "adores" his beloved, calls her his "angel," his "idol," so does the love of the Savior, of the Virgin Mary, of the saints or the adoration of idols and fetishes, appear often to be a substitution of an erotic equivalent" (*Le Corps et l'amour* [Paris: Gallimard, 1937], p. 26).

exemplar of aberrant consciousness. Well served by Rousseau's abject wish fulfillment (his professed wish to lie at the feet of an imperious mistress), Binet pathologized his literary masochism, linking the posture of submission (*assujetissement*) to fetishistic paradigms of idolatry and idealization. Binet thus transformed Rousseau's narrative deviousness into a psychiatric model of sexual deviance.

Though according to Binet almost any work of romantic fiction might offer commonplace examples of the lover's frenzied hypostatization of his beloved's relics (her handkerchiefs, a piece of her dress, a book whose cover had been caressed by her hands), Rousseau's *Confessions* were for him particularly significant from a medical viewpoint. In them the author took the crucial step toward perversion, for the choice of privileged icon could no longer be seen as simply the result of its direct or contiguous connection to the actual body of the beloved. The relic, intransitively inscribed within the consciousness of the fetishistic lover, was revered in and for itself. No longer just the signifier of an absent totality, the material object was severed from the woman's body and actually *preferred* to the living self to which it originally belonged. "Amorous fetishism" Binet surmised, "has a tendency to detach completely, to isolate (the object) from anything separating it from its cult-worship, and when the object is part of a living person, the fetishist tries to render this part an independent entity" (B 263). Freestanding, self-enclosed, and abstracted from context, Binet's fetish object bore the signs of cutting, a violent image that, in addition to prefiguring Freud's association of fetishism with castration, underscored the importance of the synecdochic gaze.

For Binet, the epistemological difference between the workings of synecdoche in fetishism and in normal love was determined by the degree to which individual parts assumed semantic autonomy within the lover's code. When the beloved herself was fragmented and objectified, outmatched by the allure of her cosmetic appurtenances, then ordinary passion crossed over into fetishism:

> Rousseau confessed that seamstresses, maidservants, and shopgirls hardly tempted him; he needed women of class. "It's not at all the vanity produced by estate or rank that attracts me, it's sensual delight; a better preserved complexion; a finer, better-made dress, a daintier shoe, ribbons, lace, hair better dressed. I would always prefer the less pretty one as long as she had more of all of that." With his customary precision, Rousseau signaled the key factor in his predilection when he said that it was not a matter of vanity but of sensual pleasure. (B 161)

Capitalizing on Rousseau's privileging of *volupté*, or unadulterated pleasure, Binet drew attention to Rousseau's onanistic mode of object worship. The discourse of pleasure, so enthusiastically elaborated by the Goncourt brothers with reference to the mores of Rousseau's century, was here specifically identified with a haptic technique of perversion. Touching and stroking the nearest object at hand, obtaining titillation from a piece of ribbon or lace, the fetishist implicitly valorized object contiguity (metonymy), or what Binet characterized in terms of the twin principles of abstraction and generalization.[13]

These pathological tropes of perversion emphasized by the doctor in Rousseau's text were systematically built up to form a kind of "Rousseau case-history," crediting the philosophe with the invention of a psychic fetishism that went beyond the extended metonymy of the body. Following step-by-step the narrative genesis of Rousseau's famous discovery of masochism at the hands of his gentle disciplinarian Mlle Lambercier, Binet dilated on the fetishist's propensity for "erotic rumination"—that is, his ability to project his object fixation to the realm of intellectual and emotional obsession (B 253). *Abjection*, that condition of total ontological submission that Rousseau would tirelessly seek to reproduce, represented a highly refined version of the fetish: "What Rousseau loves in women," Binet observed, "is not just the puckered brow, the raised hand, the severe look, the imperious attitude, it's also the emotional state of which these attributes are the exterior translation; he loves the proud, contemptuous woman, who crushes him at her feet with the weight of her royal rage" (B 256). Unlike Rétif de la Bretonne, apparently content with a simple substitution of the pretty foot for the totalized body, Rousseau found his pleasure in a foot fetishism that was a significant step removed from the physical; an idealized mode of mental flagellation analogous to the monk's mortification of the flesh or the roué's self-destructive quest for moral debasement. "To love, say the mystics, one must suffer" (B 258), Binet wrote, a phrase that in its turn would become a kind of motto for Dr. Cabanès in his treatise *La Flagellation dans l'histoire et la littérature* (1899).

For Binet, this relationship between image making and orgasm— what he called *la dynamogénie*—not only indicated Rousseau's parti-

---

13. See Edmond and Jules de Goncourt, *L'Amour au dix-huitième siècle* (later included in *La Femme au dix-huitième siècle*) (Paris: E. Dentu, 1875).

ality for "erotic rumination," a pathological condition identifiable in most perverts, but also served to characterize an entirely new genre, that of literary perversion. Without exactly characterizing it as such, Binet sketched a theory of perverse writing that, ostensibly developed on behalf of medical diagnosis, inexorably expanded to comprise the domain of writing and reading as a whole. For the normal man, he surmised, the most paltry real experience would be superior to the *jouissance* derived from masturbatory fantasy. For the *ruminants*, however, who subversively reversed the hegemony of the Real over the Imaginary, images were rendered as self-sufficient mechanisms in ejaculatory production. Drawing the now-obvious analogy between sexual fantasizing and writing, he qualified what Freud would call sublimation as a form of textual perversion:

> The same effect of dynamogeny is obtained,...by the habit of writing, that is to say by objectifying thought on a piece of paper; the mental image is in this case more intense; it has the effect on the very person who gave birth to it of seeming to come from outside. Moreover, one must not forget that spoken language, and especially written language, is a marvelous instrument for analyzing thought; the subject, seeking through this means alone to write his dream, is obliged to analyze it; a weak, vague image no longer satisfies him; everything must be sharpened and nuanced under the influence of the pen. (B 270)

In this way Binet unearthed the fetishism submerged within writing itself, associating the process of contour sharpening (a kind of focalization) with the very essence of erotic fixation. This effect of sharpening the lens, of stabilizing the image as if plunging it into a chemical bath, yielded, moreover, interesting implications for the genre of realism still prevalent as a literary fashion of the *belle époque*. Commenting on the links between realism and the stylistic technique of hyperamplification, Binet clearly articulated a role for the eroticized detail in fiction: "Witnesses to a fact of real life," he wrote of writers in general, "they seek to amplify it in order to make their readers more sensitive to it." Analyzing Adolphe Belot's best-seller *La Bouche de Madame X*... he argued that the writer "had probably seen a benign real-life case of fetishism but had exaggerated the phenomenon for the sake of the novel" (B 272).

In his evocation of real-life perversions writ large, Binet was undoubtedly referring to the way in which Zola, Maupassant, and the Goncourt brothers (among others) had raided the medical archives as source material for their experiments in clinical realism.

Even when there was no proof that nineteenth-century authors had consulted scientific documents, it is fairly evident that they appealed to the public's intuitive grasp of psychopathology. Literary works specifically cited by Binet—Gustave Droz's *La Femme gênante*; "La Maison du vent," by Dumas fils; Barbey D'Aurevilly's *Vellini*; and Georges Rodenbach's *Le Carilloneur*—all relied on fetishistic symptoms that were presumably recognizable to the lay reader. In this sense it is perhaps no wonder that time and again, in the supposedly scientific case studies of the doctors, literary examples were adduced to support experimental evidence rather than just the reverse.

In his suggestion of a pathology of realist stylistics, in his insinuation that all writers are potential fetishists, Binet thus expanded the epistemological parameters of perversion while inviting further speculation on the repertory of forms that textual fetishism might assume. By characterizing fetishism as an extreme genre of normal love Binet opened the way for all the tropes of amorous discourse to be seen as themselves fetishistic. Divinization, synecdoche, abstraction, depersonalization, and psychic fixation emerge as the preeminent defining features of fetishism, despite their appearance in normal love as well. With degree the only significant differentiating factor, the risk of "perversion" loomed perilously near.

No doubt sensing the need to remarginalize this outlaw edge of sexuality, Binet had recourse to further medicalization of the lover's discourse. His strategy, once again highly literary, consisted of defamiliarizing the commonplace bourgeois codes of romanticism: the conventions of idolatry, idealization, and hyperbole. Stendhal's *De l'amour*, for Binet an omnipresent intertext, thus became in his hands a manual detailing the stages and modalities of fetishism rather than seduction. The magical *déclic*, the sign on the lover's body that ignites attraction and fuels the quest to reproduce the image in the Other (even a defect, a disfiguring smallpox mark, could function in this way according to Stendhal), became within the confines of Binet's theory the fixative moment, the fetishistic primal scene to be found both in every normal ritual of enamoration and in its representation. Without knowing, perhaps, where his reading of textual perversion would lead him, Binet made a "pervert" of Everyman: lover, reader, and writer.

.

Variety and instruction—these values ascribed to the linguistic anomaly picked up and assiduously stored over the years like an amusing bagatelle by the master nineteenth-century lexicographer Emile Littré—may be seen as the twin raisons d'être for a clinical realism that pervaded late-nineteenth-century prose.

> Like a highly experienced doctor, who, perusing the diary of his cases at the end of his career, pulls out those he considers to be particularly instructive, so I have opened my journal, my dictionary, that is, to select a series of anomalies which struck me or embarrassed me even when I wrote them.... This proliferation of little facts, dispersed throughout my dictionary, are here subject to sustained scrutiny. They have the interest of variety, and at the same time, since they are facts, they have the interest of reality. Variety amuses, reality instructs.[14]

In this way Littré's *pathologie verbale*, with its didactic "little real" placed on exhibit, exemplifies the word itself made stigma. Connoting an image of language "on the couch," or in the clinic, this expression was also symptomatic of a zeitgeist enamored of scientisms impossible to subsume under one rubric yet uniformly maniacal even in their eclecticism. A unique coalescence of positivism, Darwinism, sociopathology, tabloid reporting, medical jurisprudence, anthropo-criminology, national chauvinism, pessimism (Schopenhauer), exoticism, racism, mysticism, sexology, naturalism, and decadence fomented an intellectual culture in which Binet's essay on fetishism was fully contextualized.[15] To enable us to appreciate the extent to which fetishism, as a form of verbal pathology, became identifiable as a style of writing legible to a broad reading public, a brief review of this medico-literary culture may be helpful.

Following in the French positivist tradition of physiological psychology, from Balzac's *Physiologie du mariage* (1829) to Paul Bourget's *Physiologie de l'amour moderne* (1889), Remy de Gourmont's book on the "physic of love" (translated as *The Natural Philosophy of Love*) typifies the psychobiological tendency within nosological realism at the turn of the century. Written between 1901 and 1903 his "essay on sexual instinct" heralds the new field of what he refers to as "sexual ethnography." *Physique de l'amour* places itself under the sign of the maxim *more bestiarum* (bestial love) —"love is profoundly

14. Emile Littré, *Pathologie verbale ou lésions de certains mots dans la cours de l'usage* (Paris: Société des Amis de la Bibliothèque Nationale, 1986), pp. 8–9.
15. Though it would require a separate study to investigate fully the myriad intellectual genealogies present in this mid-fin de siècle, a brief overview (following on the heels of important historical studies of crime, medicine, and madness by Elisabeth Roudinesco, Robert Nye, Jan Goldstein, Ruth Harris, and Roger Williams) may illuminate sources of a nosological consciousness inclusive of fetishistic realism.

animal, and that is its beauty."[16] De Gourmont documented the sexual life of plants and animals and introduced the word *scissiparity* as a kind of presciently psychoanalytical concept mediating between ego-splitting, sexual difference, and gender instability: "sexual attitudes are attributed by Nature to both sexes: there is no ordained male or female role,... each can don the same costume, wear the same mask, wield the same weapon, tool or sabre,... and short of consulting Life's archives, we may never know if a sex is masquerading or performing a natural role" (*P* 61). The great travesty, the grand "parade" of seduction common to animal and human species alike, signified for de Gourmont that which was "true" in love. Ludic sexuality, recast through Darwinism as an appetite-enhancing ruse of nature, emerges as the norm of love's "physic" (or motor) at the expense of modesty, chastity, and asceticism. These last, so vaunted by religion, are dismissed as unnatural acts. De Gourmont would later parody this epistemological inversion of normal and perverse in his play *Lilith* (1906), in which the human race is perpetuated only when Satan's mistress solicits fecundation from a timorous Adam. Quivering, panting, and moaning, drawing Satan himself *in vulva infernum*, Lilith personifies an essentialist vision of the animal nature of the female much like Rachilde's throbbing heroine in *L'Animale* (1903), who sees herself in the mirror as a woman-beast, with red eyes and paws, pendulous breasts, and a "splendid fleece."[17]

Citing Schopenhauer, who had used as an analogy to the external laws of nature the example of a putrid flower (*arum muscivorum*) that could "fool" cadaver-seeking flies with its scent, Remy de Gourmont associated the mating instinct with the metaphysical workings of a blind, indifferent will. In its fusion of pessimism, natural philosophy, and sexology, *Physique de l'amour* could be bracketed on the literary side by Zola's *La Bête humaine* (featuring Lantier's struggle against innate urges to rape and kill) and Proust's *Sodome et Gomorrhe* (opening with the famous fertilization scene between the bumblebee [Jupien] and the orchid [Charlus]). On the medical side, it fit into a canon including Prosper Lucas's *Traité de l'hérédité* (1850); Herbert Spencer's *Principes de psychologie* (1855); Auguste Bénédict Morel's *Traité des dégénérescences* (1857); Théodule Ribot's

16. Remy de Gourmont, *Physique de l'amour: Essai sur l'instinct sexuel* (Paris: Les Editions 1900, 1989), p. 17. Further references to this work will be abbreviated *P*.
17. Rachilde (Marguerite Valette), *L'Animale* (Paris: Mercure de France, 1903), p. 307.

De l'hérédité (1872), *Maladies de la volonté* (1884), and *La Philosophie de Schopenhauer* (1890); Cazalis's *Le Livre du néant* (1872); Max Nordau's *Dégénérescence* (1893); Jules Dallemagne's *Dégénérés et déséquilibrés* (1894); Emile Laurent's *L'Amour morbide* (1895); Charles Féré's *L'Instinct sexuel* (1899); and Otto Weininger's misogynistic *Sexe und Charakter* (1904).

In addition to providing the medical underpinnings for a positivist literary heredito-degenerescence theory of character popularized by Hippolyte Taine and Zola, this corpus raised new questions pertaining to the role of the senses in aesthetic appreciation (as in Henri Bergson's study of laughter) that in turn intersected with Krafft-Ebing's notion of physiological fetishism. Citing Binet and Max Dessoir (who published an article in German on the fetishism of love), Krafft-Ebing delineated the broader sphere of fetishistic sensualism—the idolatry of physical qualities in the Other, whether eye, voice, smell, or touch. Théodule Ribot's description of a kind of "inner haptic" (*Gemeingefühl*)—an "internal touching by which we are made aware of the state of our organs, the tension of our muscles, the degree of our lassitude or sensual delight"—may be interpreted in this light as a fetishism of the interior body.[18] As if taking this interiorized fetishism as his program, the exoticist novelist and poet Victor Segalen shuttled conceptually between internal and external aesthetic phenomenologies of the body in a thesis outline planned while he was a medical student in 1900. The first chapter was to be dedicated to a comparison between clinical and naturalist case histories; the second proposed an examination of manias, hysterical fits, and hallucinations in novels such as *Salammbô*, *Le Horla* (an anagram of Dr. Cazalis's pen name, Lahors), *La Faustin*, and *A rebours*. A third intended to explore "sensorial synaesthesias" in the symbolist school. Heredity and degenerescence as portrayed in Zola's *Le Docteur Pascal*, drug use and alcoholism in works by Daudet and Théophile Gautier, the morbid psychology of crowds in Gérard Hauptmann's *Les Tisserands*, and, perhaps most interesting, a reading of Pierre Loti's *Le Rêve* as a case study of déjà-vu—each was allotted its section in this ambitious project. In the resulting book, *Les Cliniciens ès lettres*, Segalen (though considerably narrowing the focus) argued convincingly that realists and naturalists had made the medicalized body a topos of destiny in the

---

18. Théodule Ribot, *L'Hérédité psychologique* (Paris: Librairie Germer Baillière, 1882), pp. 90–91.

novel. In this regard he quoted Edmond de Goncourt's letter to Zola on the day following Jules de Goncourt's gruesome death from syphilis, referring to how detailed medical descriptions of the disease presented in their novel *Charles Demailly* retrospectively seemed to have uncannily foretold the untimely death of the author: "When we wrote *Charles Demailly* together, I was more ill than he was. Alas! He has hanged himself since. *Charles Demailly*! It really is most bizarre, the fact that he wrote his own story fifteen years before!"[19]

Constituted on the one hand by the writer's appropriation of medical jargon (de Gourmont lamented that while physicians in Molière's time spoke Latin, in his own they spoke Greek), and on the other by a scientific tradition sensitive to the literariness of the medical gaze (an astonishing number of doctors published novels under pseudonyms), the medico-esthetic stylistics of anatomy were also reinforced by a proliferation of scholarly studies concentrating fetishistically on body parts. Gilles de la Tourette's *Traité clinique et thérapeutique de l'hystérie* (1891–95) contained, for example, a chapter on "the hysterical breast" that chronicled the case of a patient whose facial blush was matched by mammarian spotting and swelling.[20] Paul Richer, an artist who collaborated with Charcot in developing an iconography of seized-up postures and morphological malformations in hysterics, also played a crucial role in generating a visual lexicon of the stigmata-riddled medical body. Subscribing to the principle of *similia similibus curantur* (the same are cured by the same), Richer took his cue in providing exact copies of the hysterical body from "primitive" artists who depicted pathological divinities afflicted by the wounds they were supposed to heal. In addition to fashioning plaster casts of "hysterical contractures" (*le pied bot, le pied tors*) he left writings with titles such as "Notes on the Fold of the Buttocks" (1889) that seem now like virtual parodies of naturalist depictions of the convulsive body part. Karl Kraus's quip, "There is no more unhappy being under the sun than a fetishist that pines for a boot and has to content himself with an entire woman," could easily be applied to Charcot and his disciples, all obsessively dedicated to the clinical methodology of "pictorial" focalization on an

19. Edmond de Goncourt as cited by Victor Segalen, *Les Cliniciens ès lettres* (1902; Montpellier: Fata Morgana, 1980), p. 76.
20. Gilles de la Tourette, *Traité clinique et thérapeutique de l'hystérie*, vol. 2 (Paris: Plon, 1895), p. 492.

isolated part of the body.[21] Clearly, the supernatural severed hand in Maupassant's "La Main écorché" (1875) and Zoë Bertgang's foot in Wilhelm Jensen's *Gradiva: A Pompeiian Fantasy* (1903) formed part of a larger episteme of fetishism grounded in medico-anatomical synecdoche.

Within the encompassing genre of nosological realism, fetishistic synecdoche may be distinguished from medicalized description in general by its textual eroticism. Inanimate objects registered as erogenous zones in the narrator's eye, bodily extremities tinctured with redness or "split" in a mock-staging of castration, repulsive details, miming the fetishist's putative tendency to wallow in disgust, and physical mutilation, these are among the signs of a metonymic poetics encoded as fetishistic.

.

From Monsieur Nicolas's high-heel worship to Emma Bovary's revered slipper or Thérèse Raquin's attention-snatching boot, foot fetishism has attained a literary "pedigree" in the history of French literature. But rather than thematically catalog such proverbial phallic symbols as they appear in great literary works, I will examine a number of less familiar texts written in the "low-rent" realist mode. Récits and novellas by writers such as Adolphe Belot and Octave Mirbeau offer a clarified image of what I mean by the expression "fetishistic fiction," because their generic contours so closely resemble those of the archival case history. Unheroic texts of confession and talking-cure, parables of base instinct and perplexing longing told by anonymous narrators, stories of mental illness and hysteria cataloging in detail the full range of morbid symptoms, these works of a countercanon blur the line between fiction and nonfiction.[22]

---

21. Karl Kraus as cited by Jean Bellemin-Noël, *Gradiva au pied de la lettre* (Paris: Presses Universitaires de France, 1983), p. 258.
22. Literary anecdote peppered the medical case history. As an example, Dr. Paul Moreau de Tours's *Des Aberrations du sens génésique* (Paris: Asselin, 1880) traced erotomania to the allegory of Love, seen by the ancients as a kind of vengeance of love (loving too much). The doctor refers to classical tales of a Greek who became so enamored of a Cupid statue that he defiled it with his seed and left an offering of a crown. The Delphic oracle ordered his release because he paid for his pleasure. He also cites Lucan and Saint Clement of Alexandria, who told the story of a young man who falls in love with a Venus by Praxiteles, hides at night in the temple, and sullies the goddess in an outrage to public morals.

If one looks first at the proximity of clinical case histories to fiction, Freud's analyses of Dora, the Wolf-man, and the Rat-man stand out as extraordinary models of psychoanalysis as literature. But even the earliest recorded case histories of fetishism reveal a clear affinity to their literary counterparts. Charcot and Magnan's "Inversion du sens génital et autres perversions sexuelles" included the tales of several patients who ejaculated uncontrollably at the sight of shoenails, aprons, and nightcaps. Case 4, concerning the lover of *bonnets de nuit*, resembles a short story with its minute attention to the interests and habits of family and milieu. We learn that the subject's father loved books, that his sister frequented the theater, that his rebellious brother became a coachman, and that M. X himself was a collector of bibelots. This seemingly irrelevant background adds a narrative suspense to the ensuing chronicle of the patient's defeat of conjugal impotence through the fantasy of a wrinkled lady in a nightcap.[23] As in many of Krafft-Ebing's case studies, this narrative of fetishistic ritual approaches the comedic genre. Georges Lanteri Laura has pointed out that whereas records of masochism and sadism "conserve the dignity accruing to a narrative of pain," accounts of fetishism and exhibitionism always border on the ridiculous: "to risk so much for so little seems grotesque and pitiful; fetishistic clients give off the impression of being had, of paying too much for a paltry illusion."[24]

If comedy emerges as the prevailing genre of the authentic case history, then irony, its close relation, seems to be the dominant mode of case-history fiction. Consider, for example, Adolphe Belot's *La Bouche de Mme X...*, one of Binet's important paradigms of fetishistic narrative. Belot was a society writer whose best-sellers, sporting titillating titles such as *Les Baigneuses de Trouville*, *La Maison centrale des femmes*, *La Bossue*, and *La Sultane parisienne* were often set in brothels. *La Bouche de Mme X...* takes place in a specialty house of prostitution, its atmosphere of intimacy enhanced through first-person narration. The central character is a ladies' man, an expert on all international types of women, and a connoisseur of the female mouth. He is also a personal friend of Charcot, who informs him that his enigmatic passion makes him "a remarkable subject." The novel opens with the narrator's reception at the

---

23. Charcot and Magnan, *Inversion du sens génital et autres perversions sexuelles*, pp. 30–32.

24. Georges Lanteri Laura, *Lectures des perversions: Histoire de leur appropriation médicale*, (Paris: Masson, 1979), p. 43.

brothel, where he is a favored habitué. To his demand for something different, the madam proposes a society woman who seeks the transgressive pleasure of prostitution but will consent to submit only on the condition that strict rules of secrecy be observed. She will remain veiled, able to inspect the gentleman without his being able to do the same. Here the novelty obviously lies in the conceit of doubled, gender-reversed voyeurism, with the male viewer becoming, in this match, the object of a female voyeur.

When he enters the room, the narrator perceives an elegant form swathed in silk, velvet, and lace, whose only visible facial attribute is a mouth. The spectacle provides an example of scotomization, or visual distortion: veil and gloves cut the face, obscuring it from view. The framed mouth, magnetizing the reader's gaze, comes to the fore in hyperfocus. More than just a "reality effect" (an illusion of reality built up by a mass or concatenation of seemingly useless little notations), this detail acts as a spur or point of entry (*point tichique*) into the symbolic order of desire. As an eroticized synecdoche the mouth decomposes as a unified image the closer we come, causing the eye to swim in a miasma of undulating smaller synecdoches that interlock and pull the reader deeper into desire:

> Cette bouche encadrée dans le haut par le voile noir et dans le bas par des doigts gantés de chevreau, appuyés sur le menton, ressortait superbe, voluptueuse, lascive. Elle était grande, franchement dessinée, nettement arrêtée aux coins, où apparaissait un léger duvet, un duvet de blonde. Les lèvres épaisses, rouges, écartées l'une de l'autre, celle du haut relevée comme un bourrelet, s'ouvraient librement, largement sur des dents blanches, solides, bien rangées. Oui, c'était bien la bouche que j'avais toujours désirée. J'en avais beaucoup connu, beaucoup aimé, et je n'avais jamais pu trouver celle-là.

This mouth, framed above by the black veil, below by fingers gloved in kid resting on her chin, emerged superb, voluptuous, lewd. It was large, clearly outlined, cleanly demarcated at the corners, where the lightest down, the down of a blond, could be perceived. The red, thick lips, drawn apart one from the other, the upper one raised up like a cushion, opened freely, widely onto white, solid, perfectly arranged teeth. Yes, it really was the mouth that I had always desired. I had known many, loved many, but I had never been able to find this one.[25]

25. Adolphe Belot, *La Bouche de Mme X...* (Paris: Dentu, Librairie de la Société de Gens de Lettres, 1882), p. 120.

Fighting to restore a vision of totality as a means of overcoming the castratory visual bait of the scotomized face, the narrator struggles to glimpse beneath the veil. His efforts prove futile, and worse, the mouth remains inanimate, inert, and closed.[26] The part for whole symbolism here is hardly subtle, but it illustrates the way in which fetishistic synecdoche relies on a gendered scopic poetics: a voyeuristic mise-en-scène, framing conceits (the veil), visual distortion (the mouth appears temporarily out of focus), foregrounding of a singular detail ("I had known many, loved many, but I had never been able to find this one"), and excessive libidinal expenditure for the sake of a frozen, idealized image (the narrator embarks on a feverish quest for the mouth, taking him through dozens of women).

The detail also functions fetishistically in the *mise-en-abyme* or "hall of mirrors effect." An interesting example of this technique in which the fetishistic synecdoche is politicized rather than eroticized may be found in François Coppée's article "Fétichisme" (*Le Journal*, December 15, 1894). Coppée satirizes the fetishism of national heroes in the kitsch artifacts of patriotic culture, specifically as it pertains to the national cult worship of Napoleon. The officer who can smoke only a pipe emblazoned with the profile of the conqueror, or the Grand Army veteran who can take his tobacco only out of a tin with Napoleon's hat on it, must, he argues sardonically, be accused of pagan idolatry. He recounts how in passing the window of a village cabaret, he catches sight of a vial (forgotten and covered with dust), sporting a picture of the "brav' général." On closer inspection, he discovers that the image represents General Boulanger. "Forgotten so soon, though it was only yesterday that his star shone so high!" he thinks to himself, deciding that "fetishism for fetishism, I prefer that of the Grand Empereur."

---

26. The rest of the story proceeds as follows. Unable to possess the mouth, or to discover the identity of the unknown woman, the narrator enlists his friends to help him find the mouth. He checks from woman to woman, discarding the rest of their bodies in his comparative inspection of a single trait: "in short, it wasn't my mouth, or rather hers, let's not confuse them" (*La Bouche de Mme X...* 163). In despair, he repairs to the country for a rest cure. While there, he is introduced to a countess whose mouth he thinks he recognizes, but by now he is suspicious of wish-fulfilling illusions: "I was obviously mistaken, this devil of a mouth had obsessed me for so long that I saw it everywhere" (*La Bouche de Mme X...*, 183). Upon learning that she has just spent three months in Paris, he recovers hope and even thinks he discerns a ray of blush on her face. During a soirée, he spies on her, hoping to catch her looking for him. As they dance, he feels he recognizes the forms of "the goddess." A protracted period of disbelief mingled with credibility ensues until finally he elicits her confession. Avowing that she was driven to the brothel because an impotent husband was unable to satisfy her, she collapses into the arms of the narrator. The book ends with mouth on mouth.

Synecdoche, as this example shows yet again, plays a crucial role in the fetishistic récit, although in general I would argue that it must be distinguished from the *blazon* insofar as the fetish, as Kant pointed out, implies a degraded, purely materialist sign, nonrepresentative and cut off from the organic whole. In his short story "Vernissage," Octave Mirbeau emphasized this mutilated, debased poetics, personifying what Lacan called "the phantasm of the dismembered body" (*le corps morcelé*) in the character of an overzealous surgeon. Docteur Doyen becomes so famous as a "body sculptor" that fashionable women beg him to cut off their limbs (*dis*embodiment as a work of art).[27] A similar theme occurs in Mirbeau's early novel *Le Calvaire* in which the painter Lirat mutilates the body of an allegorical Venus. In the manner of one of Courbet's corpulent nudes, she is presented as coming out of a dark crevice of shadow, carried up on the wings of a beast, her body thrown back, her thighs covered with folds of fat and beads of greasy flesh, her stomach gaping, and her expression avid, greedily "all mouth." This grotesque image is set off against a crowd of leering old men with convulsed eyes and drooling mouths, a send-up perhaps, of "Susannah and the Elders."[28]

Mirbeau's grotesque realism devolves consistently around the body which seems to speak its sufferings to the eye. In the short story "Piédenat," a mother lives with her son in the apartment of a cocotte. The narrator's gaze conspicuously zooms in on her repulsive hand—symbol of swallowed pride and resignation to vice: "Sa main surtout attirait mon attention, une main courte et grasse, creusée de fossettes profondes, dont les doigts semblaient de caoutchouc, une patte répugnante de bête visqueuse qui paraissait faite exprès pour tripoter de sales choses [It was above all her hand that attracted my attention, a hand short and fleshy, furrowed with deep crevices, the fingers like rubber; it was the repugnant paw of a clammy beast that seemed made for fingering dirty things]."[29] A variation of this scopic detailism recurs in "L'Octogénaire," the gruesome tale of a denatured son who forces his aged mother to pose naked for painters. She assumes the posture of shame: "Ses mains et une partie des avant-bras plongeaient entre les cuisses rapprochées, pour cacher le bas du ventre et jeter un voile

---

27. Octave Mirbeau, "Vernissage," *Le Journal*, Feb. 16, 1902, repr. in *Des artistes* (Paris: Union Générale d'Editions, 1986), pp. 400–405.
28. Octave Mirbeau, *Le Calvaire* (Paris: Union Générale d'Editions, 1986), p. 150.
29. Octave Mirbeau, *La Pipe de cidre: Oeuvres inédites* (Paris: Flammarion, 1919), p. 27.

d'ombre épaisse sur la nudité attristante du sexe [Her hands and a part of her forearm were plunged between her squeezed-together thighs to hide the end of her stomach and to throw a veil of thick shadow over the pitiable nakedness of her genitals]."[30] As in *La Bouche de Mme X...* a visual framing technique is used to concentrate the gaze, and as in the example of the painter Lirat in *Le Calvaire* the ocularizing conceit of the painting itself guarantees a kind of self-reflexivity to the topos of looking. Lacan theorized this "laying down of the gaze" before a riveting detail:

> The painter gives something to the person who must stand in front of his painting which, in part at least, might be summed up thus—*You want to see? Well, take a look at this!* He gives something for the eye to feed on, but he invites the person to whom this picture is presented to lay down his gaze there as one lays down one's weapons. This is the pacifying, Apollonian effect of painting. Something is given not so much to the gaze as to the eye, something that involves abandonment, the *laying down*, of the gaze.[31]

In the descriptions cited thus far, Mirbeau clearly makes a comparable overture—"you want to see, well look then!"—but it is a taunt rather than an invitation. The detail that he proffers to the eye is morbid, chilling. Far from being the rewarding "glance" of light coming off an apple or candlestick in a Dutch still life, or the "pacifying, Apollonian" detail in which the aesthete's oculus luxuriates, his fetishized synecdoches resemble "shots" at the object that make the eyes smart afterward. Whether comic or tragic, alluring or repulsive, the visual pinprick of the detail constitutes an essential feature of nosological realism.

As the broad parameters of what constituted medical discourse in the nineteenth century gave way to the more specialized disciplines of psychiatry and psychoanalysis by the century's end, nosological realism was joined with case-history narrative conventions, thus constituting a new kind of writing, one that, following Freud and Sander Gilman, I have called pathography. From P. L. Jacob's *Curiosités de l'Histoire de France* (1858) to Richard von Krafft-Ebing's *Psychopathia Sexualis* (1886); from Oskar Panizza's *Pyschopathia Criminalis* (1898) to Dr. Augustin Cabanès's *Le Cabinet secret de l'histoire* (1900); and from Havelock Ellis's *Studies in the Psychology of*

---

30. Octave Mirbeau, "L'Octogénaire," in ibid., p. 99.
31. Jacques Lacan, "The Line and the Light," in *The Four Fundamental Concepts of Psycho-analysis*, ed. Jacques-Alain Miller, trans. Alan Sheridan (New York: Norton, 1978), p. 101.

Sex (1936) to Magnus Hirschfeld's *Geschlechts Anomalien und Perversionen* (1957), legendary biographies were pathologized; that is, they were built up as medical dossiers and collected like so many rare specimens.[32] Each case study was exhibited, as in a psychohistorical museum, demonstrating individually the determinative traits of a given perversion, obsession, or paranormal idée fixe, and exemplifying as a totality the taxonomy of criminal anomaly.

Despite this wealth of material, there exists, to date, no satisfactory definition of the pathography. Freud used the term provocatively in the final chapter of his *Leonardo da Vinci and a Memory of His Childhood* (1910) to defend himself against the slings of idealistic biographers intent on glorifying "great men" even at the expense of truth:

> It would be futile to blind ourselves to the fact that readers to-day find all pathography unpalatable. They clothe their aversion in the complaint that a pathographical review of a great man never results in an understanding of his importance and his achievements, and that it is therefore a piece of useless impertinence to make a study of things in him that could just as easily be found in the first person one came across. But this criticism is so manifestly unjust that it is only understandable when taken as a pretext and a disguise. Pathography does not in the least aim at making the great man's achievements intelligible; and surely no one should be blamed for not carrying out something he has never promised to do. The real motives for the opposition are different. We can discover them if we bear in mind that biographers are fixated on their heroes in a quite special way. In many cases they have chosen their heroes as the subject of their studies because—for reasons of their personal emotional life—they have felt a special affection for him from the very first. They then devote their energies to a task of idealization, aimed at enrolling the great man among the class of their infantile models—at reviving in him, perhaps, the child's ideal of his father. To gratify this wish they obliterate the individual features of their subject's physiognomy; they smooth over the traces of his life's struggles with internal and external resistances, and they tolerate in him no vestige of human weakness or imperfection. They thus present us with what is in

---

32. The most prepossessing of all these studies from a literary point of view is Panizza's, particularly the section called "Typologie de la *psychopathia criminalis.*" Here, in a wonderful tongue-in-cheek description of "l'état démentiel final" (the final state of dementia) awaiting the lapsed or deviating monarchist, he couched a biting critique of the German empire of William II. Seeming to anticipate twentieth-century instances of the psychiatrization of repression, he ironically entered the term *la mania anti-gouvernementalis* into the lexicon of terms used to describe the mental condition of political subversives.

fact a cold, strange, ideal figure, instead of a human being to whom we might feel ourselves distantly related. That they should do this is regrettable, for they thereby sacrifice truth to an illusion, and for the sake of their infantile phantasies abandon the opportunity of penetrating the most fascinating secrets of human nature.[33]

In addition to refusing the "clean," expurgated life, Freud implies that the distinguishing feature of the pathography is its attention to the sexual peculiarities of the creative artist or the minute eruptions of repressed desire in the work of art. He identifies the single most important technique developed by psychoanalysis for unlocking the "fascinating secrets of human nature" as a heightened sensitivity to detail. Noting an error made by Leonardo as to the exact time of his father's death, he remarks, "It is only a small detail, and anyone who is not a psycho-analyst would attach no importance to it," only to add didactically: "But the psycho-analyst thinks differently. To him nothing is too small to be a manifestation of hidden mental processes."[34]

Freud's pathography of Leonardo may be historically and comparatively situated in a canon of psychological fiction particularly popular in European literature from the end of the nineteenth century through the 1930s. When, in his study of Leonardo da Vinci, Freud angrily fended off the accusation that he had "merely written a psychoanalytic novel," one must remember the notoriety gained by the case-history novel. In England there were "coming out" works, such as E. M. Forster's *Maurice* and Radclyffe Hall's *The Well of Loneliness*. In Russia novels of mental instability, such as Gogol's *Diary of a Superfluous Man* and Dostoevsky's novella *The Double*, defined the literary vanguard. In Germany novellas of bourgeois neurosis and monomania, such as Stefan Zweig's "The Royal Game," "The Burning Secret," and "Amok," Arthur Schniztler's *The Confirmed Bachelor*, and Rilke's *The Notebooks of Malte Laurids Brigge*, directly inspired or were inspired by the burgeoning field of psychoanalysis. In France a host of minor naturalist works evoked the contagion of madness, psychosis, and hallucination. Forgotten

33. Sigmund Freud, *Leonardo da Vinci and a Memory of His Childhood*, Standard Edition 11:130. This passage offers an extremely rich critique of how idealization motivates literary scholarship. The case of biography is perhaps the most straightforward, but one can easily see, even in the writing of critical theory, how an author may be spurred on by his or her idealization of a mentor or rival critic.
34. Ibid., p. 119.

plays by Alfred Binet (the same who wrote on fetishism) and André de Lorde, *L'Obsession* and *L'Homme mystérieux,* and forgotten novellas, such as Jean Lorrain's *Songeuse,* Maurice Quillot's *L'Entraîné,* Léon Hennique's *Un Caractère* (not to mention Maupassant's better-known récits "Fou?," "Le Horla," "Le Docteur Heraclieus Gloss"), qualified as literary equivalents of Cesare Lombroso's "genius and madness" study *(Le Génie et la folie)* in their dissections of insanity and horror.[35]

In the Vienna Psychoanalytic Society, presided over by Freud between 1902 and 1918, the pathography flourished as a genre of psychoanalysis. In addition to his analysis of Leonardo, Freud contributed an early paper on "Psychopathic Characters on the Stage" (1905). Wilhelm Stekel's *Poetry and Neurosis* (1909), Isador Sadger's *Heinrich von Kleist: A Pathographical-Psychological Study,* Max Graf's analysis of Wagner's character as seen in *The Flying Dutchman (A Contribution to the Psychology of Artistic Creation,* 1911), Otto Rank's *The Artist,* and Theodor Reik's *Arthur Schnitzler as Psychologist* (1913)—all could be classed under the rubric of pathography.[36]

In a more contemporary critical vein, Evelyne Keitel has characterized the psychopathography as a work of fiction in which experiences such as schizophrenia, hallucination, autism, and anorexia are transcribed and transmitted through ingenious techniques of reader response:

> Psychopathographies comprise a quantity of apparently quite different texts: traditional pathographies (Freud's case histories) as well as those texts about psychoses which, as a phenomenon of contemporary literature, have not yet had the critical attention they deserve. In this book, I started out by *hypothetically* defining psychopathographies by two criteria, one of content and one of aesthetic response. Psychopathographies thematize psychotic personality dissolutions and/or psychotherapies, and are thus obligated to grapple with phenomena beyond the margins of discourse. The way in which a psychopathography translates psychotic phenomena into linguistic structures determines, in turn, the extent to which such a borderline situation can be conveyed, and even experienced, in the reading process.[37]

35. André Vial, *L'Internement de Maupassant: Documents inédits* (Paris, 1892).
36. For this bibliography I am indebted to Louis Rose, "The Psychoanalytic Movement in Vienna: Toward a Science of Culture" (Ph.D. diss., Princeton University, 1986).
37. Evelyne Keitel, *Reading Psychosis: Readers, Texts, and Psychoanalysis,* trans. Anthea Bell (Oxford: Basil Blackwell, 1989), p. 85.

Though Keitel's emphasis on the rhetoric of madness as a distinguishing trait of pathography is essential, I feel impelled to extrapolate the generic criteria to include: (1) the medicolegal dossier as transposed into fiction; (2) demonic hagiography as defined by the unsaintly life of civilization's greatest "perverts" (Gilles de Rais, Jack the Ripper, the Countess Bathory); (3) psychohistorical biography (Alexander the Great, Mohammed, Marie Antoinette) that focuses on the "dirty little secrets" of celebrated men and women; and (4) the tabloid story featuring scenes from the human circus: freak shows, gladiatorial sports, sagas of family members who commit unnatural acts, and so on. This is by no means an exhaustive delineation of this bastard genre of pathography, but it frames an exemplary gamut of turn-of-the-century texts that explore the logic of perversion and call for an interpretive approach amalgamating New History, close reading, and psychoanalysis.

CHAPTER 3

· Cabinet Secrets: Peep Shows,
Prostitution, and Bric-a-bracomania
in the Fin-de-siècle Interior

· Toward the end of the nineteenth century, when the bourgeois interior became increasingly like a museum in which curios, antiques, and personal memorabilia were lovingly displayed, a literary microgenre characterizable as "cabinet fiction" developed concurrently. The cabinet text may be seen as a sociotext subsuming all the nuances of a newly defined domestic interior. The word *cabinet* has multiple associations, from work space and display case to water closet (*la commodité, les lieux, les vécés*). As Hubert Damisch has pointed out, the *cabinet* as defined by Diderot and d'Alembert in the *Encyclopédie* designated above all a private place.[1] Indeed, the *mentalité* of the cabinet presumed an "architecture of private life" or bourgeois arrangement of domestic space, which had gradually evolved in the eighteenth century.[2] Zones forbidden to the opposite sex, such as the man's study or *salle d'antiquités* and the woman's dressing room or boudoir, served to render the cabinet a gendering divide within the interior. No doubt it was this atmosphere of the forbidden that transformed the cabinet into an architectural fetish in eighteenth-century literature. In Vivant Denon's anonymously

---

1. Hubert Damisch, "The Museum Device: Notes on Institutional Changes," *Lotus International* 35 (1982): 5.
2. For a discussion of the curiosity cabinet from the sixteenth to the eighteenth century, see Krzysztof Pomian, *Collectionneurs, amateurs et curieux. Paris, Venise: XVI–XVIII siècle* (Paris: Gallimard, 1987). See also Monique Eleb-Vidal's comprehensive and illuminating study, *Architectures de la vie privée: Maisons et mentalités, XVII–XIX siècles* (Brussels: Archives d'Architecture Moderne, 1989).

published libertine novella *Point de lendemain* (No Tomorrow; 1777), the cabinet emerges as the most erotic object in the text. A recessive, enchanted room made of glass panels on which leafy groves have been painted in trompe l'oeil, Denon's cabinet imitates a Masonic initiation chamber. Within this illusionistic box, a young man is introduced to the mysteries of love by an older woman.

Drawing on an equally encyclopedic tradition of physiognomies and physiologies (discernible in the art of facial caricature or the chronicles of the urban panorama found in Louis-Sébastien Mercier's *Le Tableau de Paris* or Rétif de la Bretonne's *Les Nuits de Paris*), this cabinet fiction was equally the result of the nineteenth-century marriage between the "pathologies of modern life" contrived by Balzac and Baudelaire and the medical literature of psychosexual mania. The curiosity shops, bazaars, and antique galleries (strikingly rendered in Balzac's *La Peau de chagrin* and Zola's *Nana*) that provided the nineteenth-century novel with commercial spaces in which to savor the visual cacophony of culturally relativized, historically dislocated commodities were matched by an archival psychiatric genre in which the doctor's most disturbing professional secrets were divulged.

The case histories of legendary sexual perverts such as Gilles de Rais (a fifteenth-century nobleman burned at the stake for sodomizing and cannibalizing scores of children) were clinically "exposed" to the prurient reader in works such as Dr. Jacob's *Curiosités de l'histoire de France* (1858) and Dr. Cabanès's *Le Cabinet secret de l'histoire* (1899).[3] The latter consisted of a peephole survey of pathographies, ranging from Marie Antoinette's putative nymphomania to Citizen Marat's diseases and the fetishism of Gambetta's eye.[4] Similarly,

---

3. See P. L. Jacob, *Curiosités de l'histoire de France* (Paris, 1858), and Augustin Cabanès, *The Secret Cabinet of History*, trans. W. C. Costello (Paris: Charles Carrington, 1897). In a similar vein, Cabanès wrote *La Flagellation dans l'histoire et la littérature* (Clermont, Oise: Daix Frères, 1899).

4. The chapter "Gambetta's Eye" is particularly choice and provides an example of how the notion of fetishism was applied in its fin-de-siècle context. "For indeed, the god (Gambetta) being dead, a new religion sprung up from his ashes. The least vestige of the great man became a fetich, an object of adoration to his disciples. One of them took his brain; another, the intestines; Paul Bert had reserved to himself the most precious portion, the heart. After the campaign led by the *Intermédiaire*, the heart of Gambetta was placed in the monument erected to his memory.... According to the minute of the proceedings, the glass bottle which contained it was enclosed in a double envelope, a leaden casket and a trunk of a fir-tree from Alsace, containing the record of the proceedings.

"How then explain that the eye of the apostle of the *Revanche* could have been permitted to escape, and that this organ can now be found neither in any private

Richard von Krafft-Ebing's landmark *Psychopathia Sexualis* (1886) afforded a terrifying glimpse into the medical chamber of horrors where every variety of erotic deviance was exhibited and cataloged. And in a more personally confidential vein, Axel Munthe's *The Story of San Michele* (1929) provided a gallery of salon portraits revealing the private neuroses and "dirty little secrets" of his fashionable *belle époque* clientele.[5]

The quasi-literary medical cabinet, a mixture of doctor's memoir, nosological observation, and *roman à tiroir* (frame novel) devolved dramatically into the fetishistic conceit of showing and telling what was in principle kept professionally sealed behind closed doors. In this respect, it bore a striking affinity to bedroom dramas or alcove pornography (descended from such eighteenth-century novellas as *Le Sopha*, by Crébillon *fils*, and Diderot's *Les Bijoux indiscrets*), which titillated the audience by lifting the curtains on forbidden scenes of adultery and libertinage. A close relation, too, of the prostitution novel, which typically featured narrative snapshots of the client choosing among girls proffered like objects in a display case, this cabinet fiction also highlighted the theme of transgressive, erotic collecting both inside and outside the protected, bourgeois confines of "home."

Often a simple room within the home, the fin-de-siècle cabinet, as a space in which assembled treasures nested and multiplied, habitually contained familial icons, objets d'art, and private papers, themselves invested with rarefied forms of eroticism. The mania of collecting and its increasingly refined, recherché developments—bric-a-bracomania, tableaumania bibliophilia—seem to have merged in the 1870s with the newly minted sexual aberration of erotomania, itself appropriated and dramatically exploited by the temple of love, from the courtesan's boudoir to the specialty house of prostitution. As the economy of venal sexuality adapted itself to those

---

collection, nor in any of our museums? For, by Gambetta's eye, we of course mean that which was enucleated in 1867 and which now wanders o'er hill and vale, without a single one of the admirers or of the friends of the illustrious deceased having ever thought to claim the right of giving it hospitality" (pp. 230–31).

5. Walter Kendrick, tracing the history of pornography, derives his notion of the "secret museum" from engravings by H. Roux in M. L. Barré's study of Pompeii, *Herculanum et Pompèi, Recueil Général des Peintures, Bronzes, Mosaïques, etc. découverts jusqu'à ce jour et reproduits d'après Le Antichita di Ercolano, Il Museo Borbonico et tous les ouvrages analogues*, 8 vols. (Paris: Firmin-Didot, 1839–1840). Kendrick notes that the last volume, containing illustrations of licentious relics, was entitled *Musée secret*. See the discussion in chapter 1 of Walter Kendrick's *The Secret Museum: Pornography in Modern Culture* (New York: Viking, 1987).

42 · Feminizing the Fetish

festering domestic pathologies that furnished the early sexologists with their experimental data, the *cabinet*, or peep show, as the French social historian Alain Corbin has noted, emerged as a special attraction within the house of ill repute:

· Witty confections of odors, sumptuous sets, multiple mirrors, a profusion of carpets and an orgy of electricity renewed the technical arsenal of pleasure. Inside the grottos of Calypso or the Sadean convents, nymphs and expert "nuns" refined their caresses. Tableaux vivants were the joy of the voyeur. These were disposed as separate cabinets, distant ancestors of the "life-show." Certain houses became highly specialized. The inroads cut by a burgeoning new science of sexology created a demand for new forms of venality. From that point on, each "perversion" had its specialists and privileged space of enactment.[6]

In *La Vie quotidienne dans les maisons closes, 1830–1930*, Laure Adler also records the extent to which voyeurism and its devices usurped the place of more traditional pleasures in the sophisticated house of prostitution:

· Most observers of the period agree that the sexual demands of the rich were progressively transformed: consumption of the sexual act was abandoned in favor of visual orgasm. Certainly voyeurism had always been an essential component of desire, but the house of ill-fame began systematically to offer tableaux vivants; in the interior of the grand salon a kind of erotic machinery set up by the madame was installed: on a large black carpet naked women were seated in suggestive poses, lit from behind by candelabras; on a rotating floor the women made their appearances, possessed of the allure of wax dolls fixed for eternity in voluptuous poses. To satisfy the voyeurs, the habitual holes pierced in the shafts of walls or inside closets no longer sufficed: through the skillful arrangement of pinned sheets or wall hangings or thanks to tubes stuck into partition walls and used by some as listening trumpets, by others as magnifying glasses, the spectator could watch and participate, seated in an armchair in the room next door.[7]

Increasingly used as a viewing station for floor shows or provocative tableaux vivants, the cabinet became a consummate metonym for the *maison close* (literally, "closed house"), itself already a subver-

6. Alain Corbin, "La Relation intime ou les plaisirs de l'échange," in *Histoire de la vie privée*, vol. 4, ed. Michelle Perrot (Paris: Seuil, 1987), p. 559.
7. Laure Adler, *La Vie quotidienne dans les maisons closes, 1830–1930* (Paris: Hachette, 1990), p. 130.

sive antiphrasis yoking the bourgeois notion of home to the morally tainted connotations of closet sexuality. As a spatial metaphor crisscrossing the high associations of connoisseur collecting with the low associations of the prostitute's peep show, the cabinet thus broadly defined received a literary pedigree from, besides other, lesser-known writers, J.-K. Huysmans, the Goncourt brothers, Zola, and Proust. Descriptions of the interior in the work of these authors demonstrate a disturbing set of slippages from object mania to erotomania, from household fetishism to brothel decadence, and from the medical genre of the doctor's secret cabinet to the voyeuristic literary representation of prostitutional curiosities.

Seen together, these slippages sharpen our understanding of how woman, and most specifically, the *fille de noce* came to be fetishized as an erotic commodity or collector's item within the fin-de-siècle Imaginary. Though in psychoanalytic terms the well-worn feminist theme of "woman as fetish object" is most frequently treated through an analysis of the masks or masquerades deployed to obscure her phallic deficiency (clothes, jewels, trinkets, maquillage, and so on), I will be experimenting here with an approach, unorthodox in strictly Freudian or Lacanian terms, that implicitly empowers the female collectible.[8] Drawing on the anthropological notion of fetish as magic talisman, I want to show how feminine "charms," whether acquired for the household or the whorehouse, possessed and infected with erotomania the very master collector whose aloofness and control were believed to be impregnable. Just as Marx, in his discussion of its workings on the economy, would evoke the hidden power or value of the commodity fetish, or Freud, in his mapping of libidinal economy, would refer to the uncanny volatility of the surrogate phallic object on which the fetishist, fearing the spectacle of maternal castration, would fix his gaze, so I will construe the fetish as a cabinet secret or hidden agent that displaces the boundaries between propriety and proprietorship.

I should also emphasize that the notion of fetishism is again being used in its broadest applications, referring at once to the cabinet as a fetishistic space of perversion, to prostitutes as market-

8. Mary Ann Doane in her article "Woman's Stake: Filming the Female Body," *October* 17 (Summer 1981), traces this concept of masquerade from Joan Rivière's important essay, "Womanliness as Masquerade" (1929: republished in *Formations of Fantasy*, ed. Victor Burgin, James Donald, and Cora Kaplan [London: Methuen, 1986], pp. 35–44) through to Lacan (*Ecrits*) and Michèle Montrelay. Doane further develops the theme in "Film and the Masquarade: Theorizing the Female Spectator," *Screen* 23, nos. 3–4 (1982).

place idols capable of reversing the viewer's objectifying gaze (thus challenging the erotic conditions of mastery), and to fetishization as a synonym for manic collecting. Whether this mania is seen as undiscriminating (as when the drive to accumulate supersedes the desire for any particular object in itself) or highly selective (as in the case of aestheticist antiquarianism, finicky and exclusive), in both instances a passion for possession dominates the entire life of the fetishist-collector. A morbid fixation or *monomania* (as defined by Jean-Etienne Dominique Esquirol in the early nineteenth century), conveyed by Faustian scenes of the object's procurement at any cost (even murder, as in Flaubert's Nodier-inspired short story "Bibliomanie" of 1836), emerges as the thematic constant of the cabinet genre and provides, as well, a theoretical connection between fetishism and mania in sociohistorical and psychoanalytical terms. Moving intentionally between Marxist and Freudian ascriptions of the fetish, I hope to explore as well how these two discourses, the one materialist, the other psychoanalytic, meet and become intertwined on the body of the fin-de-siècle courtesan.

Perhaps the most fetishistic cabinet in French literature is that portrayed in Huysmans's *A rebours*, inside the chateau of his protagonist Des Esseintes. Replete with an embalmed alcove, sacred ornaments, and an altar dedicated to poetry, Huysmans's womblike haven provides a consummate illustration of the bourgeois idolatry of art. Its heavy, dark red drapes festooned with golden tassels show that Huysmans's neurasthenic hero is clearly inspired as a decorator by the ideal house that Edgar Allan Poe, in his *Philosophy of Furniture*, put forth as an antidote to the crass, nouveau-riche apartment that was encroaching in his day on the domain of aristocratic taste. The first "physiognomist of the interior," according to Walter Benjamin, Poe stamped his domestic space with the inimitable stylistic flourishes of his literary haunted houses, but more important for our discussion, he equipped it with the trappings of hidden surveillance:[9] "The walls are prepared with a

9. "The interior was not only the private citizen's universe, it was also his casing. Living means leaving traces. In the interior, these were stressed. Coverings and antimacassars, boxes and casings, were devised in abundance, in which traces of everyday objects were molded. The resident's own traces were also molded in the interior. The detective story appeared, which investigated these traces. The *Philosophy of Furniture*, as much as his detective stories, shows Poe to have been the first physiognomist of the interior. The first criminals of the first detective novels were

glossy paper of a silver-gray tint, spotted with small Arabesque devices of a fainter hue of the prevalent crimson. Many paintings relieve the expanse of the paper.... But one mirror—and this is not a very large one—is visible. In shape it is nearly circular—and it is hung so that a reflection of the person can be obtained from it in none of the ordinary sitting places of the room."[10] Des Esseintes's study competes with Poe's room in its generous use of opulent, sensuous materials. Where Poe calls for walls covered with an expensive silvery paper patterned with arabesque designs, Des Esseintes strives for an equally baroque sensibility, binding his walls (like a book) in gilded Moroccan leather. Poe's mirror, suspended like an all-seeing eye in a place where no visitor can espy his reflection, is also mimed by the vividly colored ceiling cove of Des Esseintes's study, which resembles a bull's-eye window (*oeil-de-boeuf*) through which the master voyeur, in the position of the Almighty, contemplates the scenes of his delectation.

These decadent cabinets, with their murky light, heavy crimson curtains, crevices, cavities, and plethora of "seeing eyes," already seem to theatricalize erotic fantasy, imaging, through decorative accoutrements such as the *oeil-de-boeuf* that facilitate the voyeuristic gaze, the "look" of the bordello client trained on feminine wares. Léo Taxil, an anticlerical pundit writing in 1884, confirmed this valorization of the gaze in his sociohistorical account of the daily workings of a prototypical *maison clandestine*. A judas, or peep hole, allowing the madame to appraise her customers in advance, confronted the prospective visitor, who, on being admitted, was treated to an enticing spectacle of female bodies exhibited as in a vitrine. Taxil's description, echoing the novelistic renderings of a prostitute's interior in Edmond de Goncourt's *La Fille Elisa* and Huysmans's *Marthe*, underscored the importance of the scopic encounter.[11] Forbidden to speak, the *filles de joie* inaugurate a transaction by attempting to lock the roving eye of the client into their own:

---

neither gentlemen nor apaches, but middle-class private citizens." (Walter Benjamin, "Louis-Philippe or the Interior," in *Charles Baudelaire: A Lyric Poet in the Era of High Capitalism*, trans. Harry Zohn [London: New Left Books, 1973], p. 169).

10. Edgar Allan Poe, *The Complete Tales and Poems of Edgar Allan Poe* (New York: Modern Library, 1965), pp. 465–66.

11. For a broader discussion of woman's ontology within the fin-de-siècle interior, and particularly of the "sexual politics of looking," see the chapter "Modernity and the Spaces of Femininity," in Griselda Pollock's *Vision and Difference: Femininity, Feminism, and the Histories of Art* (London: Routledge, 1988), pp. 50–90.

As soon as he plants his feet in the corridor, a voice rings out: "Close the doors!" The serious client [Taxil's argot term *miché* has a cruder ring than "client"] makes his entrance. Not one of the women is allowed to make him a verbal invitation, but all send him a flaming look, sway their hips, assume sexy poses, smile, and even flick their tongues, so as to make it perfectly clear that they are putting a thousand refinements of pleasure at the disposal of the client. The *miché* traverses with his gaze the lines of these priestesses of Venus, fixes his choice on one of them and gallantly offers her his hand. It is a true mise-en-scène.[12]

Taxil's description emphasizes the extent to which the inner sanctum of prostitution, like the *maison d'artiste* of the Goncourt brothers or collector's apartment, catered to visual feasting. In Octave Uzanne's exemplary depiction of a *boîte à femmes* ("girlie box") the bordello seems to resemble a toy or miniature theater whose contents are emptied out and scrutinized at will. In contrast to the sordid and solitary *cabinet obscur*—workplace of *la basse prostitution* in which could be found only "a wretched couch, hard as wood and garnished only by a pillow,—the instrument of work,—a chair, some towels and, on the floor, pans for ablutions lost amidst an archeology of bottles"—Uzanne's bustling "girlie box" is a "live" cabinet:

Veritable pandemonia these "girlie boxes" asleep until nearly noon and filled all day with the comings and goings of uncombed creatures in dirty camisoles, shrieking, laughing, swearing at each other, dragging their slippers along the stairs, catching each other out with dirty boys, smoking cigarettes, ordering up absinthe and, until the time for "work," that is, roughly five in the evening, gambling among themselves.[13]

In his portrayal of off-duty hours Uzanne reveals to the inquisitive eye a behind-the-scenes glimpse of what is already a clandestine existence. Painterly and literary representations of courtesan and client only reinforce this effect of double voyeurism: you will recall Manet's famous portrait of Nana (a premonition of the novel to come, since at the time Manet painted the picture in 1876–1877, Zola had described Nana only as a young girl in *L'Assommoir*), in

12. Léo Taxil, *La Prostitution contemporaine: Etude d'une question sociale* (Paris: Librairie Populaire, 1884), p. 100.
13. Octave Uzanne, *Etudes de sociologie féminine: Parisiennes de ce temps* (Paris: Mercure de France, 1910), pp. 370, 379.

which the patron, bifurcated by the picture's frame, gluttonously savors his private view of Nana's generous posterior. Nana, in deshabille and seeming to ignore him, holds a powder puff aloft and gazes tenderly out of the canvas directly at the viewer.[14] The picture perfectly captures the built-in stereoscopy of the cabinet: a scene of secret beholding is itself "caught in the act of looking" because of the projection of an imaginary spectator, who, though anonymous and intangible, is no less fully present.

This voyeuristic *mise-en-abyme*, composed of viewer-gazing-at-viewer-gazing-at-object-of-desire, emerges as one of the many initiatory optical devices that Zola used to enhance his literary rendering of visual fixation and to underscore the variety-show aspect of his presentation of prostitutional sensations to the readers of *Nana* (1880). In an extended boudoir scene, the novelty of feminine autoeroticism is brought to the foreground, as Count Muffat fetishizes the sight of Nana fetishizing herself; kissing her own reflection and fondling the favored parts of her own body. As a female reader of the scene, I find myself divided between assuming the narrative perspective of masculine fetishism defined by the gaze of the Count and identifying with Nana's narcissistically defined female fetishism.

As the novel progresses and the reader becomes more blasé, bestiality is introduced as the ultimate attraction. Modeling his depiction of sadomasochistic ritual on Hippolyte Taine's description in *La Littérature anglaise* of Thomas Otway's *Venus Preserved*, and foreshadowing his theme of *la bête humaine*, or human beast, Zola transforms the reader, masculine or feminine, into a spy. Much like the unlicensed lay reader of the sexological document, this spy is implicitly troubled by the sight of such explicit sex.

> Ce ne fut pas cruauté chez elle, car elle demeurait bonne fille; ce fut comme un vent de démence qui passa et grandit peu à peu dans la chambre close. Une luxure les détraquait, les jetait aux imaginations délirantes de la chair. Les anciennes épouvantes dévotes de leur nuit d'insomnie tournaient maintenant en une soif de bestialité, une fureur de se mettre à quatre pattes, de grogner et de mordre. Puis, un jour, comme il faisait l'ours, elle le poussa si rudement, qu'il tomba contre un meuble; et elle éclata d'un rire involontaire, en lui voyant une bosse au

---

14. Charles Bernheimer has insightfully analyzed this painting in his *Figures of Ill-Repute: Representing Prostitution in Nineteenth-Century France* (Cambridge: Harvard University Press, 1989), pp. 231–33. This book provides important psychoanalytical interpretations of the culture of sexuality and consumerism that surrounded nineteenth-century prostitution.

48 · Feminizing the Fetish

front. Dès lors, mise en goût par son essai sur La Faloise, elle le traîta en animal, le fouailla, le poursuivit à coup de pied.

"Hue donc! hue donc!...Tu es le cheval...Dia, hue! sale rosse, veux-tu marcher!"

D'autres fois, il était un chien. Elle lui jetait son mouchoir parfumé au bout de la pièce, et il devait courir le ramasser avec les dents, en se traînant sur les mains et les genoux....

Et lui aimait sa bassesse, goûtait la jouissance d'être une brute. Il aspirait encore à descendre, il criait: "Tape plus fort...Hou! hou! je suis enragé, tape donc!"

It was not cruelty in her case, for she was still a good-natured girl; it was as though a passing wind of madness were blowing ever more strongly in the shut-up bedroom. A storm of lust disordered their brains, plunged them into the delirious imaginations of the flesh. The old pious terrors of their sleepless nights were now transforming themselves into a thirst for bestiality, a furious longing to walk on all fours, to growl and to bite. One day, when he was playing the bear, she pushed him so roughly that he fell against a piece of furniture, and when she saw a lump on his forehead she burst into involuntary laughter. After that, her experiments on La Faloise having whetted her appetite, she treated him to an accompaniment of kicks.

"Gee up! Gee up! You're a horse. Hoi! gee up! Won't you hurry up you dirty screw!"

At other times, he played the dog. She would throw him her perfumed handkerchief in the far corner of the room and he would run and fetch it in his teeth, dragging himself on his hands and knees....

And he loved his abasement, and delighted in being a brute beast. He longed to sink still further, and would cry, "Hit harder. On, on! I'm wild! Hit away!"[15]

The repeated references in this passage to the "shut door," "shut-up bedroom," and strange, unnatural atmosphere incubating within suggest that the room itself is as much an accomplice in these antics as the couple itself. Indeed, the entire scene, with its eerie specularity and infernal duo of dominatrix and willing victim, prefigures Proust's House of Sodoma in the final (unfinished) volume of *A la recherche du temps perdu*.

This notorious episode, in which the Baron de Charlus orches-

15. Emile Zola, *Nana*, trans. Ernest Boyd (New York: Modern Library, 1927), pp. 510–11. Henri Mitterand claims in a note to this edition that the details of this scene were taken directly from the tragedy *Venus Preserved* by the Restoration dramatist Thomas Otway. Whipped by the courtesan Aquilina, the old senator Antonio first plays the cow and then the dog.

Cabinet Secrets · 49

trates his own beating, syncopating blows in unison with the apocalyptic rhythm of an imagined German bombardment of Paris, is witnessed by the narrator Marcel through two extremely devious espionage contraptions. World War I is on, and a general suspicion toward German sympathizers pervades the social ethos: "Was this hotel being used as a meeting-place of spies?" Marcel asks himself after stumbling on a flourishing establishment in the midst of an abandoned neighborhood.[16] Little by little, like a spy, he pieces together the sinister goings-on within the different rooms. A center for advanced debauchery, ingeniously planned by Charlus's factotum Jupien, this bastion of male prostitution is explored, room by room, through the hidden camera of the narrator's surreptitious gaze. The word *curiosity*, reiterated throughout the Sodom section of *Le Temps retrouvé*, yields the image of a Pandora's Box perforated through a secret opening. This is what Marcel sees through the fortuitously discovered *oeil-de-boeuf*:

- Tout d'un coup, d'une chambre qui était isolée au bout d'un couloir me semblèrent venir des plaintes étouffées. Je marchai vivement dans cette direction et appliquai mon oreille à la porte. "Je vous en supplie, grâce, grâce, pitié, détachez-moi, ne me frappez pas si fort, disait une voix, Je vous baise les pieds, je m'humilie, je ne recommencerai pas. Ayez pitié.—Non, crapule, répondit une autre voix, et puisque tu gueules et que tu te traînes à genoux, on va t'attacher sur le lit, pas de pitié", et j'entendis le bruit du claquement d'un martinet probablement aiguisé de clous car il fut suivi de cris de douleur. Alors je m'aperçus qu'il y avait dans cette chambre un oeil-de-boeuf latéral dont on avait oublié de tirer le rideau; cheminant à pas de loup dans l'ombre, je me glissai jusqu'à cet oeil-de-boeuf, et là, enchaîné sur un lit comme Prométhée sur son rocher, recevant les coups d'un martinet en effet planté de clous que lui infligeait Maurice, je vis, déjà tout en sang, et couvert d'ecchymoses qui prouvaient que le supplice n'avait pas lieu pour la première fois, je vis devant moi M. de Charlus. (*PR* 394)

- Suddenly from a room situated by itself at the end of the corridor, I thought I heard stifled groans. I walked rapidly towards the sounds and

---

16. Marcel Proust, in "Time Regained," trans. Andreas Mayor, p. 838, in *Remembrance of Things Past*, vol. 3, trans. and ed. C. K. Scott Moncrieff and Terence Kilmartin (New York: Vintage, 1982). Further references will be to this edition (Mayor translation) and will be abbreviated *R*. Citations in French are taken from Marcel Proust, *A la recherche du temps perdu*, vol. 4, ed. Jean-Yves Tadié et al. (Paris: Gallimard, 1989). Further references to this edition will appear in the text abbreviated *PR*.

put my ear to the door. "I beseech you, mercy, have pity, untie me, don't beat me so hard," said a voice. "I kiss your feet, I abase myself, I promise not to offend again. Have pity on me." "No, you filthy brute," replied another voice, "and if you yell and drag yourself about on your knees like that, you'll be tied to the bed, no mercy for you," and I heard the noise of the crack of a whip, which I guessed to be reinforced with nails, for it was followed by cries of pain. At this moment I noticed that there was a small oval window opening from the room on to the corridor and that the curtain had not been drawn across it; stealthily in the darkness I crept as far as this window and there in the room, chained to a bed like Prometheus to his rock, receiving the blows that Maurice rained upon him with a whip that was in fact studded with nails, I saw, with blood already flowing from him and covered with bruises which proved that chastisement was not taking place for the first time—I saw before me M. de Charlus. (R 843)

As if lifted to the letter from the rites of religious penitents or the technical descriptions of *algolagnia* (pleasure in pain) found in Krafft-Ebing's *Psychopathia Sexualis*, this scene of flagellation capitalizes on the narrator's voyeurism, tracing with careful realism each detail of Charlus's punishment as it becomes imprinted on Marcel's greedily gratified retina. The *oeil-de-boeuf*, or peephole, which allows him (and us the readers) to infiltrate the walls of "la chambre 14b" attains an even deeper symbolic significance when it is exchanged against another seeing-eye mechanism. This miracle of spying artistry, fashioned by Jupien for the Baron and called, for lack of a more precise term, a *vasistas*, refers to a kind of trapdoor transom window or one-way glass permitting the viewer to see without being seen:

· On entendit des pas lents dans l'escalier. Par une indiscrétion qui était dans sa nature, Jupien ne put se retenir de me dire que c'était le baron qui descendait, qu'il ne fallait à aucun prix qu'il me vît, mais que si je voulais entrer dans la chambre contiguë au vestibule où étaient les jeunes gens, il allait ouvrir le vasistas, truc qu'il avait inventé pour que le baron pût voir et entendre sans être vu, et qu'il allait, me disait-il, retourner en ma faveur contre lui. (PR 402)

· Slow footsteps were heard on the stairs. With the indiscretion that was natural to him, Jupien could not refrain from telling me that it was the Baron who was coming down, and at all costs he must not see me, but that if I liked to go into the bedroom adjoining the ante-room where the young men were, he would open the ventilator [*vasistas* in the original

French], a device which he had fixed up so that the Baron would see and hear without being seen, and which he said he would use in my favour against him. (R 852)

Misleadingly translated by Andreas Mayor in the Kilmartin edition as a "ventilator," the *vasistas* emerges as a key word of cabinet fiction, for, deriving as it does from the German "Was ist das?" this singular spy-window breaks down into one of the major questions of psychoanalysis (and of the fetishist in particular): What is it? What is the object of (perverse) desire?[17] The reply seems to reside in the very *secrecy* of the contract binding the members of the "perverse couple" (in this case, Charlus and Jupien). As the psychoanalyst Jean Clavreul has argued:

> In the normal relationship one speaks of suffering, the infidelity of the partner, and the waste of time; the third party has no other role than to register the failure. But for the pervert, to the extent that only the "secret" kept from the third party constitutes the foundation of the contract, it will not be the infidelity, the suffering, the indifference of one of the partners, or the waste of time that will lead to the breakup. It will be the failure to keep the secret, the telling of a third party, and the ensuing *scandal* that will bring about the breakup....
>
> We cannot overestimate the importance of such a secret contract, without which we could not begin to understand how the most extreme perverse practices can be perpetuated for such a long time, leaving the occasional spectator fascinated and finally an accomplice because he cannot give away the secret.[18]

In the scene just evoked, the *vasistas*, cousin of the judas (a term for peephole deriving from the name of Christ's traitorous disciple), emerges as the means by which Jupien violates his contract with Charlus. Introducing a "third party" (Marcel) into the private space of perversion, and turning the psychoanalytical question "Was ist

---

17. "Ventilator" (at least in one nineteenth-century French-English dictionary that I have come across) is included as a plausible equivalent for *vasistas*, but in the Proustian context (which emphasizes its status as a homemade instrument of pornographic viewing) it seems to be an infelicitous choice. In the earlier, Scott Moncrieff edition, *The Past Recaptured* was translated by Frederick A. Blossom. Blossom prefers "peep-hole" to "ventilator," which, though more accurate, sacrifices some of the uniqueness of the mechanism described.

18. Jean Clavreul, "The Perverse Couple," in *Returning to Freud: Clinical Psychoanalysis in the School of Lacan*, trans. and ed. Stuart Schneiderman (New Haven: Yale University Press, 1980), p. 219.

das?" back on Charlus—the very onlooker who sought to deflect its castrating implications by spying on others—this strange piece of voyeuristic paraphernalia thus betrays a cabinet secret.

Perceiving Charlus's abjectly presented backside through the *vasistas*, Marcel encounters that "disgust" which Freud claimed, in his *Three Essays on the Theory of Sexuality*, excites scopophilia (love of looking) in the voyeur.[19] Freud suggested that fetishist and voyeur alike, resisting passage to the oedipal symbolic order, become fixed regressively in the anal-erotic stage and therefore fixated on some object of coprophilic disgust. "Seeing," which, Freud argues, "derives from touching," has an immense capacity to arouse perverse sexual interest. The Baron's whipping, a performance of anal eroticism satisfying the visual-haptic appetite to perfection, thus exemplifies the Freudian paradigm of sexual aberration.

Though its psychoanalytical legibility is uncontestable, I would argue that Freud's scopophilic answer to the question "Was ist das?" is hardly exhaustive. One could argue that, within the cabinet, this loaded question remains suspended, unanswered, or, alternatively, answered on an individual basis. As in the pre-Freudian medical cabinet, which assigned abstruse names to every exotic strain of perversion (Foucault, in his *History of Sexuality*, enumerates the "zoophiles, zoorasts, auto-monosexualists, mixoscopophiles, gynecomasts, presbyophiles, sexoesthetic inverts and dyspareunist women" who populated the annals of sexual deviancy), Proust's Pompeian-style House of Sodoma seems to revel in the display of sexual differences.[20] Matched according to type and taste, each eccentric desire is coordinated with the object that it requires for satisfaction:

> On entendait des clients qui demandaient au patron s'il ne pouvait pas leur faire connaître un valet de pied, un enfant de chœur, un chauffeur nègre. Toutes les professions intéressaient ces vieux fous, dans la troupe toutes les armes, et les Alliés de toutes nations. Quelques-uns réclamaient surtout des Canadiens, subissant peut-être à leur insu le charme d'un accent si léger qu'on ne sait pas si c'est celui de la vieille France ou de l'Angleterre. A cause de leur jupon et parce que certains rêves lacustres

---

19. Freud wrote, "this pleasure in looking (scopophilia) becomes a perversion (a) if it is restricted exclusively to the genitals, or (b) if it is connected with the overriding of disgust (as in the case of *voyeurs*)" (*Three Essays on the Theory of Sexuality*, Standard Edition 7:157).

20. Michel Foucault, *The History of Sexuality*, vol. 1: *An Introduction*, trans. Robert Hurley (New York: Vintage, 1980), p. 43.

s'associent souvent à de tels désirs, les Ecossais faisaient prime. Et, comme toute folie reçoit des circonstances des traits particuliers, sinon même une aggravation, un vieillard dont toutes les curiosités avaient sans doute été assouvies demandait avec insistance si on ne pourrait pas lui faire faire la connaissance d'un mutilé. (PR 402)

- Clients could be heard inquiring of the *patron* whether he could introduce them to a footman, a choir-boy, a negro chauffeur. Every profession interested these old lunatics, every branch of the armed forces, every one of the allied nations. Some asked particularly for Canadians, influenced perhaps unconsciously by the charm of an accent so slight that one does not know whether it comes from the France of the past or from England. The Scots too, because of their kilts and because dreams of a landscape with lakes are often associated with these desires, were at a premium. And as every form of madness is, if not in every case, aggravated by circumstances, an old man in whom curiosity of every kind had no doubt been satisfied was asking insistently to be introduced to a disabled soldier. (R 852)

Proust accentuates the humorous effect of this description by intertwining the clichés of tourist travelogues and geographical color supplements with a specialized cornucopia of masculine perversions. On one level, he may be teaching us a great deal about the psychology of sex—the flourishing of fantasy around some cultural mytheme or idée fixe (a favorite literary conceit, perhaps epitomized on the bourgeois side by Paul Bourget's fashion-conscious classification of mistresses, flirts, and coquettes in his *Physiologie de l'amour moderne* of 1889).[21] On another level, Proust alerts us to a kind of museal eroticism embedded in the spectacle of object choice and passive availability. The fact that the juxtaposition of disparate nationalities, sensual temperaments, and body types characterizes artistic collection and bordello interior alike only reinforces the epistemological connection between the two species of cabinet. The Baron de Charlus goes so far as to make this connection (unwittingly) explicit in his attempt to disguise a complicated negotiation for a particular style and type of gigolo by a loud expostulation: "Yes, in spite of my age, I still keep up a passion for

21. See in particular Bourget's sketches of "la chercheuse," "la comédienne," "la littéraire" (redoubtably "Sandiste"), "la vaniteuse," "les snobinettes," "l'imitatrice," "la voyageuse," "la dominatrice," "l'ennuyée," etc. This literary display case of demimondaines certainly belongs to the enumerative, classificatory, collective genre that we are calling cabinet fiction (Paul Bourget, *Physiologie de l'amour moderne* [Paris: L'Intelligence, 1906], pp. 95–104).

collecting, a passion for pretty things." Proust describes the manner in which the Baron "shouted his words so loud that this charade should in itself have been enough to reveal what it concealed."[22] Substituting boy for object and object for boy, Charlus performs the necessary inversion of erotomania and collectomania implicit in the cabinet secret.

Both Edmond de Goncourt and Huysmans, writing in the same year (1878) about the life of the lower-class *fille soumise* (indentured prostitute), but each claiming not to be cognizant of the other's novel, described the contents of the brothel in terms evoking the heaped-up merchandise inside a new-fangled department store. Though both authors were ostensibly concerned to demystify the harlot's life, showing her to be part of a conglomeration of sorry humanity, defamiliarized and uncannily objectified through exploitation and overuse, they nonetheless relied for their effect on the commodifying gaze. In de Goncourt's *La Fille Elisa*, the reader is shepherded to the back of the room:

- Au fond, tout au fond de la salle resserrée et profonde et ayant l'infini de ces corridors de lumière d'un grossier palais de féerie, confondues, mêlées, épaulées les unes aux autres, les femmes étaient ramassées autour d'une table dans une espèce d'amoncellement pyramidant et croulant.

- At the very back of a deeply recessed chamber, in which flicker infinite corridors of light typical of a vulgar fairy palace, jumbled together, splayed shoulder to shoulder, women were gathered around a table forming a kind of crumbling, pyramidal embankment.[23]

In Huysman's *Marthe*, through the girl's own jaded eyes, a similar pile-up effect is generated. After failing to recognize her own body shamelessly prostrated on a couch with lips swollen and rouged and gaping flesh hanging out of its bodice like a lure, Marthe

- regardait avec hébétement les poses étranges de ses camarades, des beautés falotes et vulgaires, des caillettes agaçantes, des hommasses et

22. Marcel Proust, *The Cities of the Plain*, vol. 2 of *Remembrance of Things Past*, trans. C. K. Scott Moncrieff (New York: Random House, 1932), part 2, pp. 275–76.
23. Edmond de Goncourt, *La Fille Elisa* (Paris: Flammarion, 1878), p. 109. Further references to this work will be abbreviated *FE*.

des maigriottes, étendues sur le ventre, la tête dans les mains, accroupies comme des chiennes, sur un tabouret, accrochées comme des oripeaux, sur des coins de divans, les cheveux édifiés de toutes sortes: spirales ondées, frisons crêpelés, boucles rondissantes, chignons gigantesques, constellés de marguerites blanches et rouges, de torsades de fausses perles, crinières noires ou blondes, pommadées ou poudrées d'une neige de riz.

· looks groggily at the strange poses of her companions, vulgar and wan beauties, irritating, skinny, almost mannish little quails, crouched like dogs, on a stool, pinned like tattered clothing, on the corners of sofas, their hair built up into every kind of edifice: undulated spirals, crimped waves, rounded curls, gigantic chignons constellated with white and red daisies, and twisted knots of fake pearls, manes of black or blond hue, pommaded with a snowfall of rice-powder.[24]

First represented as an assemblage, a kind of composite of differences (what the French call *l'hétéroclite*), which must be separated out and selected as the eye grows more focused, the bodies of these women are next given over to the fetishizing, fragmenting poetics of synecdoche. Huysmans focuses obsessively on the incredible phallic headdresses worn by his inebriated muses. The same props of a grand feminine masquerade may be found in *La Fille Elisa*: "Each girl, on top of two kiss-curls, had built up the scaffolding of an extravagantly high coiffure in which were intertwined vine leaves made out of gilded paper" (*FE* 110) The image of woman as commodity and rare specimen, who, as a bonus, wards off castration anxiety with her prosthetic coiffure, is emphasized in strikingly similar ways by both authors.

From the general to the particular, from the female menagerie to the chosen girl, the prostitutional cabinet appears to revolve as a literary genre around the dynamic of ocularization, as subordinated to the fetishization of the objectified female body. In this respect it becomes the ideal space for the propagation of object manias— particularly that virulent form of attachment to things which the nineteenth century dubbed *érotomanie*.

Erotomania was an aberrational condition common to men and women, and identified in the nineteenth-century case literature with severe outbreaks of erotic frenzy culminating, in the most severe instances, in physical attacks on the beloved. When the

---

24. J. K. Huysmans, *Marthe* (Paris: Union Générale d'Editions, 1975), p. 49. Further references to this work will be abbreviated *M*.

sufferers were women, erotomania, like its parent neuroses—"uterine fury" and hysteria—was used as a medical euphemism for inadequately mastered sexual urges. Symptoms such as exaggerated nervosity, convulsions, and exaggerated lewdness, when detected in the behavior of bourgeois women were thus discretely sanitized with the help of a professional lexicon. By contrast, the same symptoms were frequently classified as generic temperamental defects of the "born prostitute" by "experts" such as Cesare Lombroso and his assistant Gina Ferraro. What I want to explore now is the extent to which this disease of aggravated, toxic desire inadvertently created a link between the prostitute and the collector in the popular consciousness of the period.

The theoretical predecessor of fetishism, erotomania was elaborated in the early 1880s by the doctors Moreau (de Tours), Charcot, Magnan, and Ball.[25] From 1883 to 1887, Ball published a tripartite article entitled "Erotomania or Erotic Madness," which both consolidated prior classifications and set forth a series of case studies that would be treated by subsequent psychiatry as essential paradigms.[26] Ball distilled a number of symptoms typical of erotomaniacs, most of them involving a central delusion projected by the subject onto a living person often so remote from the patient that he or she was reduced to the status of an inanimate object or fetish substitute.[27] Ball described in detail how erotomaniacs whom he had observed became "fou par amour," or, literally, "mad with love," tyrannically lording over the surrogate object of desire. Lacan's teacher, the eccentric psychiatrist G. G. de Clérambault, further elaborated Ball's definition by exploring the erotomaniac's self-figuration as the Other's supplement, the only element missing in what was otherwise a perfect and self-sufficient figure of alterity. In the words of Jacques-Alain Miller, Clérambault's female erotomaniac was "constituted in her delusions as (the Object's) lack, passionately sought after. She is thus what is lacking in the Other who lacks

25. See Paul Moreau (de Tours), *Des Aberrations du sens génésique* (1880), and Jean-Martin Charcot and Valentin Magnan, "Inversion du sens génital et autres perversions sexuelles," *Archives de Neurologie* 3 (Jan.–Feb. 1882): 53–60, and 4 (July 1882): 296–322.
26. Benjamin Ball, "De l'érotomanie ou folie érotique," *L' Encéphale* 3 (1883): 129–39, and "La Folie érotique," *L' Encéphale* 7 (1887): 188–97 and 257–415.
27. For a fascinating discussion of the *object* (of fixation) prefiguring the Lacanian object of fixation, see the work of Lacan's teacher Gatian de Gaeton de Clérambault. Vol. 1 of his *Oeuvre psychiatrique* (published posthumously through the editorial efforts of Jean Fretet in 1942 by PUF) is almost exclusively devoted to a discussion of erotomania as *psychose passionelle*.

nothing."[28] This description brings erotomania closer to Freudian fetishism, with its simultaneous avowal and disavowal of lack. Though Ball and Clérambault concentrated more on the psychotic, paranoid workings of object delusion (as when the patient would construct a *roman* (novel) around some farfetched conviction such as "the Queen of England loves me") than on the libidinal investment of actual inanimate objects within an economy of sexual fixation, both nonetheless projected an almost caricatural image of the frenzied relay between lack and desire characterizing the erotomaniac's behavior.

Given its congeniality to caricature, it is perhaps no surprise that so many writers appeared to have appropriated this medical discourse to describe the collecting furor that swept through Europe during the latter half of the nineteenth century. Already, in the romantic period, long before psychiatric case studies of either fetishism or erotomania would furnish detailed descriptions of abnormal passions for things, Charles Nodier and the circle around his *Bulletin du Bibliophile* (founded in 1834) had established the classic récit of collectomania.[29] Flaubert's "Bibliomanie," Balzac's *Le Cousin Pons*, Charles Asselineau's *L'Enfer du bibliophile* (1860), Huysmans's *A rebours*, Anatole France's *Le Crime de Sylvestre Bonnard*, Henry James's *The Spoils of Poynton*, and Borges's "Library of Babel" (among many others) can all be seen as part of a direct line whose origins lie in Nodier's narratives of bibliomania.[30] In Nodier's exemplary short story "Le Bibliomane" (1831), the protagonist takes ill on discovering that he has mistaken the day of an important auction. All the rare and precious books have been sold off to his rivals. As if pastiching the medical genre to come, Nodier introduces the character of an ambitious doctor who publishes a

---

28. Jacques-Alain Miller, "Teachings of the Case Presentation," in Schneiderman, *Returning to Freud*, p. 52.

29. For a full account of Nodier's "bibliomania," including its literary sources and the subsequent writers it influenced, see Didier Barrière, *Nodier, l'homme du livre* (Bassac: Plein Chant, 1989).

30. See the important collection of texts assembled under the title *Les Livrets du bibliophile*, ed. Alexandre Alphonse Marius Stols (Maestricht: A.A.M. Stols, 1926). Dedicated to the memory of Nodier, the collection contains Nodier's "Le Bibliomane"; Paul Claudel's "La Philosophie du livre" (a lecture given in Florence in 1925); Anatole France's essay on typography, "Le Livre du bibliophile"; Claude Aveline's "'Les Désirs' ou le livre égaré"; Stéphane Mallarmé's "Quant au livre"; Paul Valéry's "Notes sur le livre et les manuscrits"; Flaubert's "Bibliomanie"; Valery Larbaud's "Ce vice impuni, la lecture"; Charles Asselineau's "L' Enfer du bibliophile"; and Georges Duhamel's "Lettre sur les bibliophiles."

report in the *Journal des Sciences Médicales*, designating Théodore's obsessive affliction under the name of "*monomanie du maroquin, ou de typhus des bibliomanes*" ("monomania of Morocco leather, or bibliomaniacs' typhus").³¹

Writing in *Le Gaulois* in 1883, Maupassant, perpetuating the conceit of medicalizing bibliophilia, compared bric-a-bracomania to a fatal epidemic: "Of all the passions, of all without exception, the passion for the bibelot is perhaps the most terrible and invincible of all. The man smitten by an antique is a lost man. The bibelot is not only a passion, it is a mania, an incurable mania."³² What was perceived in the eighteenth century as an aristocratic pursuit of the connoisseur or sophisticated dilettante was for Maupassant and his generation a democratized fad, in which "even women" participated: "Everybody collects today," Maupassant complained, "everybody is or thinks he is a connoisseur; because fashion has got mixed up in it. Practically all the actresses have contracted the rage of collecting; all the great houses resemble museums encumbered by filthy fetishes [*saletés séculaires*]."³³ Between its increasing "feminization," on the one hand, and its resemblance to a secular cult, on the other, the high art of collecting was fast becoming a virulent petty-bourgeois sickness in the eyes of Maupassant and his (primarily male) contemporaries.³⁴ Though his negative voice was countered by the injunctions of popular fashion counselors (as in Gustave Droz's exhortation to the young housemaker, "Let your nest be cozy, let us feel you in your thousand little nothings," or Paul Ginisty's apostrophe to "le Dieu Bibelot" [the God Bibelot]), Maupassant articulated a fin-de-siècle object fetishism that paralleled a masculine view of the prostitute's putative sexual anhedonia.³⁵

31. Charles Nodier, "Le Bibliomane," in *Nodier: Contes* (Paris: Garnier Frères, 1961), p. 504. Nodier, himself a famous sufferer from bibliomania, was even said to have circulated a fabricated Spanish *fait divers* (tabloid story) (concerning a bookseller who agrees to confess to the assassination of his competitor only on the condition that his library be left intact), which Flaubert unknowingly used as a factual basis for his short story "Bibliomanie." See Barrière, *Nodier, l'homme du livre*, pp. 14–15.

32. Maupassant, "Bibelots," in *Chroniques*, vol. 2 (Paris: Union Générale d'Editions, 1980), p. 183.

33. Ibid.

34. Asa Briggs has discussed this vogue of collectomania in England in *Victorian Things* (Chicago: University of Chicago Press, 1989).

35. Gustave Prou (pseud. Gustave Droz?), *Monsieur, madame, et bébé* (Paris, 1866), as cited by Anne Martin-Fugier, "La Douceur du nid: Les 'Arts de la femme' à la belle époque," *Urbi* 5 (1982): 114, and Paul Ginisty, *Le Dieu Bibelot* (Paris: A. Dupret, 1888). Ginisty in his preface evocatively heralds the modern consumerist religion of

If, for Robert de Montesquiou, the exquisite taste of the collector was expressed in the arrangement of ornaments according to color, decorative compatibility, and their poetry in space ("the fragile," "the frozen," and "the fossilized" were his preferred classifications), for others, collecting took on a more psychosexual undertone.[36] No one more than Octave Uzanne, society writer, bibliophile historian of women's fashion, and sociologist of prostitution, captured the depiction of collecting as both virus and obsessional vice.[37] In his highly ironical set piece "Le Cabinet d'un eroto-bibliomane," framed inside a larger work called *Les Caprices d'un bibliophile* (1878), he merged the medical codes of erotomania with the pornographic conventions of closet erotica, thus creating a kind of whorehouse inside the doctor's cabinet, or bordello of the book.[38] The collector, cast in the role of brothel client and/or depraved medical man, loses his professional cover and becomes prey to the basest instincts, little better than the species of lust-stricken woman he collects. The implicit equivalence between collector and prostitute established by Uzanne represents a significant dislocation of the male collector/ female collectible opposition. As when the voyeur was betrayed by

---

bibelot collecting: "This is a strangely modern cult whose altars are bedrooms where, in an amusing pell-mell, a pretty and titillating pile of very ancient things is displayed,... The Trinket God has he too, his temple, his rites, his mysteries, his solemnities.... But, more favored than the religions that have disappeared in today's skepticism, the Trinket God has friendly Parisians for worshipers and beautiful society ladies for priestesses. A happy God is he!" (p. 6). See Alain Corbin's detailed compendium of the degenerative, pathological traits attributed to the "born prostitute" (*Les Filles de noce* [Paris: Flammarion, 1982], pp. 440–52). It has been pointed out to me that one obvious explanation for this masculine construction of the prostitute as a woman completely prey to uncontrollable desires lies in the fact that it assigns power and control to the role of the man. A purely simulated lust on the part of the prostitute would imply, rather, that she is in control.

36. See Didier Coste, "Robert de Montesquiou, poète critique: La Cristallisation du décoratif," *Romantisme* 42 (1983): 103–117. I am grateful to Rae Beth Gordon for drawing my attention to this article. Gordon's forthcoming book on ornament in French fin-de-siècle literature elaborates many of the themes explored in this chapter.

37. Uzanne's writings provide a rich and hitherto neglected sociocritical source for reconstructing the nineteenth-century woman and her place in the context of fin-de-siècle *mentalités*. See in particular *Caprices d'un bibliophile* (1878), *Le Bric-à-brac de l'amour* (1879), *La Française du siècle: Modes, moeurs, usages* (1885), *Les Zigzags d'un curieux* (1888), *Le Paroissien du célibataire* (1890), *L'Art et les artifices de la beauté* (1902; esp. the section on "le cabinet de toilette"), and perhaps most interesting of all for its section on prostitution, *Etudes de sociologie féminine: Parisiennes de ce temps* (Paris: Mercure de France, 1910).

38. Octave Uzanne, *Caprices d'un bibliophile* (Paris: Edouard Rouveyre, 1878), pp. 127–46.

the *vasistas,* becoming the self-reflexive object of his own spying, so here, the master of the cabinet is unmasked by his own love of looking.

The real-life counterpart to Uzanne's fictive hero could have been Edmond de Goncourt, self-nicknamed the "John-the-Baptist of modern neurosis."[39] Paul Bourget called the Goncourt brothers "the first moderns of the museum" and placed at their feet the full weight of their culture's frenzy for collecting and taste for anachronistically collaged decorative styles:

> The bibelot—refined mania of an uneasy epoch in which the lassitudes of boredom and the maladies of nervous sensibility have led man to invent for himself the artificial pleasures of the collector. In the meantime this complicated intimacy renders him incapable of tolerating the generous, healthy simplicity of the former things surrounding him! To his jaded look one must pose the pretty, the cute, the bizarre.... This singular taste for the bibelot is gaining on those who normally are indifferent to a work of art.... In the windows of the department stores which boast the latest novelties and which form a colossal résumé of the habits of a people in anticipating their desires, what do you encounter? The bibelot again, and again the bibelot.... It's a fashion that will disappear like any other, but the analyst of contemporary society can no more ignore it than the historian of the *grand siècle* could pass over in silence the pruned landscapes of Versailles.[40]

Writing about his own home in *La Maison d'un artiste* (1881), Edmond confessed to his fatal passion for collecting in terms that unwittingly linked him to the very characterological prostitute type that he and his brother had misogynistically portrayed so many times, from their multivolumed *Journal* to their novel of a sluttish, bestial maid-of-all-work, *Germinie Lacerteux* (1865).[41] In a preamble

---

39. "The critics may say what they like about Zola, they cannot prevent us, my brother and myself, from being the John-the-Baptists of modern neurosis," in *Pages from the Goncourt Journal,* trans. and ed. Robert Baldick (New York: Penguin, 1984), p. 238 (Tuesday, April 23, 1878).

40. Paul Bourget, *Essais de psychologie contemporaine,* 2 vols. (Paris: Librairie Plon, 1895), 2: 146-48.

41. The character of Germinie was modeled, as is well known, on the Goncourt brothers' personal domestic, Rose Malingre. In 1862 they were astounded by revelations following her death of her "secret life." Jules wrote: "Those bills she signed, those debts she left with all the tradesmen, all had an unbelievable, horrifying explanation. She had lovers whom she paid. One of them was the son of our dairywoman, who fleeced her and for whom she furnished a room. Another was given our wine and chickens. A secret life of dreadful orgies, nights out, sensual

to the domestic inventory comprising *La Maison d'un artiste*, Edmond wrote:

> Seated beside this hearth, during breaks from work, a cigarette between my lips, my eyes roving over all the bric-a-brac that surrounds me, I often question myself about this passion for the bibelot which has rendered me miserable and happy all my life. And remembering the months of privation that my brother and I endured, years at a time spent in cheap painter's hostels in order to pay off an extravagant purchase, and finding in my memory those feverish days of insane buying from which one walked away still unsatisfied, feeling like one had been up all night gaming and suffering that bitter-taste in the mouth that only the water of a dozen oysters could cleanse, I would ask myself if this sickness were an accident, an evil contracted by chance, or whether it were rather some kind of hereditary illness, a contagion similar to madness or gout.[42]

The gentle and sad atmosphere that prevails in this cabinet, sanctified by the atmosphere of mourning for his dead brother, contrasts sharply with Edmond's comparison of his collecting fever to the devastating effects of hereditary disease. It is as if the specter of syphilis, fatal cause of Jules's premature death, had suddenly intruded into the private room. So ominous is this "malady" of collecting that it recalls the spasms of mortal agony of the dying Jules (in effect "killed" by his dalliance with disease-carrying prostitutes) or the convulsive attacks of "uterine madness" experienced by the erotomaniac maidservant Germinie. From this inadvertent fusion of collector and prostitute, subversive psychohistorical consequences arise: masculine changes places with feminine, prostitute (alias Germinie Lacerteux) becomes collector (of lovers), and the cabinet itself is gradually transformed into a not-so-secret museum of erotic curiosities.

The double conversion of prostitute into collector and collector into prostitute invites further investigation into those narrative scenarios featuring the courtesan's revenge on the patron through her own manipulation of object fetishes. The example of Nana

---

frenzies that prompted one of her lovers to say: 'It's going to kill one of us, me or her!' A passion, a sum of passions, of head, heart, and senses, in which all the unfortunate woman's ailments played their part: consumption, making her desperate for satisfaction, hysteria, and madness" (Baldick, *Pages from the Goncourt Journal*, pp. 75–76).

42. Edmond de Goncourt, *La Maison d'un artiste* (Paris: Charpentier, 1881), p. 354.

again seems appropriate. Taking great delight in spoiling or smashing the priceless gifts bestowed on her by her smitten suitors, Nana seems to flaunt the very hollowness of the hidden commodity value of sex that she herself embodies. In addition to providing a symbolic gloss on the political theme of libidinal expenditure for expenditure's own sake—a veritable psychosexual conundrum—Nana's contemptuous collecting also inscribes the masterplot of the prostitute's "decline and fall" within a Second Empire allegory of capitalist self-destruction, itself the result of a nation's delusionary worship of consumerist idols.

If the prostitute's body stands as the *locus amoenus* of psychoanalytic and materialist demystification (a place where paradigms of false value are reversed and exposed), then the cabinet emerges as space that absorbs the transgressive aura of these transactions. In this "literary closet" the reader is often induced to "re-dress" the prostitute (reassigning her pathological lust to more respectable folk) while concomitantly "undressing" or defrauding the appearances of the bourgeois home.[43] From the prostitute's closet to the pathologized house the transfer is direct.

Such a transfer was perhaps at work in the interiors of Doctor Charcot's personal apartments.[44] As Debora Silverman has shown in *Art Nouveau in Fin-de-Siècle France*, Charcot evinced a sinister fondness for death's-head imagery, mutant bibelots, and the grotesque, art-nouveau patterns of a fevered consciousness. His house, which he himself crafted, designed, and choreographed in the Renaissance manner, boasted a collection of croquis depicting *Blaps mortisaga*, ("presages of death"). Exemplary of what Derrida has allusively referred to as "cadaverization" (tropes of death associated with coffins, cabinets, and cartouches), as well as of what Walter Benjamin has called "a fancier's value, rather than use value," Charcot's house, as recorded by his colleague Henri Meige, was a

---

43. Here I have applied the terms developed by Peggy Kamuf in her trenchant reading of dressing and fetishization within the cabinet in Jean-Jacques Rousseau's *La Nouvelle Héloïse* ("Inside *Julie's* Closet," *Romantic Review* 69 [Nov. 1978]: 296–306). My thanks to Nancy K. Miller for alerting me to this provocative article.

44. Debora Silverman's chapter "Psychologie nouvelle" contains a richly researched section on Charcot as interior designer. Silverman suggests precise connections between his theory of hysteria and his practice of art nouveau. See her *Art Nouveau in Fin-de-Siècle France: Politics, Psychology, and Style* (Berkeley: University of California Press, 1989), pp. 100–106.

repository of historically dislocated artifacts, idiosyncratic relics, and emblems of erotic mysticism:[45]

> Eager to remain faithful to his artistic credo, he took great pains during his travels and museum visits to inspect the decorative relics of the past.... Thus he became the master of a kind of atelier of decorative arts, situated in his very own home. From this space were born sculptures with deformed contours or bas-reliefs, chiseled or embossed ornaments, painted or gilded table-settings, stained-glass windows, enamelware, furniture with carved, engraved or varnished panels, bookbindings, coffers, armchairs, tables, a whole profusion of fantastic bibelots, antiqued, waxed, and refinished,... a curious family museum in which Charcot experienced his best moments, realizing his Shakespearean ideal "A little too much of everything."[46]

Charcot's Shakespearean motto "Un peu de trop" defines the fin-de-siècle baroque interior in terms of an aesthetic of hyperbolic accumulation. In the formal *écarts*, or deviations of line toward the margin, in the proliferation of zigzags and twisting shapes, we find in Charcot's domestic sanctuary the very signs of nervosity associated with the "born prostitute" or female hysteric. Formerly confined to the medical cabinet, these subliminally legible patterns of perverse excess spill over and contaminate the private, bourgeois dwelling.

As a space showcasing in objectified form the de-repressed phantasms of a doctor-gone-mad, Charcot's study anticipated scenes from Hans Janowitz and Carl Mayer's famous film *Das Cabinet des Dr. Caligari* (released in 1920). Siegfried Kracauer, commenting on the set designs for *The Cabinet of Dr. Caligari*, linked the representation of eroticism and mental instability to the film's expressionist aesthetic. "The settings amounted to a perfect transformation of material objects into emotional ornaments," he noted. At a time

---

45. Walter Benjamin, "Louis-Philippe or the Interior," in *Charles Baudelaire: A Lyric Poet in the Era of High Capitalism*, trans. Harry Zohn (London: NLB, 1973), p. 168. In this fragment on the interior, Benjamin defined this "fancier's value" in terms of an absence of commodity value: "The interior was the place of refuge of Art. The collector was the true inhabitant of the interior. He made the glorification of things his concern. To him fell the task of Sisyphus which consisted of stripping things of their commodity character by means of possession of them. But he conferred upon them only a fancier's value, rather than use-value. The collector dreamed that he was in a world which was not only far-off in distance and in time, but which was also a better one."

46. Dr. Henri Meige, *Charcot artiste* (Paris: Masson, 1925), pp. 21–24.

when Freud was theorizing (as verbal parapraxis) the lapses, double-entendres, and unintended puns that erupted into normal speech, expressionist architecture seems to have generated a companion lexicon of discombobulating, deconstructive forms. Kracauer, undoubtedly taking his cue from the psychoanalytical theory in the air, encouraged the viewer to accord expressivity to the sharp angles, abstract configurations, and distorted perspectives of *Caligari*'s backdrop:

> With its oblique chimneys on pell-mell roofs, its windows in the form of arrows or kites and its treelike arabesques that were threats rather than trees, Holstenwall resembled those visions of unheard-of cities which the painter Lyonel Feininger evoked through his edgy, crystalline compositions. In addition, the ornamental system in *Caligari* expanded through space, annulling its conventional aspect by means of painted shadows in disharmony with the lighting effects, and zigzag delineations designed to efface all rules of perspective. Space now dwindled to a flat plane, now augmented its dimensions to become what one writer called a "stereoscopic universe."[47]

Caligari's "stereoscopic universe" seems to have its origins in the camouflaged viewing devices and paradigms of "looking at looking" highlighted by the cabinet episodes in Zola, Proust, and so many of their epigones. Put simply, the collector's house and the psychiatrist's house (themselves anticipated by Goethe's witches' kitchen or Balzac's fantastic antiquary's shop in *La Peau de chagrin*) seem early on to have epistemologically collided and converged, thus helping to spawn an increasingly fashionable psychiatrization of style. The emergent pathological interior, progressively synonymous with the bourgeois "home," was no longer a romantic haunted house, no longer a chamber of symbolist nightmares, no longer even a Freudian "uncanny" house plagued by recursive repression; rather, it emerged as a singularly "possessed" apartment, fostering the folly, caprice, and *érotomanie* of its spellbound master.

47. Siegfried Kracauer, *From Caligari to Hitler: A Psychological History of the German Film* (Princeton: Princeton University Press, 1970), p. 69.

CHAPTER 4

· Unmasking the Masquerade:
Fetishism and Femininity from the
Goncourt Brothers to Joan Riviere

· The feminist ideology of the masquerade and the Freudian discourse of fetishism could hardly be more antithetical on first consideration. The former, as constituted by Luce Irigaray, Michèle Montrelay, Mary Ann Doane, and Judith Butler, in response to Joan Riviere's pivotal essay "Womanliness as a Masquerade" (1929), aims at a destabilization of masculinist psychoanalysis, whereas the latter in its vivid imaging of castration anxiety qualifies as one of Freud's most explicitly phallocentric essays. And yet, the masquerade and fetishism in their shared dependency on the lexicon of phallic surrogation prove to be curiously compatible at specific theoretical junctures. Both theories may be characterized in terms of a defensive posture toward the symbolic order of castration, and both articulate surrogation in a language of veils, prosthetic appendages, and sexual travesty.

In addition to examining the rather strange points at which femininity and fetishism, or feminism and psychoanalysis, dovetail, collide, and mutually refract (nodes where patriarchal Freudianism loses a measure of its phallocentrism, moments where feminist theory confronts some of its own theoretical inconsistencies and lacunae), this study of sartorial language in the Goncourt brothers and Baron Octave Uzanne also entails an engagement with what Joan Copjec has provocatively termed the female "sartorial superego." Beginning with an investigation of mid-nineteenth-century idioms of fashion, material culture, and female consumerism, I want to experiment with grounding a feminist ontology of femininity in the constructions, both erotic and social, of a certain kind of *Verkleidungstrieb* ("will to dress," "sartorial drive") or clothing fetishism.[1]

The debate over the impossibly vexed question What is femininity? seems more rather than less elusive with each new attempt within psychoanalysis and feminism to theorize the female subject. In the late twenties and early thirties many important women psychoanalysts endeavored to extend or challenge Freud's writings on femininity (Jeanne Lampl-de-Groot, Helen Deutsch, Ruth Mack-Brunswick, Marie Bonaparte, Karen Horney, Joan Riviere, to mention only the most well known), but successive generations would find even the more unorthodox among them too timid when it came to articulating female sexuality as something other than a second-best version of its masculine counterpart. Though since the thirties the validity of femininity as a category for understanding the feminine has become increasingly the target of skepticism, there has also been a concern to preserve the history of its representations.

With a rather curious consistency, nineteenth-century authors strategically retrieved representations of eighteenth-century woman, projecting her as fiction, fixture, and even fetish of the feminine. In the Goncourt brothers' *La Femme au dix-huitième siècle* and in the fashion writing of Octave Uzanne, literary portraits of eighteenth-century libertinage and sartorial pomp are often used to praise and at the same time to pathologize (implicitly) a high culture of flirtation, seduction, and masquerade. These writings provide an interesting illustration of how one century's reading of another leads to epistemological shifts or new developments within adjacent disciplines, demonstrating, specifically, how the nineteenth century's reading of eighteenth-century woman created a vision of femininity that in turn passed into early psychoanalysis.

As in the case of "cabinet fiction," an important microgenre of nineteenth-century literature may be defined in the Goncourts' proleptically New Historical reconstruction of eighteenth-century feminine culture. Coining the expression "elegant reality" (*la réalité élégante*) for a descriptive mode devoted to foregrounding "the pretty" and "distinguished" detail, Edmond de Goncourt matched style to content in his examination of what he called *féminilité*.[2]

---

1. Jann Matlock introduces the notion of *Verkleidungstrieb* in "Masquerading Women, Pathologized Men: Cross-dressing, Fetishism, and the Theory of Perversion, 1882–1935," in Emily Apter and William Pietz, eds. *Fetishism as Cultural Discourse: Gender, Commodity, and Vision* (Ithaca: Cornell University Press, forthcoming).
2. Edmond de Goncourt, prefaces to *La Faustin* and *Chérie*, in Edmond de

Applied to the intangible qualities of a woman's innermost being (her initiation into coquetry, the dawning of secret effusions, the recesses and shadows of deception), "femininity" emerges as an essentialist label that subordinates subtle permutations of psychological sensibility to outward clichés of women's culture fixed by mid-century convention. Similarly Uzanne, a kind of "lesser Goncourt" in his literary career, made a point of resuscitating the terms *féminie* (roughly, all that falls in the domain of woman: beauty, ornament, love) and *femmenie* (accenting *la femme* herself as circulating temptation [*poupée d'Eros*] within the Gallic "commerce of gallantry") from the neglected pages of Littré's dictionary.³ Uzanne's texts on "les artifices de la beauté" equally constitute a distinctive genre in which metonymies of costume, natural physique, and attitude coalesce in an eroticized sentimental prose. Here the mimological rhetorical conventions by which fin-de-siècle writers represented feminine narcissism, worldliness, and display are clearly placed in view. By focusing on a genre that might be called (after the Goncourts) *elegant realism*, we can clarify the history of gender clichés and better understand its imprint on psychoanalytical assumptions.

Jules and Edmond de Goncourt were far more notorious for their virulently misogynistic view of the female species, which they placed on a par with the animal order in the evolutionary chain, than for any sympathetic investigation of womanliness. Novels such as *Germinie Lacerteux* (1865) or *Manette Saloman* (1867) capitalized on sensational illustrations of the insatiable sexual urges of women. And as Elisabeth Badinter has shown, the *Journal* was equally replete with depictions of women psychically enslaved to their physical morphologies and bodily functions. "All the life juices, the whole evolution of woman flows downward toward the inferior parts of the body: the pelvis, the rump, the thighs," they wrote in 1855.⁴ Possessed of feeble intelligence, superficial, agents of the Revolution, and emblems of nineteenth-century depravity—these characterizations of

---

Goncourt and Jules de Goncourt, *Préfaces et manifestes littéraires*, ed. Hubert Juin (Paris: Slatkine, 1980), pp. 57–62.

3. Octave Uzanne, *Féminies* (Paris: Académie des Beaux Livres, 1896), p. 190.

4. Edmond de Goncourt and Jules de Goncourt, *Journal*, Oct. 13, 1855, as cited by Elisabeth Badinter in her preface to *La Femme au dix-huitième siècle* (Paris: Flammarion, 1982), p. 11. Further references to *La Femme* will be abbreviated *F*. Badinter's preface is highly informative and suggestive; I am indebted to it for a number of ideas presented in this chapter.

women repeatedly surfaced in the Goncourts' multitomed journal.

As naturalist writers who lingered over the most scrofulous particulars of disease, the Goncourts not only contributed to the general nineteenth-century medicalization of eighteenth-century literature but they also pathologized the much-trumpeted libertinage of ancien-régime aristocrats. To the debauchery indulged in by ladies of noble station the Goncourts attributed a psychopathology of emptiness, ennui, vapors, hypochondria, hysteria, and what they referred to as "a kind of intellectual libertinage [*une sorte de libertinage de pensées*]" (*F* 316). In brief, as their posthumous reception bears out, a prudish but no less prurient habit of diagnosing the consequences of promiscuity informed their historical panoramas, even at the risk of placing their idealized vision of the ancien régime in jeopardy.

Despite the fact that Madame du Barry, Madame de Pompadour, and Marie Antoinette had set redoubtable examples of licentiousness before the populace, the Goncourts' documentation of the eighteenth-century aristocrat, with her cultivated mien and seductive allure, afforded some kind of narrative reprieve from their characteristically gynophobic vituperation. As Juliette Adam, one of the few women spared their contempt, would write: "The Goncourts so loved and frequented eighteenth-century women that they despised the women of the nineteenth... consigning them to wickedness, debauchery or imbecility."[5] Published in 1862, *La Femme au dix-huitième siècle* marks the culmination of a series of works by the Goncourt brothers dedicated to the nostalgic recuperation of ancien-régime political and aesthetic values. *Histoire de la société française pendant la Révolution et pendant le Directoire* had appeared in 1854, *Histoire de Marie-Antoinette* in 1858, portions of *L'Art au dix-huitième siècle* in 1859, and *Les Maîtresses de Louis XV* in 1860. In this fruitful period of a collaboration that critics unfailingly describe as incestuous, they elaborated an ideal of feminine beauty, charm, and even intelligence matched by a prose style at once frothy and rhetorically fetishistic.

In this context, the expression *rhetorical fetishism* refers to the taste for epithet, mannered syntax, and tropes of hyperbole and accumulation commonly used by the Goncourts to render the codes of *féminilité*. As in the language of fetishization, whereby the verbal substitute for the phallic referent is reified to the point where its

---

5. As cited by Badinter, *La Femme*, p. 16.

origin is forgotten, so the Goncourts' idiolect of womanliness replaced the patriarchically inflected signifier with a hypostatized, essentialist sign of the feminine:

> *Etonnant! miraculeux! divin!* ce sont les épithètes courantes de la causerie. Une langue d'extase et d'exclamations, une langue qui escalade les superlatifs, entre dans la langue française et apporte l'enflure à sa sobriété. On ne parle plus que de *grâces sans nombres,* de *perfections sans fin.* A la moindre fatigue, on est *anéanti;* au moindre contre-temps, on est *désespéré,* on est *obsédé prodigieusement,* on est *suffoqué.* Désire-t'on une chose? On est *folle à perdre le boire et le manger.* Un homme déplaît-il? C'est *un homme à jeter par les fenêtres.* A-t-on la graine? on est d'une *sottise rebutante.* On applaudit *à tout rompre,* on loue à *outrance,* on aime *à miracle.* Et cette fièvre des expressions ne suffit pas; pour être une femme "parfaitement usagée", il est nécessaire de zézayer, de moduler, d'attendrir et d'efféminer sa voix, de prononcer, au lieu de *pigeons* et de *choux,* des *pizons* et ces *soux.*
>
> *Astonishing! miraculous! divine!* these are the common epithets of (woman's) chatter. An idiom of ecstasy and exclamations that goes beyond superlatives, enters the French language and brings turgidity to its sobriety. One speaks only of *infinite charms,* of *endless perfections.* At the slightest fatigue, one is *reduced to nothing;* at the slightest contretemps, one is *in despair,* one is prodigiously *obsessed,* one is *suffocated.* Does she desire something? She is *crazed to the point of bringing up her food and drink.* A man displeases her? He is *a man to be thrown out the window.* Has she gone to seed? She is *revoltingly stupid.* She applauds *to breaking point,* she praises *to the limit,* she loves *miraculously.* And even this fever of expressions is not enough: to be a woman "perfectly in the know," it is necessary to lisp, to inflect, to soften, and to effeminize one's voice, to say in the place of *pigeons* and *cabbage,* "*pizons*" and "*soux.*" (F 71; authors' italics)

Here it is perhaps no accident that the paradigm of feminine speech is predicated on error (of pronunciation)—for the discourse of womanliness seems destined to the regime of surrogation.

The Goncourts complemented this rhetorical fetishism with a more clinical fetishization of the female body typically found in the work of eighteenth-century authors. Their portrait of eighteenth-century woman often derived from writers such as Marivaux, Rousseau, and Rétif de la Bretonne. From the world of Marivaux's *La Vie de Marianne,* with its titillating scenes of sartorial strategy in love, they took inspiration for the theme of the mask.[6] A device of dupery designating the veiling of ulterior motives in the game of love through skillful manipulation of multiple visages, *marivaudage* was treated as the ensign of phallic woman. Like painters preparing fastidious physiognomical and characterological studies for each genre of feminine beauty (and reinforcing this technique with constant allusions to Boucher, Fragonard, and Watteau), the Goncourts developed prototypes of the eighteenth-century seductress. As a fleshy, bovine, Venus evolves through the century, imperiled by the "orgies of the Palais-Royal," only to reemerge under the brushstrokes of Boucher as a smirking nymph, she is evoked as "le masque de ses amours [the mask of her loves]" (*F* 254). The *marivaudage* of the feminine facial mask, at least in rather simplistic Freudian terms, suggests an artful incognito designed to prolong the male viewer's distraction from the absorbing prospect of a hypothetical female phallus.[7] Evoking Marivaux again in a manner that strikingly foreshadows the twentieth-century psychoanalytical debate on the masquerade, the Goncourts identified eighteenth-century woman's ultimate refinement as the ability to appear as if she were no longer wearing a mask: "She can say: that's how nature made me. What she will leave visible, as if by negligence or oversight, will have the irritating charm of a modest, veiled copy of the original; and the veil that she preserves is so light, so transparent, that it hardly creates a barrier to the male imagination" (*F* 270). In the qualifiers "*comme* par négligence" and "qu'il ne sera *presque* pas un obstacle," the psychosexual innuendos of veiling (as in Nietzsche) shine through; woman masquerades as essential femininity ("telle que la nature m'a faite"), but her essentialism is only a more invisible form of the mask.[8]

6. The roster of theoretical voices contributing to the philosophical treatments of the mask is long. From phenomenological and anthropological analyses (elaborated in the 1940s and 1950s by Roland Kuhn, Georges Buraud, Gaston Bachelard, and the early Foucault) to Derrida and Lacan's post-Nietzschean interpretations of the veil as trope of the woman's phallic prevarication and its feminist critique (Jacqueline Rose, Gayatri Spivak, Mary Ann Doane) there have been seemingly endless reappropriations of this discourse.

7. It is this aleatory technique of delay without consummation that Roland Barthes would assign to *marivaudage* in his *Fragments d'un discours amoureux*: "To speak amorously is to expend without an end in sight, without a *crisis*; it is to practice a relation without orgasm. There may exist a literary form of this *coitus reservatus*: what we call Marivaudage" (Barthes, *A Lover's Discourse*, trans. Richard Howard [New York: Hill and Wang, 1978], p. 73.

8. The use of the veil as a metaphor for womanliness and philosophy alike has been a recurrent theme in the discourses of deconstruction and feminism. From

If Marivaux captured the ethic of falsity implicit in the feminine masquerade and Rousseau epitomized the cult worship of erotic synecdoche (from the stolen ribbon to the famous deformed nipple), it was nevertheless Rétif de la Bretonne who most influenced their portrayal of femininity. Like no other writer he appreciated the inherently fetishistic nature of the prosthetic appendages favored by eighteenth-century fashion.[9] Many of his texts sexualized the extremities of the female anatomy and its sartorial extrusions: corsets, crinolines, and, most especially, shoes. In his novella *Un Joli Pied*, for example, the elegant shoe completely upstages the charms of its wearer:

> Elle s'assit et posa son joli pied sur une chaise, de sorte qu'on le voyait en entier. Rien de si charmant dans la nature par sa petitesse, par la grâce et l'élégance de sa chaussure: c'était un soulier de couleur puce brodé et garni d'un cordonnet en argent sur les coutures; le talon mince était assez haut, mais placé de manière qu'il ne faisait pas refouler le pied; la forme par devant était la plus mignonne qu'on puisse voir. Saintepallaie était hors de lui-même.

> She sat down and placed her pretty foot on a chair, so that one could see the whole foot. Nothing in nature was ever so charmingly small, graceful, and elegant as her shoe; it was footwear of puce brocade garnished with silver braid along the seams; the thin heel was quite high, but placed so as not to compress the foot; the shape in front was the most adorable sight imaginable. Saintepallaie was beside himself.[10]

Passages of this kind furnished the Goncourts with conceits for rendering the psychology of fashion. As they built up a language of libidinously charged vestimentary details in *La Femme au dix-huitième siècle* they cited Rétif's *Le Pied de Fanchette*:

> Nous entrons dans le règne des artistes en tout genre, des modistes de génie, aussi bien que des cordonniers sublimes, uniques pour *monter* un pied et le faire valoir, lui donner la petitesse, la grâce, la tournure, la "lesteté" si vantée, si goûtée, si souvent chantée par le dix-huitième siècle, le je ne sais quoi enfin de ce pied de Mme Lévêque, la marchande

---

Nietzsche to Derrida, Luce Irigaray, and Gayatri Spivak a genealogical discussion can be traced, culminating in Spivak's notion of the "feminization of philosophizing."

9. The Goncourts used Rousseau as an exemplar of hyperbolic sentimental display, localized in passionate attachments to feminine bagatelles (we have only to recall the famous episode of the stolen ribbon).

10. Rétif de la Bretonne, *Un Joli Pied*, as cited by J. Avalon and Albert Charpentier, "Restif de la Bretonne fétichiste," *Aesculape* (Apr. 1912), p. 89.

de soie à la *Ville de Lyon*, qui inspire à Rétif de la Bretonne le *Pied de Fanchette*.

At this point we enter into the realm of art in every sphere, from the couturier of genius to those sublime shoemakers, unique in their ability to *raise up* and thereby enhance the foot, endowing it with the smallness, grace, shape, and "lightness" so celebrated and enjoyed, so lyrically praised by the eighteenth century; it was this "je ne sais quoi" of the foot of Mme Lévêque (a silk merchant in the town of Lyon) that inspired Rétif's *Foot of Fanchette*. (F 275)

Ultimately one might argue that the Goncourts' reading of Rétif allows us to supplant the notion of *mask* with the modern figure of *construction*, and here we mean to literalize the Foucauldian (and now feminist) figure of social construction so as to designate the actual props, cages, stays, and struts appertaining to the eighteenth-century female body.

It is of course the extravagant, preposterous coiffure that constituted the most familiar cliché associated with the period. The full symbolism of mounted piles of hair, as prolongation of the female body and verbal constellation of fetishistic signs, is, however, less well understood. As Chantal Thomas has recently remarked in her analysis of the names for hair fashions popularized by Marie Antoinette and her followers, "the coiffeur not only had to have the talent of an architect, he also had to show himself capable of chronicling the daily news."[11] *La Femme au dix-huitième siècle* offers an exhaustive glossary of what the Goncourts referred to as "les coiffures parlantes" (speaking hairstyles), from "le pouf au sentiment," in which strands of hair from deceased loved ones were interwoven; to "les coiffures à l'insurgent," commemorating seismic political events; to "la coiffure à la Dauphine," an image of gender crossover with its phallic resemblance to *une queue de paon*, or "peacock's tail" (F 282–87). Instead of signifying a timeless, essential femininity, which may have been what the Goncourts wished to evoke, the exaggerated coiffures of the eighteenth-century French noblewoman disclosed the historically commodifying conditions of her erotic construction, one that was, of course, essentially nineteenth century in its character and function.

In the section of his *Passagen-Werk* on fashion, Walter Benjamin claimed that it was hard to find a more erotic fetish than the

---

11. Chantal Thomas, *La Reine scélérate* (Paris: Seuil, 1989), p. 88.

enhanced head of hair, which, in its negotiation between the dead realm of inert consumer artifacts and the enticing, animated domain of sexual stimulants, fostered a psychoanalytical mediation of material culture and gender differentiation. He gave the example of the multiple erotic significations that were "dissimulated" beneath the feminine hat. As opposed to the strict political codes of rigidly typified male headgear, women's hats suggested infinite possibilities of meaning beyond the simple symbolization of the sexual organs. Thus, he noted the peculiarly mimetic agency of the *capote*, a form of bonnet contemporary with the crinoline: "The wide brims of the *capote* are turned up, in this way suggesting how one should turn up the crinoline so that the man might the more easily have sexual relations with the woman."[12] This penchant for an eroticism of the *retroussé*, or "turned up," was turned inward in the case of the corset, described by Benjamin as a *passage* for the torso (a kind of *Passagen-Werk* of the female anatomy).[13] The corset, Benjamin claimed, was a particularly freighted signifier for nineteenth-century eroticism, for it gave off the aura of the *renfermé* (closed-in) associated with clandestine prostitution.

Anticipating Benjamin, the Goncourts dismantled the apparent eroticism of coiffure, corset, and crinoline. Consider, for example, their rendering of a panier:

- Cette toilette, avec son incroyable déploiement de jupe, représente le *panier* dans l'ampleur, la grandeur, l'énormité de son développment. Le panier que les princesses de sang vont bientôt porter si large qu'il leur faudra un tabouret vide à côté d'elles, le panier commence à grandir sur le modèle des paniers de deux dames anglaises venues en France en 1714; et chaque année il est devenue plus usité, plus exagéré, plus extravagant. Il s'est étoffé de façon à couvrir les grossesses de la Régence: il s'est répandu par toute la France comme un masque de débauche, pendant ces jours de folie.

- This dress, with its incredible unfolding of the skirt, represents the hoop in its full amplitude, grandeur, and monstrosity. Worn so wide that princesses of noble birth soon needed an empty stool beside them, modeled after a petticoat sported by two English women who came to France in 1714; this panier has each year become progressively wide-

---

12. Walter Benjamin, *Gesammelte Schriften* (Frankfurt am Main: Suhrkamp Verlag, 1982), 1: 131. Benjamin is summarizing an argument made by Helen Grund in her *Vom Wesen der Mode* (Munich: Privately printed, 1935).
13. Benjamin, *Gesammelte Schriften* 1: 510.

spread, exaggerated, and extravagant. Upholstered to disguise the pregnancies of the Regency, the panier spread all over France like a mask of debauchery during these days of folly. (*F* 261–62)

In this image of a furnished feminine persona (identified as "debauchery's mask"), all traces of seduction are forfeited. As the beaux-arts critic Charles Blanc argued in a section of his aesthetic analysis of women's fashion, *L'Art dans la parure et dans le vêtement (Art in Adornment and Dress)*, this eighteenth-century fondness for amplitude ultimately defeated its purpose, calling femininity's bluff by revealing its attempt at empowerment through sartorial bulk:

> To exaggerate width would be to run counter to the proposed end, it would be to miss the goal by overstepping it; because excess, which can only be produced by an increase of size, would end in spreading out the figure and overwhelming it, unless in order to balance the enlargement of the figure that puffs and paniers would give it, a structure of curls and feathers were erected on the head, like those worn by the Princesse de Lamballe and Marie Antoinette during the reign of powder.[14]

Like the oversized falbala, constricting corset, or spiky, totemic hair ornament, the panier afforded a caricature of mythic femininity. In the spread of the woman's hips, merging with the footstool used to prop up her volumnious skirts, femininity seems to evaporate by virtue of its overly emphasized materialization. Again and again, in their representations of eighteenth-century fashion, the brothers called attention to the charade of femininity by highlighting the structural supports and surface drapery sustaining and simultaneously exposing the illusion of a swollen, imperious, expansive, incorporating female body. In contrast to the nineteenth-century body—that pert, coquettish, curvaceous female form that, as Debora Silverman has recently observed, became embedded as a design motif in the art-nouveau furniture and interiors that the Goncourts helped to anticipate—this eighteenth-century body defied domestication.[15] This is of course probably why the Goncourts seemed so

14. Charles Blanc, *Art in Adornment and Dress* (London: Chapman and Hall, 1877), p. 59.
15. "Archaeologists of material culture," as Debora Silverman has described them, the Goncourts distinguished themselves as masters at creating a rhetoric of plasticity and texture—upholstery, drapery, lacquer—which both feminized domestic artifacts and literalized woman as material construction. "La mode" is portrayed as the "furniture" of women's bodies, an extensive "frame" that inadvertently demystifies the masquerade of womanliness in its nomenclature. Silverman has noted, "the

intent on denaturalizing its impression—the obviousness of feminine artifice (as in Baudelaire's aesthetic of *maquillage*) guarantees the failure of an autonomous (nonpatriarchal) definition of femininity.

But there are risks in underscoring the feminine mask, for this exposed transparency of artifice also reveals the extent to which masculinity relies for its own mythic gender on a contrivance of gender in the opposite sex. As Judith Butler has observed, masculinity is equally vulnerable to the masquerade critique, especially when it is "taken on by the male homosexual who, presumably, seeks to hide—not from others, but from himself, an ostensible femininity."[16] This over-exposed quality of the gender masquerade serves to explain why the Goncourts' gongoristic idiom of eighteenth-century fashion occasionally seems to come undone much in the way that their social snobbery and bourgeois monarchism appear to be undercut by their moving fictional portraits of exploited working-class women. Ostentatious articles of clothing rendered with colorful adjectives or meticulously matched to fascimiles of feminine speech patterns come apart at unexpected moments in their texts, revealing a latent instability of sexual identity. In *Les Maîtresses de Louis XV*, for example, they described "la Pompadour" appointed as Venus in a gown of metallic blue. The way in which the train of her dress aspires to phallic stiffness serves to overlay a masculine persona on the feminine frame:

· Elle était la mère des Amours, Vénus elle-même, dans un habit de mosaïque d'argent, festonné de taffetas peint, chenillé d'argent et bleu, frangé d'argent, et traînant avec la majesté d'un manteau royal une grande queue d'étoffe bleue à mosaïque d'argent.

· She was the mother of Love, Venus herself, attired in a mosaic of silver, festooned with painted taffeta, wrapped around in silver and blue,

---

Goncourts clarified how the rococo interior was inseparable from its female identity, for the Louis XV *style moderne* was initiated to oppose the *grand goût* of Louis XIV with the ethos of *la grâce*, a petite, amorous, and explicitly female form.... Furniture with anthropomorphic female names multiplied: *la causeuse*, 'the chatterer'; *la bergère*, 'the shepherdess'; *la chiffonnière*, 'the dresser'; *la marquise brisée*, 'the divided marquise'; *la chaise à la reine; la chaise longue*; and especially *la toilette*. The feminization of rococo furnishings culminated here, as *toilette* named both the small dressing table for women and the art of women's preparation of their bodies for display" (*Art Nouveau in Fin-de-Siècle France: Politics, Psychology, and Style* [Berkeley: University of California Press, 1989], pp. 27–28).

16. Judith Butler, *Gender Trouble: Feminism and the Subversion of Identity* (New York: Routledge, 1990), p. 51.

fringed in silver and dragging, with the majesty of a royal cloak, a huge train of blue and variegated silver material.[17]

Though as a general rule Edmond and Jules reveled in the aesthetic contrasts between mistresses, Madame du Barry is similarly masculinized in the costume of the hunt:

> Toutes les métamorphoses conviennent à cette beauté, comme aux divinités de la Fable; et que demain elle quitte le grand habit de Versailles pour un déguisement de chasse; qu'elle mette l'habit d'homme aux larges parements battus par la dentelle d'Angleterre qui fait le tour de son col nu; qu'elle porte ses cheveux plats, et que deux ou trois mouches jetées çà et là dans sa figure où relèvent la mutinerie: elle sera Vénus chasseresse.

> All metamorphoses suit this beauty, as they do the gods of Fable; and tomorrow may she shed the raiment of Versailles for a hunting costume; may she don masculine dress with a large, English-lace collar encircling her bared throat; may she wear her hair straight, and may there be two or three patches thrown here and there on a face that speaks unruliness: she will be a Venus of the hunt.[18]

Commentators on cross-dressing have often insisted that men's clothing when worn by women only enhances the spectacle of femininity. In this case, however, it would seem that Madame du Barry has so entered the spirit of her travesty that her character, in its forcefulness and projection of a predatory will, attests to some kind of veritable sex change.

In their portrait of Marie Antoinette the Goncourts took this gender ambivalence yet a step further, obliquely associating the scandal of the Diamond Necklace Affair (in which the queen was implicated in a conspiracy to buy one of the most valuable jewels in France for resale on the black market) with the stony dazzle of Marie Antoinette's character, and discerning a natural disposition to power in the queen's body. Here it is the unadorned, essential body that functions like some kind of underwire support structure for the royal social construction.[19] Marie Antoinette's upright carri-

17. Edmond de Goncourt and Jules de Goncourt, *Les Maîtresses de Louis XV*, 2 vols. (Paris: Librairie de Firmin Didot Frères, 1860), 1: 230.
18. Ibid., bk. 3, vol. 2, p. 172.
19. In a paper entitled "Adorning Marie-Antoinette" (delivered at the Modern Language Association annual meeting, Washington, D.C., December 27, 1989), Pierre Saint-Amand described the way in which the masquerade of the royal

age ("as if made for the throne," according to Madame de Polignac) and the way in which her blond hair settles on her head like an organic crown ("le diadème d'or pâle de ses cheveux blonds") suggest a subliminal monarchism—an overdetermined will to rule— that decidedly corroborates the female sovereign's primordial masculinity.[20]

In *La Femme au dix-huitième siècle* the Goncourts gave this transvestite female ruling class a globally imperialist socioeconomic status, attributing the French fashion industry's "domination" and "seduction" of Europe to the Frenchwoman's ingenuity and exigence in the field of frippery: "all of Europe is under the sway of our fashions" (*F* 274). A patriarchal tendency to export culture and conquer markets is here imputed to the lady skilled in feminine wiles. Finally, in an astonishing passage framed in the context of a political allegory equating the demise of the aristocracy with female empowerment, the same creature who passes for the consummate embodiment of feminine charm is also unmasked as a paragon of maleness:

> Cette influence, cette domination sans exemple, cette souveraineté de droit presque divin, à quoi faut-il l'attribuer? Où en est la clef et l'explication? La femme du dix-huitième siècle dut-elle seulement sa puissance aux qualités propres de son sexe, aux charmes de sa nature, aux séductions habituelles de son être? La dut-elle absolument à son temps, à la mode humaine, à ce règne du plaisir qui lui apporta le pouvoir dans un baiser et la fit commander à tout, en commandant à l'amour? Sans doute, la femme tira de ses grâces de tous les temps, du milieu et des dispositions particulières de son siècle, une force et une facilité naturelles d'autorité.... Il y a dans toutes ces physionomies la résolution et l'éclair d'une idée virile, une profondeur dans la mutinerie même, je ne sais quoi de pensant et de perçant, ce mélange de l'homme et de la femme d'état dont vous retrouverez les traits jusque sur la figure d'une comédienne, de la Sylvia....

---

persona was in a sense extended, hardened, and further materialized in the narcissistically erotic space of Trianon. Saint-Amand writes, "Theater, balls, fashion shows, Trianon was a seductive paradise. Everything was constructed in order to reflect back the queen's image to herself. Mirrors were everywhere, and more were put in at night to mask the windows. The space was saturated with ornamentation." For an interesting analysis of the Diamond Necklace Affair, see Sarah Maza, "The Diamond Necklace Affair Revisited (1785–1786): The Case of the Missing Queen," in Lynn Hunt, ed., *Eroticism and the Body Politic* (Baltimore: The Johns Hopkins University Press, 1991), pp. 63–89.

20. Edmond de Goncourt and Jules de Goncourt, *Histoire de Marie-Antoinette* ([1858]; Paris: Flammarion/Fasquelle, n.d.), pp. 101–102.

78 · Feminizing the Fetish

> Quittez les portraits, ouvrez l'histoire: le génie de la femme du dix-huitième siècle ne démentira pas cette physionomie. Vous le verrez s'approprier aux plus grands rôles, s'élargir, grandir, devenir, par l'application, l'étude, la volonté, assez mâle ou du moins assez sérieux pour expliquer, légitimer presque ses plus étonnantes et ses plus scandaleuses usurpations.

> · This influence, this domination without example, this sovereignty of near divine right, to what must it be attributed? Where is the key to the explanation? Did eighteenth-century woman owe her power solely to the innate qualities of her sex, to the charms of her nature, to the habitual seductions of her being? Or did she owe it exclusively to her epoch, to the fashion, to the reign of pleasure that brought her power in a kiss and allowed her to rule everything in ruling love? Without a doubt, woman will draw from the graces of every century, from the milieu and particular temperaments of her age, a strength and a natural facility for authority.... In all these physiognomies, there is the clarity and resolution of a virile idea, a profundity even in rebelliousness, an "I don't know what" of perspicuity and thoughtfulness, this mixture of the man and woman of state that you can trace through to the features of the actress Sylvia....
> Put the portraits aside, open up history: the genius of the eighteenth-century woman will never give the lie to this physiognomy. You will see it take over the largest roles, grow bigger, become, through application, study, and sheer force of will, male enough, or at the very least, serious enough, to explain, and legitimate, even its most astonishing and scandalous usurpations. (F 294–95)

This masculine face stamped indelibly on period physiognomies of women, this "scandalous" propensity to usurp male prerogative, this fundamental commutability of femininity and masculinity, ultimately implies that there is absolutely no fixed sociopolitical basis for sexual difference. Woman's social construction is revealed as just that: no more than an evanescent agglomeration of codes and commonplaces, no less than a materially ornamental construct that gives narcissistic pleasure to the female subject by enhancing her body in her own eyes.

Half a century later Proust would render this idea in one of his portraits of Swann's mistress. Odette emerges as an impossible construction, for she is made from clumsy sheaths and unadhering parts. In the gaping seams of her mechanical body, we glimpse the emptiness of her feminine essence:

> · Il faut d'ailleurs dire que le visage d'Odette paraissait plus maigre et

plus proéminent parce que le front et le haut des joues, cette surface unie et plus plane était recouverte par la masse de cheveux qu'on portait alors prolongés en "devants", soulevés en "crêpes", répandus en mèches folles le long des oreilles; et quant à son corps qui était admirablement fait, il était difficile d'en apercevoir la continuité (à cause des modes de l'époque et quoiqu'elle fût une des femmes de Paris qui s'habillaient le mieux), tant le corsage, s'avançant en saillie comme sur un ventre imaginaire et finissant brusquement en pointe pendant que par en dessous commençait à s'enfler le ballon des doubles jupes, donnait à la femme l'air d'être composée de pièces différentes mal emmanchées les unes dans les autres; tant les ruchés, les volants, le gilet suivaient en toute indépendance, selon la fantaisie de leur dessin ou la consistence de leur étoffe, la ligne qui les conduisait aux noeuds, aux bouillons de dentelle, aux effilés de jais perpendiculaires, ou qui les dirigeait le long du busc, mais ne s'attachaient nullement à l'être vivant, qui selon que l'architecture de ces fanfreluches se rapprochait ou s'écartait trop de la sienne, s'y trouvait engoncé ou perdu.

It must be remarked that Odette's face appeared thinner and more prominent than it actually was, because her forehead and the upper part of the cheeks, a single and almost plane surface, were covered by the masses of hair which women wore at that period, drawn forward in a fringe, raised in crimped waves and falling in stray locks over her ears; while as for her figure, and she was admirably built, it was impossible to make out its continuity (on account of the fashion then prevailing, and in spite of her being one of the best-dressed women in Paris) for the corset, jetting forwards in an arch, as though over an imaginary stomach, and ending in a sharp point, beneath which bulged out the balloon of her double skirts, gave a woman, that year, the appearance of being composed of different sections badly fitted together; to such an extent did the frills, the flounces, the inner bodice follow, in complete independence, controlled only by the fancy of their designer or the rigidity of their material, the line which led them to the knots of ribbon, falls of lace, fringes of vertically hanging jet, or carried them along the bust, but nowhere attached themselves to the living creature, who, according as the architecture of their fripperies drew them towards or away from her own, found herself either straitlaced to suffocation or else completely buried.[21]

21. Marcel Proust, A la recherche du temps perdu, vol. 1 (Paris: Gallimard, 1987), p. 194. Swann's Way, trans. C. K. Scott Moncrieff (New York: Random House, 1970), p. 151. Kaja Silverman has also analyzed this passage in terms of the feminine sartorial construction in her "Fragments of a Fashionable Discourse," in Tania Modleski, ed., Studies in Entertainment (Bloomington: Indiana University Press, 1986), pp. 138–52. See also Diana Festa-McCormick, Proustian Optics of Clothes: Mirrors, Masks, Mores (Saratoga, Calif.: Libri, 1984), pp. 11–13.

Prefigured here as he was so often by the Goncourt brothers, Proust's picture of absent femininity has the phallic woman as its corollary: the raised-up mass of crimp curls, the imaginary stomach over which the corset ends in a point, the fetishistic bows and tapering curtain of dark beads, the explicit allusion to a "loss" of the female body, all conspire to give the impression of phallic uncertainty, "to keep the reader from ever being able to answer the question: is woman castrated?" as Naomi Schor, paraphrasing Barthes, has put it.[22]

This undecidability over what Freud called the "fact" of castration (a fact that unravels quickly into a highly unlikely hypothesis, as Charles Bernheimer has reminded us) constitutes, as we know, the defining feature of psychoanalytic fetishism. What is brought to the fore by the Goncourt brothers' masculinized representation of eighteenth-century femininity is the extent to which this undecidability was featured all along in the culturally endorsed clothing fetishism of an entire epoch. *La Femme au dix-huitième siècle* leads, one could say, to a reappraisal of vestimentary female fetishism and its hitherto suppressed connections to masquerade.

Interestingly enough, it was Freud who inaugurated this undertaking in a little-known lecture delivered to the Vienna Psychoanalytic Society in 1909. Going against the conventional ban on female fetishists, he suggested that "all women...are clothes fetishists" because fashion, by magnetizing the gaze, both represses and de-represses a woman's desire to show herself:

> In the world of everyday experience, we can observe that half of humanity must be classed among the clothes fetishists. All women, that is, are clothes fetishists. Dress plays a puzzling role in them. It is a question again of the repression of the same drive, this time, however, in the passive form of allowing oneself to be seen, which is repressed by clothes, and on account of which, clothes are raised to a fetish. Only now we understand why even the most intelligent women behave defenselessly against the demands of fashion. For them, clothes take the place of parts of the body, and to wear the same clothes means only to be able to show what the others can show, means only that one can find in her everything that one can expect from women.[23]

---

22. Naomi Schor, "Fetishism and Its Ironies," *Nineteenth-Century French Studies* 17 (Fall–Winter 1988–89): 94.

23. "Freud and Fetishism: Previously Unpublished Minutes of the Vienna Psychoanalytic Society," ed. and trans. Louis Rose, *Psychoanalytic Quarterly* 57 (1988): 156.

This new addition to the Freud archive (buried until recently in Otto Rank's personal papers) offers a fetishism ingeniously dissociated from castration anxiety. The female superego (or to defer again to Joan Copjec's expression, the "sartorial superego") that emerges assimilates fetishism into narcissism and in the process takes away many of narcissism's pejorative connotations.[24]

Copjec's notion of the sartorial superego (derived from J. C. Flugel's 1930 classic *The Psychology of Clothes* and applied to the functionalist *ethics* of dress codes in the modern age, particularly as they appertain to that curtailing of male display that Flugel calls "The Great Masculine Renunciation") invites us to consider the "low" culture of fashion writing (along with its massive upsurge in consumer appeal in the fin de siècle) as the source of an ethic of womanliness as masquerade. Though Flugel applied the term to an ascetic turn in dressing rather than to appanages of decadent display, one could say that in the high pageantry and "exotic magnificence" that Flugel emphasized in eighteenth-century costume there was a ceremonial aura approaching religious decorousness. Paradoxically, puritanical dress codes shared with ancien-régime splendor a general tendency to subordinate the human body itself. As Flugel noted: "during the period of artificiality that distinguished the eighteenth century, the body was largely to serve as a support for gorgeous clothes."[25] This anaclitic, purely supportive social body describes, on the one hand, the dependency of the female masquerader on a masculine social gaze that mandates subordination of the female body, but on the other, it prepares the ground for redefining the notion of "support" as an anchoring, stabilizing ontology for the female subject, what Flugel called "the extension of the bodily self." The latter option might allow us to reread fashion writing not as a genre of egregiously reductive female typecasting but as the literary support structure of a critical femininity.

One of the most adept and prolific devotees of the genre was, of course, Octave Uzanne, whose apostrophes to muffs, gloves, parasols, and the fan so delighted the public that, to his consternation,

24. Joan Copjec, "The Sartorial Superego," *October* 50 (Fall 1988): 57–96.
25. J. C. Flugel, *The Psychology of Clothes* (New York: International University Press, 1969), p. 158.

they overshadowed his subsequent "serious" publications on *la féminité psychologique* (psychological femininity).[26] Like the Goncourt brothers Uzanne codified the tropes of feminine sensibility already in place within the courtly tradition of French letters or within a popular journalism of the 1830s perhaps best exemplified by the *Chroniques parisiennes* of Delphine de Girardin.[27] Certainly he was not alone: without even attempting to enumerate the myriad professional contributors to fashion bulletins destined for a female readership, we have only to evoke the names of Flaubert, Baudelaire, Théophile Gautier, Remy de Gourmont, Mallarmé, and Paul Bourget to see that Uzanne was in the best of company when it came to perpetuating the genre of "elegant realism."

Uzanne situated himself in a line of "women's" poets famous for privileging rhetorical preciosity over concision and pith:

- Le style compact du savant ou de l'archéologue ne convient guère à un sujet où les grâces seules doivent régner, où un poète ami de la femme, un Ovide, un Pétrarque, un Musset ou un Swinburne trouvait assurément d'assez subtils vocables pour traduire la pensée dans une forme exquise.

- The compact style of the scholar and archeologist hardly suits a subject on which only the graces should reign supreme, only poets such as Ovid, Petrarch, Musset, or Swinburne, true friends of woman, find vocables sufficiently subtle to translate the idea of so exquisite a form.[28]

Fashion, he vehemently insisted, was woman's only "literature" and he himself the only true "historian" of this art form. The names of clothes were in themselves poetic vocables ("The muff!" he exclaimed. "It's name alone has something adorable, downy, and voluptuous about it.")[29] Uzanne described new outfits ("costumes inédits") as unpublished masterpieces, avenues for fantasy and escape for the imagination, subjects over which women argued and "epilogued." If in some instances he applied the language of textuality to fashion,

26. In his preface to a new edition of *Les Ornements de la femme* (Paris: Librairies Imprimeries Réunies, 1892), originally published in 1882, Uzanne complains that he was henceforth referred to exclusively as "l'Auteur de l'Eventail" (the author of the Fan).
27. Delphine de Girardin, *Chroniques parisiennes, 1836–1848*, ed. Jean-Louis Vissière (Paris: Editions des Femmes, 1986); see in particular her "La Parure est un langage" (1839), pp. 210–17; "Féminitude" (1840), pp. 243–51; "Recettes de beauté" (1844), 384–87; "Masculin, féminin" (1845), pp. 393–96; and "Les Pompiers du bal" (1847), pp. 398–412.
28. Octave Uzanne, *L'Art et les artifices de la beauté* (Paris: Juven, 1902), p. 181.
29. Octave Uzanne, *Les Ornements de la femme*, p. 239.

in other instances he generated a poetics directly out of neologisms afforded by the images of fashion plates: "Oh! les divines chemises cintrées et ajustées, fanfreluchées de larges collerettes plongeaient l'esprit dans l'inquiétante obsession des formes qu'elles devaient revêtir! [Oh! those divine close-fitting chemises, frilled with wide lace collars, how they plunged the spirit into a disquieting obsession with the forms that they were destined to array!]."[30] Adjectives such as *fanfreluche* (from the Latin *fanfaluca*, meaning "bagatelle," and the German *pompholux*, "air bubble"), turned here as a past participle so as to heighten the power of sartorial affect, add a mimologically "feminine" mannerism to Uzanne's hackneyed repertory of mythological allusions. They also serve to underscore the dark, obsessive side of clothing mania that Uzanne understood to be the secret bond between himself and his female reader.

What stands out in Uzanne's belletristic tributes to the narcissistic female fetishist (perhaps more than in the works of his canonical rivals) is an almost palpable will-to-be woman, a desire to write himself as woman through the art of sartorial describing. The effect of his rhetoric can be almost uncanny; even if one rejects the cloying, overly "artistic" undulations of his style it comes back at us with the force of a shocking reflection. Uzanne (much like Clérambault, rumored to have secretly dressed up in the Muslim veils that he so delighted in photographing on Algerian women) doubles the already doubled feminine masquerade, creating a masculine travesty or cross-dressed impersonation of women in prose.

Uzanne began his most renowned work—a history of the fan—with a statement indicating his pleasure in rhetorically "trying on" women's garb: "L'auteur de *l'Eventail* ose se présenter à vous dans le négligé du *home* [The author of *The Fan* dares to present himself to you in the deshabille of home]."[31] Alternately speaking as a woman and to a woman, he shifts from the role of transvestite to lover, cajoling his addressee in the confidential tones of an *habitué* of the boudoir: "Causons donc, s'il vous plaît, de cette causerie intime qu'un terme plus malpropre qu'impropre appelle le *déboutonné* de la conversation [Let's chat then, if you will, about that intimate patter which might itself be called, using a term more malapropric

---

30. Octave Uzanne, *L'Art et les artifices* p. 215.
31. Octave Uzanne, *L'Eventail* (Paris: A. Quantin, 1882), p. 1. Further references to this work will be abbreviated *LE*.

than improper, the 'unbuttoned' conversation]" (*LE* 2). Elsewhere, he adopted the voice of the fetishist regressing, as Freud described him, to that last moment when the mother could still be regarded as phallic. Infantile phantasms of the most blatant variety hover around this memory of the "maternal muff":

· Tout enfant, nous aimons à jouer avec le grand Manchon maternel, à passer les mains au rebours dans l'électricité des longs poils, à plonger notre visage dans l'odeur fauve et capiteuse du pelage et à nous servir de ce sac fourré dans des espiègleries inconcevables, en y faisant cache-cache avec des menus objets ou en y enfouissant le chat familier qui s'acagnarde en sa tiédeur.

· As a small child, we loved to play with the big maternal Muff, stroking and touching the electricity of its long hairs; plunging our face into the heady, animal scent of its skin; getting up to unthinkable monkey-tricks with this furry sack, from playing peek-a-boo with small objects to burying our dear cat inside to snuggle in its warmth.[32]

When Freud wrote of hair and fur becoming a fetish for his juvenile subject, he would hardly have found a more appropriate example than this quasi-autobiographical passage by Uzanne. What is perhaps more interesting, however, is the way in which this *blazon* of the muff succeeds in personifying femininity even as it blocks perception of the mother by privileging the sartorial part over the living whole. The muff flirts! *Despite* the safely distancing effect of fetishistic displacement, the woman's dangerous sexuality shines through, communicated through the very medium chosen to thwart its immanence.[33] One could say that in this description and those like it throughout Uzanne's work, the fetish *is* the feminine; their languages are one and the same.

Following in the steps of the Goncourt brothers, Uzanne evolved his discourse of femininity out of the nostalgically reconstructed, extremity-enhanced body of eighteenth-century woman:

· Du Manchon, ornement du dehors, je conduirai le lecteur à la Chaussure, à l'ensorcelante petite Mule, cette friponne qui cache son museau

---

32. Uzanne, *Les Ornements de la femme*, pp. 239–40.
33. Uzanne created a similar effect in the section "Furs" in *Les Ornements de la femme*: "Thus amid her furs, woman, this adorable plant, this *mimosa pudica*, releases a beauty more mysterious, more gentle, more alluring, more envelopped and enveloping, as if the electricity of this furry skin were wafting into the air surrounding this provocative daughter of Eve, a sensuality enticing like a subtle caress that lightly brushes our senses as it passes" (p. 41).

de soie ou de maroquin sous le flot des dentelles et que Fragonard nous fait voir dans *les Hasards de l'escarpolette,* lancée gracieusement en l'air, s'envolant plutôt que tombant à terre, avec un esprit et une volupté de facture qui ne se retrouvent plus que dans les peintures des Cythères d'autrefois. Ne sera-t-il pas charmant de se complaire dans l'histoire de ces coquets Souliers de femme, qui eurent toujours leurs fanatiques admirateurs et qui inspirèrent à Restif de la Bretonne le roman du *Pied de Fanchette* qui débute comme un chant de poème épique: *Je suis l'historien véridique des conquêtes brillantes du pied mignon d'une belle?*

· From the Muff, an external ornament, I will lead the reader to the shoe, to that enchanting little Mule, this minx who hides her silk or leather snout under a cascade of lace and who Fragonard invites us to see in *The Little Swing* flung gracefully into the air, taking off rather than dropping to earth, with a spirit and voluptuousness of facture that one only finds in the bygone paintings of Cythera. Wouldn't it be charming to gratify oneself with the history of these stylish feminine shoes, footwear that has always had its fanatical admirers, inspiring Restif de la Bretonne's novel *Fanchette's Foot* which begins like an epic poem: "I am the truthful historian of the brilliant conquests of a beautiful woman's adorable foot?" (*LE* 4–5)

Like Maupassant's character Olivier Bertin (a ladies' man and society painter) in *Fort comme la mort* (1889), the narrator of *The Fan* warrants the sobriquet "realist Watteau," for in addition to reviving the eighteenth-century taste for scenographies of feminine frivolity, he is as guilty as Bertin of garnering favor as a "photographer of dresses and coats."[34]

There are several possible explanations for Uzanne's strategic revival of a *clothed* rather than a partially naked eighteenth-century female body (and certainly Fragonard and Boucher provided ample visual examples of the latter). His foremost concern was to counteract the encroachment of the execrated "modern nude" (as in Manet's *Olympia* or Degas's bathers) on the aesthetic taste of the fin de siècle. Uzanne complained that "la nudité qu'elle expose exprime une beauté malsaine et sincère, une volupté perverse, une

---

34. Guy de Maupassant, *Fort comme la mort* (Paris: Gallimard, 1983), p. 104. Bertin exhibits all the symptoms of Uzanne's confessed affliction—*vestignomia*, or clothing mania. He penetrates the secrets of *féminilité* with his intimate knowledge of "the thousand little nothings" comprising a woman's toilette; he experiences vertigo and a sense of religious awe upon entering the commercial "sanctuaries" where feminine accessories are displayed; his eyes become uncontrollably riveted by fabric, and his hands reach for lace like those of the kleptomaniac fetishists described in criminological records of the 1880s.

manière de sadisme délirant et capiteux [the nudity displayed by the modern nude was an overly sincere, unhealthy beauty, a perverse voluptuousness, a sadistic manner at once ecstatic and heady]."[35] Vampiric, gaunt, anemic, chlorotic, convulsive, and above all hystericized, this decadent *nu pathologique* excited hallucinatory flights of eloquence in Uzanne's "sociology of women," published in 1910.

Seen in this light, Uzanne's *Verkleidungstrieb* may be interpreted as part of a deep compulsion to keep the specter of the "essential" naked female body at bay. Pathologizing the nude was an ingenious technique for sustaining the fetishistic illusion of an idealized femininity. In *Son Altesse la femme* (*Her Highness the Woman*; 1885), the narrator prostrates himself accordingly before a hieratic goddess whose aloofness, in contrast to the vulgarly available "modern nude" inspires reverence and awe. The work is imbued with a nostalgic cult of the woman of yesteryear, specifically the eighteenth-century type designated as *la Caillette*. "*La Caillette!*" Uzanne teases his reader, "ce joli mot vous trouble et vous surprend, très curieuse Lectrice!... Ce mot résume dans sa plus haute et sa plus mignonne expression le type gracieux, évaporé et fripon de la femme au XVIII siècle. [The Rennet! this pretty word provokes and surprises you, curious reader! This word resumes in its highest and most appealing expression the gracious, vaporous, roguish type of eighteenth-century woman]."[36] Vapid, frivolous, feckless, pervious ("She takes on a lover like a new dress, because it's the custom"), debauched ("In her person there is a kind of exquisite depravity of sentiment and expression"), and flighty—a cross between a quail (*caille*) and a pebble (*caillou*)—*la Caillette* emerges as the most fetishizable male fantasy of the masquerading woman to be found, identifiable (as Uzanne notes) in the works of every major libertine author of the eighteenth century: Duclos, Casanova, Crébillon fils, Marivaux, Rétif de la Bretonne, and the marquis de Caraccioli (*A* 117–18).

For Uzanne *la Caillette* looms large as a historic reminder of an age of erotic theatricality long gone. He implicitly pays homage to the "constructed" eroticism of the eighteenth-century female body

---

35. Octave Uzanne, *Etudes de sociologies féminines: Parisiennes de ce temps* (Paris: Mercure de France, 1910), p. 50.

36. Octave Uzanne, *Son Altesse la femme* (Paris: Quantin, 1885), p. 114. Like most of Uzanne's deluxe publications, this edition contains arresting illustrations by Henri Gervex, J. A. Gonzalès, L. Kratké, Albert Lynch, Adrien Moreau, and Félicien Rops. Further references to this work will be abbreviated *A*.

when he lingers over the nomenclature of hairstyles in his history of coiffure in the age of Louis XVI. Here Marie Antoinette receives special praise for ushering in "un système d'outrance, de retroussis, de boursouflure qui, en quelques années, prit de pyramidales proportions [a system of excess, of curling, of puffing up, that, in a few years, took on pyramidal proportions]."[37] In their expenditures and disregard for functionalism, the coiffures of eighteenth-century woman transparently signify sexual pleasure enjoyed in and for itself; a disinterested, gratuitous gratification forever insubordinate to civilization's reproductive aims.[38]

If eighteenth-century fashion was occasionally harnessed in the service of an apology for libertinage, it was also evoked for purely aesthetic purposes. Uzanne dilated on the "heroism" of eighteenth-century woman's grand *tenue*: "On observe son héroisme, ses stratagèmes d'amour, ses coquetteries, son mépris de l'opinion, son extravagance dans les modes, et à la fois sa science de fée pour draper un chef-d'oeuvre de costume avec quelques mètres d'étoffe sans valeur [One observes her heroism, her strategies in love, her coquetry, her contempt for opinion, her extravagance in fashion, and her fairy genius in draping a masterpiece of costume in meters of priceless cloth]" (*A* 267). In the monumentalization of falling drapery, in the exorbitant spectacle of fabric thrown in abundance over horizontally extending poufs, the rococo acquires a solemnity and pomp normally reserved for the classical sublime. Eighteenth-century woman's grandeur "freezes" an erotic credo of perpetual foreplay in time and testifies to the mysterious process by which raw materiality is converted into the value-saturated commodity fetish. Equally, we can see in his larger-than-life shroud an allegorical representation of the female body's transformation into woman-

---

37. Octave Uzanne, *La Parure excentrique époque Louis XVI: Coiffures de style* (Paris: Edouard Rouveyre, 1895), pp. 16–17. This tiny, jewel-like book contains marvelous illustrations of the most remarkable eighteenth-century fashions in hairdressing.

38. Uzanne's endorsement of this symbol of nonutilitarian, antibourgeois sexuality forms a piece with his apology for an *ethic* of libertinage in *Le Bric-à-brac de l'amour* (Paris: Edouard Rouveyre, 1879), p. 126. In a chapter on libertinage Uzanne bemoans the nineteenth-century censorship and medicalization of open sexual practices: "Today we understand sexual libertinage to be 'a sensual derangement and a bodily intemperence' when we would rather hear only 'tasteful delicacy and delectation of pleasure,' variants on this spinet of love which, alas, possesses no more than a single octave" (p. 126). Forced to go underground, undermined by the sickly nineteenth-century taste for sentimentality, libertinage has suffered many setbacks, according to Uzanne. His chapter concludes with a plea to bring back the pleasures of a grand century.

liness: *nothing* becomes *something*; a lifeless robe becomes an aura-soaked veil.

For Uzanne, as for Georg Simmel, writing a mere decade later, the veil was perhaps the preeminent sign of the feminine, the image behind the image of his cherished fan: "In the gesture of the fan, in the glistening of precious stones or the fold of the veil, is there not, for sensitive souls, the whole secret of the heart?" "The little veil is a total symbol," he wrote; "when a mistress takes it off or puts it on, glimmers of abandon, hope, and tenderness if not melancholia and inexpressible sadness pass through her gaze."[39] Rarely did he miss an opportunity to expatiate upon the seductive symbolism of this most mysterious feminine accoutrement. Entering a sanctuary of intimate apparel he confesses:

· Je ne sais rien de plus troublant, de plus cajoleur à l'oeil, de plus souple, de plus adorable, de plus chatouilleux au toucher que tous ces voiles légers, brillants et superfins.... Au course d'une récente visite à une maison de grande lingerie de luxe, il me sembla vivre dans un milieu Edénique où les houris auraient laissé leurs voiles de lumière.

· I know of nothing more troubling, more cajoling to the eye, more soft, adorable, and tickling to the touch than these light, sparkling, transparent veils.... During a recent trip to one of the great lingerie shops, it seemed that I was living in an Edenic milieu where the houris might have left their veils of light.[40]

Refuting the symbolism of Nietzsche's misogynist veil, Simmel observed that the "girdles and petticoats that fulfill the function of a fig leaf" paradoxically render concealment itself ornamental.[41] As

39. Uzanne, *L' Art et les artifices*, pp. 181, 227.
40. Ibid., p. 215.
41. Georg Simmel, "Flirtation (Die Koketterie)," in *Georg Simmel: On Women, Sexuality, and Love*, trans. Guy Oakes (New Haven: Yale University Press, 1984), 147–48. "Die Koketterie" was first published by Simmel in *Philosophische Kultur: Gesammelte Essais* (Leipzig, 1911). In speaking of Nietzsche's "misogyny" I am referring specifically to passages in *Beyond Good and Evil* and *The Gay Science* in which Nietzsche claimed that woman's self-adornment and concern with beauty were the emblems of philosophical mendacity. For a critique of the veil as philosophical metaphor of femininity (linking the discourse of the veil to fetishism as "faked orgasm"), see Gayatri Chakravorty Spivak's essay "Displacement and the Discourse of Woman," in *Displacement: Derrida and After*, ed. Mark Krupnick (Bloomington: Indiana University Press, 1983), pp. 169–95. More recently, Mary Ann Doane has examined these problems in relation to film theory in her essay "Veiling over Desire: Close-ups of the Woman," in *Feminism and Psychoanalysis*, ed. Richard Feldstein and Judith Roof (Ithaca: Cornell University Press, 1989), pp. 105–41.

if picking up where Uzanne left off, he located the mystery by which femininity acquires value in a chain of dual significations: "consent and refusal," "giving and not-giving," and "having and not-having." Flouncing, waving, winking, veiling—all these gestures are for Simmel the legible expressions of a dual signification that places the male possession of woman enticingly into question:

> It seems to be the universal experience of male sensibility that the woman—indeed, the deepest, most devoted woman, whose charm is inexhaustible—holds back some ultimate, indecipherable and unattainable quality even in the most passionate offering and disclosure of herself. ... From the perspective of the man, however, the woman's mode of being appears as a Not-Yet, an unredeemed promise, an unborn profusion of obscure possibilities that have not yet developed far enough beyond their psychic location to become visible and apprehensible.[42]

If one follows Simmel's optimistic association of ornamental secrets with the outlines of an untapped feminine potentiality, then one might say that Uzanne's *vestignomia* leads not to an alienated pantomime of masculinity (foregrounded by the Goncourts) but, rather, in the direction of a nuanced intimation of the female sartorial superego.[43] Using Simmel, then, we might interpret Uzanne's fetishistic language of clothes as referring to a "Not-yet" of femininity—a fullness without emptiness.

I have used Uzanne and the Goncourt brothers' readings of eighteenth-century woman to demonstrate the historical relativism of femininity as a literary and psychoanalytical invention. It seemed to me that their texts provided particularly clear illustrations of how certain stereotypical attributes of womanliness came to be codified in such a way as to survive into our own time. The Goncourts' *La Femme au dix-huitième siècle* exemplified the unmasking of discursive femininity by the eruption of masculinity onto the

---

42. Simmel, "Flirtation," pp. 147–48.
43. Pierre Saint-Amand's emphasis on the ornamented body of Marie Antionette leads in this direction. He makes the case that "the history of Marie Antoinette could be reconstituted according to a series of adornments, each one corresponding to a crucial moment in her short life. Framing her flight to Varennes and ultimate beheading as a staged set piece, an act called "The Final Wardrobe," Saint-Amand reads the fullness of her character as she stands disheveled, badly dressed, her hair shockingly white before the crowd. Paradoxically, he argues, the crowd makes of her lack of adornment a kind of martyrized ornament.

sartorial image. By contrast, Uzanne's speaking fetishes blur the gender distinctions habitually assigned to specific apparel, as in R. Redelsperger's "Memoirs of a Corset," in which the narrator, personified as a talking corset stay, is both feminized as it shapes itself to the female body and masculinized as it competes with a jealous husband for the attentions of his lingerie-smitten wife.[44] Uzanne's cross-dressed writing of the feminine may ultimately be read through a feminist perspective as a send-up of gendered textuality, a pastiche or "performance" of sartorial pleasure that serves to unfix ontological gender codes.

By investigating these representations of the constructibility of femininity, I hoped to underscore its tenuousness as a masquerade of gender. But the theory of the masquerade itself has proved to be inextricable from essentialist commonplaces associated with femininity. As we all know, Joan Riviere's articulation of "womanliness as a masquerade" has endured, renewed by film critics such as Mary Ann Doane as part of her effort to define the psychology of female spectatorship. What remains somewhat unclear to me is just why one would want to retain such a theory. With its language of veils, masks, and sexual travesty, the discourse of the masquerade seems always to participate in the very obfuscation of femininity that it seeks to dispel. Though invented by a woman psychoanalyst to explain the "flaunting of femininity" on the part of intellectual women, the theory of the masquerade—associated with the art of camouflaging masculine as feminine—may ultimately qualify as just another mask of phallocentric psychoanalysis. Even if one wants to argue that the masquerade provides a "screen-test" for a female superego, the psychohistorical perplex remains: if femininity, in its most historically flamboyant incarnation ultimately reverts to masculinity (as the Goncourts' text seems to suggest), then in what does the construct of femininity inhere?[45] How did woman come to be identified with womanliness and then trapped behind the mask of the masquerade? Is the masquerade feminism's fetish?

44. R. Redelsperger, "Mémoires d'un corset," *L'Art et la Mode* (1880): 33–36. The corset speaks throughout in the first person, bragging of his intimate knowledge of women, recounting his seduction of a married lady and near destruction at the hands of the husband who tugs too hard on the laces.

45. Jane Gaines also addresses these questions in her introduction to a volume of essays entitled *Fabrications: Costume and the Female Body*, ed. Jane Gaines and Charlotte Herzog (New York: Routledge, 1990), pp. 20–27. This book, published after I had written my section on the masquerade, makes a number of similar points with respect to contemporary culture and the fashion industry.

Joan Riviere's powerful essay "Womanliness as a Masquerade," presented as a response to Ernest Jones's paper "The Early Development of Female Sexuality," appeared in the *International Journal of Psycho-Analysis* in 1929. As Stephen Heath has pointed out, no thorough examination of Riviere's life and contribution to the history of psychoanalysis exists to date.[46] She was analyzed by Ernest Jones (with whom, according to Heath, she probably had an affair), by Freud (whose collected papers she translated), and later by Melanie Klein. After she herself became an analyst, D. W. Winnicot became one of her patients. A bibliography of her work appeared in the *International Journal of Psychoanalysis* in 1963, but aside from the masquerade essay her writings remain shrouded in oblivion.

That Riviere's theory of the masquerade has secured so privileged a place in contemporary critical thought seems all the more curious when one rereads the piece closely—it contains some bizarre twists and leaves issues unresolved. Riviere's premiere analysand was "an American woman engaged in work of a propagandistic nature which consisted principally in speaking and writing."[47] Later we learn that this lady propagandist is a southerner, plagued by the fantasy of seducing a black man intent on raping her. Riviere (who was English and for a time educated in Germany) makes no mention of the American sociocultural context of racism, fear, and bigotry so clearly at work in the fantasy life of her patient. The woman dreams of washing off her guilty pleasure after sex with the black man (a masquerade of innocence according to Riviere), but the question of her erotic negrophobia—and by extension, of psychoanalysis and race—are never alluded to in Riviere's elaborations of the case (nor, to my knowledge are these issues addressed by subsequent critics, with the exception of Mary Ann Doane).[48] At the very least, the lesson we might draw here is that the chosen prototype of the masquerading woman is a problematic figure—

---

46. Stephen Heath, "Joan Riviere and the Masquerade," in *Formations of Fantasy*, ed. Victor Burgin, James Donald, and Cora Kaplan (New York: Methuen, 1986), pp. 45–61.

47. Joan Riviere, "Womanliness as a Masquerade," in *Formations of Fantasy*, p. 36. Further references to this essay will be abbreviated "WM."

48. Mary Ann Doane, "Masquerade Reconsidered: Further Thoughts on the Female Spectator," *Discourse* 2 (Fall–Winter 1988–89): 48. Doane's article on her earlier essay (a response prompted by Tania Modleski's critique in *The Women Who Knew Too Much: Hitchcock and Feminist Theory* [New York: Methuen, 1988]) contains a succinct account of the problems posed for feminist thought by Riviere's masquerade essay. Further references to this essay will be abbreviated "MR."

abstracted from history and culture and blind to the psychosexual politics of racism.

Riviere's paragon of femininity is a successful career woman, an exemplary wife, an accomplished homemaker, and an elegant dresser. The only signs betraying her suppressed inward instability are those of sartorial extravagance and what Riviere refers to as a tendency toward "compulsive ogling and coquetting," particularly manifest during her delivery of public lectures ("WM" 37). Riviere's interpretation of the jarring contrast between her intellectual seriousness and her simpering, flirtatious manner emphasizes theatricality and gender crossover: "The exhibition in public of her intellectual proficiency, which was in itself carried through successfully, signified an exhibition of herself in possession of the father's penis, having castrated him. The display once over, she was seized by horrible dread of the retribution the father would then exact. Obviously it was a step towards propitiating the avenger to endeavor to offer herself to him sexually"("WM" 37). Though the explanation is somewhat crude and fails to contest the primacy accorded castration and *Penisneid* in Freudian theory, what is perhaps of far greater concern in her argument is its elliptical logic, a logic leading away from rather than toward any resolution of the famous "riddle of femininity." Womanliness is construed as an effect of masked masculinity, as the passage most often cited by feminist critics attests:

> Womanliness therefore could be assumed and worn as a mask, both to hide the possession of masculinity and to avert the reprisals expected if she was found to possess it—much as a thief will turn out his pockets and ask to be searched to prove that he had not stolen the goods. The reader may now ask how I define womanliness or where I draw the line between genuine womanliness and the "masquerade." My suggestion is not, however, that there is any such difference; whether radical or superficial, they are the same thing. ("WM" 38).

Clarifying the contours of the empty representation lying at the very core of Riviere's notion of womanliness, Stephen Heath has written of this passage: "In the masquerade the woman mimics an authentic—genuine—womanliness but then authentic womanliness is such a mimicry, *is* the masquerade ("they are the same thing"); to be a woman is to dissimulate a fundamental masculinity, femininity is that dissimulation."[49] A double cover-up, a make-believe sem-

---

49. Heath, "Joan Riviere," p. 49.

blance of womanliness superimposed on a pretend masculinity, a camouflage of persiflage—this notion of womanliness (recalling the Goncourts' portrait of the phallic *femme d'état*) exhibits the structural logic of fetishism insofar as the (Freudian) fetish functions as a substitute for something that was never there in the first place. Riviere herself encourages this analogy when she implies that the male equivalent of the female masquerade is fetishism. Summarizing the case of a transvestite she noted: "The excitation was produced by the sight of himself with hair parted in the center, wearing a bow tie. These extraordinary 'fetishes' turned out to represent a *disguise of himself* as his sister; the hair and bow were taken from her" ("WM" 40; author's emphasis). One might conclude here that fetishism is failed masquerade, for when the man dons the mask of womanliness it remains an unconvincing representation of femininity, whereas the opposite is true when women adopt a cover-up for masculine attributes—their travesty appears to be entirely believable.

What impresses me in all this is not so much that the sex anatomically endowed with a penis seems perverse when it tries to pretend not to have it (implicitly reinforcing the security in being male) in contrast to the woman (who instinctively, "naturally" veils her lack) but, rather, that the disguises adopted by both man and woman refer back to a travestied masculinity, or as Lacan would say, to a veiled "phallus" possessed by nobody.[50] Femininity remains devoid of content except insofar as (1) the layers of its dissimulation are stripped away to reveal a fundamentally masculine Imago; (2) it slides into masochism (as in the case of female Harlequin romance readers who, as Ann Douglas has observed, enjoy "the titillation of seeing themselves, not necessarily as they are, but as some men would like to see them: illogical, innocent, magnetized by male sexuality and brutality"); and (3) it mimics what Lacan termed "virile display."[51]

Lacan, rather underhandedly, returns the masking function to masculinity even as he springs sexual identity loose from biological essentialism. In "La Signification du phallus," he uses the masquerade to corroborate Freud's "view that there is only one libido, his

---

50. Doane also notes that Riviere's argument "makes femininity dependent on masculinity for its very definition" ("MR" 47).

51. Ann Douglas, "Soft-porn Culture," *New Republic* 30 (Aug. 1980): 29, as cited by Tania Modleski in *Loving with a Vengeance: Mass-produced Fantasies for Women* (New York: Routledge, 1982), p. 30. Jacques Lacan, "La Signification du phallus" in *Ecrits II* (Paris: Seuil/Points, 1971), p. 115.

text clearly indicating that he conceives of it as masculine in nature."[52] Riviere's essay, as we have said, seems to suggest that there are only differing guises of an essential masculinity common to both sexes. Lacan's appropriation of Riviere points to a similar conclusion despite its distortion of her argument. Where Riviere had described the masquerade of womanliness in blindly heterosexualist terms as a compensatory feint for a phallicism that risks tabulation to lesbianism, Lacan sees (heterosexual) woman as successfully obtaining a semblance of manliness through masquerade:[53]

> Paradoxical as this formulation might seem, I would say that it is in order to be the phallus, that is to say, the signifier of the desire of the Other, that the woman will reject an essential part of her femininity, notably all its attributes through masquerade. It is for what she is not that she expects to be desired as well as loved. But she finds the signifier of her own desire in the body of the one to whom she addresses her demand for love. Certainly we should not forget that the organ actually invested with this signifying function takes on the value of a fetish.

With Lacan's formulation, we come full circle from male fetishism as female masquerade *manqué* to women masquerading as fetishes, that is, as false phalluses that permit the imaginary phallus which both sexes want, but which neither sex has, to continue functioning as a *manque à être* ("lack in being") that generates desire as it is brought into being.[54]

In her analysis of the costumes in Federico Fellini's film *Juliette of*

---

52. Lacan, "La Signification du phallus," trans. Jacqueline Rose under the title "The Meaning of the Phallus," in *Feminine Sexuality: Jacques Lacan and the école freudienne* (New York: Norton, 1985), p. 85: "The fact that femininity takes refuge in this mask because of the *Verdrängung* inherent to the phallic mark of desire, has the strange consequence that, in the human being, virile display itself appears as feminine" (p. 85).

53. Lacan, "The Meaning of the Phallus," p. 84. Judith Butler's reading (*Gender Trouble*, p.84) of Riviere as "fearful of her own phallicism" provides a crucial antiheterosexualist critique of the masquerade theory. She says; "the donning of femininity as mask may reveal a refusal of a female homosexuality and, at the same time, the hyperbolic incorporation of that female Other who is refused—an odd form of preserving and protecting that love within the circle of the melancholic and negative narcissism that results from the physic inculcation of compulsory heterosexuality" (p. 53).

54. Butler offers important critiques of Lacan's model of woman masquerading as a fetish. "At least two very different tasks can be discerned from the ambiguous structure of Lacan's analysis," she argues. "On the one hand, masquerade may be understood as the performative production of a sexual ontology, an appearing that makes itself convincing as a 'being'; on the other hand, masquerade can be read as a denial of a feminine desire that presupposes some prior ontological femininity regularly unrepresented by the phallic economy" (*Gender Trouble*, p. 47).

the Spirits, Michèle Montrelay, elaborating on Lacan, describes how, when woman masquerades as a fetish, the results are unremittingly negative: "In this mountain of crazy objects, these feathers, hats, and strange, baroque constructions rising up like so many silent insignia, a dimension of femininity is clarified which Lacan, appropriating Joan Riviere's term, designated as masquerade. But it must be noted that this masquerade takes 'saying nothing' as its only end. Absolutely nothing. And to produce this nothing, woman disguises herself with her own body."[55] Here the female body is fetishistic insofar as it functions as a disguise or foil that lures the male subject into wanting something that he does not really desire (woman) in order to preserve free and clear the erotic territory of the ideal phallus (*le manque à être*) that he continues to covet elsewhere. Whether as prosthesis or personification of "nothing" the masquerading woman appears in the self-depreciated role of lack sustainer, a kind of supporting "cast" or "mainstay" of one in the theater of phallocentric illusion.

In the first of two important essays on the female film spectator, Mary Ann Doane attempts to redress this negative turn despite an initial avowal that "the mask of femininity conceals a non-identity."[56] Her interpretation, influenced by the body poetics of Irigaray (though diverging sharply from Irigaray's use of *la mascarade* to indicate the female mimicry of the Oedipus complex, of woman's induction into the male libidinal economy), hinges on a question of nearness/farness. The masquerade, she claims, "in flaunting femininity, holds it at a distance. Womanliness is a mask which can be worn or removed. The masquerade's resistance to patriarchal positioning would therefore lie in its denial of the production of femininity as closeness, as presence-to-itself, as, precisely, imagistic" ("FM" 81–82). For Doane, the wearability of the masquerade—the beguiling ease with which such cladding is removed—affords women a critical distance from the claustrophobia of their own bodies. It also advances a feminist project: the masquerade proves to be an uneasy spectacle for the masculine viewer, serving both "to defamiliarize female iconography" and "to disarticulate male systems of viewing" ("FM" 82). In this piece, Doane takes us to the

---

55. Michèle Montrelay, *L'Ombre et le nom: Sur la féminité* (Paris: Minuit, 1977), p. 71.

56. Mary Ann Doane, "Film and the Masquerade: Theorizing the Female Spectator," *Screen* 23, no. 3–4 (1982): 81. Further references to this article will be abbreviated "FM."

brink of an undermined patriarchal positioning. She concludes her article optimistically prophesying the advent of a female spectator, but this spectator remains a specter awaiting definition.

Returning to the topic six years later, Doane is more circumspect toward the pitfalls involved in trying to use the masquerade as a counterdiscourse to that of the female screen fetish ("her status as spectacle rather than spectator"), yet even here the argument concludes on a futuristic, hypothetical note:

> Riviere's patient, looking out at her own male audience, with impropriety, throws the image of their own sexuality back to them as "game," as "joke," investing it, too, with the instability and the emptiness of the masquerade. Heath refers to this as a "strong social-political, feminist joke" in the manner of Virginia Woolf in *Three Guineas*. As long as she is not caught in her own act. As long as she does not forget that the masquerades of femininity and masculinity are not totally unreal or totally a joke but have a social effectivity we cannot ignore. We still need to tell our own jokes, but hopefully they will be different ones. *Structurally* different ones. ("MR" 52–53; author's emphasis)

In this "joke" we see the glimmering outlines of an ironic, sexually volatile, politically feminist subject with some chance of survival but little protection against the risk of getting "caught in her own act." In the end, her "act" depends too much perhaps on Doane's laconic contention that masquerade can generate femininity from within, eschewing reference to masculine essentialisms and the fetishistic conceit of the present/absent phallus.

Where does this leave us theoretically? Freud, Riviere, Lacan, Montrelay, and Doane all seem to concur that femininity, handicapped by its lack of a visual signifier equivalent in symbolic import to the phallus and historically relative in the forms of its social construction, disappears upon close inspection into a conceptual void, or at best, survives as a surrogate masculinity.[57]

---

57. Alice Jardine reconfigures this void in another way when she applies fetishism (as a synonym for oscillation and "a demand for doubling") to the ambivalence within contemporary feminism over "essential" differences. In contrast to paranoia (which for her implies that women know what they are in knowing that they are different), feminist fetishism, oscillating between "Women are different" and "No, they are not," reinvents the epistemological "dark continent" of womanliness. Jardine's feminist fetishist, it appears, is plunged anew in darkness; deprived, on the one hand, of an empowering, "fetishistic" illusion of masculinity, and on the other, of the small comfort afforded by womanliness as a masquerade. See Alice Jardine, "Notes for an Analysis," in *Between Feminism and Psychoanalysis*, ed. Teresa Brennan (New York: Routledge, 1989), p. 75.

If the "womanliness as a masquerade" controversy sounds a pessimistic note in the quest for an enabling articulation of femininity, a different tactic may be in order. A return to the earlier problematic contained in Freud's singular conception of the universal female clothes fetishist may in fact provide an alternative approach. Despite its patronizing undertone, Freud's stark announcement "All women...are clothes fetishists" allows us to think of woman's sartorial autoreification as the symptom of an extended, projected affirmation of female ontology.

Citing Louis Flaccus's "Remarks on the Psychology of Clothes" (1906), Flugel offers specific strategies for imparting an ethic to this narcissistic female fetishism: "Whenever we bring a foreign body into relationship with the surface of the body...the consciousness of our personal existence is prolonged into the extremities and surfaces of this foreign body, and the consequence is—feelings, now of an expansion of our proper self, now of the acquisition of a kind and amount of motion foreign to our natural organs, now of an unusual degree of vigour, power of resistance, or steadiness in our bearing."[58] By reading sartorial augmentation as a complex sensation—an inmixture of prolongation, vigor, resistance, steadiness, and thrilling contact with the "foreign"—Flaccus anticipated the notion of a sartorial superego. Years later, in a similar vein, the Lacanian analyst Bela Grunberger offered a revised look at feminine narcissism:

> If woman, following the tendency toward increased social homogenization and the effacement of sexual difference, seeks to benefit from a certain sexual liberty (the same enjoyed by men), then she cannot help investing her love life in a narcissistic mode. She will valorize her corporal superego in the most extended sense, going from her body, her clothes, and her adornments toward her "interior," her house and everything that functions as material support for her love life.[59]

In this context, Grunberger's notions of physically extended subjectivity and "material support" *literalize* sartorial figures of speech as they recode them within the rhetoric of feminist psychoanalysis. Such a rhetoric allows female subjectivity to be theorized in terms of an aesthetics of ornamentation without immediate recourse to a

---

58. Louis Flaccus, "Remarks on the Psychology of Clothes," *Pedagogical Seminary* 13 (1906): 61, as cited by Flugel, *The Psychology of Clothes*, p. 34.

59. Bela Grunberger, "Jalons pour l'étude du narcissisme dans la séxualité féminine," in *La Sexualité féminine*, ed. Janine Chasseguet-Smirgel (Paris: Petite Bibliothèque Payot, 1964), pp. 105–106.

compensatory emphasis on phallic cover-up. As Georg Simmel wrote in what looks like a prescient effort to wean gender theory from its fixation on feminine lack: "It is, of course, a mistake to regard this 'lack of differentiation' simply as a deficiency and a condition of inferiority. On the contrary, it is the thoroughly positive mode of being of the woman, which forms its own ideal and has no less legitimacy than the 'differentiated state' of the man."[60] Foreshadowing Irigaray's utopian dream of an asymmetrical sexual difference beyond sameness, Simmel's "thoroughly positive mode of being of the woman" encourages the unmasking of the masquerade as a theoretical "get-up" for defensive womanliness but falls short of dispensing with it altogether. Simmel's affirmation of ornament, recalling the Goncourts' exultation in "cette mode de parade, de magnificence, d'éclat, imposée par l'étiquette aux femmes de la cour [this fashion of parade, magnificence, show, imposed by etiquette on ladies of the court], imparts an ethic of sartorial presence to the aesthetic of masquerade. In this sense we might reread the theory of the masquerade as corrected, so to speak, by sartorial female fetishism, which supplants the notion of femininity as empty content or infinitely layered veil, to replace it with a theory of materialized social construction.

60. Simmel, "Flirtation," p. 148.

CHAPTER 5

· Splitting Hairs: Female Fetishism
and Postpartum Sentimentality
in Maupassant's Fiction

· Maupassant's short story "Une Veuve" opens during hunting season at the château de Banneville.¹ Outside all is wet and dreary, and the guests, gathered inside the salon, tell stories in an effort to stave off boredom. The stories fail to amuse or distract—"the women wracked their brains but never managed to discover the imagination of Scheherazade." But suddenly a young woman notices a curious ring of hair on the hand of a maiden aunt: "Tell me, Aunt, what is that ring? One would think it the hair of a child," she remarks. "It's sad, so sad that I never want to speak of it. It is the cause of all the sadness of my life," the aunts replies.² Their curiosity finally roused, the guests implore her to divulge the mystery, and after much postponed gratification, she relents and tells her tale.

This classic prelude, a typical Maupassant frame-text, immediately sets the tone for a lachrymose drama of mourning, melancholia, and manic collecting. The lugubrious nineteenth-century practice of preserving the relics of departed loved ones, from keepsakes and love letters to nail clippings and locks of hair, is here pastiched through *postiche*, literally through a piece of hair, figuratively through the atmosphere of artifice, simulation, and ersatz reproducibility,

---

1. I am grateful to Lynn Hunt for inviting me to present an initial version of this chapter in a conference, "Eroticism and the Body Politic," at the University of Pennsylvania, Apr. 1988. Naomi Schor and Carla Hesse offered particularly useful and provocative criticism in the course of our discussion.
2. Guy de Maupassant, *Contes et nouvelles*, 2 vols., ed. Louis Forestier (Paris: Gallimard, 1974–79), 1:533.

which impregnates Maupassant's ironic evocations of late romantic nostalgia.³ Close in ethos to the bric-a-brac-cluttered world of Baudelaire's spleen poems, Maupassant's "Une Veuve" invites classification as gynotextual fetishism, that is, a female fetishism traversing literary and psychoanalytical boundaries and defined from a woman's point of view.⁴ Maupassant's descriptions of feminine neurosis, modeled on his own actual observations of Charcot's choreographed exhibitions of female hysteria at the Salpêtrière hospital, frequently highlight the frenetic, erotic mourning rituals of women.⁵ Despite a male narrative perspective, the case-history value of his texts on the feminine—some narrated in the first-person feminine voice, others projecting a feminine Imaginary through third-person omniscient narration—becomes increasingly apparent when read in conjunction with feminist theory. Legible in the fanatical attachments of his female protagonists to the secret contents of their *secrétaires* and *tiroirs* (as in, for example, his stories "La Relique" ["The Relic"], "Souvenirs" ["Memories"], and "Vieux objets" ["Old Things"]), discernible in the maternal reliquary fashioned to enshrine childhood relics (*Une Vie* [*A Woman's Life*]), and manifest in the erotically charged "fantasms of the exquisite cadaver" through which his male characters conflate women and sepulchral desire ("Les Tombales" ["Graveyard Sirens"], "L' Apparition" ["An Apparition"], "La Morte" ["Death"]), the outline of a sentimental sickness emerges akin to the great feminine pathologies of the nineteenth century: hysteria, hypochondria, somnambulism, and frigidity.⁶

3. The word *postiche* (from the Italian *posticcio*, or *part*) is defined by Littré's dictionary as "une sorte d'ornement," and generally refers to "false hair," or hair piece. The figurative connotations of the word ("se dit de ce qui est factice, simulé, qui cache quelque chose sous des apparences trompeuses" [cf. Larousse]) suggest a strong affinity to the term *fetishism*, which derives from the Latin *facticius*, meaning "artificial." For French histories of hair fashions offering illuminating descriptions of the fin-de-siècle fascination with artificial tresses (often called *anglaises*), see A. Chantoiseau, *Le Coiffeur et la Chevelure* (Paris: Ed. Ulysse Boucoiran, 1938), and René Rambaud, *Les Fugitives: Précis anecdotique et histoire de la coiffure féminine à travers les âges* (Paris: S.E.M.P., 1955). See also Pamela A. Miller, "Hair Jewelry as Fetish," in Ray B. Brown, ed., *Objects of Special Devotion: Fetishes and Fetishism in Popular Culture* (Bowling Green, Ohio: Bowling Green University, 1982).

4. For an essay treating fetishism in general (as opposed to female fetishism) in Maupassant's oeuvre, see Philippe Lejeune, "Maupassant et le fétichisme," in *Maupassant, miroir de la nouvelle,* ed. Jacques Lecarme and Bruno Vercier (Paris: Presses Universitaires de Vincennes, 1988), pp. 91–109. This chapter is indebted to my discussions of fetishism in Maupassant with Philippe Lejeune.

5. For a discussion of Maupassant's psychoanalytical education, see Elisabeth Roudinesco, *La Bataille de cent ans: Histoire de la psychanalyse en France*, vol. 1: *1885–1939* (Paris: Seuil, 1986), pp. 79–81.

6. Maria Torok, "Maladie du deuil et fantasme du cadavre exquis," *Revue*

Though eighteenth-century philosophy had recognized *l'âme sensible* (the sensitive soul) as the mark of a healthy sentimentalism essential to the elevated moral character of the enlightened individual, nineteenth-century psychology saw such excessive outpourings of tenderness as bordering on the perverse.[7] Maupassant's representation of this ailment, which he characterized in *Une Vie* as "une sorte d'instinct héréditaire de sentimentalité rêveuse [a kind of hereditary instinct of dreamy sentimentality]" not only provides the foundation for correcting the gender-biased definitions of fetishism developed by Freud and his medical precusors but also offers an invaluable portrait of sentimental obsession in the nineteenth century.[8]

The fin-de-siècle representation of feminine collecting belongs to a broader European genre, including the Biedermeier novel in Germany (best typified by Adalbert Stifter's *Der Nachsommer* [*Indian Summer*]) and British hearth-and-home fiction (filled with descriptions of what Asa Briggs has called "Victorian things," as in Dickens's *Old Curiosity Shop* [1841]). Stylistically realist, its narrative surface worked over with a mosaic of painstakingly observed domestic details, this literary fetishism features characterizations of women who vented their phobias and passions through reverent attachments to nostalgic souvenirs. *Une Vie*, already powerfully analyzed from a feminist viewpoint by Naomi Schor, provides a clear example of the genre.[9] Even though the female protagonist tends to confirm outmoded stereotypes of feminine behavior, many of these very stereotypes, in addition to having historical value as images

---

Française de Psychanalyse 4 (1968): 715–33.

7. In her discussion of "healthy sentimentality" in the eighteenth century, Jan Goldstein, in her *Console and Classify: The French Psychiatric Profession in the Nineteenth Century* (Cambridge: Cambridge University Press, 1987), has defined its place within Enlightenment codes of sensibility: "Thus certain stereotypic marks—tenderness for little children, the blissful harmony ascribed to the family circle, tears flowing freely and copiously in response to familial joys or sorrows—connect the moral treatment and its proponents' concept of human nature to the eighteenth-century cult of sentimentality.... Pinel's Rousseauism takes on an added dimension when seen from this vantage point. The author whose *Nouvelle Héloïse* had called forth floods of "delicious" tears from his grateful readers would have special significance for the physician who regarded an appropriately tearful sentimentality as a definitive sign of mental health" (p. 118).

8. Guy de Maupassant, *Une Vie* (Paris: Garnier-Flammarion, 1974), p. 150; trans. H.N.P. Sloman, under the title *A Woman's Life* (Harmondsworth: Penguin, 1982). In characterizing the baroness's affliction of hypersentimentality, Maupassant also uses the more medicalized expression "une hypertrophie du coeur." Further references to the French edition will be abbreviated *UV*; to the English, *WL*.

9. Naomi Schor, *Breaking the Chain: Women, Theory, and French Realist Fiction* (New York: Columbia University Press, 1985).

drawn on by early psychiatry, have been, if not rehabilitated, then at least reevaluated by contemporary feminist psychoanalysis in its search for alternatives to masculine norms of sexuality.

Within the nineteenth-century epistemology of perversion there was, as we have seen, a fairly clear demarcation between feminine pathology and male perversion. With the exception of female homosexuality, practices such as fetishism, sadomasochism, exhibitionism, and voyeurism required a male agent in the early chronicles of deviant practice. After stating explicitly that the "hair of man, especially the beard, the emblem of virility, the secondary symbol of generative power—is a predominant fetish with woman," Krafft-Ebing foreclosed all clinical seriousness as far as female perversion was concerned by adding, "The author has thus far not succeeded in obtaining facts with regard to pathological fetishism in women."[10] As defined by the early psychoanalysts, fetishism was the decadent creation of a male erotic imagination spurred by castration anxiety or repressed homosexuality. And despite his admission at the Vienna Psychoanalytic Society in 1909 that "all women...are clothing fetishists," Freud tended to reinforce this male homosexual typecasting with his theory of the coprophilic drive.[11] Typical fetish objects such as feet and hair (associated with dirt or animal odors) were seen as evidence that the subject was arrested at the anal stage of development.[12] Regressive (in returning to that last infantile moment at which the illusion of a phallic mother reigned supreme) and predisposed to anal eroticism (hence his homosexual leanings), the fetishist and homosexual alike failed, according to Freud, to acquire that immunizing disgust so necessary to socialization.

Feminist critics have been hard-pressed to furnish case histories of female fetishism. Naomi Schor, discussing typologies of male

---

10. Richard von Krafft-Ebing, *Psychopathia Sexualis*, trans. Dr. Harry E. Wedeck (New York: Putnam, 1965), p. 41.
11. Freud, "Fetishism" (1927), *Standard Edition* 21:152–57. See also the important essay "Splitting of the Ego in the Process of Defence" (1938), in which Freud describes a typical instance of phallic displacement as it is performed by a male subject on the female body: "This displacement, it is true, related only to the female body; as regards his own penis nothing was changed" (Freud, *Standard Edition*, 23:278).
12. "Psychoanalysis...has shown the importance, as regards the choice of a fetish, of a coprophilic pleasure in smelling which has disappeared owing to repression. Both the feet and the hair are objects with a strong smell which have been exalted into fetishes after the olfactory sensation has become unpleasurable and been abandoned" (Sigmund Freud, *Three Essays on the Theory of Sexuality*, *Standard Edition* 7:155).

fetishism in the work of George Sand, acknowledges that "female fetishism, is, in the rhetoric of psychoanalysis, an oxymoron."[13] Among the first to address the issue, Schor is fully aware of the contradictions that arise when Freudian or Lacanian terms are applied and criticized at the same time. Her own textual interpretations consistently pose the problem of how one stands both inside and outside the Freudian lexicon, invoking its normative frameworks while questioning its oedipally centered premises. Schor does succeed, however, in compiling a bibliography of case histories: G. A. Dudley, she notes, "dephallusized the fetish," arguing that the "fetish may... be a substitute for other infantile objects besides the penis." George Zavitzianos claimed that for his female fetishist (who seems to have adopted a male sexual identity and adapted the Electra complex) the fetish corresponded to the paternal phallus. Gérard Bonnet, using Lacan's distinction between "having and being" the phallus, refers to the case of a female fetishist who, in Schor's words, "responds to her mother's desire by wanting to be her (missing, absent) phallus."[14] Schor also mentions Piera Aulagnier-Spairani, a feminist Lacanian, who imputes a kind of female fetishism to conditions of acute jealousy in which women suspect not just female rivals, but all objects (animate or inanimate) capable

13. Naomi Schor, "Female Fetishism: The Case of George Sand," in *The Female Body in Western Culture*, ed. Susan Sulieman (Cambridge: Harvard University Press, 1986), p. 263. In her introduction to this piece, Schor specifies that her concern "is not to counter phallocentrism by gynocentrism, rather to speculate on modes of reading that might be derived from the female body, a sexual body whose polycenteredness has been repeatedly emphasized by feminist theoreticians." I have followed Naomi Schor in the exploration of fetishism as a "polycentered" (and polymorphous) perversion, but where Schor keeps the main outlines of a male-centered Freudian fetishism intact (dislocating Freud's definition by examining its workings in the writing of a woman author and a female character), I have pursued the opposite course: revising the Freudian definition away from phallocentrism with the help of literary descriptions of female fetishism provided by a male author.

14. Like Freud, Lacan argued that fetishism was not a problem for women: "Since it has been effectively demonstrated that the imaginary motive for most male perversions is the desire to preserve the phallus which involved the subject in the mother, then the absence in women of fetishism, which represents the virtually manifest case of this desire, leads us to suspect that this desire has a different fate in the perversions which she presents." Though Lacan does acknowledge sexual difference in relation to the problem of fetishism ("For to assume that the woman herself takes on the role of fetish, only raises the question of the difference of her position in relation to desire and to the object"), he still reverts to the image of a phallus-envying female homosexual ("giving what she does not have") as a counterpart to the male fetishist (Jacques Lacan, "Guiding Remarks for a Congress on Feminine Sexuality," in *Feminine Sexuality*, ed. Juliet Mitchell and Jacqueline Rose, trans. Jacqueline Rose [New York: Norton, 1985], p. 96).

of attracting male attention.¹⁵ Here, female fetishism, synonymous with the reification of women by women, reveals itself to be an extension of some profound, masochistic will to self-objectification (evident, at a superficial level, in a woman's desire to make herself into a sex object). One may infer that for Aulagnier-Spairani, women are ontologically fetishistic because of the ease with which they operate in the realm of the simulacrum: parure, doll-like affectations, narcissistic displays of isolated parts of the body, and the faked orgasm are just so many modalities of this essentially artificial sexuality.¹⁶ Schor concludes that no matter how one tries to define female fetishism, it remains, if it exists at all, an "appropriation" ("a sort of 'perversion-theft'") of a dominantly male disorder and thus disconcertingly close to "the latest and most subtle form of 'penis-envy'."¹⁷

To my knowledge, the only other truly novel attempt to theorize female fetishism otherwise has been Elizabeth Grosz's conjugation of lesbian fetishism. Grosz compares the male fetishist to the woman with a "masculinity complex" by means of their common disavowal of castration:

> Freud suggests that although the masculinity complex may not necessarily imply lesbianism, nevertheless many lesbians can be classified under this label. Where the so-called "normal" path to femininity involves accepting her castration and transferring her libidinal cathexes from the mother to the father (via penis envy), with the accompanying transformation of her leading sexual organ from the clitoris to the vagina (with its associated position of passivity), the woman suffering from the masculinity complex retains the clitoris as her leading sexual organ and the position of activity it implies.¹⁸

As Grosz makes clear, the lesbian fetishist hermeneutically empowers the clitoris as a means of not giving up the phallus.¹⁹ If the

15. Ibid., p. 365.
16. Piera Aulagnier-Spairani, "Remarques sur la féminité et ses avatars," in *Le Désir et la perversion* (Paris: Seuil, 1967), pp. 53–90. This volume also contains other excellent pieces on fetishism, most notably Guy Rosolato's "Etude des perversions sexuelles à partir du fétichisme."
17. Schor, "Female Fetishism," p. 371.
18. Elizabeth Grosz, "Lesbian Fetishism," in *Fetishism as Cultural Discourse: Gender, Commodity, and Vision*, ed. Emily Apter and William Pietz (Ithaca: Cornell University Press, forthcoming). Further references to this essay will be abbreviated G.
19. Naomi Schor also makes the case for "clitoral hermeneutics" broadly defined as a mode of interpretation focusing on the detail and grounded in the textual extrapolation of the female body. See her "Female Paranoia: The Case for Psychoanalytic Feminist Criticism," *Yale French Studies*, no. 62 (1981): 204–19.

phallus is to be relinquished (and of course, as Lacan reminds us, it is retained by neither sex), the lesbian fetishist, like the male fetishist, will continue to love the phallus "elsewhere": "She takes on a substitute for the phallus, an object outside her own body" (G 14). This substitute phallus, Grosz provocatively suggests, can take the form of another woman—"a 'phallic' woman, a woman precisely, one may suspect, with a masculinity complex." Preserving her ideal of a preoedipal phallic mother, the lesbian subject makes a fetish of woman, and in the process, depreciates Freud's penis-envy hypothesis by changing the referential status of the phallus from penis to clitoris.

Though female narcissism and lesbian fetishism have their place in my reading of Maupassant's fiction, the interpretive emphasis falls on what the contemporary artist Mary Kelly has gently satirized as the modern housewife's preoedipal, precapitalist object cathexis. This love, involving what Kelly calls an "archaizing of the drives," veers toward domestic artifacts stamped with the coprophilic odors of the real: flowers, clothing, keepsakes, baby relics. The close resemblance between this figure of the female fetishist and Freud's historic coprophilic homosexual fetishist seems hardly coincidental. Clearly there was a place for this female "pervert," who, alongside her male counterpart, suffered from castration anxiety and yearned to regress to the anal erotic stage. Clearly there were female fetishists whose manic collectomania was never recognized as perverse because it was naturalized as a typical feminine pastime.

Why, one might ask (along with Schor and Grosz), would one want to revise the historical record so as to allow women to be fetishists? Part of the answer is that the male gendering of this perversion always seems to entail some complementary theory of female "genital deficiency."[20] Wilhelm Stekel, classifying fetishism in 1923 as a form of homosexuality, maintained that "fetishism always develops into a depreciation of the female, regardless of the causes, and the same is true of the few cases of female fetishism

20. See Freud's argument in "Femininity," in *Standard Edition* 22:132 and 134, where he argues: "The effect of penis-envy has a share, furthermore, in the physical vanity of women, since they are bound to value their charms more highly as a late compensation for their original sexual inferiority," and "Shame, which is considered to be a feminine characteristic *par excellence* but is far more a matter of convention than might be supposed, has as its purpose, we believe, concealment of genital deficiency." See also Luce Irigaray's important critique of these passages in chap. 1 of *Speculum of the Other Woman*, trans. Gillian C. Gill (Ithaca: Cornell University Press, 1985), pp. 112–13.

which I have been able to observe."[21] Another response to this genuinely irksome question centers on the conviction that a current rereading of historical femininity dislocates essentialism through the instantiation of perversion. In this case, then, a woman's search for *jouissance* in the socially sanctioned rituals of object veneration would be seen no longer as a manifestation of a tame, essential femininity but, rather, as the semiosis of a subversively erotic practice, thoroughly "perverse" in its own terms.

The first theorist of female fetishism in the history of psychiatry was Gaëtan Gatian de Clérambault.[22] A descendent of Descartes and Alfred de Vigny, an iconoclastic contemporary of Freud, and a teacher of Jacques Lacan, Clérambault left a body of work on the obsessive gaze that was the foundation, many have surmised, for Lacan's theory of the mirror stage. His own suicide provides a macabre gloss: when he shot himself in front of a mirror, the bullet exited through his eye. Clérambault's clinical career demonstrated the cliché of the "doxic" doctor who suffers from the very psychosis that he specializes in curing.[23] Fixated on cloth textures and draped fabric, he wrote on Greek costume and photographed Moroccan women mysteriously enshrouded in their chadors and veils. Clérambault also diagnosed this same *passion des étoffes* in his female patients. Jacqueline Rose's description of scopophilic desire aptly describes the particular kind of specular blindness that characterized Clérambault's analytical pose: "The relationship of the scopic drive to the object of desire," she writes, "is not simply one of distance but of externalisation, which means that the observing subject can become object of the look, and hence elided as subject of its own representation."[24]

Though subject to the whimsy of his own ocular distortions (he was also the author of *Souvenirs d'un médecin opéré de la cataracte* [Memoirs of a doctor operated on for cataracts]), Clérambault's

---

21. Wilhelm Stekel, *Sexual Aberrations: The Phenomenon of Fetishism in Relation to Sex* (New York: Liveright, 1930), p. 3.
22. Feminist critics have just begun to work on Clérambault. Joan Copjec provides an incisive Lacanian analysis of Clérambault's photographs in her article "The Sartorial Superego," *October* 50 (Fall 1989): 57–95. Jann Matlock historically situates Clérambault's work within nineteenth-century psychiatry and draws connections between his female fetishism and medical commentary on cross-dressing in her essay "Masquerading Women, Pathologized Men: Cross-dressing, Fetishism, and the Theory of Perversion, 1882–1935," in Apter and Pietz, *Fetishism as Cultural Discourse*.
23. Roudinesco, *La Bataille* 2:121–27.
24. Jacqueline Rose, *Sexuality in the Field of Vision* (London: Verso, 1986), p. 196.

theoretical reflections on his feminine case histories, published as early as 1908, offers a haptic or touch-oriented eroticism that also appears to have been the first gender-free conception of fetishism. This theoretical advance was made, however, *en pleine dénégation* (in full disavowal), for Clérambault refused in principle to admit women into the elite precinct of male perversion. In his "Passion érotique des étoffes chez la femme" [The erotic attraction to drapery in women] he took great pains to uphold a hairsplitting distinction between male and female sexual fantasy:

> A remarkable trait of fetishists, sadists, homosexuals, and masochists is the extreme abundance of their dreams relative to the object of their passion. Even beyond onanism, they devote themselves to veritable debaucheries of the imagination the object of which is their favorite act; they celebrate it in writing and drawing; throughout masturbation with the fetish they project splendid scenes.
>
> ... In the case of our three [female] patients, we find nothing of the kind; they masturbate with silk, with no more fantasy than a solitary epicure savoring a delicate wine.[25]

Clérambault's hypotheses that women alone require this type of tactile stimulation and that pieces of cloth constitute inadequate vehicles of orgasm are radically put into question when we consider his own lovingly handled photographic albums of draped females (rumored to number well over a thousand images) or his personal collection of feminine wax figurines. Moreover, his transcriptions of case histories blatantly contradict his claim that women possess less erotic imagination than men.

Where Clérambault was hampered by psychoanalytical and sexist prejudices that weakened the value of his observations, Maupassant, never one to underestimate the capacity of either sex for "veritable debaucheries of imagination," proved to be the more reliable analyst. Hair fetishism, for example, surfaces in two exemplary tales, one told from a masculine, the other from a feminine, point of view. In "La Chevelure," an antique collector, thrilled by the purchase of a seventeenth-century Italian chest, is brought to fever pitch upon discovering a tress of hair in one of the drawers:[26]

25. G. G. de Clérambault, *La Passion des étoffes chez un neuropsychiatre*, ed. Yolande Papetti et al. (Paris: Solin, 1981), pp. 34–35.
26. For an interesting reading of a medieval analogue to Maupassant's *La Chevelure*, see Jean-Charles Huchet's psychoanalytical interpretation of the fabliau *Des Tresces* in his article "De la perversion en littérature," *Poétique*, no. 71 (Sept. 1987): 272–80.

> Oui, une chevelure, une énorme natte de cheveux blonds, presque roux, qui avaient dû être coupés contre la peau, et liés par une corde d'or.
> Je demeurai stupéfait, tremblant, troublé! Un parfum presque insensible, si vieux qu'il semblait l'âme d'une odeur, s'envolait de ce tiroir mystérieux et de cette surprenante relique.
> Je la pris, doucement, presque religieusement, et je la tirai de sa cachette. Aussitôt elle se déroula, répandant son flot doré qui tomba jusqu'à terre, épais et légère, souple et brillant comme la queue en feu d'une comète.

> Yes, a head of hair, an enormous plait of blond hair, almost red, which must have been cut off against the skin and tied together by a gold cord.
> I remained stupefied, trembling, perturbed! An almost anesthetizing perfume, so old that it seemed to be the soul of an odor, flew from this mysterious drawer as well as from this amazing relic.
> I picked it up, gently, almost religiously, and I took it from its hiding place. Immediately, the tress unfurled, spilling its gilded wave which fell to the ground, thick and light, supple and brilliant, like the fiery tail of a comet.[27]

Maupassant's staged description, replete with a figure of phallic displacement ("la queue en feu"), a coprophilic attraction to odor, and a brilliant shine (approximating Freud's famous "Glanz auf der Nase"), seems to parody rather than to anticipate Freud. Like the flower fetishist in "Un Cas de divorce," or the libertine haunted by a lady's birthmark in "Une Inconnue," the antique dealer joins the ranks of male characters distinguished by their aberrantly focused erotic "regard."[28] But lest one believe that this textbook fetishism is restricted to male personnages, one need only read "La Moustache," in which the female narrator recounts her singular fixation on male facial hair:

> D'où vient donc la séduction de la moustache, me diras-tu? Le sais-je? D'abord elle chatouille d'une façon délicieuse. On la sent avant la bouche et elle vous fait passer dans tout le corps, jusqu'au bout des pieds, un frisson charmant. C'est elle qui caresse, qui fait frémir et tressaillir la peau, qui donne aux nerfs cette vibration exquise qui fait pousser ce petit "ah!" comme si on avait grand froid.

27. Maupassant, *Contes et nouvelles* 2:110.
28. An interesting interpretation of these short stories in relation to *La Chevelure* was made by Philippe Lejeune in his talk "Maupassant et le fétichisme," at a conference titled "Maupassant et la nouvelle" at Cerisy-la-salle, July 1986.

> Where then does the seduction of the mustache come from, you ask me? Do I know? At first, it tickles in a delicious fashion. One feels its contact before the mouth and it sends a charming shudder through the body, to the tips of the toes. It's the mustache that caresses, making the skin quiver and tremble, giving the nervous system an exquisite vibration that provokes that little "ah!" as if one had suddenly caught cold.[29]

As in "La Chevelure," the hirsute object of desire inserts itself in a trichophilic literary tradition including Mathilde's impassioned sacrifice of "a whole side of her beautiful head of hair" to her lover Julien Sorel in *Le Rouge et le noir;* Charles Bovary's lonely death with "a long strand of black hair" clasped between his hands like a book of prayer (and this despite his humiliating discovery of Emma's infidelities); Baudelaire's evocations of the intoxicating odors and serpentine movements of his mistress's heavy tresses in "La Chevelure," "Parfum exotique," *Fusées,* and *Les Paradis artificiels;* or the scene in act 3 of Maeterlinck's *Pelléas et Mélisande,* which begins with Mélisande's seductive call: "My hair awaits you the length of the tower," and culminates in Pelléas's fevered declaration: "All your hair, Mélisande, all your hair is falling from the tower! I am holding it in my hands, against my mouth, in my arms.... It lives like birds between my fingers, and it loves me, loves me more than you." Where each of these precedents depends on a male hair fetishist, the narrator of "La Moustache" stands out as transgressively different. Certainly an aura of transgression prevails in the passages cited above, a transgression preserved in the subversive term "bisextuality," adapted by Naomi Schor to characterize a "perverse oscillation, a refusal... firmly to anchor woman—but also man—on either side of the axis of castration."[30] In deploying this neologism, Schor implicitly endorses Sarah Kofman's Derridean notion of textual "oscillation," or undecidability. In "Ça cloche," Kofman had called for "un fétichisme généralisé," positively valorized ("bref pourquoi c'est si mal d'être fétichiste [in short, what's wrong with being a fetishist]") and no longer bound to a single gender.[31]

Kofman seeks to raze the negative history of the fetish, removing it from its Kantian ascription as a degraded sublime ("a trifle"), erasing its Marxist connotations as a spectral figure of alienated value (commodity fetishism), and displacing it from the feminist

---
29. Maupassant, *Contes et nouvelles* 1:919–20.
30. Schor, "Female Fetishism," p. 369.
31. Sarah Kofman, "Ça cloche," in *Les fins de l'homme: A partir du travail de Jacques Derrida* (Paris: Galilée, 1981), p. 99.

lexicon where it denotes the exploitative, anatomically decorticating male gaze found in pornography, advertising, and art.[32] In her reediting of fetishism, Kofman challenges its phallocentric orientation, arguing that, regardless of sex, the fetish is generated as a guarantee against the disappearance of an idealized phallus, itself already a representation. A representation of a representation, itself representative of radical undecidability, the fetish is thus redeemed; formerly a degraded truth-value and icon of sexist psychoanalysis, it is now recast as the foundation for an ironic, gender-free metaphysics.

Kofman succeeds in demasculinizing fetishism through theory but in the process dispenses almost entirely with sexual difference. Female fetishism, insofar as it could even be epistemologically distinguished according to her terms, is subsumed within the neutered modalities of textual indeterminacy. Such an indeterminacy is exemplified in Maupassant's fiction in "Clochette", a story that puts the title of Kofman's own essay, "Ça cloche" (emphasizing the analogy between the bipolar movement of the clapper and the "bitextuality" of Derrida's *Glas*, Kofman's master text of "oscillation"), ironically into play. Clochette is the name of a family seamstress whose hairy face makes her an interesting specimen of "bisextuality":

- C'était une haute femme maigre, barbue, ou plutôt poilue, car elle avait de la barbe sur toute la figure, une barbe surprenante, inattendue, poussée par bouquets invraisemblables, par touffes frisées qui semblaient semées par un fou à travers ce grand visage de gendarme en jupes. Elle en avait sur le nez, sous le nez, autour du nez, sur le menton, sur les joues; et ses sourcils d'une épaisseur et d'une longueur extravagantes, tout gris, touffus, hérissés, avaient tout à fait l'air d'une paire de moustaches placées là par erreur.

- She was a tall, thin woman, bearded, or rather, hairy, since she had patches of beard all over her face—an amazing, unexpected beard, growing in unbelievable clumps, in curly clusters that seemed sowed by a madman across the visage of this gendarme in skirts. She had hair on her nose, around the nose, on her chin, on her cheeks; and her

---

32. For an interesting discussion of the philosophical history of fetishism and its links to the eighteenth-century study of religion in "primitive" societies, see William Pietz, "The Problem of the Fetish, I," *Res* 9 (Spring 1985): 5–17. For an interesting critique in art of fetishism in advertising and pornography, see catalogs of two shows held at the New Museum of Contemporary Art in New York: *Difference: On Representation and Sexuality* (1984) and *Damaged Goods* (1986).

eyebrows, of a preposterous thickness and length, all gray, shaggy, and spiky, had the air of a pair of mustaches put there by mistake.[33]

Clochette's visage may be read as a résumé of fetishisms: situated in the netherworld of sexual identity, neither man nor woman, she literalizes the trope of *dénégation* or disavowal ("ni...ni"), which Freud saw as the general condition of the fetishist, affirming through his very denial of repression the presence of the repressed fetish. In textual terms, this denial corresponds to a kind of castrated narrative description. Cut, isolated and displaced, each tuft on Clochette's face becomes the object of intense visual focalization. As the text-face breaks into defamiliarized fragments, the reader imagines an act of mutilation on the female body. This sadistic *coupure*, typical of fetishistic pornography, is enlarged in the tragic conclusion of the story. Clochette was so nicknamed for her lame foot (*cloche-pied*), a result of a self-inflicted wound. As a young servant girl, she had thrown herself out of a window to save the reputation of a pusillanimous lover. The maimed foot, signifier of castrated femininity, is symbolically compensated for by the displaced mustache—a masculine signifier tacked onto a female face, as if to form a grotesque carnival mask (something like what Derrida, in *Glas*, has called "une plaie postiche").[34] The bearded lady thus becomes identifiable as a burlesque supplement, a prosthesis, fantasmatically guarding against separation and loss while at the same time derepressing an image of both the split ego and the text's rift.

A comparably "bisextual" servant figure, named, appropriately enough, "Barbe," appears in Georges Rodenbach's *Bruges-la-morte* (1892), the story of a widower whose despair is etched against the watery, grisaille backdrop of a Flemish city. This period piece, stylistically retro before its time, circles obsessively around the image of a dead woman's hair sealed in a bell jar (*une cloche*), and worshiped as a votive object:

> Pour la voir sans cesse, dans le grand salon toujours le même, cette chevelure qui était encore Elle, il l'avait posée là sur le piano désormais muet, simplement gisante—tresse interrompue, chaîne brisée, câble sauvé du naufrage! Et, pour l'abriter des contaminations, de l'air humide qui

---

33. Maupassant, *Contes et nouvelles* 2:851–52.
34. Jacques Derrida, *Glas* (Paris: Galilée, 1974), p. 250.

l'aurait pu déteindre ou en oxyder le métal, il avait eu l'idée, naïve si elle n'eût pas été attendrissante, de la mettre sous verre, écrin transparent, boîte de cristal où reposait la tresse nue qu'il allait chaque jour honorer.

In order to have this head of hair which was still Her continually in view in the large, unchanged salon, he had it placed on the piano, which would remain forever silent, faintly moaning—this interrupted tress, this broken chain, this cable saved from the shipwreck! And, so as to shelter it from any contamination, from the humid air that would have discolored or oxydized the metal, he had had the idea, seemingly naive if it had not been so endearing, of putting it under glass, a transparent casket, a crystal box in which the naked tress would sleep and to which he would pay homage every day.[35]

Like Clochette's face, blocked out in pieces, each site of hair geographically discrete, the tresses of the departed wife are similarly discomposed. Hugue's perception of her hair as an "interrupted" continuity—"une chaîne brisée"—connotes the revulsed or strabismic vision of the Freudian fetishist, who, unable to sustain contemplation of the maternal void, "interrupts" his gaze by refocusing on the nearest contiguous object. After falling for a dancer because of her golden mane (seemingly a replica of the dead woman's, later revealed to be a dyed *postiche*), Hugue is deserted by his pious servant. It is as if the hair of the deceased were taking its revenge through a *barbe,* itself displaced to a "cloche," which acts as a mediating trope between religious hats (*mantes, coiffes, cloches*) and bells. "Elle exultait," one learns of Barbe, "de s'acheminer vers son cher Béguinage, d'un pas encore alerte, dans sa grande mante noire à capuchon, oscillant comme une cloche [She exulted in going to her dear Beguinage, with a brisk footstep, in her huge black hooded cape, oscillating like a bell]" (*BLM* 57). Barbe "oscillates," a figure of undecidability, whose movement is gradually taken up by the incessant clanging of the bells:

Cela lui faisait mal, ces cloches permanentes—glas d'obit, de requiem, de trentaines; sonneries de matines et de vêpres—tout le jour balançant leurs encensoirs noirs qu'on ne voyait pas et d'où se déroulait comme une fumée de sons.

It got to him, those endless bells, obituary death knells, of the requiem, of the thirty-day mass; the ringing of matins and vespers—all day

---

35. Georges Rodenbach, *Bruges-la-morte* (Paris: Flammarion, 1987), p. 20. Further references will be abbreviated *BLM*.

swinging their black censers, which one did not see and from which emanated what seemed to be a cloud of sounds. (*BLM* 75).

Psychologically destabilized by the persecuting death knell, Hugue murders his mistress, strangling her with the golden locks of his beloved. "La relique," states Pierre Fédida, commenting on this episode, "retient en elle une puissance de meurtre [The relic retains within itself the power of murder]."[36] The story provides a macabre fictional analogue to the actual suicide of Maupassant's mother, Laure Le Poittevin, rumored to have strangled herself with her own hair.

Kofman's notion of fetishism lends itself to a rigorously hermeneutical approach to psychoanalysis because of its emphasis on the analytical structures of Freudian *Verleugnung* (disavowal) and *Verneinung* (negation)—that is, the fetishist's attempt to refute absence by fabricating an image that he knows to be false but which he believes in nonetheless.[37] In searching for a more exclusively female fetishism, however, we are better served by the contemporary work of the feminist artist Mary Kelly. Kelly's *Post-Partum Document*, both a physical installation and a text, transforms the rites of childhood burial into the theory and aesthetic practice of female fetishism.[38]

---

36. Pierre Fédida, "La Relique et le travail du deuil," *Nouvelle Revue de Psychanalyse*, no. 2 (Autumn 1970): 250.

37. On this fetishistic logic of *dénégation*, see Octave Mannoni's "Je le sais bien, mais quand même...," in *Clefs pour l'Imaginaire ou l'Autre Scène* (Paris: Seuil, 1969), pp. 9–33.

38. Elizabeth Cowie has written an excellent analysis, "Introduction to Post-Partum Document," *m/f*, no. 5–6 (1981): 115–23. In a section entitled "Motherhood, Loss, Fetish," she provides an interesting discussion of the visual absence of mother, father, and child: "the Post-Partum Document is not concerned with *a* personal history but with the problem of the 'personal history' of motherhood. The deliberate absence of the human figure, of direct photographic images of Mary, the father Ray Barrie, or her son Kelly himself in the series is thus important. This strategy further underlines the work of the exhibition as representation rather than reflection and further distances it from autobiography. The fullness of identification with the image as realist representation, the human face, is refused. Instead we must make do, indeed work with the series of constructions of this personal history, to grasp it as constituted in a series of representations, markings, approximations, symbolisations and discourses. The personal experience of motherhood is the material for an exploration of motherhood in our society. That experience, of Mary Kelly's as a mother, is not however any self-evident truth, but appears as markings or traces, and in the gaps, losses and separations produced across the juxtaposition of the material of the exhibition. It is a process of representation by which the individual subject comes to be placed. Mary Kelly has suggested of Documentation IV,

Questioning, like Derrida and Kofman, "the fetishistic nature of representation itself," Kelly takes deliberate steps toward shifting fetishism from its male-biased perspective. Within her theoretical mise-en-scène, the traditionally pictured upward gaze of boy to mother yields to the downward gaze of mother to child:

> According to Freud, castration anxiety for the man is often expressed in fantasy as the loss of arms, legs, hair, teeth, eyes, or the penis itself. When he describes castration fears for the woman, this imaginary scenario takes the form of losing her loved objects, especially her children; the child is going to grow up, leave her, reject her, perhaps die. In order to delay, disavow, that separation she has already in a way acknowledged, the woman tends to fetishise the child: by dressing him up, by continuing to feed him no matter how old he gets, or simply by having another "little one." So perhaps in place of the more familiar notion of pornography, it is possible to talk about the mother's memorabilia—the way she saves things—first shoes, photographs, locks of hair or school reports.[39]

Basing her definition of maternal fetishism on Freud's discussion of feminine narcissism (the child qua maternal appendage becomes a means of restoring lost plenitude), Kelly hardly seeks to invalidate the proverbial equation of female fetishism with penis envy. Her aesthetic fabrication of a miniature museum of infantile detritus, however, privileges women in the role of (gender) constructors, preservationists, and caretakers. *Post-Partum Document* ironically frames a historic allegory of "motherhood," caught in a moment of ritual mourning for passing "babyhood." Kelly, it would seem, even goes

---

that 'to refuse to signify the mother through her image, photographic or otherwise, is not to erase her presence from the scene, but rather to locate her desire precisely in the field of the Other through the presence of the child.' 'Furthermore, because the figure of the mother is not present in the work, it does not suggest that the representation of femininity can escape the "corruption," the fetishistic implications, of conventional codes by evacuating the image. In the Post-Partum Document the realism which is repressed in the realm of the look returns in the form of the diary text.' The narrative capture, the story told, the titillating intimacy of confession are presented in these texts. But the 'story' actually only appears in the juxtaposition of these texts with the objects, becoming a statement of a process of positioning of mother and child in social relations. The objects and texts of the exhibition are important transitory, substitutive objects in this circulation. 'Her "memorabilia" and the child's "transitional objects" are emblems which testify to the threatened loss of mutual enjoyment, but the desire in which they are grounded can only be caused in the unconscious by the specific structure of phantasy'" (pp. 120–21).

39. Mary Kelly, *Post-Partum Document* (London: Routledge and Kegan Paul, 1985), p. xvi.

so far as to endorse the manic tendencies of the Freudian melancholic whose collecting and conservation express a deep-seated need to appropriate and thereby incorporate the qualities of the elusive love object. Stripping away and ironically aestheticizing the negative associations surrounding the rituals of melancholia, Kelly transforms the maternal reliquary into a feminized poetics of mnemic traces, constitutive in turn of a (now positively valorized) genre of sentimentality.[40]

Comprehended in these terms, Maupassant's novel *Une Vie* (1883) offers itself to today's female reader as a fin-de-siècle pendant to Kelly's twentieth-century museological exhibitions. *Une Vie* chronicles the successive deceptions and depredations of a woman's life: starting with the discovery on her wedding night of the animal brutality of sex, and ending with the dreary solitude of widowhood and filial neglect. Jeanne contracts melancholia like some hereditary disease from her own mother, whose greatest masochistic pleasure is to sift through the wreckage of "billets doux" shored up in her "secrétaire aux têtes de sphinx" (*UV* 155):

· Elle passait des jours à relire *Corinne* ou les *Méditations* de Lamartine; puis elle demandait qu'on lui apportât le tiroir "aux souvenirs". Alors ayant vidé sur ses genoux les vieilles lettres douces à son coeur, elle posait le tiroir sur une chaise à côté d'elle et remettait dedans, une à une, ses "reliques", après avoir lentement revu chacune. Et, quand elle était seule, bien seule, elle en baisait certaines comme on baise secrètement les cheveux des morts qu'on aima.

· She spent whole days re-reading *Corinne* or Lamartine's *Meditations;* or she would ask for her "relic drawer"; and having emptied out on her lap the old letters that were so precious to her, she put down the drawer on a chair by her side and replaced the "relics" one by one after slowly perusing each one. When she was alone, quite alone, she even kissed certain of them, as one kisses the lock of hair of someone whom one once loved and who is now dead. (*UV* 149; *WL* 123).

In response to her daughter's concern upon finding her mother in tears, the baroness replies: "Ce sont mes reliques qui m'ont fait ça.

---

40. Kelly gives us a feminist transposition of what might be called the "discourse of the museum," a discourse grounded in literary representations of the collection (through techniques such as *ekphrasis*, the *blason*, enumeration, the *hétéroclite*, the literary "passage" or "exposition universelle") by writers such as Balzac, Baudelaire, Flaubert, Zola, Henry James, Proust, Benjamin, and Adorno.

On remue des choses qui ont été si bonnes et qui sont finies!... Tu connaîtras ça plus tard [It's my "relics" that do this to me. The memory of things that were so good once but are no more is stirred!... You'll experience the same thing later on yourself]" (*UV* 149; *WL* 123). With her "tu connaîtras ça plus tard," Jeanne's mother condemns her daughter to learning the coded language of morbid grief, with its hyperbolic, hyperfeminine rhetoric of nostalgia, self-pity, and loss. Though Jeanne dutifully learns to speak this language, she transposes it into a maternal dialect, commemorating her son's absence, for example, by turning his nickname—"Poulet" —into a verbal relic:

· Et, tout bas, ses lèvres murmuraient: "Poulet, mon petit Poulet", comme si elle lui eût parlé; et, sa rêverie s'arrêtant sur ce mot, elle essayait parfois pendant des heures d'écrire dans le vide, de son doigt tendu, les lettres qui le composaient. Elle les traçait lentement, devant le feu, s'imaginant les voir, puis, croyant s'être trompée, elle recommençait le P d'un bras tremblant de fatigue, s'efforçant de dessiner le nom jusqu'au bout; puis, quand elle avait fini, elle recommençait.

· She kept whispering: "Pullet, darling little Pullet!" as if she were talking to him. His name sometimes put an end to her dreams, and she would spend hours trying to write the letters of his name in the air with an outstretched finger. She traced the letters slowly in front of the fire, imagining that she could see them; then, thinking that she had made a mistake, she began again with the P, her arm trembling with fatigue, forcing herself to complete the name; when she had finished it, she began all over again. (*UV* 219; *WL* 193–94)

Tracing the letter *P* Jeanne substitutes the missing love object with a "mnemic trace" that is added in its turn to an already assembled collection of infant souvenirs. Most cherished of all objects is the "Poulet ladder"—knife-marks on a wood panel recording her child's development on the order of Mary Kelly's computation of fecal traces.

Jeanne's museological mania corresponds to what Stekel, in gender-biased terms, describes as the fetishist's "harem cult." "Every fetish adept," he wrote, "has his harem of handkerchiefs, drawers, shoes, braids, photographs, hair, corsets, garters, etc. Each single fetish loses its enchanting qualities as a fetish and the devotee quickly and hungrily finds himself another sample only to drag forth the old one again after a while; all just like a pasha in his harem."[41] A female counterpart of Stekel's pasha, Jeanne collects frenetically, joyfully rediscovering and resurrecting the "little nothings" assembled by her in the past. Her gallery includes shattered cups, mother's lantern, father's broken cane, warming pans and water bottles, old calendars, her own gold hairpin, and Poulet's hallowed growth chart, which, like an epitaph, is festooned with loving inscriptions:

- Toutes les légères marques grimpaient sur la peinture à des intervalles inégaux; et des chiffres tracés au canif indiquaient les âges, les mois, et la croissance de son fils. Tantôt c'était l'écriture du baron, plus grande, tantôt la sienne, plus petite, tantôt celle de tante Lison, un peu tremblée. Et il lui sembla que l'enfant d'autrefois était là, devant elle, avec ses cheveux blonds, collant son petit front contre le mur pour qu'on mesurât sa taille.
 Le baron criait: "Jeanne, il a grandi un centimètre depuis six semaines."
 Elle se mit à baiser le lambris, avec une frénésie d'amour.

- The lines on the paint went up at different intervals and the figures scratched with a penknife gave her son's age in years and months and his height. Sometimes it was in the Baron's large writing, sometimes in her smaller script, sometimes in Aunt Lison's rather shaky hand. She pictured him there in front of her, a fair-haired boy, as he was in those days, pressing his little forehead against the wall for them to measure his height. "Jeanne!" cried the Baron, "he's grown half an inch in the last six weeks," and she began to kiss the panel in a frenzy of affection. (*UV* 224; *WL* 199)

The saccharine tone of this passage, coupled with the reified, already quoted quality of the baron's phrase, recalls the lachrymose parsing of stock tombstone etiquettes or mourning mottos. Maupassant would later use this conceit—what one might call the lapidary verbal fetish—to greatest effect in his description of four engravings adorning a widow's parlor in *Pierre et Jean* (1888). With their maudlin captions, ironically signifying "widowhood," these pictures form a *mise-en-abyme* of the kitsch bourgeois culture of mourning. Funeral wreaths, miniatures in lockets, household shrines, mantelpiece urns, widow's crepe, mortuary figurines, letter packets, locks of hair, in short, the entire junkheap of personalized *pompes funèbres*,

---

41. Stekel, *Sexual Aberrations*, p. 21.

when seen through Maupassant's satirical lens, emerges as a fetishistic iconography linked to feminine object cathexis.

The vaguely necrophilic aura surrounding these commemorative markers of loss has been derived by Maria Torok (glossing Ferenczi, Abraham, and Freud) from "the feeling of an irreparable sin: the sin of having been invaded by desire, of having been caught by an outpouring of libido at the least appropriate moment, the moment where it is befitting to abandon oneself to pain and despair."[42] Though Torok herself never restricts this *maladie du deuil* (sickness of mourning) to the second sex, and though her signature paradigm of the return of the repressed—the phantasm of the exquisite cadaver—need in no way be identified as a feminine imago, her description of mourners who fixate on objects as representations both of loss and sepulchral desire fits easily into a model of female fetishism.[43]

Such a model, as we might now construe it, gives special weight to the woman's need for what Sandor Ferenczi called "objectal inclusion"; for "incorporation," "introjection," or encrypting, for anatomical self-reification (a kind of dismembered narcissism), and for sexual gratification through objects.[44] In *Une Vie,* each of these

---

42. Maria Torok, "Maladie du deuil," p. 717.

43. Hair fetishism and necrophilia are linked in Maupassant's "La Chevelure" and "La Tombe," both published in 1884. In the latter, told from a first-person male point of view, the hair is identified with the coprophilic allure of organic decay (*Contes et nouvelles* 2:216):

"She! It was she! I was seized with horror. But I put out my arm and caught her hair to pull this monstrous face towards me! It was at that moment I was arrested.

"All night I carried with me, as one retains the perfume of a woman after a sexual embrace, the filthy smell of this putrefaction, the odour of my beloved!" (*The Collected Novels and Stories of Guy de Maupassant,* trans. Ernest Boyd [New York: Knopf, 1923], p. 105).

If, in *La Tombe,* the fetish emerges as a singularly masculine necrophilic fantasm, typical, according to the Freudian construct, of the fetishist's urge to return to the infant utopia of anal eroticism and fecal "gifts," in *Apparition,* published a year earlier, death, hair, and female longing are configured. Here, in a haunted house, a feminine specter awaits release from this world when a man arrives to dispose of her effects. "Voulez-vous?... Voulez-vous?" she repeats, entreating him passionately to "rendre un grand service." *Apparition* is a tale of necrophilia in reverse: instead of a male protagonist satisfying his lust through intercourse with a dead woman, here we have a female corpse imposing sexual demands on the living (*Contes et nouvelles* 1:785): "'Comb my hair, oh! comb my hair; that will cure me; it must be combed. Look at my head—how I suffer; and my hair hurts me so!'... Why did I receive that comb with a shudder, and why did I take in my hands the long, black hair which gave to my skin a gruesome, cold sensation, as though I were handling snakes?" (*The Collected Novels and Stories of Guy de Maupassant,* p. 225).

44. Sandor Ferenczi, "Introjection and Transference," in *First Contributions to*

dimensions is present in Jeanne's cloying habit of touching, fingering, and clinging to old things. "Elle apercevait mille bibelots connus jadis,... des riens qu'elle avait maniés,... Jeanne les touchait, les retournait, marquant ses doigts dans la poussière accumulée [She saw a thousand knickknacks, which she had known in former days... things which she had handled, trivial little things that had been lying around her.... Jeanne touched them and turned them round, dirtying her fingers in the accumulated dust]" (*UV* 201–2; *WL* 176–77). Jeanne's gestures correspond to the notion of *cramponnement*, that "instinct of clinging," that "rhythm of little jerks," that oscillating sequence of strokes which Derrida situated "between crochet needles" ("entre crochets.")[45]

Derrida himself relates such *cramponnements* to fetishism, discerning in *les maniements*, or manic clinginess, a desire to fix, immobilize, and reify a truth-value that is constantly slipping away toward its parodic double, or *postiche* representation. But if we accept this argument, it means that we are willing to grant Derrida (and Kofman) their gender generalized fetishism of oscillation and undecidability. If one prefers a theory accenting a distinctly female fetishism, the notion of *cramponnement* might alternatively be affixed to the feminine expression of postpartum sentimentality. This particular mode of sentimentality, applied to an indifferent lover rather than a lost child, is discernible in Maupassant's magnum opus *Bel-Ami* (1885), where the aging wife of a newspaper magnate, about to be abandoned by the ruthless, arriviste Du Roy, manages to ensnare him, to encrypt him, so to speak, with a ring of hair:

· Elle frottait lentement sa joue sur la poitrine du jeune homme, d'un mouvement câlin et régulier, et un de ses longs cheveux noirs se prit dans le gilet.
Elle s'en aperçut, et une idée folle lui traversa l'esprit, une de ses idées superstitieuses qui sont souvent toute la raison des femmes. Elle se mit à enrouler tout doucement ce cheveu autour du bouton. Puis elle en

---

Psycho-Analysis (London: Hogarth Press, 1952), pp. 40–43. J. Laplanche and J. B. Pontalis have defined incorporation, introjection, and their close relationship as follows: "Incorporation contains three meanings: it means to obtain pleasure by making an object penetrate oneself; it means to destroy this object; and it means, by keeping it within oneself, to appropriate the object's qualities.... Introjection is close in meaning to incorporation, which indeed provides it with its bodily model, but it does not necessarily imply any reference to the body's real boundaries (introjection into the ego, into the ego-ideal, etc.)" (*The Language of Psychoanalysis*, trans. Donald Nicholson-Smith [New York: Norton, 1973], pp. 212, 229).
45. Jacques Derrida, "Entre crochets," *Digraphe*, no. 8 (1976): 97–114.

120 · Feminizing the Fetish

> attacha un autre au bouton suivant, un autre encore à celui du dessus. A chaque bouton elle en nouait un.

> She was slowly rubbing her head to and fro against the young man's chest, gently stroking him, and one of her long black hairs caught in his waistcoat.
> She noticed it and a wild notion suddenly came into her head, one of those superstitious ideas which are often a woman's only form of reason. Very gently she started to wind the hair around the button. Then she fastened another one to the next button and another one to the button above. To each of his buttons she attached one hair.[46]

Rubbing against him with short, regular movements Madame Walter mimes the work of knitting needles. This masturbatory gesture, *entre crochets*, announces a fantasy as perverse as that of any male fetishist—a fantasy confusing the real and the simulacrum, a hypersentimentalized clinging to a surrogate sex or prosthesis. But is this substitute sex simply a figure of her own sex?

> Il emporterait quelque chose d'elle sans le savoir, il emporterait une petite mèche de sa chevelure, dont il n'avait jamais demandé. C'était un lien par lequel elle l'attachait, un lien secret, invisible! un talisman qu'elle laissait sur lui.

> And without knowing it he would take away something of hers, a little lock of hair, a thing for which he had never asked. It was a link by which she would be binding him to her, a secret, invisible link, a talisman that she was leaving with him. (*BA* 283; *B* 326–27).

Though Madame Walter abases herself before her lover there is nonetheless a kind of narcissism and self-aggrandizement in this circular figuration of hair. The ring connotes a noose leading back to its owner, or, at the very least, to an image of woman enclosed on herself, involved, like the classic male fetishist, in a self-referential erotic fantasy.

Indeed, it is this narcissistically ordered female fetishism that acquires specular form in *Bel-Ami*. As Du Roy moves from one mistress to the other, he is caught out by the hair, which claims him like a sticky trace of the dead. While undressing him, Clotilde

---

46. Guy de Maupassant, *Bel-Ami* (Paris: Garnier-Flammarion, 1959), p. 283; trans. Douglas Parmée as *Bel-ami* (Harmondsworth: Penguin, 1975), p. 326. Further references to the French edition will be abbreviated *BA*; those to the English, simply *B*.

discovers the strand, fingering and inspecting it like a detective. After unwinding the third knot, she pales, exclaiming: "Oh! tu as couché avec une femme qui t'a mis des cheveux à tous tes boutons [Oh, you've been to bed with a woman who's put hairs on all your buttons]" (*BA* 286; *B* 330). Clotilde *recognizes* the fetishism of the other woman where Du Roy fails to do so. "Elle avait deviné, avec son instinct rusé de femme, et elle balbutiait, furieuse, rageant et prête à pleurer:—Elle t'aime, celle-là...et elle a voulu te faire emporter quelque chose d'elle [Her woman's crafty instinct told her what had happened and, furious with anger, on the point of tears, she stammered: 'She's a woman who loves you...and she wanted you to take something of hers away with you]' (*BA* 286; *B* 330–31). "Vouloir faire emporter quelque chose d'elle"—this repeated construction epitomizes a kind of gynotextual fetishism in the second degree. In the figure of two women meeting invisibly over the buttons of their common lover we have a sudden revelation of the female fetishist no longer "split" by the gaze of a male Other but, rather, absorbed and reified in an identical and mutually identified look. This circular gaze is reinforced by the recurrent image of a ring of hair: "Garde ta vieille femme...garde-là," rails the outraged Clothilde, "fais-toi faire une bague avec ses cheveux...avec ses cheveux blancs....Tu en as assez pour ça [You can stick to your old woman...stick to her...have a ring made with her hairs...her white hairs....You've got enough of them to do that]" (*BA* 287; *B* 331).

With its emphasis on a frozen moment of *peripeteia* (unmasking the complicity of two women in the making and unraveling of a lover's discourse), this scene highlights the specular nature of feminine longing. Anticipating Luce Irigaray's *Speculum of the Other Woman*, Maupassant's characters suffer a violation of trust at the hands of men, but at the same time discover in their pantomime of each other a "language of their own."

Using this language of a gynotextual desire that recognizes the feminine relic as symbolizing something both more than and less than a simple compensatory object, we might better understand the polysemic character of female fetishism. Whether standing in for lover, parent, child, or female double, the female fetish belongs to an erotic economy of severance and disappropriation, itself less fixed on a fiction of castration anxiety. In interpreting Freud's statement that the "horror of castration sets up a sort of permanent memorial to itself by creating this (fetish) substitute," I am tempted to retain his concept of a memorial or marker to which the female subject "clings" but would want to question the preeminence of a "castrated" site within the female fetishist's Imaginary.[47]

Having attempted to challenge the obsession with emasculation so frequently evinced in male-biased psychoanalysis, and having tried, concordantly, to establish epistemological categories for thinking female loss as something other than just penis envy or a masqueraded castration anxiety, I have come increasingly to value Mary Kelly's pioneering "work of mourning." In her *Post-Partum Document*, the accent on woman's "genital deficiency" is displaced by a poetics of loss, fluids, and ghostly stains, which themselves paradoxically acquire conceptual bulk. For Kelly, the transgressively eroticized mourning of missing love objects becomes substantial in its own right, weaned from supraphallic explanation.

And these repetitively phallic explanations certainly continue to prevail. As recently as 1981, for example, the French psychoanalyst Gérard Bonnet offered an account of his own patient's history of female fetishism, which, though enlightened in regard to the need to redress the lack of material on female perversion, nonetheless reaches conclusions not so dissimilar from those of Clérambault. Bonnet begins by recognizing the extent to which the salient points of his subject's case—the substitution and surinvestment of an inanimate object, the necessity of the object to the production of *jouissance*, the elaboration of a "perverse" mise-en-scène—match the requisite coordinates of male fetishism. "Lucie" experiences orgasm, much like Clérambault's female silk fetishists, only when the relics of an ancient bathrobe are placed between her thighs. Ingeniously, Bonnet traces the choice of fetish object to a vestigial *text*—Octave Mirbeau's *Le Journal d'une femme de chambre*—introduced to the patient by her mother, who had bragged that she herself had performed services for a foot fetishist much like the maid in this turn-of-the-century novel. Correlating the words *robe de chambre* with *femme de chambre*, in the context of Lucie's absent father, Bonnet at first sees her "possession" of the dressing gown as a symbolic formulation of "having" the *paternal* phallus. But having provided the grounds for decentering the Freudian emphasis on the male fetishist's problematic of "having and not-having" the *maternal* phallus, Bonnet reverts to a more orthodox line of interpretation. Pointing out to Lucie that the consonants in *RoBe de*

---

47. Freud, "Fetishism," p. 200.

CHamBRe yield *BoRD de BRanCHe*, or "wood plank," he concludes that her bathrobe fetish discloses a phantasm of wishing to "be" that maternal supplement or strut ("une planche de salut") that is traditionally projected by the male fetishist. In a manner disquietingly close to that of Clérambault, Bonnet rephallicizes the female fetishist's inner arena of the symbolic, arguing that she is "fétichée" (fetishized for and by her mother) rather than "fétichiste."[48] Though Bonnet, like Kofman, opts for the "undecidability" hypothesis in relation to female fetishism, arguing that Lucie's symptoms signify a perpetual oscillation between maternal and paternal phallus, his case study ends in equivocation. Lucie is "not *not*" a fetishist. Though her robe functions like a "transitional object" (and here Bonnet, like so many analysts, implicitly infantilizes women "perverts" by placing them regressively in the realm of the Kleinian preoedipal), it also shares the pure instrumentality of the sexual fetish object. Female fetishism, like female perversion in general, is thus estimated by Bonnet to be "furtive" and "hardly formulated [*à peine formulée*]."[49] The point could hardly be made more clearly: from Clérambault to Gérard Bonnet, the standard psychoanalytical account of female fetishism has remained woefully impoverished from a theoretical perspective.

In concluding this discussion, I am aware of the problem, inherent in my own approach, of seeming to validate a negative stereotype of female sexuality. But the purpose of this investigation has been neither to promote female fetishism (though I do think women have a right to be perverse!), nor to intimate that women are necessarily locked into rigid codes of hypersentimentality. My concern, rather, has been to experiment with recuperating what the cultural anthropologist Clifford Geertz has called "thick descriptions" of women's behavior, locating in the representation of feminine collecting (from Maupassant and Clérambault to Kelly) documents on which to draw in the task of revising sclerotic psychoanalytic configurations of female eroticism.

48. Gérard Bonnet, "Fétichisme et exhibitionnisme chez un sujet féminin," in *Voir, être vu: Etudes cliniques sur l'exhibitionnisme*, 2 vols. (Paris: PUF, 1981), 1:93–94.
49. Gérard Bonnet, *Les Perversions sexuelles* (Paris: PUF, 1983), p. 117.

CHAPTER 6

· Mystical Pathography: A Case of Maso-fetishism in the Goncourts' *Madame Gervaisais*

· The nineteenth-century medicalization of religious excess was given its greatest impetus by Jean-Martin Charcot and Paul Richer in their iconographic and clinical studies of hysteria. In Charcot's *Iconographie photographique de la Salpêtrière* (1876), *Les Démoniaques dans l'art* (1886), and *La Foi qui guérit* (1897) and in Richer's *Etudes cliniques sur la grande hystérie* (1881/85), they examined the female *imitatio christi* and classified related spiritual performatives: mystical folly, spirit-possession, the convulsionaries of Saint-Médard (a cult renowned for its collective ejaculations on the walls of the church), faith healing, exorcism rites, and attacks of ecstasy and erotic delirium. Charcot's division of hysteria into five passional attitudes— *Appel, Supplication, Erotisme, Menacé, Extase*—drew directly on the vocabulary of devotional practice. Richer, the more specialized in visual classifications of the two, deciphered the scenographies of hysterical female bodies as so many mimed stages of the cross. The Passion, or *chemin de la croix*, could be identified when the patient roamed over her bed on bent knees, head bowed, eyes wide open. Contractions and convulsions invariably followed—what Charcot and Richer called *attaques démoniaques*, in which the patient appeared to be possessed by the Devil. Then the torso would stiffen, and each arm would be flung out to the side (as if nailed to a cross) with the head dropping forward over one shoulder. This stage was dubbed the *crucifiement* and was typically succeeded by the *descente de la croix*, a state of physical exhaustion and mental disorientation. The finale was punctuated by *extase* (where the patient clasped her hands in prayer) or *délire érotique* (in which she would spread her thighs and cry out for satisfaction).

Making visible the erotic subtext of feminine mysticism, Charcot and Richer buried the blasphemous implications of their research behind the edifice of scientific investigation. Anticlerical pundits of the day had no such reticence, however, as they revealed how confession and zealous worship provided women with a perfect alibi for catering to an impulse that was principally sexual rather than spiritual. In their journal of 1854 the Goncourt brothers aired their philosophy on the "natural" connection between religion, sexuality, and femininity. In 1854 they wrote:

- La religion pour la femme n'est pas la discipline à laquelle l'homme se soumet; c'est un épanchement amoureux, une occasion de dévouement romanesque. C'est dans les jeunes filles un exutoire licite, une permission d'exaltation, une autorisation d'avoir les aventures mystiques; et si les confesseurs sont trop doux, trop humains, elles se jettent aux sévères, qui remplacent la vie bourgeoise par une vie d'émotions factices, par un martyre qui donne aux martyrisées, à leurs yeux mêmes, quelque chose d'intéressant et de surhumain.

- Religion for women is not the kind of discipline to which men submit themselves; it is a loving effusion, an excuse for romantic devotion. In young girls, it is a lawful outlet, a permission for exaltation, an authorization for mystical affairs; and if the confessors are too gentle, too humane, they throw themselves on the severe ones, who replace bourgeois life with a life of false emotions, with a martyrdom that lends to the martyred something interesting and superhuman in their own eyes.[1]

Seen as overly susceptible to spiritual *jouissance*, women were frequently portrayed as the unsuspecting quarry of charlatan men of the cloth. In *Du Prêtre, de la femme, de la famille* (1845) Jules Michelet excoriated sacerdotal sadism, which he saw as the inevitable outcome of Catholicism's negative logic of renunciation, and exposed the clergyman-interloper who placed himself between husband and wife in matters domestic and conjugal. Stronger still was a work provocatively entitled *Les Débauches d'un confesseur* (1885), by Léo Taxil and Karl Milo, in which a thoroughly corrupt Jesuit priest (based on the notorious eighteenth-century figure Père Girard)

---

1. Edmond de Goncourt and Jules de Goncourt, *Journal*, 3 vols. (Paris: Robert Laffont, 1989), 1:100 (May 20, 1854). Further references to this work will be abbreviated *J*.

plots the murder of his enemies, abuses the prerogative of the confessional, and flagellates the bare breasts of his trusting female penitent.[2] "Think.... Think hard," he admonishes his victim, as she prepares, blushing, to undress, "of the early Christian martyrs, the hermits in the desert rolling themselves naked on a bed of thorns to combat the goading of the flesh.... Think of the penitents, offering their backs to the whip, brandished by the priest."[3] Octave Mirbeau's *L'Abbé Jules* (1888) provides the portrait of an equally odious clergyman whose leather case stores the infernal contents of his sado-erotic fantasies.

The Joan of Arc–style trials of feminine martyrdom enumerated in the Goncourts' *Madame Gervaisais* (1869) perfectly complement Charcot's studies in the staging of religious hysteria. As in J. K. Huysmans's *Là-bas* (1891), in which the sex crimes and spiritual redemption of Gilles de Rais are retold, this novel exposes the Manichean psychology of religion, with its pendulum swings between idealization and abasement. Like the true-life Joan of Arc and Gilles de Rais, who reputedly fought alongside one another in the heroic battle at Orléans, so the protagonists of these pathograpies, Madame Gervaisais and Durtal, seem symbiotically bound, angelic and diabolical complements within twin allegories of Catholicism's darker side. Though in this chapter I will be concentrating on the Saint-Joan–Madame Gervaisais figure rather than on the pathography of Gilles, a brief word on the consistent intercalation of their respective sagas within twentieth-century cultural history may be in order. The canonization of Joan of Arc in 1920 sparked a host of mimological treatments. Bernard Shaw published his *Saint Joan* in 1923, Joseph Delteil's novel *Jeanne d'Arc* appeared in 1925, and Carl Dreyer's film *The Passion of Joan of Arc* was released in 1928. Gilles de Rais's story, though reserved for a more underground audience, flourished as the evil counterpart—the corrupt version of France's supreme patriotic fetish. In 1885 the Abbé Eugène Bossard

---

2. Léo Taxil's work came to my attention through Alain Corbin's provocative contribution to *Histoire de la vie privée*, vol. 4, ed. Michelle Perrot (Paris: Seuil, 1987). Corbin defines the bourgeois culture of religion in more specific terms, as it relates to marriage, baptism, and funeral practices, its vulnerability to anticlerical tradition, its role in the nineteenth-century construction of spiritual sensibility, its localized psychogeographies both in the home and throughout sacred pilgrim sights in France, and the alliances between women and the clergy—the gendering of ecclesiastical power.

3. Léo Taxil and Karl Milo, *Les Débauches d'un confesseur* (Paris: Librairie Anticléricale, 1885), p. 46.

published his thesis *Gilles de Rais, maréchal de France, dit Barbe-Bleue*. Writing in 1912 as a Jew in the wake of the Dreyfus affair, Salomon Reinach in a chapter of his monumental study of world-historical sacred practices, *Cultes, mythes et religions*, attempted to rehabilitate Gilles, marshaling evidence that he had been scapegoated.[4] There was also a play featuring a meeting between Gilles and the ghost of Joan of Arc written between 1925 and 1926 by the Chilean surrealist Vicente Huidobro.[5] Finally, Tournier's postmodern version, *Gilles et Jeanne*, stressed the bisexuality of the pair: Jeanne is portrayed as a *garçonne* whose martyrdom is mystically bound up with Gilles's subsequent need to perform acts of violent pollution. The concept of *l'inversion bénigne* is introduced not only to denote the religious convertibility of a satanic Gilles into a saintly Joan, but especially to describe the bigendered or doubly inverted figure created by their composite psycholiterary profiles.[6]

This reversibility of masculine and feminine, male and female homosexuality, good and evil, phantasm and reality, pleasure and pain, is crucial to understanding the workings of sadomasochism and its cognates: *sadi-fétichisme* (a term introduced by Paul Garnier in the 1880s) and *maso-fétichisme*. In addition to functioning as a crucible of the pathographic imagination, these two derivative perversions have important cultural implications, particularly in their mesh with religious mentalities of the fin de siècle.[7] Here I am referring specifically to Catholicism's popular rituals, including its idealization of Christ and the Virgin, its seemingly idolatrous reverence for sacred images and figurines, its fixations on martyred flesh, its arduous pilgrimages to Lourdes, its erotic intimacy of the confessional, its fashion (encouraged among bourgeois women) to macerate the body in emulation of Christ's sufferings. Félicité de Lammenais's translation of Saint Augustine's *Imitation of the Life of Jesus Christ*, Loyola's *Spiritual Exercises*, Saint François de Sales's *Introduction à la vie dévote*, and Lacordaire's *Conférences de carême*, all mentioned specifically in the Goncourts' novel as the touchstones of Madame Gervaisais's new-found religious instruction, constituted, as Frank Paul Bowman has demonstrated, *architexts* of a French

---

4. Salomon Reinach, *Cultes, mythes et religions*, vol. 4 (Paris: Ernest Leroux, 1912).
5. Vicente Huidobro, *Gilles de Raiz* (Paris: José Corti/Ibériques, 1988); for the scene with Jeanne d'Arc see pp. 142–58.
6. Michel Tournier, *Gilles et Jeanne* (Paris: Gallimard, 1983).
7. Paul Garnier, *Les Fétichistes pervertis et invertis sexuels* (Paris: J-B Baillière et Fils, 1896).

romantic sublime steeped in the "precious blood" of the Savior.[8] Citing a long passage from Lacordaire's official biography by the Dominican Bernard Chocarne (*Le R.P. Lacordaire de l'ordre des Frères Prêcheurs* [1866]), describing the ecclesiastic's entreaties to his novices to flagellate him, as well as "to slap him, spit in his face, talk to him as if he were a slave," Bowman raises the issue directly of how we read these descriptions today:

> This text was republished seven times, and translated five times during the nineteenth century. It leaves today's reader astonished. Masochism? Homosexuality? Fetishism? Exhibitionism? Chocarne is already worried about the reactions of ill-minded readers, and we have probably all become so ill-minded. But to what extent is our reading of the text unhistorical? Is the blood of the religious discourse here transformed into a lived experience, or does it simply serve to disguise perversion? (*FR* 88)

Bowman's final query invites an affirmative response: these wounds, these supplications for mortification, do indeed appear to be congruent with perverse scenarios, and it is precisely this ambiguity that authors of the later nineteenth century (that is, the Goncourts and Huysmans) refracted in their novels, upon returning with pronounced cynicism to the devotional theme so dear to their romantic predecessors. After reading Saint Augustine, the Goncourts confided in their journal that martyrdom was proof of the madness of religion (*J* 1:297).

Religious sadism (black masses, demonic pederasty, flagellation) and religious masochism (the hairshirt, anorexia nervosa) overlap in the fetishization of instruments of pain. In this schema, fetishism should no longer be perceived as a perverse end in itself but, rather, as a means to an ultimate end—a state of total excitation in which "pain pleasures." Following Freud ("The Economic Problem of Masochism" [1924]), Parveen Adams has traced this "erotogenic masochism" through to a subject-shattering fantasy of sacrifice, self-loss, and death induced by the phantasm of a silent, primal, preoedipal father. "The primal father resides," she writes, "in the silent space where the subject tries to lose himself through being

---

8. Frank Paul Bowman, *French Romanticism: Intertextual and Interdisciplinary Readings* (Baltimore: Johns Hopkins University Press, 1990); see his trenchant chapter "'Precious Blood,' in Religion, Literature, Eroticism, and Politics," pp. 81–105. Further references to this work will be abbreviated *FR*.

devoured, beaten, seduced."[9] An instrument of pain wielded by the primal father and adored by the masochist, the fetish emerges as a psychic appliance facilitating access to this primordial, cannibalistic, degree-zero state of the subject. Within the history of religious psychology, it collaborates on the project of soul suicide through the production of a crushing ego ideal. Circulating in the libidinal economy of masofetishism, the religious superego paradoxically undercuts its own interests by promoting a physical pain that affords erotic pleasure. Sadofetishism operates according to the same economy, but the fetish, agent of ego annihilation, is turned outward toward the other rather than inward against the self.

As pathography *Madame Gervaisais* offers a fictional rendering of a feminine masochism worthy of inclusion as a case history in a sexological manual. This "case" was in fact grounded in historical reality insofar as the Goncourt brothers patterned Madame Gervaisais's self-punishing addiction to God after the alarming life story of their own aunt, Nephtalie de Courmont. Elements of the drama were also borrowed from the biography of Princess Louise-Adélaïde de Bourbon-Condé (friend of a certain Marquis de Gervaisais), who, after she became Sister Marie-Joseph de La Miséricorde in 1794, founded a sororal order and published her *Vie* (1843) as an exemplum of penitence and abnegation.

Such a genre of mystical pathography intersects with fetishism on at least three levels: the first is *cultural: Madame Gervaisais* illustrates the incursion of a fundamentally idolatrous form of worship into the hallowed territory of European civilization. Indeed, the Goncourts desublimate a kind of primitivist fetishism that was there all along in Western religious practice but was covered up by the pretensions of monotheism. Their demystifying treatments of institutionalized faith ultimately promote erasure of the colonial distinction between pagan and Christian. In *Madame Gervaisais* this symbolic revenge of the Other, via fetishistic ritual, is underscored by evocations of Rome as the site of an Africanist or Orientalist Catholicism. Rome represents the "third world in the first": its jaundiced, pallid atmosphere reminds Madame Gervaisais of "paintings of Africa, of country stifled under sultry desert cloud."[10] And it is surely no accident that she takes as her spiritual counselor the obdurate Père

---

9. Parveen Adams, "Coming to Terms" (Paper delivered at the annual meeting of the Modern Language Association, Washington, D.C., Dec. 1988), p. 5.
10. Edmond de Goncourt and Jules de Goncourt, *Madame Gervaisais* (Paris: Gallimard, 1982), p. 104. Further references to this work will be abbreviated *MG*.

Sibilla, whose thirst for a tougher martyrdom has led him on civilizing missions under the "ferocious sky of Africa" (*MG* 215). As Marc Fumaroli has noted, Rome—Africa's mimetic other half—is portrayed in this work as a place of pure ethnology (*MG* 43).

On another level, fetishism may be identified with an *aesthetics* of historical backdrop, local color, ornamental style, and décor. *Madame Gervaisais* capitalizes on the mannerism of the baroque; its chiaroscuro, processual sublime, opulent church raiment, and clamor of choral accompaniment. True to their taste for eighteenth-century neoclassicism, the Goncourts forced themselves to accomplish this exercise in baroque sensibility by borrowing from a tradition of aesthetic contemplation and exegesis set out by Johann Winckelmann and Diderot. Self-consciously composing scenes, framing tableaux, inserting segments devoted to empathic "appreciations" of famous paintings and sculptures, they created an *écriture artiste* that was itself fetishistic in its celebration of artifice—the maquillage of religious culture. Anticipating Lacan's seminar in *Encore* "On the baroque," this religious aesthetic is more than a sensibility; it lends itself to a masochistic *jouissance*, that, as we shall see, becomes linked to the fetishization of divine voice.

On the *psychoanalytical* plane, both works illuminate a key aspect of fetishism's link to repression through idealization, a link that Freud elaborated not only in "Fetishism" (1927) but also in "Repression" (1915) and "Splitting of the Ego in the Process of Defence" (1938). Freud suggested in "Repression" that, "as we found in tracing the origin of the fetish, it is possible for the original instinctual representative to be split in two, one part undergoing repression, while the remainder, precisely on account of this intimate connection, undergoes idealization."[11] In his "Splitting of the Ego" he affirmed that, faced with a conflict between the instinct's demand and reality, the child may select not to choose between them, opting instead for a means of satisfying both sides. In one case, a boy punished for masturbating by his nurse with the threat of castration concedes to society by giving up the maternal phallus. At the same time he caters to his instinct by creating a "fetish" with which he continues to masturbate. All would seem resolved, except for the fact that the ego is not so easily fooled: as Freud would insist, "everything has to be paid for in one way or another, and this success is achieved at the price of a rift in the ego

---

11. Sigmund Freud, "Repression" (1915), *Standard Edition* 14:150.

which never heals but which increases as time goes on. The two contrary reactions to the conflict persist as the centre-point of a split in the ego."[12] When repression "splits" the ego, one might say, a certain amount of fallout results: an idealized fetish symbol (Freud used the example of the Virgin Mary at a meeting of the Vienna Psychoanalytic Society in 1909) rises up on one side, and a devaluation of the real (the degradation of women) occurs on the other.

Freud allowed for the full perversity of civilization's fetishization of the Virgin to shine through in "Repression," when, as we saw, he equated that which is idealized with the "remainder" or "leftover" of base instinct. In this transformation of dross into gold, we find a reprise of an important point set out early on in *Three Essays*. Claiming that the perversions were related through their common "idealization of the instinct," he identified as critical that juncture where "the instinct succeeds in overcoming the resistance to shame and disgust set up by mental forces."[13] *Madame Gervaisais* may be read as a construction of what happens when instinct, got up in the trappings of a religious superego, tricks the ego into venerating the very symbols of shame which, in principle, it places firmly outside the law.

Magnus Hirschfeld, in 1937, interpreted the Goncourts' 1857 journal entry "La religion est une partie du sexe de la femme" (*J* 1:248) in the following manner:

> The transposition of sexual impulsions into religious impulsions, their mutual substitution, is possible thanks to a certain affinity that exists between religious and sexual ecstasy. Just as the lover "adores" his beloved, calling her his "angel," his "idol," so the love for the Savior, for the Virgin Mary, for the saints or the adoration of idols and fetishes appears often as a substitute for its erotic equivalent....We can only agree with the Goncourts when they say: "Religion forms part of feminine sexual life."[14]

---

12. Freud, "Splitting of the Ego in the Process of Defence" (1938, 1940), *Standard Edition* 23:275–76.

13. Freud, *Three Essays on the Theory of Sexuality, Standard Edition* 7:161–62. If one looks back over the timespan during which Freud worked on this configuration of repression, idealization, and fetishism, it becomes clear that some (unwritten) theory explaining the links between instinctual or archaic desire, "splitting" and its visual signs, and scopic fixations on the ideal preoccupied him throughout the better part of a life career.

14. Magnus Hirschfeld, *Le Corps et l'amour* (Paris: Gallimard, 1937), p. 26.

In their portrait of Madame Gervaisais the Goncourts test out this essentialist dictum on the female body itself: their heroine's entry into religion takes place via the sexual organs. She returns from an initiatory visit to a pious, charismatic countess, "attendrie dans toutes les fibres intimes de son sexe par le je ne sais quoi de fondant [touched to the inner fibers of her sex by an ineffable melting sensation]" (*MG* 171). As if seduced by an invisible caress, her "soul" is gently uncorseted ("déliée") and decontracted ("déraidie"), pried open ("cette ouverture tendre") and moistened ("presque mouillée") (*MG* 171, 172). What penetrates her fissured heart is the language of a little book, "speaking to her in the voice of a nursemaid, addressing a Christian soul in its infancy [*l'enfance chrétienne d'une âme*]" (*MG* 171). Here this sexual awakening in a woman avowedly frigid is tallied with the infantilism that Freud associated with feminine masochism (that is, the woman's putative desire to be punished like a child).

The prayer book, demeaning to the intelligence of a woman reared on Kant, foreshadows humiliations to come. A similar ominousness can be read in the symbol of a bleeding rose: "A regarder un camélia luisant et verni, une rose aux bords défaillants, au coeur de soufre où semble extravasée une goutte de sang, ses yeux avaient une volupté [Her eyes looked with voluptuousness on a camellia, glistening and varnished, on a rose with flagging borders and a sulfur heart that seemed to ooze a drop of blood]" (*MG* 88). This allusion to the mystical flower of the Rosicrucianists, tainted at its center with sulfur, suggests the kernel of something devilish—masochism, say—lurking at the core of religious fervor.

That masochism itself can be fetishized is hardly a revelation. Hirschfeld interpreted the masochist's reduction of self to the level of inanimate object (as in cases where the man wants to "be" the carpet on which the woman puts her feet) as an instance of the masochist's "becoming" the fetish.[15] Freud's Viennese disciple Wilhelm Stekel argued along similar lines that as a substitute for religion fetishism encouraged the martyr complex (he described how when the fetishist put on a corset or constricting glove he was trying symbolically to martyr himself).[16] Every fetishist copies Christ, he

---

15. Magnus Hirschfeld, *Anomalies et perversions sexuelles (Geschlechts Anomalien und Perversionen)*, trans. Anne-Catherine Stier (Paris: Corréa and Guy Leprat, 1957). See chap. 19 on symbolic forms of masochism.

16. Wilhelm Stekel, *Sexual Aberrations: The Phenomena of Fetishism in Relation to Sex*, vol. 1, trans. Samuel Parker (New York: Liveright, 1971). See the section in chap. IX

noted, referring not only to the fetishist's predilection for idealization, altar building, and private ritual but also to his fascination with the maimed, deficient body. In *Sexual Aberrations* he chronicled the case of "Beta," "a thirty-year-old independent scholar, suffering from divers parapathic symptoms," most critical among them being "his agoraphobia and his foot fetishism" (*SA* 226): "what really interested him in the line of feet was a *bloody* one. He would often phantasy that he had stuck a nail or a splinter into his foot and that it bled. The picture of a foot with a nail in it appeared more and more frequently in his phantasies and day-dreams. In short, there appeared that phenomenon which I have found so often in parapathics: the Christ neurosis" (*SA* 232). Beta's fetishism of red, swollen, bloody feet illustrates fetishism's "masochistic tendency" as mediated by the "Christ neurosis." His initial dream and Stekel's analysis of it yield a sense of the textuality of religious maso-fetishism, both in terms of the evocative thematics and imagery of the case itself and insofar as an actual book emerges at the psychic origin of the neurosis. The power of suggestion accruing to the author's incredible name, "Dr. Bloody-Binet," is not lost on Stekel:

· He dreamt:
   I see a large wooden image of Christ before me and take a piece out of it.
   This dream is to be taken symbolically. The dreamer is still a believer, a devout believer, as a matter of fact, despite his apparent pose as a freethinker. The day before the dream, he had read a book entitled *La folie de Jésus* (Dr. Binet-Sanglée, Paris, A. Maloine, 1908), but had to stop suddenly in the middle of it. He could not say why. It was all like an obsession, like a command: stop reading. The deeper causes for this experience are revealed in the dream. He had taken something from his godliness.
   Second determination. He himself is Christ, but only a part. He adapts a part of the life of Christ for himself. He is therefore no longer flesh and blood, but wood. He can no longer give way to the passions of the flesh. Simultaneously he expresses his bipolar tendency: he is made of wood, can easily burn and go up in flames. What piece was it that he took out? He doesn't know, but we shall learn in later dream analyses. That piece which he took out of the image—might not that have been the foot? His fetish? His personal religion? His atonement? (*SA* 233)

---

on "Masochism in Fetishism" and chapter VIII, "The Bible of the Fetishist" including the section "The Sadistic Phantasies of an Ascetic." Further references to this work will be abbreviated *SA*.

Interestingly, as the progression of dreams transposed by Stekel reveals, the more Beta (marching about in sandals) becomes identified with Christ's wounds, the more he assumes the woman's position. Stekel narrates three intricated dreams: an old box filled with red splinters signifying "the cross and blood of Christ," a journey on a train during which he is asked by a conductor to share a bed with his father, and a phone call from a friend advising him about a telephone. Menstruation, sleeping with his father, "receiving" a call, these telltale subtexts point to only one interpretation: "As a female he could be passive and masochistic," Stekel concludes. "He could suffer. This phantasy leads directly to the wish to be a woman, Christ nailed to the cross. His pet phantasy is that he is nailed (possessed)" (SA 241).

One may infer from Stekel's case that masochistic fetishism prefers a female subject, or worse, that when fetishism degenerates into masochism, the subject is implicitly feminized regardless of biological gender. Certainly the Goncourts' portrait of Madame Gervaisais conforms to this psychoanalytically phallocentric model. Madame Gervaisais treats her own body much as Beta treats the lacerated foot. By the end of the novel, wracked by consumption and catalepsy, her body bears the signs of immolation. She has used what is left of her wits to devise "rare and recherché privations": filing her nails with a heavy brick, clothing herself in penitential garb, mortifying the flesh.

- Depuis quelque temps, Honorine s'étonnait de trouver, sans pouvoir deviner d'où pouvait venir cela, dans les chemises de sa maîtresse, des taches de sang au bout de brindilles d'arbuste: Mme Gervaisais avait, sur le refus du P. Sibilla de lui laisser porter un cilice, pris l'habitude de coudre, sur la toile qui couvrait sa poitrine, de petites branches de rosier dont les épines lui déchiraient la peau.

- For some time now, Honorine was astonished to find, without being able to divine from whence it came, bloodstained twigs in the shirts of her mistress: Upon Father Sibilla's refusal to allow her to wear a hair-shirt, Madame Gervaisais took up the habit of sewing little rosebush branches into her undergarments, the thorns of which tore her skin. (MG 237)

The blood that falls from her neck and shoulders hearkens back to the dripping rose. Drunk on the charms of "the discipline," mesmerized by mystical ascesis, locked into the bizarre performance of a mock Calvary, she has become a fanatical bride of Christ. How has this happened? What, in fact, has triggered the psychosis of what Luce Irigaray, following Simone de Beauvoir, has called *la mystérique?*

The Goncourts' pathography provides a fascinating array of insights into the way in which maso-fetishism burns its way into feminine consciousness by means of the beguiling aesthetics of religious "show" (*le faste*). An antique sculpture located in the Vatican acts, for example, as a psychosexual lure:

· Tout enveloppé d'une étoffe mouillée qui l'embrasse, le baigne et le serre, en se collant à tous ses membres, le voile de marbre, de la pointe des seins qui le percent de leur blancheur, glisse en caresse sur le dessin de la poitrine et la rondeur du ventre, s'y tuyaute et s'y ride en mille petits plis liquides qui de là vont, droits et rigides, se casser à terre, tandis que la draperie, presque invisible, plaquant aux cuisses, et comme aspirée par la chair des jambes, fait dessus de grands morceaux de nu sur lesquels courent des fronces, des plissements soulevés et chiffonées, des méandres de remous dans le courant brisé d'une onde.

· All enveloped in a moist material that embraces, washes over and clasps it while sticking to its every limb, the marble veil, pierced through by the white tips of the breasts, slips like a caress over the outlines of the chest and rounded stomach, fluting there, wrinkling there in a thousand little liquid folds that go down, straight and rigid, to break ground. Meanwhile the barely visible drapery, sticking to the thighs, as if sucked in by the flesh of the legs, gathers over the pieces of the naked body, swirling into raised, bunched pleats, meandering eddies in the broken current of a wave. (*MG* 144)

Gazing at the statue, Madame Gervaisais empathically experiences the adhesive "caress" of the marble shroud, savors the coquettishly revealed outline of naked female lineaments under classical folds of drapery, gasps at the contraction of cloth over the genitalia, yields to the sensation of liquefaction. Shortly thereafter, while beatifically contemplating the floating face of Christ in a portrait by Raphael, she feels engulfed by the shrouds of Veronica. Christ comes and inhabits her body, becomes "le patron de son sexe" (in the sense of patron saint of women, but also, of course, sexual master) (*MG* 148).

The Goncourts initiate the reader, just as they initiate Madame Gervaisais, into the allure of spectacular religion through a technique of vivid picture making in prose (*ut pictura poesis*). A kind of processual sublime is introduced through Madame Gervaisais's first exposure to a local Roman fete: the sun glances off the crowd and alights on banners sporting images of Christ's face weeping drops of blood. Lines of penitents, at angles to the profusion of banners, caskets, and candles add depth and perspective to the visual plane. A huge cross is held up against the stomach of a Herculean brother, sweating and groaning under the strain. Prelates in gold and silk and a novice costumed as an angel follow. Bringing up the rear, as a focal point to the scene, is an entire altar borne aloft by sixteen staggering men, its metallic glare riveted on a sacred heart pierced with seven swords. Sound effects enliven the picture: a program music of pilgrimages to the cross, covered over with the percussion of the crowd's loud, collective cries.

Disturbed by the aura of idolatry and Orientalism commingled in this pageantry, Madame Gervaisais writes to her brother:

- Je me disais: c'est pourtant la foi de la civilisation; et je ne voyais qu'une sauvage et toute brute idolâtrie d'Orient, un peu de la ruée de l'Inde sous une idole de Jaggernat! J'étais atteinte, touchée, humiliée au plus profond de moi par cette extériorité et cette grossièreté figuratives.... Je souffrais de cette scandaleuse dégradation d'un culte qui me paraissait profaner des croyances que ma vie a quittées,...j'étais *blessée* dans le sentiment élevé, délicat et pudique... tant de matérialité, tant de spectacle, tant de réalité basse, tant d'efforts de muscles d'hommes, pour faire ce qu'on appelle une religion!

- I said to myself: this is after all the faith of civilization; but I saw only the brutish, savage idolatry of the Orient, the hordes of India hurling themselves at the idol of Jaggernat! I was shocked, touched, humiliated to the inner core by this exteriorization, this crass figuration.... I suffered from the scandalous degradation of a cult that seemed to me to profane the very beliefs that my life had left behind.... It was like a wound to my sense of delicacy, modesty, and higher feeling.... so much materiality, so much spectacle, so much base reality, so many muscular efforts of men, to make what one calls a religion! (*MG* 99–100)

Here, masochism is spurred by a sadistic church, personified as a false idol that is by turns "brutish," "savage," "shocking," "humiliating," "degrading," "wounding," "base," and physically overpowering.

These associations are reinforced in a startling scene charting her "fall" into idolatry. After her son, Pierre-Charles, becomes dangerously ill, two women take her to the Church of Saint Augustine, sanctuary of the Madonna del Prato, the patron saint of mothers. As

Madame Gervaisais enters the church she dimly perceives the form of the mulatto idol. This female fetish bears the distinguishing mark of a strangely erotic, damaged foot: "a foot used up, devoured by kisses, a foot half-restored in gold, but flattened to the touch by the crush of adoring mouths, the wear of lips" (*MG* 156). As she watches in fascination, the door swings continually open and shut, admitting worshipers who march directly to the foot of the Virgin, embrace it, press their foreheads to the big toe, and genuflect. Hypnotized by the sight of a mother bending forward to let her sick child kiss the sacred foot, Madame Gervaisais suddenly flies to the pedestal and "places her own mouth to the foot, glues her forehead to the coldness of the gold: a prayer from childhood on her lips, and breaks into sobs" (*MG* 158). This conversion episode might be captioned "The Return of the Fetish," insofar as it records a moment in which Catholic ritual is symbolically "negrified," subverted from within, taken over by a dark-skinned Virgin that it sought to colonize and disable.

The scene also highlights the motif of *orality*—a kind of cannibalism or primal fantasy characteristic, according to Helene Deutsch, of the masochistic "mother who enjoys" (she refutes lack by replacing the act of coitus with the act of feeding).[17] Throughout the novel, there is a commerce between oral cavity and biblical word that seems to have a loaded meaning in the context of female *mysteria*. Inside the church of Saint John of the Lateran, for example, Madame Gervaisais highlights the female mouth in her aestheticized observation of indigenous religious custom:

- Mme Gervaisais était surprise qu'un grand artiste n'eût pas saisi cette sculpture des poses, des lassitudes, des méditations, des absorptions, l'aveuglement de cette dévotion éblouie, la stupeur presque bestiale de cette prière. Le tableau surtout la frappa des confessions élancées de femmes qui, debout, la bouche tendue, plaquée contre le cuivre du confessionnal, se soutenaient et s'appuyaient avec leurs deux mains près de leur tête, posées à plat contre le bois, dans le mouvement de ces buveuses de campagne approchant la bouche d'un filet d'eau plus haut que leur bouche.

- Mme Gervaisais was surprised that a great artist had never captured this sculpture of poses, lassitudes, meditations, absorptions, blind dazzled devotion, the almost bestial stupor of prayer. The tableau of these

17. It is Parveen Adams who makes this point in "Coming to Terms."

women confessing especially struck her, standing with their mouths pressed against the brass of the confessional box, supporting themselves with their hands near their heads, their bodies lying flat against the wood in the manner of country drinkers approaching their mouths to a trickle of water higher than their mouths. (*MG* 126–27)

This image of supplicant jaws ready to imbibe the word of God makes of the mouth a displaced ear. Gradually, the seduction through the eye produced by the dazzling veneer of baroque religious art gives way to the acoustic register as Madame Gervaisais experiences what can be described only as a kind of orgasm of the ear. As she listens to the *Miserere* in the Sistine Chapel, the choir floods her with the pain of the soul:

- Les voix ne cessaient pas,—des voix d'airain; des voix qui jetaient sur les versets le bruit sourd de la terre sur un cerceuil; des voix d'un tendre aigu; des voix de cristal qui se brisaient; ... des voix étranges et troublantes, des voix flûtées et mouillées, des voix entre l'enfant et la femme, des voix d'hommes féminisées, des voix d'un enrouement que ferait, dans un gosier, une mue angélique, des voix neutres et sans sexe, vierges et martyres, des voix fragiles et poignantes, attaquant les nerfs avec l'imprévu et l'anti-naturel du son.

- The voices did not cease—voices of brass, voices that threw onto the verses the dull thud of earth on a coffin; voices of a tender sharpness; voices of breaking crystal; ... strange and troubling voices, fluted and moist voices, the voices between child and mother, the voices of feminized men, voices of such huskiness that they made an angelic mew in the throat, the neutered, asexual voices of virgins and martyrs, fragile and poignant voices that attacked the nerves with the impromptu, antinaturalness of their sound. (*MG* 123–24)

The unnerving strangeness of this plainsong, connoting the grating falsetto of castrati, designates the sexually ambiguous presence of an *âmosexual* singer, to use the figure coined by Julia Kristeva to evoke the masochistic, "feminized" homosexual soul of Saint Sebastian (*Histoires d'amour*).[18] Perhaps it is this image of a bisexual desire, smuggled into the unconscious through music, that gently places Madame Gervaisais under the thrall of religion. In any case, this seduction by guttural threnody presages a more violently sexual encounter in the confessional box between ecclesiastical Voice and female Ear.

18. Julia Kristeva, *Histoires d'amour* (Paris: Gallimard, 1983), p. 101.

The box is a thing of terror, a shadowy coffin from which only the priest's hand, uncannily severed, emerges as it holds open the listening shutter: "a hand that never moved, a pale and chubby hand, still, smooth and impassive, cut off and seemingly nailed to the wood, a hand that caused fear, dead and eternal!" (*MG* 189). A string of forbidding imperatives issues, low and monotonous, from the box: "You have reviewed your errors, but you must not let your soul be assuaged by the malady of faith," the voice warns, then continues:[19]

- "Efforcez-vous donc... —et il mit une note presque dure dans le bénin de sa parole inlassable et coulante—... efforcez-vous donc de corriger cette opiniâtreté de votre esprit.... Prenez la résolution d'obéir fermement à votre Père spirituel, quels que soient les remords, la crainte et les appréhensions qui vous conseillent; apportez la docilité que saint Bernard prescrivait à un disciple tourmenté des mêmes scrupules que vous.... [...] Persuadez-vous donc... —et le prêtre laissa tomber ici une note presque attendrie—... qu'une âme ne peut pécher en agissant d'après les ordres et les lumières de son Père spirituel, puisque Jésus-Christ lui-même a dit aux directeurs dans la personne des apôtres: 'Celui qui vous écoute m'écoute.'"

- "Force yourself, then"—and he put an almost hard note into the benignity of the indefatigable stream of his words—"force yourself then to correct the recalcitrance of your spirit.... Resolve to firmly obey your spiritual father, whatever your regrets, fears and apprehensions; bring to him the docility that Saint Bernard prescribed to a disciple, tormented by the same scruples as you have.... Persuade yourself, then"—and the priest let fall here an almost tender note—..."that a soul cannot sin in acting on the enlightened orders of its spiritual Father, since it was Jesus Christ himself who said to his apostles: 'He who listens to you listens to me.'" (*MG* 201)

This extended one-way interview with God's proxy illustrates a disturbing relationship between feminine submission and the mystical voice, or what Kaja Silverman, in the context of film criticism, has characterized as "voice-over," "off-stage," or "off-screen" authoritative pronouncements. In *The Acoustic Mirror* she characterizes

19. Gilles Deleuze has argued: "Imperatives abound in the work of Sade and Masoch; they are issued by the cruel libertine or by despotic woman.... Words are at their most powerful when they compel the body to repeat the movements they suggest, and 'the sensations communicated by the ear are the most enjoyable and have the keenest impact' (Bataille)" (Gilles Deleuze, *Masochism: An Interpretation of Coldness and Cruelty*, trans. Jean McNeil [New York: George Braziller, 1971], p. 17).

this voice-over in terms of a "disembodied and extradiegetic male voice" that "speaks from an anonymous and transcendental vantage point, 'over' the narrative.... As [Pascal] Bonitzer observes, this voice is a pure distillate of law; not only does it 'forbid questions about its enunciation, its places and its time,' but it speaks with an unqualified authority."[20]

Using Silverman's theory of feminine acoustic castration we might rewrite the Lacanian apothegm (cited by Silverman) "In the scopic field, the gaze is outside, I am looked at, that is to say, I am a picture" with "In the acoustic register, the voice is off-stage, I am talked at, that is to say, I am ventriloquized."[21] The image of God's voice implanted in Madame Gervaisais's pliant body plays into an age-old conception of female anaclisis ("attachment," from the Greek "to lean on"), whereby the feminine superego stands in need of a symbolic prosthesis to prop itself up. As the Goncourts wrote with their usual misogynist flair: "La femme ne se suffit pas: elle ne va pas de soi; sa fébrilité a besoin d'être relancée et remontée, de recevoir une impulsion, un *la* [Woman does not suffice unto herself, it is not clear where she comes from; her nervous temperament needs relaunching, rebolstering, an extra lift, a kick]" (*J* 1:295; authors' emphasis). It seems no accident that the prod that comes from without is invisible, unaccountable, and male gendered, whereas the body which receives is tangible, capable of pain, and female. As Kaja Silverman argues, if one follows the full implications of this voice-over, it leads to a theory of sexual difference implicitly derogatory of feminine subjectivity:

> This is all another way of saying that if male subjectivity is most fully realized (or perhaps it would be more accurate to say most fully "idealized") when it is least visible—when it approaches a kind of theological threshold—female subjectivity is most fully achieved (or should I say "deidealized") when it is most visible. Through a curious kind of paradox, man, with his "strikingly visible" organ, is defined primarily in terms of abstract and immaterial qualities such as potency, knowledge and power, whereas woman, whose genitals do not appeal to

---

20. Kaja Silverman, *The Acoustic Mirror: The Female Voice in Psychoanalysis and Cinema* (Bloomington: Indiana University Press, 1988), p. 163. Further references to this work will be abbreviated *AM*. Silverman is referring here to Pascal Bonitzer's *Le Regard et la voix* (Paris: Union Générale d'Editions, 1976).

21. Jacques Lacan, *The Four Fundamental Concepts of Psychoanalysis*, ed. Jacques-Alain Miller, trans. Alan Sheridan (New York: Norton, 1978), p. 106, cited in Silverman, *The Acoustic Mirror*, p. 161.

the gaze, becomes synonymous with corporeality and specularity. (*AM* 164)

To counter feminine depreciation, one could argue that even though the female is body and the male is voice, the question remains of who upholds whom. Does the *mystérique* maintain the God-position in place or does she use God for her own pleasure? Lacan implied the latter when he described the expression of sexual bliss on the face of Bernini's statue of Saint Teresa of Avila:

- It's like Saint Teresa—you have only to go look at Bernini's statue in Rome to understand immediately that she is in sexual bliss, there is no doubt about it. And what is causing this pleasure? It is clear that the only important testimony for the mystics lay in saying what they felt, but they know not from whence this comes.... This pleasure that one feels and which remains inscrutable, isn't this what puts us on the path of ex-sistence? And why not interpret the face of the Other, the face of God, as held up by feminine *jouissance*?[22]

Though God's Other is a woman's pleasure, Lacan also managed to undermine the status of this pleasure in a seminar describing his "orgy of Churches" during a visit to Italy in 1973. Delivered three months after the more controversial "God and the *Jouissance* of t(e Woman," this lecture, entitled "On the Baroque," identifies the resuscitated body of Christ with "incorporation," or an "oral compulsion—with which Christ's wife, the Church as we call her, contents herself just fine, having nothing to expect from a copulation" (*E* 102). Lacan's conventionally gendered female church, deprived of any real sexually gratifying return, is offered spiritual fellatio as compensation for her chastity vow. Religion, he insinuates, revives itself through "la dit-mension de l'obscénité" (roughly, "the obscene utterance," "the dimension of obscenity," or "obscenity's calling"). Untranslatable wordplays throughout *Encore*, such as the conjugation of erotic spiritualism in "A Love Letter"—"*J'âme*, tu âme, il âme...jamais j'âmais... les femmes âment l'âme*"—reinforce Lacan's depiction of the female addiction to God (*E* 78).[23] He

22. Jacques Lacan, "Du Baroque," in *Le Séminaire de Jacques Lacan, Livre XX: Encore*, ed. Jacques-Alain Miller (Paris: Seuil, 1975), p. 70. Further references to this work will be abbreviated *E*.
23. For an English translation of Lacan's "Une Lettre d'âmour," see *Feminine Sexuality*, ed. Juliet Mitchell and Jacqueline Rose, trans. Jacqueline Rose (New York: Norton, 1985), pp. 149–61.

figures a soul that comes into being as the enunciation of a female body at once sacralized and disgraced: "Pour que l'âme trouve à être, on l'en différencie, elle, la femme, et ça d'origine. On la *dit-femme* [one says woman] on la *diffâme* [and (in calling her woman) one defames her soul]" (*E* 79). Lacan's bride of Christ emerges, then, as the maligned *porte-parole* of *l'âmoralité*.

Interestingly enough, a feminist theorist of the stature of Luce Irigaray seems to have agreed to become the female carrier of this subversively re-Catholicized Lacanian Word. As the following loosely translated opening passages from her *Passions élémentaires* indicate clearly, she collapses, as in her earlier writings, the distinction between vaginal and facial lips. As the lips speak, however, they seem to be making love not with other female lips but with a distant and overpowering divine voice. Irigaray the "narratrice" appears to be engaging in oral intercourse with (a female?) God:

> Ta langue, dans ma bouche, m'a-t-elle obligée à parler? Cette lame entre mes lèvres, est-ce elle qui tirait de moi des flots de paroles pour te dire? Et, comme tu voulais des mots entre autres que ceux déjà prononcés, des mots encore inouïs pour te nommer toi et toi seul, unique en ta langue, tu m'ouvrais de plus en plus loin. Tu effilais et amenuisais ton outil, jusqu'au quasi-imperceptible, pour frayer plus avant mon silence. Plus avant dans ma chair, n'allais-tu découvrir le chemin de ton être? De son encore à venir?
>
> ...Tu rentres encore une fois, une fois sans fin, au plus profond du plus profond de ma bouche, un peu plus loin que là où elle s'ouvrirait, d'où elle pourrait te dire, et tu y crées le vide. Excavation artificielle. Attente vacante du présent de ton surgissement. De toi venant construire et rendre habitable de l'encore disponible. De toi disposant de la réserve et la fécondant selon ton projet.
>
> Hors ce projet, rien n'est.
>
> ...Cette immémoriale blessure qui ne saigne que de la douleur imperceptible du rien, incrustation de ton néant au plus innocent de ma chair,...Combien de fois, sans fin, reviendras-tu disposer en moi de ce don?

Your tongue, in my mouth, did it force me to speak? This blade between my lips, is it that which took from me the flood of words to say it to you? And, as you wanted words among others already pronounced, words still wonderful to name you and you alone with, unique in your language, you open me further and further apart. You pare away and hone your instrument, to the point of the quasi-imperceptible, so as to break through my silence. Further and further into my flesh, will you not find the path of your being? of its being still to come?

...You return once more, a once more without end, to the deepest of the deepest recesses of my mouth, further than that place where it would open from, where it could tell you, and where you create an empty space. Artificial excavation. Empty wait for your surging forth. From you coming to construct and make habitable the still available. From you disposing of reserve and fecundating according to your plan. Beyond this plan, nothing is.

...This immemorial wound that bleeds only from the invisible pain of nothing, the incrustation of your nothingness on my innocent skin.... How many times, without end, will you return to dispose in me of this gift?[24]

Though the familiar topography of absences, voids, and bodily fluids in these paragraphs recalls *Speculum of the Other Woman* and *This Sex Which Is Not One*, this particular *histoire d'eau*, (with its watery poetics of blood, saliva, and sexual discharge) shockingly approximates a slave language replete with wounds, lashes, and knife cuts. References to "waiting" for the other to "fill" or "surge forth" fall neatly into the Deleuzian paradigm of masochistic discourse. Emphasizing the prevalence of waiting scenes in Leopold von Sacher-Masoch's *Venus in Furs*, Deleuze has developed a theory of suspense, doubly understood as erotic postponement, or forepleasure, and the freezing of bodily postures into lexemes of bondage.[25] Putting her body entirely at the disposal of her imaginary interlocutor so that it may do with her as it pleases, Irigaray's speaker resembles the Virgin waiting for the Annunciation, ready to prostitute herself, if need be, to the "Conception" of God.

In her docility, Irigaray, or "I," as we might be tempted to call her now, not only resembles Madame Gervaisais, but she also recalls the heroine of Pauline Réage's cult classic of female masochism, *The Story of O*:

"*You also have on too many clothes. Unfasten your stockings and roll them down to above your knees. Here are some garters.*"

By now the taxi has picked up speed, and she has some trouble managing it; she's also afraid the driver may turn around. Finally, though, the stockings are rolled down, and she's embarrassed to feel her legs naked and free beneath her silk slip. Besides, the loose garter-belt suspenders are slipping back and forth.

"*Unfasten your garter belt*," he says, "*and take off your panties.*"

---

24. Luce Irigaray, *Passions élémentaires* (Paris: Minuit, 1982), pp. 9–12. I have translated the original freely.
25. Gilles Deleuze, *Présentation de Sacher-Masoch* (Paris: Minuit, 1967).

That's easy enough, all she has to do is slip her hands behind her back and raise herself slightly. He takes the garter belt and panties from her, opens her bag and puts them in, then says:

"*You shouldn't sit on your slip and skirt. Pull them up behind you and sit directly on the seat.*"

The seat is made of some sort of imitation leather which is slippery and cold: it's quite an extraordinary sensation to feel it sticking to your thighs.[26]

O's unspeakable speech act, stylistically retrofitted, as Roland Barthes has pointed out, in the nostalgic trappings of kinky eroticism, attests to an *aural* reward for her labors. In his preface to a deluxe Italian edition of *Histoire d' O*, Barthes punned on the effect of the fractured images used by the illustrator, Guido Crepax, to depict O's subjection, calling the *bande dessinée* (comic strip) a "dessin qui bande" or "cartoon with an erection":

- Représenté, mis dans notre vision, sous notre nez, l'organe érotique de O n'est nullement son sexe (ou ses seins, ou ses fesses), c'est—chose bizarre à dire—: son oreille. Et voilà ce que Crepax a compris: il n'a dessiné (il est vrai de bien des façons dont aucune n'est auriculaire) qu'une oreille: O n'est figurée, en mille postures, et sous mille parties de son corps, que pour autant qu'elle écoute. Entendez, comme elle: "Relevez-vous et asseyez-vous....J'aimerais vous voir complètement nue....Otez votre jupe, maintenant...", etc: c'est alors que le désir passe (le désir du lecteur, du voyeur). Les yeux noyés, l'ovale du visage, le bout des seins, le petit chapeau, la tunique rétro, les hauts talons, tout s'imbibe d'écoute.
  Une métonymie tout aussi rayonnante saisit la voix que O reçoit et prend dans son désir. D'où part-elle, cette voix de l'assujetissement? De partout: moins des lèvres que de la main, des ongles, de la cigarette, des pieds nus, d'un noeud de robe de chambre, d'une fleur qui est dans la pièce. Crepax a reconstitué les trajets de l'interlocution sado-masochiste.

- Displayed, brandished before our eyes and under our nose, the erotic organ of O is not, as one might expect, her genitalia (or her breasts, or her buttocks), but rather—strange to say—her ear. And that's exactly what Crepax has understood: he has drawn an ear in countless forms, none of which directly resembles an ear. O is figured as an infinitely fragmented body contorted in a thousand positions that register what she hears. Listen, like she does: "Stand up again and sit down.... I

26. Pauline Réage, *The Story of O*, trans. Sabine d'Estrée (New York: Ballantine Books, 1965), p. 4.

would like to see you completely naked.... Take your skirt off, now...,"
etc. It's in this way that desire passes through (the desire of the reader,
of the voyeur). The drowned eyes, the oval of the face, the tip of the
breasts, the little hat and retro vest, the spike heels, everything is soaked
in the acoustic.

A metonymy so dazzling seizes the voice that O receives and takes in
her desire. From where does it come, this voice of subjugation? From
everywhere: less from the lips than from the hand, the nails, the
cigarette, the naked feet, the bathrobe tie, or a flower in the room.
Crepax has reconstituted the path of the sadomasochistic interlocution.[27]

Barthes's metonymic appraisal of O represents the far-flung fragments of her deconstituted body as the result of so many suturing oral interventions. The disjunctive, staccato commands of the God-Voice (a primal, preoedipal father?) cut the woman's body into segments each fetishized in turn in the line of the gaze. Now if we extrapolate Barthes's message to Irigaray's texts, we might conclude that the language of masochism literalizes the figure of a woman's mouth (an orifice, O) that is filled by the voice of God, such that *aural* stimulation becomes *oral* pleasure. By letting God speak through her, Irigaray has, in so many words, submitted to a "once-over" with "voice-over."

Perhaps the occupation of a female body by a God voice releases woman from the confines of essentialism. Perhaps this protean body talk yields a kind of ludic apotheosis, freeing up women to "play the mistress" or the "master" as they wish. Jane Gallop, in her book *Thinking through the Body*, intimates that an outlaw pleasure may be derived from feminist masochism, a kind of *épater le féminisme* effect.[28] Certainly the implicit argument of the lesbian sadomasochist manifestos seems to be that women are no longer in bondage; rather, it is bondage that is in drag. Seen in this light, Irigaray's *mysteria* is recast as a kind of cross-dressed Lacanianism, a feminist masquerade in which women ventriloquize the voices of divine authority.

We have apparently strayed far afield from the world of nineteenth-century Rome, with its baroque stage sets and parade of bourgeoises stricken by "theomania."[29] But the question of fetishized

27. Roland Barthes, "Crepax," in *Roland Barthes, Le Texte et l'image* (Paris: Pavillon des Arts, 1986), pp. 102–103.
28. Jane Gallop, *Thinking through the Body* (New York: Columbia University Press, 1988).
29. See Frank Bowman, "Une lecture politique de la folie religieuse ou 'théomanie,'" *Romantisme*, no. 24 (1979): 75–88.

masochism posed by the Goncourts' novel still seems remarkably relevant to debates within current feminist theory. Has Irigaray, cast as a latter-day Madame Gervaisais, exercised her will in practicing the religious *exercitium* (in the Ignatian sense of prostrated discourse)? Or is her erotic contract with the voice of God flawed, a form of blind obedience to the "exercitive" (J. L. Austin's generic category for command language), masquerading in its turn as a "commissive" or covenant language? Ultimately, I think she, like her fictional forbear, has fallen for the Ignatian promise of an erotic reprieve at the final stage of ascesis. According to Barthes, during this "anagogic" phase of the religious *exercitium* acoustic pleasure floods consciousness: "Hearing turns into its own answer, and from being suspensive, the interrogation becomes somehow assertive, question and answer enter into a tautological balance: the divine sign finds itself completely absorbed in its hearing."[30] Though this pleasure may be real enough, in the end it strikes me as coercively contracted; extracted, that is, through the exercise of divine phallogocentric muscle rather than through an agreement in which both parties are freely bound.

But to make the feminist case in a backhanded way, one could say that Irigaray's social contract exchanges her identity as a feminist theorist against that of a female mystic, one of those elect few whose masochism earns them a place in a unique pantheon of feminine letters. The transcendental female voice to which Irigaray adds her own may thus be traced back in the French literary tradition not only to *Madame Gervaisais* but to Héloïse, Madame de Lafayette's Princesse de Clèves, Gide's Alissa in *La Porte étroite*, Colette Peignot's Laure, and Pauline Réage's infamous O.[31] Such a voice, even as it seeks to blot itself out, stands out against the backdrop of the male canon, articulating a credo of feminine pleasure.

30. Roland Barthes, *Sade, Fourier, Loyola* (New York: Hill and Wang, 1976), p. 75.
31. Much could be made of the "mistress" phenomenon in French letters as far as theoretical masochism is concerned. Colette Peignot was the ill-fated "mistress" of Bataille. She died in his bed, and it is rumored that she had offered herself as the willing victim of a human sacrifice "experiment" planned (but purportedly never executed) by Bataille and several cohorts from the Collège de Sociologie. Réage was the putative "mistress" of Jean Paulhan, whose preface to *The Story of O* is included in the Ballantine edition.

CHAPTER 7

· Hysterical Vision:
The Scopophilic Garden
from Monet to Mirbeau

· In his attempt to give ocular disorders a psychoanalytical interpretation, Freud cited the tale of Lady Godiva. This "beautiful legend," he wrote, "tells how all the town's inhabitants hid behind their shuttered windows, so as to make easier the lady's task of riding naked through the streets in broad daylight, and how the only man who peeped through the shutters at her revealed loveliness was punished by going blind."[1] For Freud, the fate of the renegade voyeur illustrated how scopophilia (the "love of looking") is punished by the ego with blindness or, in the term popularized by his teacher Jean-Martin Charcot, with *scotomization* (from the Greek *skotos*, meaning "darkness"; signifying partial, distorted, or peripheral vision within the field of ophthalmology). Moving beyond the studies of hysterical vision made by Charcot and Pierre Janet between 1887 and 1889, which merely identified characteristic symptoms such as color blindness, dilated pupils, strabismus, and the twisting of the orb to reveal the whites of the eye, Freud inferred the law of *lex talionis* (*Urteilverwerfung*), literally, "retaliation," in the condemnation of a visual representation deemed sexually culpable by the faculty of judgment. This "verdict of guilty," strangely recalling the old wives' tale that masturbation leads to blindness, also evokes as its corollary the equally proverbial notion

1. Sigmund Freud, "The Psycho-Analytic View of Psychogenic Disturbance of Vision" (1910), *Standard Edition* 11:217. Further references to this essay will be to this edition and will be abbreviated "DV."

of "turning a blind eye." For Freud, however, these sayings were the folkloric expressions of a malady that was not only individual but also collective. If in the private world of the self the punishments for *Schaulust* (hunger of the gaze) imposed by the ego assumed the form of hysteria, in the public realm they signaled a crisis of judgment, an imbalance in the careful treaty made by civilization between sexual drives and their institutional sublimation.

Charcot's *scotome scintillant*, characterized as an *éblouissement de ténèbres* (dazzle of shadow) clouding the eyes of his female hysterics, became a privileged sign of personal and public psychosis within the early history of psychoanalysis.[2] Comparing the scotoma to a "fortification à la Vauban," Charcot made a drawing of this "ophthalmic migraine" as a hatched and broken spiral: "a luminous image, first circular, then semicircular, in the form of a zigzag; like the drawing of a fortification flickering in a very rapid, vibrating movement. An image sometimes phosphorescent, sometimes offering shades of yellow, red or blue of varying densities. That is what we call the scintillating scotoma."[3] This scotoma, interfering with the visual field, was associated by Charcot with the first stages of hysteria, the *douleur*, or irritation of the eye, that commenced the *aura hysterica*. From Charcot to René Laforgue, the scotoma was so matter-of-factly taken by the French psychoanalytical school as the visual sign of repression that it provoked a five-year dispute between Freud and Laforgue, who insisted, despite Freud's objections, on translating *Verdrängung* (repression) as "scotomization."[4] Lacan, perhaps complicitous with Laforgue in his desire to "re-Frenchify" denial and disavowal, revived the term *scotoma*, using it as a metaphor for consciousness.[5] Consciousness, as a variant of

2. See Georges Didi-Huberman's discussion of Charcot's drawing of the *scotome scintillant* and sensation of an *éblouissement de ténèbres* in *Invention de l'hystérie* (Paris: Macula, 1982), p. 132.
3. Jean-Martin Charcot, "Leçons sur les maladies du système nerveux," *Oeuvres complètes*, 9 vols. (Paris: Bureaux du Progrès médical, 1885–1890), 3:74, quoted in Didi-Huberman, *Invention de l'hystérie*, p. 283.
4. The debate between Freud and Laforgue can be found in their correspondence (1923–37), published in French in *Nouvelle Revue de Psychanalyse*, no. 15 (Spring 1977): 251–314.
5. Jacques Lacan, "Anamorphosis," in *The Four Fundamental Concepts of Psychoanalysis*, ed. Jacques-Alain Miller, trans. Alan Sheridan (New York: Norton, 1978), pp. 82–83. Here Lacan writes of the *scotoma*: "Psycho-analysis regards the consciousness as irremediably limited, and institutes it as a principle, not only of idealization, but of *méconnaissance*, as—using a term that takes on new value by being referred to a visible domain—*scotoma*. The term was introduced into the psycho-analytic vocabulary by the French School. Is it simply a metaphor? We find here once again the

Sartrean *méconnaissance*, slides into a model of "seeingness" (*voyure*), in which the scotoma marks the vanishing point where the eye catches itself offguard in the act of seeing itself see itself: "As the locus of the relation between me, the annihilating subject, and that which surrounds me, the gaze seems to possess such a privilege that it goes so far as to have me scotomized. I who look, the eye of him who sees me as object. In so far as I am under the gaze, Sartre writes, I no longer see the eye that looks at me and, if I see the eye, the gaze disappears" (*FFC* 84).

The scotomized Lacanian subject is caught in a contentious struggle for mastery between the eye and the gaze that parallels Charcot's dialectic between scopophilia and scotomization. Both metaphor for and visible evidence of repression, the scotoma, as Lacan uses the term, plays on an ambiguity already introduced by Charcot, where the physical sight of the brilliant *aura* was interpreted both as manifestation of, and punishment for, hysteria. Signs of the "essential vacillation of the gaze," Lacan's spots emerge throughout his writings as blind. Stains, punctiforms, sutures, splits, butterflies ("primal stripes...on the grid of desire") [*FFC* 76]), or points of irradiation from which "reflections pour forth, overflowing the ocular bowl" (*FFC* 94), these *taches*, or spots, are the unmistakable evidence of castrated vision. Within the Lacanian lexicon, male and female viewer alike hystericize the scopic field in an effort to "camouflage" (Lacan's term) the spectacle of phallic lack.

Scotomization, the process of visual occlusion that punishes private or public *voyure-isme*, was subtly politicized and institutionalized in the overlapping spheres of sexual and national politics at the end of the nineteenth century. As many recent studies have shown, women whose sexual inclinations led them to affront social mores (the example of Camille Claudel is among the most notorious) were commonly chastised with protracted sojourns in a psychiatric ward. Once there, they stood a good chance of becoming subjects in an array of casually sadistic experiments that were being performed at the time by Charcot and his disciples. Alfred Binet, for example, shortly after completing his work on fetishism, investigated the related problem of hysterical vision—what he called *la vision mentale*—through a series of tests in which the bodies of his female hysterics were scarified with needles. Jabbing the skin here

---

ambiguity that affects anything that is inscribed in the register of the scopic drive." Further references to this work will be abbreviated *FFC*.

and there to determine the nature and degree of sensation and response, pricking the "hysterically anaesthetized" zones of the anatomy (believed to demarcate lesions severing feeling from intelligence) with "the point of a compass," Binet interpreted the body's translation of pain into dizzying flickers as the cipher of inner perception (Wilhelm Wundt's *innerer Blickpunkt* or *points de fixation interne*). Attempting to decode the dense spray of variegated spots (*taches*) induced by these violent *piqûres* (punctures), he compared (with unnerving detachment) the hysteric's body to a mystic writing pad on which the doctor could transcribe at will. "If we trace a character or letter on the skin, the subject will see this same character or letter on the visual screen," he wrote of this female tracing paper. Prodding more gingerly still, he discovered that "if one presses harder, one obtains dots or spots that become darker, almost black, resembling trails of ink that would leave a stain on paper."[6]

Despite his efforts to "read" transparently the female body in pain, Binet failed to forge any significant theoretical connections between mental vision, scotomization, and fetishism. His references to Wundt's work on interior visual fixation, however, imply a fetishism no longer concentrated on exterior objects but, rather, congested and turned inward on itself. As if punished for lingering on an object of desire in the outside world, Binet's hysteric scotomizes her inner field of vision, bathing the focused image in a wash of scintillating dots. Though he himself never articulated the plausible bridge between hysterical vision and visual repression, one can discern in Binet's description of this inverted fetishism of the eye a mechanism of retribution not dissimilar to *lex talionis*.

The medical establishment's obliviousness to the mistreatment of women in the course of its investigations of hysterical vision forms a seemingly not so arbitrary counterpart to the scales that descended over the political eyes of a nation at the time of the Dreyfus affair. Here I am referring specifically to the way in which the French public, as if afflicted by hysterical vision (itself the apparent result of a blinding nationalism), refused to believe the evidence of its own eyes: that the memoranda used to inculpate Dreyfus were obvious forgeries. Looking back on some of the more significant literary

---

6. Alfred Binet, "La Vision mentale: Recherches sur les altérations de la conscience chez les hystériques," *Revue Philosophique* 27 (Apr. 1889): 347, 351. I am grateful to Jann Matlock for bringing this essay to my attention.

portrayals of the trial, we can see that both sides in the affair were conscious of the critical role played by optical repression. Proust in *Jean Santeuil* developed a disquisition on the theory of *lex talionis* in relation to the popular condemnation of Colonel Picquart, Dreyfus's solitary defender within the ranks of the French army:

· It is a sort of Law of Compensation—a *lex talionis*—in the world of moral values, that those, no matter how intelligent or how sensitive they may be, who as the result of laziness or for some other reason have no inner, no disinterested activity on which to employ their minds, inevitably in their judgments of life attach enormous importance to the merely formal.... Votes, regular attendance at meetings or sessions, indispensable calls on possible supporters, canvassing, party cries—all these are so many refuges in which we shelter from the dread necessity of turning our eyes inwards.[7]

Moving from a general theory of how outward patriotic display acts as a cover for inward ethical occlusion, to the particular blind spots applied to Picquart's trial, Proust offers a performative enactment of *lex talionis*, registering the visual "shock" provoked by the life-sized Picquart:

· There he was in the flesh, one of the general throng. It came to him [Jean Santeuil] with something of a shock that he could do nothing to modify that physical fact, each feature of which, the reddish complexion, the easy carriage of the head, made him feel almost embarrassed, such violence did they do to his imagination which so long accustomed to visualize the Colonel in a certain way had now to submit to a reality which it could not alter at will.[8]

Proust, a well-known Dreyfus supporter, was astonishingly close to his ideological opponent, Maurice Barrès, in his use of this language of visual violence to describe the affair. Barrès invoked the law of "optical aphasia" with respect to Dreyfus's assumed incapacity to respond to national values and symbols: "Il n'est point perméable à toutes les excitations dont nous affectent notre terre, nos ancêtres, notre drapeau, le mot 'honneur' [He is not remotely susceptible to the feelings roused in us by our land, our forefa-

7. Marcel Proust, "Colonel Picquart," in *Jean Santeuil*, trans. Gerard Hopkins (Harmondsworth: Penguin, 1985), p. 328.
8. Ibid., p. 335.

thers, the flag, or the word 'honor']."⁹ Though placed out of sight and for the most part out of mind on Devil's Island, Dreyfus kept resurfacing as a "fly in the eye" of the nation.

The intersection of scopic field and political hysteria, one used as specular allegory of the other, was dramatically exploited in Octave Mirbeau's Dreyfusard novel *Le Jardin des supplices* (*The Torture Garden*). Joining the ranks of better-known novels focusing on the affair by Proust, Anatole France, Roger Martin du Gard, Léon Blum, Charles Péguy, and Romain Rolland, *Le Jardin des supplices*, published in 1899, merits close reading not because its Dreyfusard message eludes decipherment but, rather, because its Dreyfusism is uncomfortably embedded in what was deemed to be a pornographic narrative.¹⁰ Political argument seems to be undercut by sadomasochistic fantasy, where (as Gilles Deleuze says of Sacher-Masoch's *Venus in Furs*) "history, politics, mysticism, eroticism, nationalism and perversion are closely intermingled, forming a nebula around the scenes of flagellation."¹¹ In Mirbeau's text, the cross-contamination of pornography and politics serves to aestheticize, to "psychiatrize," and ultimately to destabilize its ideological stance. So, for example, the critique of pathology and difference (Jews, poor people, the Orientalist Other), ostensibly the core of Mirbeau's literary project, yields to a psychopoetics of display and exhibition, a dynamic of seeing and looking that merits consideration as a kind of Lacanianism *avant la lettre*.¹² Whether the objects of scopic fascination are flowers exquisitely rendered with impressionist facture or tortured Chinese victims exposed before the public, the perverse curiosity of the gaze—the viewer's indulgence in scopophilic pleasure—is dramatically exploited even as it is put theoretically and politically into question.

---

9. Maurice Barrès, *Scènes et doctrines du nationalisme* (Paris: Félix Guven, 1902), p. 140.

10. For an analysis of literary representations of the Dreyfus affair, see Susan Rubin Suleiman's essay "The Literary Significance of the Dreyfus Affair," in *The Dreyfus Affair: Art, Truth, and Justice*, ed. Norman L. Kleeblatt (Berkeley: University of California Press, 1987), pp. 117–39.

11. Gilles Deleuze, *Masochism: An Interpretation of Coldness and Cruelty*, trans. Jean McNeil (New York: George Braziller, 1971), p. 10.

12. Rosalind Krauss provocatively treated the theme "Exhibit/Exhibitionism," in relation to Duchamp's *Etant Donné*, in a lecture delivered at a conference entitled "Mostly Modernism and Some Post," organized by Mary Ann Caws at the Graduate Center of the City University of New York, New York, Mar. 25, 1988.

Octave Mirbeau (1848–1917) was born the son of a Norman notary in the Calvados region of France. Militarist, monarchist, and xenophobe, he began his career as a journalist for newspapers of right-wing tendency. A founding editor of the weekly newspaper *Les Grimaces* in 1883, he became famous for his virulently anti-Semitic articles. He launched ad hominem attacks on the Rothschilds, pictured France the victim of speculators in league with the Jews, and accused his country of having made Judaism a state religion. In 1896, at the height of the Dreyfus affair, he made a political about-face and joined the Dreyfusards. He also became an activist surveyed by the police for anarchist causes, regularly contributing prefaces, pamphlets, and political fables to books or journals on the Left—and also a friend of Mallarmé, as well as many other symbolist writers. His *Le Jardin des supplices* is at once symbolist in tone and a parody of literary decadence. A similar ambivalence of attitude marked his articles on impressionism, through which artists such as Rodin, Cézanne, and Monet gained considerable visibility in the public eye. His plays and novels were immensely popular at the turn of the century—a stylistic mixture of naturalist metaphor and verbal invective.

Mirbeau criticized the middle-class view of poverty (as some kind of disease or anomalous condition) by using the motif of the *tache* as a fatal sign. Portraying it as a bourgeois taboo or zone of cultural fetishism surfacing on the body politic as a blight, he satirized the view of such *taches* as exteriorized manifestations of an inner social shame. In *Les Vingt et Un Jours d'un neurasthénique* (1902), a later work comprised of loosely associated vignettes much like his more famous novel *Le Journal d'une femme de chambre* (1901), poverty is diagnosed by a sadistic doctor as a cranial degeneration whose most discernible symptoms consist of "une série de taches noirâtres qui se présentèrent au cerveau et sur tout l'appareil cérébro-spinal [a series of blackish spots that manifest themselves on the brain and the entire cerebral spinal system]."[13] Doctor Triceps compares these same *taches noirâtres* to sunspots or patches of dirt that he proposes to "clean off" as part of the "cure."

In a very early political fable entitled "Tatou" (1896), poverty and misfortune leave their atavistic trace in the nickname of an exploited

13. Mirbeau, *Les Vingt et Un Jours d'un neurasthénique* (Paris: Union Générale d'Editions, 1977), p. 293.

child who comes to work as a shepherdess for the narrator. Tatou suffers from amnesia: she has no recollection of how she came by her name, her skin bears no tattoo, and her physiognomy suggests no exotic origin. When the narrator succeeds, however, in piecing together fragments of her personal history, he is amazed at the disjunction between her "tattooed" past and her innocent, "unspotted" character. Indeed, only the name is left as a signifier of a childhood "scarred" by rape and abuse.[14] With "Tatou," a story typical of the récits published by Mirbeau in the 1890s, the *tache* as a kind of tribal marking of lower-class oppression merges with its symbolism of legal and social injustice, for which the historical catalyst was the Dreyfus affair.

Le Jardin des supplices qualifies as pornographic more in terms of certain stylistic and structural similarities to a Sadian text than in terms of its erotic content. Just as the Marquis de Sade had devised a syntax of tortures and sexual perversions classifiable, repeatable, and combinatorial like the elements of a language, so Mirbeau, in his description of a Chinese prison, enumerates infinite variations of punishment and debauchery in a tone of deliberately affected irony. Starting with prosaic forms—whipping, branding, starving, or garroting—the visitors are soon initiated into more sophisticated torments: the "torture of the caress," consisting of sexually exciting the male member until the prisoner dies of pleasure, or the display in a niche of a naked woman whose genitalia have been abraded:

- Une autre femme, dans une autre niche, les jambes écartées, ou plutôt écartelées, avait le cou et les bras dans des colliers de fer.... Ses paupières, ses narines, ses lèvres, ses parties sexuelles étaient frottées de poivre rouge et deux écrous lui écraisaient la pointe des seins.

- Another woman, in another niche, her legs spreadeagled, or rather quartered, had her neck and arms in iron clamps.... Her eyelids,

---

14. In his article, "Tatou," in *Le Journal*, May 24, 1896, Mirbeau wrote: "By dint of questioning her, I finally understood that she, having left the service of these old establishments, had been employed in tasks that were repugnant and too heavy for her emaciated arms. Here, she had been abused by old men; there, beaten by frightful shrews. But she had harbored in her soul neither the mark of her degradation [*tache des souillures*] nor the hatred of the blows."

nostrils, lips and sexual parts were rubbed with red pepper and her nipples were squeezed by two screws.[15]

The skewered, pried-open figuration of the female sex, fascinating and repellent like Freud's fetish, yet far too "exposed" to function as a fetish, also foreshadows the image of the *speculum*, a term deployed by Luce Irigaray to suggest both the desecration of the female body through barbaric gynecological practice (where "inside" turned "outside" results in "over-exposure") and the more general condition of woman's occlusion throughout history.[16]

Emphasizing his lurid vision through compulsive repetition, Mirbeau replicates these infernal "niches" in miniature as display cabinets in a museum in which exquisitely crafted art treasures are sardonically presented for viewer delectation:

- Ces niches contenaient des bois peints et sculptés, qui représentaient, avec cet effroyable réalisme particulier à l'art de l'Extrême-Orient, tous les genres de torture en usage dans la Chine: scènes de décollation, de strangulation, d'écorchement et de dépècement des chairs.

- These niches contained painted and sculpted wood which, with the frightful realism peculiar to the art of the Far East, represented every genre of torture commonly used in China: scenes of decapitation, strangulation, flaying and tearing of flesh. (*JS* 148).

This museum of horrors, a grotesque counterpart of the Musée de l'Homme or Charcot's clinic, parodies the taxonomy of cultural and psychological curiosities as well as their exhibition to a prurient audience. Charcot's famous "man in a cage" feeding on raw meat before a circus public—a case history of "degeneracy"—finds its mocking parallel in Mirbeau's imprisoned poets, condemned to recite on command in return for rotten scraps.[17] The female

15. Octave Mirbeau, *Le Jardin des supplices* (Paris: Fasquelle, 1949), p. 224. Further references to this work will be abbreviated *JS*.
16. Luce Irigaray, *Speculum of the Other Woman*, trans. Gillian Gill (Ithaca: Cornell University Press, 1985). Though I do not focus here on the complex issue of gender in Mirbeau's oeuvre (he was a blatant misogynist), my use of the expression "blind spots" (*points aveugles*) intentionally "quotes" Irigaray's feminist ascription. See, in particular, her chapter entitled "The Blind Spot of an Old Dream of Symmetry."
17. J. M. Charcot, *Leçons du mardi, 1887–1888: Hystérie et dégénérescence chez l'homme*, in J. M. Charcot, *L'Hystérie*, ed. E. Trillat (Toulouse: Privat, 1971), pp. 143–45.

victims recall Charcot's bevy of performing hysterics, women like the celebrated Alphonsine Bar, Louise Glaiz, and Blanche Wittmann, who were trained to produce convulsions before a curious public.[18]

Lest one read this museum as referring exclusively to Charcot's clinic, it must be remembered that the culture of sadistic, racist iconography, diffused by anti–Third Republic newspapers such as *La Libre Parole, La Croix, Le Petit Journal, Le Courrier Français, Le Cri de Paris, Psst...!* and *Le Sifflet,* had been given a tremendous boost by the Dreyfus affair. As a freak show featuring bestial specimens of humanity, *Le Jardin* explicitly specularizes the anti-Semitic caricatures of popular artists such as Jean-Louis Forain, Adolphe Willette, Henri-Gabriel Ibels, Félix Vallotton, Caran d'Ache, and Gyp. Published in 1899 (the same year as Mirbeau's novel), during Dreyfus's second trial, a set of virulently anti-Semitic posters by the illustrator Lenepveu, marketed as a Musée des Horreurs, must also be read alongside Mirbeau's literary horror show. There is a chilling resemblance between the images of these cartoons and those of Mirbeau's novel.[19] Where Lenepveu's illustrations depict Jews and Dreyfusards as shit-ingesting pigs (Emile Zola), bovine females (Séverine), drunken elephants (Jean Jaurès), and cloven-footed demons (Picquart, Joseph Reinach, Dreyfus, and others), Mirbeau presents a breviary of dehumanized prisoners wallowing in their own excrement and confined in cages like animals in a zoo.[20]

Le Jardin's diegesis is structured, then, around the central image of a zoological museum for which the narrator must furnish new exotic specimens. A corrupt politician masquerading as a Darwinian comparative embryologist, the narrator has been implicated in a scandal and banished to the Orient to discover "the origin of life." On board ship he encounters Clara, a pre-Raphaelite femme fatale, who, after seducing him, enjoins him to accompany her to the torture garden, itself hierarchically structured like Dante's Inferno to provide a public panorama of increasingly grotesque tortures. Mirbeau's lightly veiled allegories of political corruption, presented under the guise of a visit to the East, were undoubtedly recognizable to contemporary readers; so too was the implied comparison of

---

18. For a discussion of this "living pathological museum," see Joan Copjec's "Flavit et Dissipati Sunt," *October,* no. 18 (Fall 1981): 20–40.
19. When Mirbeau reversed his position during the Dreyfus affair, many suspected him of trying to protect his place among the literary ranks that supported Zola.
20. See Kleeblatt, *The Dreyfus Affair,* pp. 244–52.

the garden to a combination of Charcot's Salpêtrière and the newly instituted Musée Guimet. Mirbeau notes the latter by name in the novel, but only for litotic effect; the Guimet Museum's famous collections are deprecatingly evoked, so as to deepen our appreciation of the truly dazzling *Gesamtkunstwerk* of suffering proffered by the Chinese garden.

The novel's frontispiece, a curious text in its own right, "exhibits" the latest fashionable theories, from Social Darwinism (*sélectionnisme*) to naturalism and anti-Semitism. Assembled in a salon, literati spar over subjects such as the destiny of the species, the female sex, and racial typology. A loquacious philosopher advances the opinion that all men are potential assassins, substantiating his claim by identifying the fatal "stigmata" ("in the look, the neck, the shape of the cranium, the maxillaries, the zygoma of the cheeks") that mark the faces of any crowd chosen at random (*JS* 10). Here again we encounter an implied political critique of the psychiatric establishment couched in a language of visual semiotics.[21] In a parody of clinical discourse, Mirbeau elides the theories of Hippolyte Bernheim and Paul Aubry—who wrote on the "contagion of murder" in the early 1890s—with the notions of criminal physiognomy developed by characterologists such as Cesare Lombroso and Gina Lombroso Ferrero. In an era when Alphonse Bertillon (an employee of the Paris police department and "handwriting expert" during the Dreyfus affair) was putting Lombroso's methods to disciplinary use, perfecting the photographic recording of criminal traits and compiling precise, detailed inventories of prisoners' handwriting, fingerprints, tattoos, and phrenological contours, Mirbeau's satire alludes implicitly

21. In 1898 Mirbeau wrote a short pro-Dreyfus allegory that differs substantially from *Le Jardin* in that sadoerotic sensationalism is notably absent. In this disturbing short story, "La Vache tachetée" (The spotted cow), however, the motif of the "blind spot" is already clearly in evidence. A Kafkaesque scenario, it revolves around the putative guilt of a man who, to his own knowledge, has committed no crime. Jacques Errant, an evident personification of the "Juif errant," is arrested and imprisoned without apparent reason. The details bear a chilling resemblance to those of Dreyfus's incarceration. From his jailkeeper Jacques Errant learns only that this is a period when the state is imprisoning all those who tell the truth: "Et que vous n'ayez pas, non plus, une vache tachetée," the guard admonishes, "parce que voilà encore une chose qui n'est pas bonne par le temps qui court [and what's more, you don't own a spotted cow, because that's another thing that is not good in these times]." Reassured because he owns no spotted cow, Errant awaits his trial. But the spotted cow, the sacred cow, or *vache d'or* (forbidden object of representation according to Mosaic law: a sign of the "erring" of the "chosen people"), is none other than Jacques himself.

to the racial caricatures of Dreyfus by cartoonists and legal experts alike.[22]

What is distinctive about Mirbeau's rendering of these pseudoscientific practices is his conversion of the particularism of traits attributed to the Jew, or "born assassin," into a generalized morphology applicable to the whole of humanity. Just as Lombroso had isolated the "born prostitute" according to hereditary abnormalities similar to those of the female "savage" in primitive societies—protuberant jaws, cysts, crooked teeth, large hips, obesity, excessive hairiness, and abundant tattoos—so Mirbeau isolates the "signs" of the murderer.[23] But by universalizing his pathology, he undermines the entire psychophysiognomical method, which depends on specificity, on the isolation of difference, deviation, and anomaly. This travesty of socioracial typology points the frontispiece to its fundamental, Dreyfusard tenet: criminality is not measurable according to positivistic methods; neither handwriting tests nor anatomical indexes defined in terms of class, race, or religion qualify as legitimate proof, for man is universally murderous and loath to relinquish his favorite sport—scapegoating. "Never," Mirbeau's philosopher pontificates, "was the passion for blood and the joy of the chase so completely and cynically displayed as in the Dreyfus affair [L'affaire Dreyfus, jamais, je crois, la passion du meurtre et la joie de la chasse à l'homme, ne s'étaient aussi complètement et cyniquement étalées]" (*JS* 15).

Displayed (*étalé*)—this choice of adjective, like the word *stigmata*, becomes increasingly significant. Linked to a cosmic theory of what might be called *thanatophilia*, the scapegoating instinct as manifest in the persecution of Dreyfus is part of a larger problem of the visual lure or bait. Like the "displayed" female sex organs in the garden, the spectacle of a martyred, battered Dreyfus attracts a hungry crowd. In the frontispiece, the philosopher evokes these visually salivating hordes as they "play" on the fairground, forsaking the merry-go-rounds and swings for target sport: "Everywhere, under

---

22. For an analysis of this classificatory tradition earlier in the nineteenth century, see Richard Sieburth's "Same Difference: The French *Physiologies*, 1840–1842," in *Notebooks in Cultural Analysis* 1 (1985): 163–200 n. 1.

23. Cesare Lombroso and Gina Lombroso Ferrero, *La Femme criminelle et la prostituée* (Paris, 1896) as cited by Alain Corbin, *Les Filles de noce* (Paris: Flammarion, 1978), p. 442. See also Hippolyte Bernheim, "La Suggestion criminelle," *Revue de Hypnotisme* 4 (1890): 243–301, and Paul Aubry, *La Contagion du meurtre* (Paris: Alcan, 1894).

the tents and illuminated boutiques, were the dummies of corpses [*des simulacres de mort*], parodies of massacre, representations of hecatombs.... Were these good people ever happy!" (*JS* 11). The reflections of Lacan on the workings of *invidia*, or the evil eye, provide a particularly appropriate gloss on Mirbeau's "games": "How could this *showing* satisfy something, if there is not some appetite of the eye on the part of the person looking?" he queries. His own answer, with its continuation of the gustatory trope, seems to echo the equation between hunger and sight set up in *Le Jardin* during the initial Tantalus episode: "This appetite of the eye that must be fed," Lacan writes, "produces the hypnotic value of painting. For me, this value is to be sought on a much less elevated plane than might be supposed, namely, in that which is the true function of the organ of the eye, the eye filled with voracity, the evil eye" (*FFC* 115). Consonant with the Lacanian evil eye, the restless orb of Mirbeau's heroine ("with a glint drunk with joy") projects the image of its own appetite, even as it "feasts" on the voracious stares of the starving prisoners: "simultaneously, twenty eyeballs, each starting out of their sockets, were hurled at the meat, shooting red glances, fixated glances of hunger and fear" (*JS* 145). The entire spectacle, reflected *en abyme*, is witnessed by a covey of society ladies enticed by this *comédie bouffe*: "Curious women followed the movements of this cruel game with an attentive and delighted air [Des curieuses suivaient toutes les péripéties de ce jeu cruel, d'un air attentif et réjoui]" (*JS* 146–47).

Through its black representation of popular pastimes, *Le Jardin* reinforces the notion of the crowd's scopophilic attraction to mangled and mutilated quarry. A sado-erotic rhetoric prevails, featuring murder (the ultimate "lure" of desire) as an end to sexual fever and tortuous insatisfaction:

- Et c'est l'homme-individu, et c'est l'homme-foule, et c'est la bête, la plante, l'élément, toute la nature enfin, qui, poussée par les forces cosmiques de l'amour, se rue au meurtre, croyant ainsi trouver hors la vie, un assouvissement aux furieux désirs de vie qui la dévorent et qui jaillissent, d'elle, en des jets de sale écume!

- And it's man-individual, and it's man-crowd, and it's the animal, the plant, the element, all of nature in the end, which, prompted by the cosmic forces of love, hurls itself at murder, hoping to find outside of life, a means of satisfying the furious desires within life, desires that devour and spurt, like jets of dirty foam! (*JS* 231).

Here, the "dirty foam" (*sale écume*), the sperm of a frustrated nature, which—as a result of being so long imprisoned—turns to blood, doubles as the politically valorized master *tache*—the "ineffacable red spot"—that appears, as in *Macbeth*, on the ghostly bodies of the narrator's past acquaintances, all innocent victims like Dreyfus.

Mirbeau's intersection of scapegoating and *voyure-isme* reveals the pornographic cast of anti-Semitism, emphasizing its identification in the popular unconscious with visual obscenity and implicating, as accessories to the crime, all reader-viewers "caught in the act of looking." Mirbeau's scopic critique was directed, however, not only at the immediate scandal of the Dreyfus affair, but also toward the domestic repercussions of the colonial expansion of previous decades. While Dreyfus himself was banished to a distant colony, a tropical wasteland where he languished for five years in a fetid hut, his legs in shackles and his lucidity dissipated by swamp fever, Mirbeau was intent on demonstrating that the most deplorable wasteland, the moral one, was located in the heart of France. To the heinous sin of scapegoating, he added the crimes of empire: colonial exploitation, enslavement, racism, and the annihilation of indigenous cultures. Systematically, he brought the catalog of barbaric practices associated by the average Frenchman with tribal societies—human sacrifice, idolatry, rape, cannibalism—home, so to speak, to Europe.

Thus in the course of a motorcar tour through Belgium in *La 628-E-8* (1907), Mirbeau conflated French anti-Semitism and "primitive" human sacrifice. Picaresque in genre and jovial in tone, the novel yields suddenly and unexpectedly to an account of the pogroms in Russia narrated by an old Jew in the city of Anvers. Tsarist brigands sack his store, rape and murder his wife, shoot his sons, and commit atrocities on his daughter: "his daughter, poor Sarah, was found on his stall, dead among the vegetables and crushed fruits, and they even had the force to ram the stumps of her legs into her gaping stomach."[24] Here again Mirbeau employs the shocking device of display, scotomizing the horrified, hypnotized gaze of the reader-viewer. Wincing at the spectacle, we divert our gaze, only to have our eyes fall on another chilling vignette, entitled "Red Rubber." In this story, a kind of Baudelairean *flâneur* traps us beguilingly with a visual curiosity in the course of an innocent urban promenade:

24. Octave Mirbeau, *La 628-E-8* (Paris: Union Générale d'Editions, 1977), p. 183. Further references will be abbreviated *L6*.

Hysterical Vision · 161

- Je m'arrête devant une petite boutique, dont l'étalage est étrange: des pyramides de petits meubles, petits cubes, petits cylindres, petits parallélipipèdes, petits pains d'une matière mate, alternativement grise et noire. Rien d'autre. Pas d'indication. Aucune étiquette.

- I stop in front of a little boutique whose display is strange: there are pyramids of little objects, little squares, little cylinders, little parallelepipeds, little mounds of dull matter, alternately gray and black. Nothing else. No sign. No label. (L6 146)

The banality of these objects, displayed in the window of an ordinary hardware store in Belgium, is contradicted by the narrator's inexplicable fixation on them: "I couldn't tear my eyes away from these pieces of rubber," he confesses (L6 147). Following an intuition ("'Congo, right?' 'Yes,' the shopkeeper replied simply, but proudly"), he ascertains the strange and forbidding origin of the rubber. As if not wanting to believe the evidence of his own eyes, but impelled nonetheless, he projects before our already traumatized retina a scene of unsuspecting African men and women, one minute smiling, dancing, and marveling at the array of European goods, the next moment butchered by the colonizer:

- Nettement, dans une plaque grise, dans une boule noire, j'ai distingué le tronc trop joli d'une négresse violée et décapitée, et j'ai vu aussi des vieux, mutilés, agonisants, dont craquent les membres secs. Et il me faut fermer les yeux pour échapper à la vision de toutes ces horreurs, dont ces échantillons de caoutchouc qui sont là, si immobiles, si neutres, se sont brusquement animés.

- In the bits and pieces of gray and black rubber, I clearly distinguished the beautiful torso of a raped and decapitated negress, and I also saw old people, mutilated and agonizing, their dry limbs cracking. And I had to close my eyes to escape the sight of all these horrors, hidden in the rows of rubber there in front of me, so still, so neutral, so suddenly animated. (L6 148)

Smitten by *lex talionis*, the narrator no longer succeeds in obfuscating his perception of flesh transformed into rubber. The dull, neutral mass of inert matter that goes into the making of seemingly anodyne and ubiquitous industrial materials—tires, cables, and telephone wires—becomes, like the fetish in Freud's definition, uncannily "animated." A signifier of colonial enslavement as well as of the repressed evidence of European murder (instinctively "blinded" or censored by the Western eye as it navigates the city street), "red rubber" emerges as yet another trope of hysterical vision. Stained by the "red blot" of native blood, the neat stacks of goods that line the shelves of European shops, a kind of demonic transubstantiation, attest to the distortion of vision that has to have occurred in order for Western commerce to accept the debasement of human life to the level of its use value as product, *Stoff*, expendable substance. "If negro blood oils our tires and wires, how good for business!" the narrator expostulates in a simulation of the stalwart burgher whose profit motive triumphs in every European capital. "Can we," he adds, "better assimilate the inferior races to our own civilization, or more usefully absorb them into our lives and commerce?" (*L6* 149). The note of intensified cynicism that accompanies this inversion of barbarism and civilization echoes that of *Le Jardin des supplices*, especially the moment when the master executioner bemoans the "waste of death," that is, the killing *without* torture, characteristic of modern times.

Wherever brutality appears comfortingly distant in an exotic setting—Africa or the Orient—Mirbeau relentlessly re-displaces it back to Europe, thereby underscoring civilization's universal blindness to cruelty. But this blindness, in the context of Mirbeau's moral critique of inhumanity, never remains at the level of simple ignorance. The narrator of *Le Jardin des supplices*, like the enlightened *flâneur* of "Red Rubber," has the scales of oblivion removed from his eyes only to lose the didactic drift of the horrifying spectacle before him. As if "forgetting" the conclusion he is meant to draw at the sight of Clara's sadistic *jouissance*, the narrator is seduced (drawn in, as if by a "lure") by her sublime aesthetic of cruelty. Swathed in fashionable *belle époque* colors, Clara's gilded person comes at the price of the viewer's moral anaesthetization. Mirbeau heightens this dilemma by crafting a demonic analogy between the blood-red highlights of her hair and the "spots of blood" that stain her elegant footwear as, a Gradiva of the East, she glides through the debris of rotting skulls, quivering brains, and fresh pools of blood in the torture garden. Even this staining of the foot is a double profanation, for Clara is shod in slippers of fine, yellow leather, fashioned from the skin of murdered Oriental victims. For Mirbeau, it would seem, the stain marks the spot where scotomization *fails* to censor, and where scopophilia triumphs by showering the eye with a dazzling, decadent spectacle of color and light.

When the narrator first visits the garden of tortures his eye is dazzled (*ébloui*) in a manner that strangely recalls the *éblouissement de ténèbres* (blinding by shadows) identified with Charcot's hysterical scotoma:

> Je regardais, ébloui de la lumière plus douce, du ciel plus clément, ébloui même des grandes ombres bleues que les arbres, mollement, allongeaient sur l'herbe, ainsi que de paresseux tapis; ébloui de la féerie mouvante des fleurs.... Je regardais avidement, sans jamais me lasser.

> I looked, dazzled; dazzled by the sweetest light, the clearest sky, dazzled even by the great blue shadows that the trees laid softly on the grass, like voluptuous carpets; dazzled by the shimmering phantasmagoria of the flowers.... I gazed greedily, never tiring. (*JS* 161)

Such a representation, almost painterly in its evocation of an impressionist scene, returns us to Lacan's characterization of "how the appetite of the eye ... produces the hypnotic value of a painting." Hysterical vision and hypnotic fixation come together in this impression-showered garden. Was Mirbeau, then, adding impressionism as yet another level of symbolic pastiche to his multitiered specular allegory? As before, it is the spot that draws the reader into complicity with scopophilic looking.

It was a commonplace of late-nineteenth-century criticism to characterize the impressionists as "spot makers."[25] The Goncourt brothers employed the term in a pejorative sense in *Manette Salomon*, when Coriolus conquers the public with an Ingres-style painting that allows him to transcend the category of a mere *faiseur de taches* (maker of spots). Akin to another preferred keyword of the Goncourts, *plaque* (meaning "plaster appliqué," "veneer"), *tache* correlated impressionist impasto with the flaky epidermis of a syphilis victim.[26]

---

25. In the Goncourts' *Journal* (May 8, 1888) we find the following references to the impressionists as "faiseurs de taches:" "Ah! the good impressionists! There are no artists like them! Amusing artists who have never been able *to realize* much of anything.... Because the difficulty of art is in the realization: the work of art pushed to this degree of completion that goes beyond the outline or the sketch in order to make a picture.... Yes, these sketchers, these makers of spots, and still more spots that they haven't invented, spots stolen from Goya and the Japanese" [my translation]. Edmond de Goncourt and Jules de Goncourt, *Journal*, 3 vols. (Paris: Robert Laffont, 1989), 3:121. All further references will be abbreviated *J*.

26. See Jean-Pierre Richard, "Deux écrivains épidermiques: Edmond et Jules de Goncourt," in *Littérature et sensation* (Paris: Seuil, 1954), pp. 266–83.

The critic Albert Wolff evoked this image of cadaverous skin in reference to Renoir's variegated rendering of shadow: "Just try," he urged in his article on the second major impressionist show (1876), "to explain to M. Renoir that a woman's torso is not a discomposing mass of flesh covered with black and blue marks and conjuring up a putrefied corpse!"[27] The *tache* was also maligned by Claretie, who castigated Manet for his reliance on this egregiously nonrepresentational sign.[28]

Huysmans, reiterating the general reaction in his *L'Art moderne*, and availing himself of a self-ironizing rhetoric of excess not unlike Mirbeau's, saw in the impressionist effort to paint the depth, transparency, and evanescence of light and color nothing but opacity—a sickly pallor that clung to the surface of the canvas. Subjecting Monet's feminine subjects to a gaze both violent and violating, Huysmans, as is well known, saw these *femmes-fleurs*, with their faces congested by an infernal blush or chalky with layers of makeup, as resembling the inmates of a clinic, an intimation of his imbricated analogy between madness and impressionism. Referring to the paintings as "touching follies," Huysmans asserted that the "works derived their inspiration from physiology and medicine." Finally, he alluded to Charcot directly despite a stated resolve not to name names: "most of the paintings corroborate Dr. Charcot's experiments on changes in color perception which he noted in many of his hysterics at the Salpêtrière.... They had a malady of the retina."[29]

In ascribing to the impressionists a "malady of the retina," a form of color blindness, Huysmans appears to have been following Charcot, who had himself joined the pathology of hysteria to the study of art. Ranging through the history of art, from medieval *grottesche* to the postures of torture or spiritual euphoria used in conventional hagiography, to his own sketches of female hysterics in positions of anguished contortion, Charcot saw in the iconography of demonic possession a common thread of visual disturbance. Charting each clownish, savage, giddy, or agonistic gesture, Charcot always registered the changes to the eye. In the prelude to the hysterical attack he noted, among other symptoms, the habitual occurrence of an "obnubilation of vision." A drifting into somno-

---

27. As cited by Gustave Geffroy, *Claude Monet: Sa vie, son oeuvre* (Paris: Macula, 1980), p. 87.
28. Ibid., p. 71.
29. J. K. Huysmans, *L'Art moderne* (Paris: Union Générale d'Editions, 1975), p. 103.

lence, or clouding over of consciousness, was followed, according to Charcot and Richer, by visual revulsion: the eye, flipping backward into the head, would send up white shutters as if in retaliation (*lex talionis*) against some terrible mental or moral shock.[30] It was with such a state of scotomization that Huysmans hyperbolically characterized Monet: "occasionally a landscape artist of talent, more often, a man off his rocker, someone who rams his finger into his eye up to the elbow."[31]

The "resolution" of the hysterical attack was, Charcot argued, punctuated by the closing of the eyes, and the entire crisis subject at any moment to the effects of "hallucinations." He referred to the "sad pictures" that moved before his patients' eyes; pictures of fires, wars, revolutions, and assassinations, which, like the hellish images of the torture garden, were spattered everywhere with spots of blood. It is easy to see in these spots the macabre version of Charcot's "dazzling scotoma." In *Les Démoniaques dans l'art* he and Richer noted: "During the happy phase, the patient thinks that she has been transported to a magnificent garden, a kind of Eden, where the flowers are *red* and the inhabitants *clothed in red*" (*D* 102; authors' emphasis)

The "hysterical" spots of the impressionists and Charcot's hallucinatory flowers were to be merged, in Mirbeau's satire of symbolist synaesthesia, with the fatally scented flowers of the garden of tortures itself. But on another level, the comparison between madness, impressionist technique, and the flower garden was literally forced by the existence of that most hallowed of impressionist landscapes—Monet's Giverny—a garden that in turn served Mirbeau as the real model for his own Oriental enclosure.

In their plans, Giverny and the torture garden exhibit a disturbing similarity. Giverny was divided into symmetrical sections, each containing carefully aligned flower beds. The path running down the middle sported a succession of arches festooned with climbing roses, and led to the heart of Giverny—the *jardin d'eau* containing the broad *bassin* on which floated elusive islands of *nymphéas* (waterlilies). The pool was surrounded by luxuriant foliage—outstretched *agapanthes*, or "love-flowers," iris, lilies, and *glycines*—Oriental blossoms suspended from the Japanese bridge. Mirbeau's garden mirrored this layout virtually element for element:

---

30. J. M. Charcot and Paul Richer, *Les Démoniaques dans l'art* (Paris: Macula, 1984), p. 94. Further references to this work will be abbreviated *D*.
31. Huysmans, *L'Art moderne* p. 106.

> Un vaste bassin que traverse l'arc d'un point de bois, peint en vert vif, marque le milieu du jardin au creux d'un vallonnement où aboutissent quantité d'allées sinueuses.... Des nymphéas, des nélumbiums animent l'eau de leurs feuilles processionelles et de leurs corolles errantes jaunes, mauves, blanches, roses, pourprées; des touffes d'iris dressent leurs hampes fines... des glycines artistement taillées s'élèvent et se penchent, en voûte au-dessus de l'eau qui reflète le bleu de leurs grappes retombantes et balancées.

> A vast pool crossed by the arch of a bright green wooden bridge marks the center of the garden in a hollow of the valley where a number of sinuous alleys and paths converge.... water-lilies and nelumbos animate the water with their trailing leaves and floating corollas in yellow, mauve, white, pink, and purple. Tufts of iris lift their slender stalks.... Artistically trimmed canopies of wisteria extend their vault over the water, which reflects their blue, swaying clusters. (*JS* 159–60)

Edmond de Goncourt, reminiscing on afternoons spent at Giverny with Monet and Mirbeau, sensed the "unnatural parentage" between the two gardens: "Et qui sait si ce n'est pas ce cher souvenir des fleurs qui exhalera, un jour, au dessus du charnier du *Jardin des supplices*, sa senteur de lotus et de paletuviers [And who knows if it wasn't the dear memory of these flowers that one day exhaled their aroma of lotus and mangrove over the charnel-house of *Le Jardin des supplices*]."[32] Edmond's conjecture may be substantiated not only by Mirbeau's personal passion for gardening ("I love the compost-heap as I love a woman") but also by the fact that it was a gardener recommended by Mirbeau who supervised the upkeep of Giverny when Monet became sufficiently solvent.[33] In their letters to each other, painter and writer sympathetically exchanged accounts of their horticultural triumphs and failures.

An art critic of some repute, Mirbeau both collected and wrote on painting and sculpture.[34] His essays, turned with spontaneity

---

32. As cited by Edmond Pilon, *Octave Mirbeau* (Paris: Bibliothèque Internationale, 1903), p. 8.

33. See Claire Joyes, *Claude Monet et Giverny* (Ste. Nlle: Chêne, 1985), p. 100. Mirbeau's "J'aime le terreau comme on aime une femme" (cited by Joyes, p. 28) comes from an undated letter to Monet (1884), in *Les Cahiers d'Aujourd'hui*, vol. 9 (1923): 168.

34. In 1919 part of Mirbeau's collection was sold, including painting and sculpture by Monet, Cézanne, Sisley, Van Gogh, Rodin, Pissarro, Vuillard, and Bonnard. For further details, see Françoise Cachin, "Un Défenseur oublié de l'art moderne," *l'Oeil* 90 (June 1962): 50–55. See also a commemorative issue of *Les Cahiers d'Aujourd'hui*, vol. 8 (1922), which, in addition to containing significant portions of Mirbeau's

and brio (masking their lack of intellectual depth), appeared regularly in *Le Figaro, L'Echo de Paris,* and *Le Journal.* Converting his misogyny into a set of aesthetic criteria, he composed fanciful diatribes against the sickly, "effeminate" tendencies of pre-Raphaelite painting, travestied the provocative feminine curves of art nouveau, and promoted those artists he deemed robust and virile, from Delacroix, Pissarro, Van Gogh, Gauguin, Cézanne, and Maillol, to his particular favorites, Rodin (whose wash drawings from an edition of *Le Jardin* published by Ambroise Vollard in 1902 constitutes, according to Frederic Grunfeld, "one of Rodin's rare forays into book illustration") and Monet.[35]

Nothing in Mirbeau's first essay (1889) on Monet (lauding the impressionist's translucent color and natural, "virginal" freshness) prepares us for *Le Jardin*'s literary tableau of a grotesque, lubricious, "de-repressed" Giverny.[36] In Mirbeau's novel, Monet's preferred flowers are systematically transformed into savage freaks of nature. The parody begins on a linguistic level where plant names traditionally personified by means of their composite Latinate roots are reformulated by Mirbeau in literal evocations of sexual function and character type. Writing in a virtual dialect of botanical onomastics, Mirbeau evokes "giant luzules which mixed their leaves with the *phalliforme, vulvoid* blossoms of the most stupendous arroïdées," and "a *menisperme* embracing a stone column whose base was covered by *nudicaules delphiniums*" (*JS* 159, 204). If here Mirbeau seems to invent his own floral language of the Jabberwocky, else-

---

correspondence with Monet (roughly between 1884 and 1886) also includes reminiscences by distinguished artists and critics: Gustave Geffroy, who compares Mirbeau to Goya, Swift, and Daumier in his mastery of caricature; Frantz Jourdain ("he had a cult for flowers"); and Thadée Natanson, "a collector who derived more pleasure from thinking about the painter than amassing their works" (pp. 105–72).

35. Frederic V. Grunfeld, *Rodin: A Biography* (New York: Henry Holt, 1987), p. 274. As Grunfeld points out, Rodin's nudes are surprisingly unerotic. Grunfeld explains what happened as follows: "The result [of the collaboration between Rodin and the master lithographer Auguste Clot] was one of the most striking *livres d'artiste* of the century, though most of the drawings have only the most tenuous connection with the text. According to the humor magazine *le Canard Enchaîné* Rodin had neglected to read the novel before delivering the illustrations. Actually he did make some preparatory studies of nude women undergoing torture, but these were left out of the book: where the text speaks of agonies and ecstasies Rodin merely shows calm, lyrical nudes that may well have come from his existing stock of such drawings, already mounting into the hundreds" (p. 397).

36. Mirbeau, "Claude Monet," *Le Figaro,* Mar. 10, 1899, quoted in *Des artistes* (Paris: 10/18, 1986), pp. 88–96. Mirbeau also wrote the preface to a catalog for Monet's show "Vues de la Tamise à Londres," held from May 9 to June 4, 1904, at the Galéries Durand-Ruel.

where he pastiches the style and stock characters of fin-de-siècle *boudoir* literature: "La fleur n'est qu'un sexe, milady," states the executioner. "Ces pétales merveilleux...ces soies, ces velours...ces douces, souples et caressantes étoffes...ce sont les rideaux de l'alcôve...les draperies de la chambre nuptiale...le lit parfumé où les sexes se joignent [The flower is nothing but a sex milady.... These marvelous petals, these silks, these velvets, these soft, supple, and caressing materials, are the curtains of an alcove, the draperies of the bridal bed where the sex organs come together]" (*JS* 191–92).

Mirbeau's mordant satire continues with the transformation of the gardener into a grafter and sculptor of human flesh. This figure of Père Hortus was originally conceived by Mirbeau in a newspaper story as a breeder of floral monsters (he causes his hibiscus to "miscarry").[37] In *Le Jardin* he is recast as the chief executioner, who, comparing himself to a surgeon or artist, boasts of having "rebuilt a man from head to foot," and, most diabolical of all, of sculpting a woman out of the detached skin of a man ("D'un homme j'ai fait une femme...Hé!...hé!...hé...") (*JS* 179, 180). Parodying the encyclopedic commonplaces of the nineteenth-century "Traités du jardinage" and the symbolist vogue of sexual androgyny, Mirbeau's genetic experiments culminate in the crossbreeding of women with Baudelairean flowers of evil. The result is a species of foliated vulva whose stem is nourished by human detritus and whose petals are spackled with the blood of the innocent. But however horrible this specimen strikes us in the context of the torture garden, it appears more sinister still when resituated in the context of Mirbeau's second essay on Monet (written in 1891, some eight years prior to *Le Jardin*). If, on first reading, the article appears to be an anodyne "appreciation," it gradually reveals itself as a sinister prolepsis of the garden of scopic perversion.

37. "Do you know what I've just done? he told me. I've just fertilized a hibiscus.... The hibiscus detests music.... And so! I played the trombone to her just at the moment of fecundation. This bothered her, this bored her, this made her drop the ball...and she was fertilized backwards, that is to say that she gave me seeds from which will grow a species of frivolous monster which will be a hibiscus without being one, a plant the likes of which one has never seen" (as cited by Emile Gallé, "La Floriculture lorraine au concours régional" [Oct. 1894], in *Ecrits pour l'art* [Marseille: Lafitte Reprints, 1980], p. 87). Gallé cites Mirbeau as part of a response to the journalist's insult to the "begonia of Nancy," which he claimed was one of those "stupid, impoverished flowers to whom gardeners communicated their contagious stupidity." Gallé undermined his slight by insinuating that Mirbeau had erroneously identified the flower: "Mr. Mirbeau's gardener has, it seems, planted an abominable *Zinnia* in his garden of letters instead of the begonias asked for by the master!"

In this similarly titled article, "Claude Monet," the flowers, with their inexhaustible sexual appetites provide a milieu of nature in heat out of which are born Monet's own strange progeny. Both garden and painting merge in Mirbeau's imagination, pictures themselves almost alive and filled with undercurrents of "troubling mystery."[38] In a carefully staged *expositio* of three images drawn from Monet, Mirbeau creates a sense of the taboo, insidiously undermining the apparently carefree and sun-filled world of impressionist flower painting. The gentle, shaded, river, with its obligatory skiff and two young girls, turns, beneath its surface, into a contorted mingling of algae and vegetation, resembling nothing less than the knotted mass of a woman's hair; gorgons with "bizarres chevelures" writhe in the depths of this placid pool. A second picture, "Jeune fille à l'ombrelle," gives rise to an equally disturbing image, as Gradiva-like, and coquettishly wielding her umbrella, she has the air of a phantom, emerging, shaded like the stream, into the brilliant sunlight. A third, similarly enveloped in mysterious shade, depicts a young girl seated at a table, on which stands a vase holding three huge sunflowers: her sad and delicate beauty is, for Mirbeau, "strange...troubling, and a trifle terrifying." These enigmatic beauties are, finally, compared to the uncanny phantom of Poe's Ligeia with her complexion betraying the pall of the tomb.

Phrase by phrase, by way of Baudelaire's translation of Poe, Mirbeau draws Monet's girls into complicity with the shadow of living death. Like Ligeia, with her elegant tread—"j'essayerais en vain de dépeindre la majesté, l'aisance tranquille de sa démarche et l'incompréhensible légèreté, l'élasticité de son pas [In vain will I try to describe the majesty and tranquil ease of her walk, the incomprehensible lightness, the elasticity of her step]"—Mirbeau's is "a thin, light woman," an "aerial apparition," whose "soaring footstep" makes her seem to glide over the grass. Poe's "elle venait et s'en allait comme une ombre...sa beauté était fort exquise et fortement pénétrée de cette étrangeté [she came and went like a shadow... her beauty was exquisite and strongly infused with an air of the uncanny]" becomes in Mirbeau: "Elle est étrange comme l'ombre qui l'enveloppe toute.... Involontairement, l'on songe à quelque Ligeia, fantômale et réelle [She is as strange as an all-

---

38. Mirbeau, "Claude Monet," in *L'Art dans les Deux Mondes*, no. 16 (Mar. 1891): 183–85.

enveloping shadow.... Involuntarily, one thinks of some Ligeia figure, both real and phantom]."[39]

These modern specters, in their gardens of impressionist *taches*, are also forms of flowers; the umbrella, hovering above the young girl "like a huge flower," and the three sunflowers merge in Mirbeau's fantasy with their human counterparts to form female faces, ghostly souls like those evoked in the poems of Stéphane Mallarmé. Through a chain of associations that encompasses the entire symbolist heritage up through T. S. Eliot, Mirbeau joins Poe-Baudelaire to Poe-Mallarmé to Giverny-Monet by way of the epithet, Homeric and satanic at once, "hyacinth hair." From Poe, whose Ligeia has *chevelure d'hyacinthe*, to Mallarmé's translation of Poe's *Helen*, who likewise has *chevelure hyacinthe*, we are returned to the first frame of Mirbeau's vision of Giverny, with its death-bringing spring—"dead are the hyacinths"—a foreboding that itself echoes the occult presence of Huysmans's Hyacinthe, companion of Durtal's satanic rites in *Là-bas*.[40]

Of all the flowers in Monet's garden, none was more enthralling than the *nymphéa*, the painting of which was to become like a second signature for Monet, an evident sign of the feminine and substitute for the female models denied him (as legend would have it) by his possessive second wife, Alice Hoschedé.[41] It is significant that each of the two major cycles of *nymphéas* seems to have been precipitated by the death of a beloved muse—his adopted daughter in 1899 and his wife in 1911—confirming the intimate relays between mourning and erotic sublimation in these flower women. Technically defined as a "water-lily with white flowers," the *nymphéa* was deeply rooted in Oriental mythology and its reinscription by the symbolists. The most famous of the species, the sacred lotus of the Egyptians, was conjured in its white purity by Mallarmé as virgin and "ideal flower" in an image dedicated to the hardly virginal Méry Laurent, his mistress, Monet's subject, and a model for Proust's Odette.[42] For Mirbeau, the interplay of purity and

---

39. Ibid., p. 183; Edgar Allan Poe, *Oeuvres en prose*, trans. Charles Baudelaire (Paris: Gallimard, 1951), pp. 242–43.

40. Stéphane Mallarmé, "Stances à Hélène," *Oeuvres complètes* (Paris: Gallimard, 1945), p. 193.

41. On Madame Monet's jealousy, see Daniel Wildenstein, "Giverny ou la conquête de l'absolu," in *Monet à Giverny: Au-delà de l'Impressionisme* (Paris: Herscher, 1983), p. 15.

42. Mallarmé's prose poem "Le Nénuphar blanc" (1885) evokes the flower as a "creuse blancheur" or "negative tache" mirrored in the "virginally absent gaze" of a nymph as cold and arresting as Hérodiade (see Mallarmé, *Oeuvres complètes*, p. 286).

perversion, remote and understated in Mallarmé and Monet, becomes a leitmotif in *Le Jardin des supplices*, where the *nymphéa*, with all its sacred and profane associations, is brutally "exposed" as Clara's "nympho-mania." It is at this point that the visual lure of the painted flower is bluntly and brutally exchanged for the sexual lure of a no longer aestheticized female sex.

Informed by the botanical vogue that swept through the garden of Bouvard and Pécuchet, the hothouses of Zola and Maeterlinck, Huysmans and Proust, or the art-nouveau interiors of Emile Gallé, Mirbeau's treatment of Clara's plantlike instincts implies a theory of feminine sexual rapacity. Literally fertilized by flowers, the woman-flower, an aesthetic hybrid resembling the sexualized flowers of Huysmans's *A rebours*, mimics the popular studies of the mating rituals of flora and fauna that were the outgrowth of Darwinism and the scientific venture into ethology. Most famous of the literary versions of these studies were Remy de Gourmont's *Physique de l'amour* (1903) and Maeterlinck's *L'Intelligence des fleurs* (1907), which, though published after *Le Jardin*, provide an index to botanical concepts on which Mirbeau also drew. Maeterlinck's thesis that the survival instinct in plants could be interpreted as a form of "intelligence" (hotly contested by Gide, another amateur botanist) was generously illustrated with examples of their sexual practices, and the remarkable nymphomania of certain female floral species—notably those related to the *nymphéa*—find their analogue in Mirbeau's caricature of Clara's libidinal excess.[43] Of the *ruta graveolens*, or "flower in heat," Maeterlinck wrote: "At the conjugal hour, obeying female orders heard from on high, the first male approaches and touches the stigmata, then the third, the fifth, the seventh, and the ninth, until all the odd numbers have inseminated. Next, it is the turn of the evens, the second, fourth, sixth, etc. It really is love on command."[44] As if satirizing in advance the preciosity of Maeterlinck's floricultural behaviorism, Mirbeau makes a natural scientist out of his Chinese executioner, whose reflections on the female orgasm are substantiated by the sexual codes of flowers:

> Il écarta les pétales de la fleur, compta les étamines chargées de pollen, et il dit, encore, les yeux noyés d'une extase burlesque:
> —Voyez, milady!... Un... deux... cinq... dix... vingt... Voyez comme

[43]. See André Gide, "Notes pour les livres de Maeterlinck," in *Journal, 1889–1939* (Paris: Gallimard, 1951), pp. 806–10.
[44]. Maurice Maeterlinck, *L'Intelligence des fleurs* (Paris: Editions d'Aujourd'hui, 1977), p. 35.

elles sont frémissantes!...Voyez!...Ils se mettent quelquefois à vingt mâles pour le spasme d'une seule femelle!

> He separated the flower's petals, counted the pollen-laden stamens and said, again, his eyes swimming in a comical ecstasy: Look, milady! One, two, five, ten, twenty. See how they quiver! Look! Sometimes twenty males are required for the spasm of a single female! (*JS* 192)

Mirbeau's parody of the phylogenetic makeup of the feminine species-being culminates in the image of Clara quivering with lust as she blindly obeys the signals of the mating ritual—the "male odor" excreted by a peony. Yielding to an attack of nymphomania induced by the scent, Clara drifts inexorably to a Chinese bordello teaming with women who throw themselves, in an act of devotion to their cult, on the multisexed statue of Priapus—"L' Idole aux Sept Verges":

> Criant, hurlant, sept femmes, tout à coup, se ruèrent aux sept verges de bronze. L'Idole, enlacée, chevauchée, violée par toute cette chair délirante, vibra sous les secousses multipliées de ces possessions et de ces baisers qui retentissaient pareils à des coups de bélier dans les portes de fer d'une ville assiégée. Alors, ce fut autour de l'Idole une clameur démente, une folie de volupté sauvage, une mêlée de corps si frénétiquement étreints et soudés l'un à l'autre qu'elle prenait l'aspect farouche d'un massacre.

> Shouting, screaming, seven women suddenly hurled themselves on the seven-fold phallus. The Idol, bound, whipped, and violated by all this delirious flesh, shook under the multiple shocks of so many possessions and the kisses, which rang out like the blows of a battering ram on the iron gates of a besieged city. Then there was a maddened clamor around the idol, an insanity of savage abandon, a storm of bodies, so frantically clasped and welded together that the whole scene took on the wild appearance of a massacre. (*JS* 247–48)

In this climactic spectacle of Bacchae in heat, Mirbeau scapegoats woman as the purveyor and mirror of the reader-spectator's scopophilia, a "love of looking" which, throughout the narrative, has been "feeding itself" on scenes whose erotic content is progressively augmented. But, like the female hysteric in Charcot's paradigm, the viewer is punished for his *Schaulust* through an increasingly hystericized vision, textually reinforced by adjectives of insanity and erotic excess: "furious," "delirious," "demented," "savagely voluptuous."

Clara's nymphomania, thus subsumed within the genetically defined "feminine" malady of hysteria, goes on display at the end of *Le Jardin des supplices* as if it were part of the staged exhibitions at the Salpêtrière. Applying, virtually to the letter, the successive stages and permutations of the hysterical attack as specified by Charcot in *Les Démoniaques*, Mirbeau crafts a literary equivalent of the molds illustrating the postures of hysteria cast by the artist Paul Richer under Charcot's supervision. True to the precursory signals alluded to by Charcot—"She becomes taciturn, melancholy, or held in the grip of extreme excitation" (*D* 92)—Clara's attack is announced by similar signs of nervousness: "Clara threw herself on the cushions. She was extraordinarily pale and her body trembled, shaken by nervous spasms" (*JS* 239). She then proceeds to Charcot's "tonic phase," typified by a "tetanic immobilization" and a flashing of the whites of the eye: "Clara didn't move anymore.... Beneath her pulled-back lids, her revulsed eyes revealed nothing but their white orbs" (*JS* 243). The period of contortions and "large movements" was referred to as *clownisme* by Charcot. Here the hysteric would show herself at her most capricious, one moment acting like a child ("she [Clara] would let out small, poorly articulated words, just like a child"), at another moment enacting the passionate attitudes that Charcot recognized from religious art—supplication, ecstasy, crucifixion, self-mortification (*JS* 243). The first and last are enacted by Clara: supplication, as she assumes the facial expression of the very torture victims that she had formerly reviled, and self-mortification, as her wrists are pinned "in a way that would prevent her from tearing her own face apart with her nails" (*JS* 250). At the climax of the crisis, Charcot's hysteric performed great feats of acrobatic skill: "the patients showed a suppleness, agility, and muscular force that seemed made to astonish the spectator" (*D* 97). Accordingly, Mirbeau's heroine attains the zenith of her frenzy in the "rainbow" posture: "In a final convulsion, her body arched, from the heels to the neck" (*JS* 250). Entering the last phase (*stertorique*), Clara succumbs to a less dramatic but ultimately more sinister mode of disequilibrium, what Charcot called *l'état du mal*. A form of blindness, this malaise is portrayed in *Le Jardin* as the eerie coma into which Clara falls, a coma punctuated only by the refrain from Poe's *The Raven*: "Nevermore!"

Here we are returned to Freud's critical reformulation of Charcot's theory of hysterical blindness, in a fragment written in honor of the Viennese ophthalmologist Leopold Königstein. Rejecting the simple identification of hysterical blindness with spontaneous autosuggestion, a kind of mirror of hypnosis, Freud proposes a model of opposition that puts the ego drives in competition with the sexual drives for control of the organs of taste and sight. Thus, "the eyes perceive not only alterations in the external world which are important for the preservation of life, but also characteristics of objects which lead to their being chosen as objects of love—their charms" ("DV" 216).[45] Where these two fundamental instincts become disunited, and the ego maintains a repression of the sexual component, pathological consequences occur, of the kind identified in the phenomenon of hysterical vision: "Let us suppose that the sexual component instinct which makes use of looking—sexual pleasure in looking [scopophilia]—has drawn upon itself defensive action by the ego-instincts in consequence of its excessive demands, so that the ideas in which its desires are expressed succumb to repression and are prevented from becoming conscious; in that case there will be a general disturbance of the relation of the eye and the act of seeing to the ego and consciousness" ("DV" 216). In this model, Clara's repeated "Nevermore!" echoing the interior voice of talion punishment, would seem to illustrate what Freud here describes as the ego's overrepression: "It looks as though the repression had been carried too far by the ego,...the ego refuses to see anything at all anymore, now that the sexual interest of seeing has made itself so prominent" ("DV" 216). Clara, like the reader-viewer, would seem to have been "overpunished" for her *voyure-isme*. But Freud goes further: this refusal to see is not just the result of overrepression by the ego but, rather, reflects the active revenge against the ego of the repressed instinct, that of "pleasure in looking." This would be as if "a punishing voice was speaking from within the subject, and saying: 'Because you sought to misuse your organ of sight for evil sensual pleasures, it is fitting that you should not see anything anymore'" ("DV" 217). Clara would then have been justly punished, like the witnesses of Dreyfus's trial or the lone spy on Lady Godiva, for having "seen too much." Her vision has been jarred out of focus so that images appear as sickly *taches*—flower-shaped bloodspots or alluring sexual stains. Finally, her scotomized eye might be understood to be not simply the result of her "love of looking," but rather, of her "love of (looking at)

45. It is significant that, as the translator of the *Standard Edition* notes, Freud uses the German *Reize*, meaning both "charms" and "stimuli."

cruelty," a conclusion supported by the particular strain of dehumanized voyeurism represented in *Le Jardin des supplices*. Mirbeau's extended reflection on the scotomizing *après-coup* of scopophilia would seem in this way to have anticipated Freud's extended German "answer" to the French school.

It is perhaps not incidental that the obsessional neurosis of one of Freud's most celebrated patients, the Rat-man, was fueled by the recounting of "a specially horrible punishment used in the East," the introduction of a starved rat into the anus of a bound prisoner, a retelling of one of Mirbeau's sublimely horrible tortures.[46] Freud, who was forced to supply the words for this story's second retelling, despite his insistence that he "had no taste for cruelty," noted that while the Rat-man was struggling with his narrative: "his face took on a very strange, composite expression. I could only interpret it as one of *horror at pleasure of his own of which he himself was unaware*."[47]

The obsessional neurosis, in Freud's characterization, "only a dialect of the language of hysteria," was itself prey to the scopophilic desire, one that was itself perhaps not entirely repressed in Freud's own fascinated refusal of the optic in favor of the psychic. Mirbeau's play with Sade, ostensibly a political allegory couched in psychoerotic terms, would lead us, then, to the discovery of a "Freud avec Sade," the hidden underbelly of Freudian *Schaulust*.

46. Freud, *L'Homme aux rats: Journal d'une analyse*, trans. Elza Riberio (Paris: PUF, 1974), pp. 41–45. The *Journal* records the Rat-man's fear of a captain of his regiment who "manifestly loves cruelty" and who recounts what he has recently read of a terrible punishment used in the Orient, evidently the *Jardin des supplices*.

47. Sigmund Freud, "Notes upon a Case of Obsessional Neurosis" (1909), *Standard Edition* 11:166–67.

CHAPTER 8

· Master Narratives/Servant Texts: Representing the Maid from Flaubert to Freud

In a celebrated scene from Mirbeau's *Le Journal d'une femme de chambre* (*Diary of a Chambermaid* [1901]), so often cited as a paradigmatic example of foot fetishism, the specific nature of the fetish object itself is at first far from clear.

· Ainsi, cela ne vous déplaît pas que je vous appelle Marie?... C'est bien entendu?...
—Mais oui, Monsieur...
Jolie fille... bon caractère... Bien, bien!
Il m'avait dit tout cela d'un air enjoué, extrêmement respectueux, et sans me dévisager, sans fouiller d'un regard déshabilleur mon corsage, mes jupes, comme font, en ·général, les hommes. A peine s'il m'avait regardée. Depuis le moment où il était entré dans le salon, ses yeux restaient obstinément fixés sur mes bottines.
—Vous en avez d'autres?... me demanda-t-il, après un court silence, pendant lequel il me sembla que son regard était devenu étrangement brillant.
—D'autres noms, Monsieur?
—Non, mon enfant, d'autres bottines...
Et il passa sur ses lèvres, à petits coups, une langue effilée, à la manière des chattes.
Je ne répondis pas tout de suite. Ce mot de bottines, qui me rappelait l'expression de gouaille polissonne du cocher, m'avait interdite. Cela avait donc un sens?

· "You don't mind then if I call you Marie, it's understood?"
"Of course, Monsieur."

"Pretty girl, good character. Very good indeed."

He had said all this to me with a playful, extremely respectful air, without a look that undresses you, like most men give. From the moment he walked into the salon, his eyes remained obstinately fixed on my boots.

"You have others?" he asked me, after a short silence, during which it seemed to me that his gaze became peculiarly brilliant.

"Other names, Monsieur?"

"No, my child, other boots."

And he passed his tapered tongue quickly over his lips like a cat.

I didn't answer right away. The word *boots*, reminding me of the vulgar wisecracks of the coachman, struck me dumb. Did it mean something?[1]

A deliberate confusion in the ascription of names to things generates an initial uncertainty as to what precisely might be the object of Monsieur Rabour's fetishistic vision. On the level of possible substitutions the alternatives are at least threefold: "Célestine," the personal first name of the maid, has been exchanged for "others" (*d'autres*), that is, other more impersonal and conventionally attributed maids' names such as "Marie" or "Rose." In this simple operation the maid loses her individuality and assumes the institutional nonidentity of the domestic. Second, if one follows the obsessional and exclusive direction of the master's gaze, a metonymic article of her traditional uniform has been substituted for the maid herself. The boot, visually detached from the rest of her body, stands in as the sign of her sexual role, more important than the directly accessible but less fetishistic blouse. Like the apron, another object of desire in classic scenarios of sexual fantasy, the boot operates as a casing, or *cache-sexe*, for the invisible feminine phallus, acquiring through contiguity a value as a substitution for a substitution. A double metonymy then, or is it in fact triple? For it is not just the boot, symbolizing the missing phallus or the missing identity of the maid, but also the name of the boot—"ce mot de bottine"—that in itself refers to a wide circumference of pathologies characterizing the rapport between master and servant in the turn-of-the-century bourgeois household.

As an exemplary description of foot fetishism, this episode of Mirbeau's novel, written prior to Freud's theory, conforms virtually

1. Octave Mirbeau, *Le Journal d'une femme de chambre* (Paris: Garnier-Flammarion, 1983), p. 38. Further references to this work will be to this edition and will be abbreviated *JF*.

point for point to a Freudian case history of fetishism. In this regard, it throws into relief once again the close relationship between literary chronicles of perversion, pathology, criminal anomaly, and the genres of medical and criminological reportage. The criminologist Raymond de Ryckère, for example, began his study *La Servante criminelle* (1908) with a detailed textual explication of Mirbeau's *Le Journal d'une femme de chambre*. But the fact that literary and nonliterary case studies cross-reference each other during this period comes as no surprise. What constitutes a more interesting problem, it would seem, is the way in which servitude, erotic submission, and foot fetishism are curiously enmeshed within a complex system of representation centering on the maid. On one level the characterization of the maid signals problems of class structure within literary hierarchy itself—questions concerning textual agency, typology, and stereotype, boundaries holding between "master narratives" and "servant texts." On another level, the strangely suppressed power of the *récit de la bonne* allows for a revisionist reading of the role of the female domestic within Freudian theory; for, as we shall see, though the housemaid enters and exits frequently in Freud's case histories, her role within bourgeois neurosis is barely touched upon. One must look to Mirbeau's novel for a ramified "reading" of domestic fetishism, both in the sense of an interiorized, domesticated psychopathology, and in the sense of a servant-inspired erotic economy expressed through specific laws, codes, and semiobscured or scotomized iconographic insignia.

In Mirbeau's novel, Célestine muses on the signification of the word *bottine* ("Cela avait donc un sens?") and one might begin examining the role of the boot as a figure of fetishism by pursuing the direction of her speculation. Is the boot not a boot in the same way that Magritte's pipe is not a pipe? That is, a referential disavowal, a word, according to Foucault's assessment, that denounces its object as a false representation?[2] Certainly insofar as the boot is the name of a fetish it possesses a doubly negative value, referring to what the maid is not: neither just an employee for domestic chores, nor the embodiment of desire, but something "split" between the two. Like Magritte's pipe, which might indeed turn into a boot if placed upside down such that its bowl becomes a heel and its stem the container for the sole of the foot, the boot is

2. Michel Foucault, *Ceci n'est pas une pipe* (Saint-Clément-la-Rivière: Fata Morgana, 1975).

not a boot, but a visual bait, an object of voyeuristic fancy whose symbolic value depends entirely on the viewer.

In this respect, what is important in Mirbeau's account is not so much the maid, her name, or her boot but simply the "strangely dazzled look" of the master, for foot fetishism, as Freud defined it, involves a certain posture, glossed by Derrida as an "orientation," or "*situation orientée*, la syntaxe d'un mouvement vers le haut, depuis le très-bas, le plus-bas [*oriented situation*, the syntax of a movement toward the top, from the very bottom, the lowest]."[3] In his 1927 essay "Fetishism," Freud elucidated the crucial role of this attitude in the subject's choice of a fetish object:

> One would expect that the organs or objects selected as substitutes for the penis whose presence is missed in the woman would be such as act as symbols for the penis in other respects. This may happen occasionally, but it is certainly not the determining factor. It seems rather that when the fetish comes to life, so to speak, some process has been suddenly interrupted—it reminds one of the abrupt halt made by memory in traumatic amnesias. In the case of the fetish, too, interest is held up at a certain point—what is possibly the last impression received before the uncanny traumatic one is preserved as a fetish, or part of it, to the circumstance that the inquisitive boy used to peer up the woman's legs towards her genitals.[4]

According to Freud, the shoe becomes a potential fetish not so much because it imitates the form of the absent phallus but rather because it emerges as an indexical (pointing upward) or metonymical object placed *in the line of vision* of the curious boy whose gaze travels from below ("le très-bas, le plus-bas") to above. This approach from the base may be interpreted alternatively as part of a larger vertical structure of idealization and idolatry typifying the fetishist's attitude to his maternal phantasm, or as an active form of debasement when read as a virtual synonym of the master's approach to the family chambermaid. Conventionally, he attacks from behind, furtively lifting her skirts as she bends over to dust or straighten a household object. This bestial posture, in addition to providing a perfect paradigm of class exploitation, also implies a mock or counter version of the gentlemanly pastime of the hunt,

---

3. Jacques Derrida, *La Vérité en peinture* (Paris: Flammarion, 1978), p. 305. See "Restitutions" for Derrida's reading of foot fetishism.
4. Sigmund Freud, "Fetishism" (1927), in *Standard Edition* 21:149.

with its sado-erotic paraphernalia of riding crops, laced-up saddles, bridles, spurs, and high boots.

The answer to Célestine's question "what does the boot signify?" is thus partially answered in her own name ("celestial," that which tends toward the ideal) and partially by the bias of Monsieur Rabour's axial and anatomically disjunctive vision—qualified by Freud as upward and occlusive, and by Jean Bellemin-Noël, elaborating on Freud, as "asymptotic," following the parallel lines of the legs disappearing into the shoes:[5]

- Il s'agenouilla, baisa mes bottines, les pétrit de ses doigts fébriles et caresseurs, les délaça.... Et, en les baisant, les pétrissant, les caressant, il disait d'une voix suppliante, d'une voix d'enfant qui pleure: —Oh! Marie... Marie... tes petites bottines... donne-les-moi tout de suite.

- He fell to bended knee, and kissed my boots, kneading them with his feverish, fondling fingers, unlacing them.... And, while kissing, kneading, and fondling them, he said in a cajoling voice, the voice of a whimpering child: "Oh! Marie, Marie, your little booties—give them to me right now."
(*JF* 39)

Like the maternal breast the boots are supplicated with childish promises of gifts and caresses; and, as if to complete this pre-Freudian mise-en-scène of a Freudian case history, the verb *battre*, "to beat," is used by the narrator to describe the flickering, upward gaze of Monsieur Rabour, as if betraying an inner phantasm of flagellation: "Monsieur s'emballait encore. A mesure qu'il parlait, ses paupières battaient, battaient comme des feuilles sous l'orage

---

5. Jean Bellemin-Noël, *Gradiva au pied de la lettre* (Paris: PUF, 1983), pp. 108–109. The name of the boot is also suggestive in terms of its own range of etymological significations. *Bottine*, the diminutive form of *botte*, has as its root a condition of podalic deformity, or clubfoot (*bot*), also active in the peasant's *sabot*, which, since the Middle Ages has connoted a vulgar, ungainly worker's shoe. The conjunction between lameness and the social underclass, with the associations ranging from one-leggedness (*boiteux*), signaling beggars or pilgrims on crutches, to the wooden leg (*jambe de bois*), described by Krafft-Ebing as a standard prop of the bordello, is only reinforced by the innuendos surrounding a secondary meaning. As tube, barrel, or drainpipe (cf. Littré, "tuyaux des lieux d'aisance"), the *bot* projects images of fecal evacuation and the maid's habitual corvée of emptying the chamber pot. This in turn is compatible with the stereotype of servants in the popular imagination as either born from or destined to "a life of the gutter." Linked through its Anglo-Saxon derivation to *booty*, meaning purse or money (*bourse*), the *botte* also evokes the theme of avarice, specifically that of the bourgeois master perennially bent on obtaining maximum labor for minimum cost. Finally, in vulgar parlance, it refers to the scrotum. In this context, the trivial expression "I would not want to be in your shoes" ironically projects the deeper nuances of castration anxiety.

[Monsieur got excited again. As he spoke, his eyelids were batting, batting like leaves in a storm]" (*JF* 39).

The quest for humiliation, part of the complex, inverted nature of fetishistic pleasure, is encapsulated by Mirbeau in the master's desire to polish the boots of the maid ("And it's I who will polish your booties, your little booties, your darling little booties..." [*JF* 39]. As the agent of role reversal, with master becoming slave, the boot draws its value from classic depictions of the bootblack, head bent and body lowered in the posture of servitude, busying himself, as in Louis Aragon's arresting vignette in *Le Paysan de Paris*, with "putting suns" on shoes that are as dark as his profession.[6] Monsieur Rabour's "strangely dazzling look" accordingly invites conjugation with that brilliant shine referred to by Freud as an attribute of the fetish. In the 1927 essay, he begins with the famous "Glanz auf der Nase," with the English pun on *glance* on the one hand evoking the primitive associations of the patient's mother tongue (English rather than German)—proof yet again of infantile fixation and the centrality of the sighting instinct—and on the other hand pointing to the disguise of shininess (as in the German *Schein*, or false appearance), used by the fetishist to divert attention from the essentially anal-erotic nature of his perversion.[7] As Krafft-Ebing reported in his *Psychopathia Sexualis*, a certain aristocrat, seduced in childhood by a French governess who had aroused him with her boot, confessed attraction only to the elegant boots of his social station, the first and archetypal artifact being characterized by the glossy sheen of its black leather.[8] Karl Abraham, in a case study that both drew from and greatly edified Freud, entitled "Remarks on the Psycho-Analysis of a Case of Foot and Corset Fetishism" (1910), also treated as significant his patient's avowed excitation when presented with patent-leather high-heeled shoes of the kind worn by prostitutes.[9] And Janine Chasseguet-Smirgel, in her obser-

    6. Louis Aragon, *Le Paysan de Paris* (Paris: Gallimard, 1978): "C'est le cireur, cela ne coûte que douze sous et nous sortirons de là avec des soleils au pied" (p. 86). ["It is the shoeshine parlour; let us make a brief halt there, it will cost us a mere sixty centimes, and we shall leave the place wearing suns on our feet": *Paris Peasant*, trans. Simon Watson Taylor (London: Picador, 1980), p. 82.]
    7. Freud, "Fetishism," p. 150.
    8. Richard von Krafft-Ebing, *Psychopathia Sexualis*, trans. Harry E. Wedeck (New York: Putnam's, 1965), pp. 228–29.
    9. Karl Abraham, "Remarks on the Psycho-Analysis of a Case of Foot and Corset Fetishism" (1910), in *Selected Papers of Karl Abraham*, trans. Douglas Bryan and Alix Strachey (New York: Basic Books, 1953), p. 126.

vations of the frequency with which waxed surfaces, satin undergarments, and gleaming boots are coupled with malodorous sense impressions, concludes that the fetish has an essentially double nature: grotesque and excremental, ideal and pristine.[10]

This brings us to what is perhaps the most salient link between the boot and the maid—the common association with dirt. In a famous note added in 1915 to *Three Essays on the Theory of Sexuality* Freud provided an explanation for this association in his discussion of the coprophilic origins of foot fetishism: "Both the feet and the hair are objects with a strong smell which have been exalted into fetishes after the olfactory sensation has become unpleasurable and been abandoned. Accordingly, in the perversion that corresponds to foot-fetishism, it is only the dirty and evil-smelling feet that become sexual objects."[11] Reverting to a stage of development prior to the repression of his scatological instincts, Monsieur Rabour plays the part of boot-licker, pandering to his desire to taste his own dirt accumulated on her boots. At the closure of Mirbeau's set piece, he lies dead, the boot, fittingly enough, having choked him to death:

> Monsieur était mort!... Etendu sur le dos, au milieu du lit, le corps presque entièrement nu, on sentait déjà en lui et sur lui la rigidité du cadavre.... Spectacle terrifiant qui, plus encore que ce visage, me secoua d'épouvante... Monsieur tenait, serrait dans ses dents, une de mes bottines, si durement serrée dans ses dents, qu'après d'inutiles et horribles efforts je fus obligée d'en couper le cuir, avec un rasoir pour la leur arracher.

> Monsieur was dead! Stretched out on his back, in the middle of the bed, his body almost entirely naked, one could already feel on him the rigidity of the corpse.... And then, a terrifying spectacle, one which, even more than his face, sent shock waves of horror through me... Monsieur held, clenched between his teeth, one of my boots, so firmly clenched between his teeth, that after much useless and horrible effort, I was forced to cut through the leather with a razor in order to tear out the boot. (*JF* 40)

In addition to affording a virtual textbook illustration of fetishism

---

10. Janine Chasseguet-Smirgel, *Ethique et esthétique de la perversion* (Seyssel: Champ Vallon, 1984), pp. 285–89.
11. Freud, *Three Essays on the Theory of Sexuality*, in *Standard Edition* 7:155.

as coprophilia, this macabre tableau can be read as a castration drama in reverse: the boot, a displaced female phallus whose absence excites Monsieur Rabour's castration anxiety, symbolically returns (albeit in the wrong place), conjuring up Roland Barthes's conception of a text as a fetish object that desires him ("Le texte est un objet fétiche et *ce fétiche me désire*").[12] A materialized lack, a fetish that "bites back," the boot becomes the agent by which the female phallus is symbolically reappropriated by its original owner, as Célestine, after overcoming her disgust, proceeds pragmatically to cut out the boot with a razor.

The motifs of mutilation, violation, and corporal dismemberment must certainly be added to the list of fetishistic topoi foreshadowed in the novel by this central episode. But what makes the episode more than just a miniature, concentrated version of the entire novel, and more than just a literary rendering of a pathological case history that influenced the psychiatric community in the early twentieth century, is its value *as a theory* of the particular relation of fetishism to the representation of the female domestic. Charcot, Binet, Krafft-Ebing, and Freud all record examples in which a maid or governess appears. All systematically neglect, however, to explore the relevance of the maid qua maid in her position as either maternal surrogate or medium of power transfer from servitude to domination in their study of specific perversions. In his essay "The Role of Fetishism in Love," Binet refers to boot nails, aprons, nightcaps, underlinen, and the white headband traditionally worn by the French maid as a class of objects provocative to fetishists but fails to discern in this vestimentary code the classic costume of the maid.[13] Although in one case history he notes the presence of an old servant, he passes over the detail with no comment: "The nightcap lover recounts that at the age of five he slept in the same bed as one of his parents, and that when the parent donned a nightcap, he would get a continual erection. Around the same time, he saw an old servant get undressed, and when she put her nightcap on, he would get very excited and again become erect."[14]

Freud drew on this very passage in tracing the etiology of fetishism to fixations of early childhood, differing with Binet only in his belief that the complex could be formed prior to the age of

12. Roland Barthes, *Le Plaisir du texte* (Paris: Seuil, 1973), p. 45.
13. Alfred Binet, "Le Fétichisme dans l'amour," *Revue Philosophique* 24(1887): 163.
14. Ibid., p. 166.

five.[15] Yet he too ignored the possible importance of the old servant, just as he did the governess in an unpublished paper entitled "A Case of Foot Fetishism," read before the Vienna Psychoanalytic Society in 1914.[16] This case, according to Ernest Jones, "concerned a man of forty-five who had always been impotent," a condition presumably caused by "premature excitation of (the foot) by a very abnormal mother who used to caress and kiss it to excess."[17] Threatened by his father with castration, the boy became obsessed with the specter of the absent phallus:

> As a child he would lie with his head between his sister's thighs, and the sight of the female genital organ increased his fear of castration. When he was married he would dream that his wife was equipped with male organs. The sister in question had deformed legs from rickets, and it was her small foot that constituted his first ideal of a lovely, attractive organ—the foot. The perversion was evidently fixed by his seventh year, when he fell in love with his governess's foot. By then it had acquired the symbolic meaning of a male genital organ.[18]

Though the rickets and deformity of the foot (recalling the boot's etymological derivation from *clubfoot*) merit inclusion in the repertory of factors deemed significant in the case, the role of the governess as object of transference from the sister is not among them.

A similar obliviousness marked Freud's exhaustive analysis of Jensen's *Gradiva* in "Delusion and Dream in Jensen's *Gradiva*" (1907). While endeavoring to verify the plausibility of the antique Gradiva's step—"the left foot had advanced, and the right, about to follow, touched the ground only lightly with the tips of the toes while the sole and heel were raised almost vertically"—Norbert Hannold is hindered in his research by the long-skirted fashion of the upper-middle classes, "for almost no one but housemaids wore short skirts and they, with the exception of a few, because of their heavy shoes, could not well be considered in solving the problem."[19]

---

15. Freud, "Delusions and Dreams in Jensen's *Gradiva*," *Standard Edition* 9:47.
16. The Vienna Society had taken up the question of fetishism a number of times before, most notably in 1909. See above, note 23, Chapter 4.
17. Ernest Jones, *The Life and Work of Sigmund Freud*, vol. 2, *1901–1919* (New York: Basic Books, 1955), p. 306.
18. Ibid.
19. Freud, "Delusions and Dreams," pp. 46–50. For an interesting reading of the Gradiva's foot, see Alain Roger, *Hérésies du désir: Freud, Dracula, Dali* (Seyssel: Champ

The boots of the servant class could thus in no way be adduced as evidence for a girl "splendid in walking." Freud, while recognizing Hannold's "fetishistic erotomania" (prompting him to venerate the Gradiva as an idealized statue on a pedestal and to endue her with an exalted genealogy as the daughter of a patrician "associated with the temple service of a deity"), also avoids investigating the particular connections between the lower-class maid's boot and the upper-class lady's foot.[20]

Freud ignored the maid again in his analysis of the "French Nurse's Dream" taken from a Hungarian comic strip discovered by Sandor Ferenczi that bore this caption and added to *The Interpretation of Dreams* (1899) in 1914. The cartoon features a child in the company of his nurse urinating prodigiously against a wall like Gargantua on the city of Paris: "The stream of water produced by the micturating boy becomes mightier and mightier. In the fourth picture it is already large enough to float a rowing boat; there follow a gondola, a sailing ship and finally a liner."[21] The final frame shows the nurse awaking and attending to the distressed child—his urgent need to relieve himself having apparently been transposed into her wet-dream. Freud passed over the symbolism of the nurse as object of infantile anal-eroticism, despite the fact that his own dreams contained imbricated analogies between feet and bedwetting (in the "Dream of Count Thun" the Count translates the German flower "cat's foot" as *pisse-en-lit*); between maids and "dirty feet"; and between maids, nurses, and childhood exhibitionism. These analogies come most sharply into focus in one of the staircase dreams (and here one must not forget the transition from *gradus* (step) to "Gradiva"), a dream in which Freud, in a state of undress, experiences painful embarrassment upon encountering a maid on the staircase: "I was glued to the steps and unable to budge from the spot."[22] Analyzing his sense of shame he remained perplexed by the fact that it was an "older...surly and far from attractive" maidservant who had prompted such feelings. Further reflection reminded him of his ongoing warfare with a concierge over the installation of a spittoon on the stair of a house where he

---

Vallon, 1985).
20. Freud, "Delusions and Dreams," pp. 50–51.
21. Freud, *The Interpretation of Dreams* (1899), *Standard Edition*, 4-5:367.
22. Ibid., p. 238.

frequently visited a patient. Freud would expectorate on the staircase in protest of the absence of a receptacle, and the concierge, lying in wait, would berate him for his impropriety. Here, in the paradigm of dirt versus cleanliness, Freud found the clue to the maidservant, for she had appeared in a prior dream complaining: "You might have wiped your boots, doctor, before you came into the room today. You've made the red carpet all dirty again with your feet."[23] Noting the structural affinity between these points of the dream and the legend, read as a child, of Odysseus "when he appeared, naked and covered with mud, before the eyes of Nausicaä and her maidens," Freud, delving still deeper, recalled the memory of his own nurse:

> According to what I was told not long ago by my mother, she was old and ugly, but very sharp and efficient. From what I can infer from my own dreams her treatment of me was not always excessive in its amiability and her words could be harsh if I failed to reach the required standard of cleanliness. And thus the maid-servant, since she had undertaken the job of carrying out this educational work, acquired the right to be treated in my dream as a reincarnation of the prehistoric old nurse. It is reasonable to suppose that the child loved the old woman who taught him these lessons, in spite of her rough treatment of him.[24]

The significance of this "prehistoric old nurse," object of conflicted affection, has been until recently curiously underestimated in terms of its psychoanalytic import. Freud evinced a consistent distrust toward feminine domestics, even when analyzing the banal accidents committed by servants while cleaning up:

> When servants drop fragile articles and so destroy them, our first thought is certainly not of a psychological explanation, yet it is not unlikely that here, too, obscure motives play their part. Nothing is more foreign to uneducated people than an appreciation of art and works of art. Our servants are dominated by a mute hostility towards the manifestations of art, especially when the objects (whose value they do not understand) become a source of work for them.[25]

While Freud cites this type of casual destruction allusively, that is, in conjunction with the Jewish marriage ritual of breaking the vessels,

23. Ibid., p. 239.
24. Ibid., p. 247–48.
25. Freud, *The Psychopathology of Everyday Life* (1901), Standard Edition 6:173.

and while he recognizes its everyday symbolic import as an act of displaced class conflict, he submerges what would seem to be an obvious connotation: the sexual initiation or "breaking in" customarily performed by the maid on the young master. The reason for his suppression of this social cliché may perhaps lie in the matrix of partial avowals and disavowals surrounding the role of his own nursemaid during his early sexual education. In the course of his self-analysis in 1897 he confided to Fliess that his *Urheberin* (translated as "primary originator" or, more literally, "the first woman to raise up") "was my teacher in sexual matters and complained because I was clumsy and unable to do anything."[26] Though the implications of this confession for the oedipal theory have been explored in Jim Swan's "Mater and Nannie: Freud's Two Mothers and the Discovery of the Oedipus Complex," though its relevance to the controversy surrounding the literalness of Freud's abandoned "seduction theory" has been acknowledged (cf. Masson and McGrath), and though its analogous structure to the relationship between analyst and (female) analysand has been elucidated, it is primarily in Freud's analysis of a case not his own, but strangely parallel, that the full significance of such a screen memory is adumbrated.[27]

In his presentation of the case of the Wolf-man, narrative suspense accrues around the question of who induced the Wolf-man's fear of castration. First it appears to be an English governess, alcoholic and sadistic, who, gathering up her skirts behind her, cried, "Do look at my little tail!" But despite her threatening behavior, the real object of fantasy is identified as the Wolf-man's sexually precocious sister. The servant is nonetheless reinscribed in the initial paradigm of displacement when we learn that the sister's sexual rebuff prompts the Wolf-man to choose as surrogate a housemaid bearing the first name of his sibling. Freud attached considerable importance to this love choice, observing that "all the

26. *The Complete Letters of Sigmund Freud to Wilhelm Fliess (1887–1904)*, trans. and ed. Jeffrey Moussaieff Masson (Cambridge: Harvard University Press, 1985), p. 268.
27. A small bibliography on the role of the nursemaid or governess in Freud's work includes Jim Swan, "Mater and Nannie: Freud's Two Mothers and the Discovery of the Oedipus Complex," *American Imago* 31 (Spring 1974): 1–64; Kenneth Grigg, "All Roads Lead to Rome: The Role of the Nursemaid in Freud's Dreams," *Journal of the American Psychoanalytical Association* 21 (1973): 108–26; Jane Gallop, "Keys to Dora," in *In Dora's Case: Freud-Hysteria-Feminism*, ed. Charles Bernheimer and Claire Kahane (New York: Columbia University Press, 1985), pp. 214–16; William J. McGrath, *Freud's Discovery of Psychoanalysis: The Politics of Hysteria* (Ithaca: Cornell University Press, 1986); and Nicolas Abraham and Maria Torok, *Cryptomanie: Le Verbier de l'Homme aux Loups* (Paris: Aubier Flammarion, 1976).

girls with whom he subsequently fell in love—often with the clearest indications of compulsion—were also servants, whose education and intelligence were necessarily far inferior to his own."[28] As the story progresses, suspicion falls on the Wolf-man's "Nanya," who, according to Freud, evinced an "untiring affection" for her charge, treating him as a "substitute for a son of her own who had died young." His attempts to seduce "Nanya" by masturbating in her presence provoke her warning against an eventual "wound in the place." Yet, Nanya's comment, like that of the English governess, diminishes in importance next to the images associated with Grusha, a third housemaid, retrieved at an advanced stage of the analysis. Grusha is the prototype of the wolf. Her animal posture, "on the floor engaged in scrubbing it...kneeling down, with her buttocks projecting and her back horizontal," perfectly matches the posture of the boy's mother, viewed *a tergo* in a primal scene.[29] To "debase" (Freud's term) Grusha, and then later "Matrona" (another family servant whose maternal name Freud does not fail to note), is thus revealed as part of a traceable urge to debase or punish both mother and intellectually superior sister. But immediately as Grusha emerges as the agent of transference from the sister or mother to a surrogate object of anal eroticism, Freud, treating her like a servant, relegates her once more to the status of vehicle, useful for clarifying the analysis but no longer an integral part of the Wolf-man's psychic history: "It was true that there could be no doubt about the scene with Grusha, but, I suggested, in itself that scene meant nothing; it had been emphasized *ex post facto* by a regression from the circumstances of his object-choice, which, as a result of his intention to debase, had been diverted from his sister on to servant girls."[30]

The contemptuous claim that Grusha's scene "meant nothing" brings us back to an earlier moment in Freud's career to a draft of "The Architecture of Hysteria," enclosed in 1897 in a letter to Fliess. Here we find under the heading "The Part Played by Servant Girls" a statement of the housemaid's pure instrumentality in Freud's mind; her position as a kind of psychoanalytical "hired help" or "second hand," subordinate to a "master" pathology:

28. Muriel Gardiner, *The Wolf-man by the Wolf-man* (New York: Basic Books, 1971), p. 167.
29. Ibid., p. 234.
30. Ibid., p. 236.

> An immense load of guilt, with self-reproaches (for theft, abortion), is made possible by identification with these people of low morals who are so often remembered, in a sexual connection with father or brother, as worthless female material. And, as a result of the sublimation of these girls in fantasies, most improbable charges against other people are contained in the fantasies.... There is a tragic justice in the circumstance that the family head's stooping to a maidservant is atoned for by his daughter's self-abasement.[31]

The complex imbrication of fear, disdain, and culpability that surfaces in this passage helps to explain Freud's consistent suppression of the maid once she appeared in her unmasked state as maternal castrator. This suppression has been remarked upon by a number of critics from Peter Stallybrass and Allon White (*The Politics and Poetics of Transgression*) to Hélène Cixous and Catherine Clément.[32] The latter two, in *The Newly Born Woman*, excoriate Freud for his exclusion of the maid. "She is the hole in the social cell," Cixous remarks; "'It' goes through 'that,' it goes through her body. In 'Dora' what was terrifying was that these archetypal servants were put by Freud himself in 'the maid's room'—that is, in the notes."[33] While Cixous and Clément are here concerned to oppose a "mistress" language to the discourse of mastery, they themselves stumble over the maid, whose "station," beneath the mistress, proves difficult to dislodge. Ultimately, they too are implicated as intellectual mistresses when they shift the burden of class insensitivity onto Freud. "Freud in relation to Dora was in the maid's place," claims Cixous, referring to the fact that he was fired by Dora, just as a servant girl is fired by her mistress.[34] If Freud is a maid, if the analyst is seen as subordinate to the analysand rather than the reverse in this heretical feminist scheme, a class injustice is certainly redressed. But by focusing on Freud, we once again elide the imago of the maid. An objective correlative of the return of the repressed, a living embodiment of the commodity fetish (and here it must be recalled that the "possession" of servants functioned as a mark of

---

31. *Letters of Freud to Fliess*, p. 241.
32. For an analysis of the maid that closely parallels my own (and which came to my attention after I had written this chapter), see Peter Stallybrass and Allon White's section entitled "Below Stairs: The Maid and the Family Romance," in *The Politics and Poetics of Transgression* (Ithaca: Cornell University Press, 1986), pp. 149–70.
33. Hélène Cixous and Catherine Clément, *The Newly Born Woman*, trans. Betsy Wing (Minneapolis: University of Minnesota Press, 1986), p. 150.
34. Ibid., p. 152.

prestige and wealth, as much decorative as functional), the maid seems doomed to displacement and emargination.

Though Cixous, Clément, Gallop, and Stallybrass and White have done much to counter the tendency within psychoanalytical (master) narratives to ignore issues of class and gender, one might go even further in this direction. The maid as quintessential fetish object, both instigator of, and antidote to, castration anxiety, merits consideration as a significant theoretical agent within a more historicized understanding of psychoanalysis. Representing the maid, however, proves to be no simple task. Her portrait may be constituted from the outlines of her absence in the master narratives, or, alternatively, from a neglected genre of servants' tales in nineteenth- and twentieth-century literature: Lamartine's *Geneviève* (1850), the feuilleton *Bécassine*, Zulma Carraud's *Une Servante d'autrefois* (1866), and Paul Bourget's *Une fille-mère* (1928), as well as the more familiar works by Zola, the Goncourts, Flaubert, Maupassant, Proust, and Genet.

In the late-nineteenth-century culture in which Freud's theories took root, the body of the maid became increasingly present in the phantasms, paranoias, and phobias of the middle class. As a result of its direct physical contact with the secret detritus of the bourgeois household, the maid's body became symbolically contaminated by the *taches*, or traces of dirt, that it was her *tâche*, task or work, to efface. A magnet for microbes—the newly discovered agent of infection that every decent bourgeois fought to expunge—the maid was to be eschewed, alienated like a carrier of smallpox or syphilis, which she was also presumed to attract through a wanton life-style of promiscuity and nomadism.[35] These associations were most powerfully captured by Zola in *Pot-Bouille* (1882), where the scullery maid, Adèle, lowest in the servant hierarchy, is referred to continuously as a creature of filth, a "slattern" (*souillon*), a "rag" (*torchon*), "a dirty, ungainly beast on whom the whole household beat up ["une bête sale et gauche sur laquelle la maison entière tapait]."[36] Avoided by all except the master and his son, who take turns with her in her bed (the father, Duveyrier, having been banished from his wife's

---

35. See chap. 3, "Le Camouflage de la maladie," in Isabelle Grellet and Caroline Kruse, *Histoires de la tuberculose: Les Fièvres de l'âme, 1800–1940* (Paris: Ramsay, 1983), for discussion of how the new organization of the bourgeois house introduced the radical separation of the maid's quarters. For an account of the links between domestic service and prostitution, see Anne Martin-Fugier's *La Place des bonnes: La Domesticité féminine à Paris en 1900* (Paris: Grasset, 1979), pp. 317–31.

36. Emile Zola, *Pot-Bouille* (Paris: Gallimard, 1982), p. 136.

boudoir because of the repugnant "bleeding spots on his forehead"), Adèle becomes the repository of these very *taches*, of all that is deemed untouchable by the rest of the household.[37] The cruel nickname "rag" perfectly conveys her dehumanized status as that which "wipes away" the "hidden family dirt [les ordures cachées des familles]" lurking in the pestiferous courtyards and kitchens of the bourgeois residence.[38]

In *Madame Bovary*, the coordinates of this typology had already been set. At the peak of Emma's affair with Rodolphe, her maid, Félicité, is charged with cleaning off her adulterous taint: "Il fallait que la domestique fût sans cesse à blanchir du linge [The maid was constantly at work cleaning her linen]." Eventually the roles of servant and mistress are ironically confused as when Emma, submitting to her lover, describes herself as a maid: "Je suis ta servante et ta concubine! [I am your servant and your concubine!]."[39] If here Emma evokes enslavement and subordination with romantic idealism, suggesting a suppressed longing to recover the fatal spot that she has passed off onto her servant, the reverse occurs within the monologues of Genet's Claire. While playing the role of "Madame," she histrionically reviles the scum of servitude:

- Je hais les domestiques. J'en hais l'espèce odieuse et vile. Les domestiques n'appartiennent pas à l'humanité. Ils coulent. Ils sont une exhalaison qui traîne dans nos chambres, dans nos corridors, qui nous pénètre, nous entre par la bouche, qui nous corrompt. Moi je vous vomis.... Vos gueules d'épouvante et de remords, vos coudes plissés, vos corsages démodés, vos corps pour porter nos défroqués. Vous êtes nos miroirs déformants, notre soupape, notre honte, notre lie.

- I loathe servants. A vile and odious breed, I loathe them. They're not of the human race. Servants ooze. They're a foul effluvium drifting through our rooms and hallways, seeping into us, entering our mouths, corrupting us. I vomit you!... Your frightened guilty faces, your puckered elbows, your outmoded clothes, your wasted bodies, only fit for our castoffs! You're our distorting mirrors, our loathsome vent, our shame, our dregs![40]

---

37. Ibid., p. 162.
38. Ibid., p. 137.
39. Gustave Flaubert, *Madame Bovary* (Paris: Garnier Flammarion, 1966), pp. 216, 219.
40. Jean Genet, *Les Bonnes*, as cited by Martin-Fugier, *La Place des bonnes*, p. 193; Genet, *The Maids*, trans. Bernard Frechtman (New York: Grove Press, 1962), p. 86.

In this self-hating impersonation there lies a full spectrum of thematic variations on the maid's *tache*: a ubiquitous odor that trails through the house, invisible yet felt as a discomfiting presence; a disease that trickles down from the cramped, unhealthy quarters of the sixth floor; a sign of the social pariah who survives, like carrion, on human waste; a clown, outfitted in the rags and castoffs of its noble superior, and as such, the grotesque double of the class it serves.

Each of these motifs is extensively treated as part of the historical biography of a maid's life recorded in *Le Journal d'une femme de chambre*. In an act of absolute devotion to a young, sickly master, Célestine yields to a dangerous embrace. Her charge, afflicted by tuberculosis, has lost all interest in life until the day when she initiates him in love. From then on, their passion grows proportionally with the boy's expenditure of force until, a mere skeleton, he dies in her arms in a paroxysm of desire. Before he expires, however, Célestine affirms her willingness to render the supreme "service":

> Mon baiser avait quelque chose de sinistre et de follement criminel.... Sachant que je tuais Georges, je m'acharnais à me tuer, moi aussi, dans le même bonheur et dans le même mal.... Délibérément, je sacrifiais sa vie et la mienne.... Avec une exaltation âpre et farouche qui décuplait l'intensité de nos spasmes, j'aspirais, je buvais la mort, toute la mort, à sa bouche... et je me barbouillais les lèvres de son poison.... Une fois qu'il toussait, pris, dans mes bras, d'une crise plus violente que de coutume, je vis mousser à ses lèvres un gros, immonde crachat sanguinolent.
>
> —Donne... donne... donne!
>
> Et j'avalai le crachat, avec une avidité meurtrière, comme j'eusse fait d'un cordial de vie.

> My kiss had something sinister and madly criminal in it. Knowing that I was killing Georges, I threw myself into killing myself, myself also, with the same pleasure and the same pain.... Deliberately I sacrificed his life and mine... With a bitter, wild exultation that increased the intensity of our spasms tenfold, I drank, I inhaled death, all of death, from his mouth.... I sullied my mouth with his poison. At the point where he was coughing, seized, while in my arms, by a particularly violent fit, I saw a huge, bloody glob of spit foam over his lips.
>
> "Give it to me!... Give it to me!... Give it to me!"
>
> And I swallowed the spittle with murderous greed, as if it was a potion of life. (*JF* 160)

Clearly a travesty of biblical parables of abasement, particularly that of Christ and the lepers reworked by Flaubert in *La Légende de Saint-Julien l'hospitalier*, this scene borders on the pornographic with its intimations of fellatio and incest (the latter if it is recalled that Célestine acts as a maternal surrogate to Georges). The aura of transgression is reinforced by the sacrificial communion where poison is imbibed with fervor. This ignominious *crachat* (sputum) brings us once again to that expectoration on the stairs, which, in a footnote, Freud admitted to "over-interpreting." The semantic slippage of *spuken*, meaning "haunting," toward its homonym *spucken*, or spitting on the stairs, yielded, according to Freud, the expression *esprit d'escalier*.[41] Though Freud neglects to recognize the maid in this figure of the staircase genie (despite the sense of shame that overcomes him when they meet), she appears not so distant from Mirbeau's Célestine. Both are associated with defilement and abjection.

Though it may be tempting to read this scene simply as evidence of Mirbeau's misogynist contempt for the sexual appetites of women, all of whom in his eyes resemble his working-class heroine insofar as they are "slaves to passion" and even capable of "killing a man with their lust," it should also be approached as a pure parody of the stock low literature of the nineteenth century, featuring the maid as a servant of God. Heroic feats of selflessness constituted the standard trope of the genre, which was especially popular for obvious propagandistic reasons among the clergy, the bourgeois matron, and the directors of employment agencies for the placement of domestics. Typically, the servant risked her life for that of the master's children, as when, in Flaubert's *Un Coeur simple* (an example of the theme percolating up into high literature), Félicité braces a raging bull and survives only by throwing clumps of earth into its eyes. Similarly, in Lamartine's *Geneviève* (1850), the outer limits of self-abnegation are attained when, having sacrificed love, fortune, and honor for the sake of a perfidious sister, she is imprisoned, branded as a social outcast, and ultimately forced to submit to the final humiliation of serving the family of her former suitor, now married and prosperous. A "paschal lamb" whose unflagging resignation indeed approximates that of a "beast of burden" (held up as an ideal model of comportment for the servant throughout this literary genre), Geneviève is nonetheless equaled in trials by Fanchette Madoré in Zulma Carraud's *Une*

---

41. Freud, *The Interpretation of Dreams*, p. 281.

Servante d'autrefois (1866). In this novel by a close friend of Balzac, one discovers what may have been the precedent for Mirbeau's description of the gob of spit in Fanchette's "cure" for smallpox, administered lovingly on the child of her mistress:

> Le médecin ayant dit qu'Elisabeth serait très défigurée si elle en réchappait, Fanchette se souvint d'avoir entendu dire à sa grande-mère qu'en perçant chaque bouton avec une aiguille fine, et qu'en ayant le courage d'en aspirer le contenu, la maladie ne laissait aucune trace. La brave fille se mit à l'oeuvre aussitôt qu'elle se trouva seule avec l'enfant, et persévera sans la moindre répugnance jusqu'à ce que les boutons fussent desséchés.

> The doctor having said that Elisabeth would be very disfigured after her recuperation, Fanchette remembered hearing someone say to her grandmother that by piercing each pimple with a fine needle, and courageously sucking the contents, the illness would leave no trace. The plucky girl set to work as soon as she was alone with the child, persevering without any repugnance until all the spots were drained.[42]

As in *Le Journal d'une femme de chambre*, the transcendence of physical repulsion proves to be the test of true fidelity; but where Célestine is at least allowed a shred of egoism in her fear of contagion, Fanchette is permitted none. Moreover, unlike Célestine, she is cruelly remunerated for her supreme act of Christian virtue with the contraction of the disease:

> Mais la pauvre fille ressentit bientôt, elle aussi, les symptômes de la contagion. Elle fut très malade à son tour, et très affectueusement soignée par Mme. Sionnet et ses deux filles aînées. Moins heureuse que l'enfant, ella porta toute sa vie des marques qui la défigurèrent.

> But soon, she too, poor girl, contracted the contagion's symptoms. In due course, she became very ill and was very kindly attended to by Mme. Sionnet and her two daughters. But less fortunate than the child, she would wear the disfiguring scars for the rest of her life.[43]

Fanchette's disfigurations emerge paradoxically as the very figurations of her masochistic humility, a pathological humility that accuses the master as it constitutes, on another level entirely, a

---

42. Zulma Carraud, *Une Servante d'autrefois* (Paris: Hachette, 1884), p. 16.
43. Ibid., p. 17.

variant of the "semiology of the spot" as posited by Barthes in his essay on the signs of medical discourse. "These spots," notes Barthes, referring to the marks of disease on the face of a sick man, "refer to nothing else but themselves; they therefore necessitate no further reading or extended interpretation."[44] The same may be said of Fanchette's, as, only surface deep, they refuse the traditional transparency between external flaws and inner defects. But where for Barthes the physiognomy of sickness points indexically to nothing but sickness, Fanchette's blemishes represent a maudlin sentimentality, if not nostalgia, for the loyal, self-effacing *servante d'autrefois*.

Lamartine's maid, Carraud's maid, or Freud's maid, whether covered with spots or blanked out by scopic fixations on other images, remains "invisible," a figment of agency, an "invisible hand." One could argue that insofar as her text is an "enabling discourse" in the literal sense of that term, that is, a discourse that helps "empower" the master narrative, then her "genre," as servant's text, is as marginal as her topological representation. Certainly this definition of her status is supported by literary history. As Erich Auerbach has argued, the maid in her original incarnation played the role of confidante, a receptive ear to the monologue of the mistress, a voice capable of expressing the sexual, reproductive, and materialistic urges suppressed by the master, and a facilitator of dramatic action, much like the stage directions or exordia appended to the great plays of the classical theater.[45] But earlier I suggested that the maid's discourse eventually destabilized

---

44. Roland Barthes, "Sémiologie et médecine" (1972), in *L' Aventure sémiologique* (Paris: Seuil, 1985), p. 281. See also Michel Schneider's concept of the *lisible plaie* for a psychoanalytical rather than a semiological interpretation of corporal scripture in *Blessures de mémoire* (Paris: Gallimard, 1980), pp. 264–65.

45. Erich Auerbach, *Mimesis: The Representation of Reality in Western Literature*, trans. Willard R. Trask (Princeton: Princeton University Press, 1973). In his discussion of Molière, Auerbach wrote: "He [Molière] did not avoid the farcical and the grotesque, yet with him too any real representation of the life of the popular classes, even in such a spirit of aristocratic contempt as Shakespeare's, is as completely out of the question as it is with Boileau. All his chambermaids and servingmen, his peasants and peasants' wives, even his merchants, lawyers, physicians, and apothecaries, are merely comic adjuncts; and it is only within the frame of an upper bourgeois or aristocratic household that servants—especially women—at times represent the voice of down-to-earth common sense. But their functions are always concerned with their masters' problems, never with those of their own lives. Not the slightest trace of politics, of social or economic criticism, or of an analysis of the political, social and economic bases of life is to be found" (p. 365).

that of the master, and if we follow Bruce Robbins's analyses of Victorian fiction, this too is borne out by literary history.[46] A. J. Munby's "secret life" reveals the perverse imagination of a literary lawyer obsessed with a maid-of-all-work who continued to call him "Massa" even after their illicit marriage.

Munby recounts an extraordinary dream during which he justifies his love for a servant to her scandalized employer. With its language of crawling and lifting, abasement and condescension, affective debit and credit, this dream narrative highlights all the ambiguities of hierarchy and control implicit in the relationship between master and servant. A kind of domestic colonialism, this relationship is fraught with tensions created by the close personal contact of class and gender differences.

> And as I was speaking she had softly withdrawn from my side, and crossed the room and gone behind her master's seat: and suddenly I saw her reappear from *under* the sofa, crouched upon her hands and knees. Her face was pressed against the floor, between her outstretched arms; she moved forwards towards me, crawling on all fours, prone along the ground, as if she would abase herself to the utmost. I knew what was in her heart: I trembled with indignation at myself for letting her lie so low, with love and intense delight at the loveliness of her humility. So she crept up to my feet, and flung her lips upon them, and would have *licked my boot*.
>
> Oh divine condescension to me unworthy! Her humiliation is glorious—my lordliness is tyrannical and base. I know it, and rejoice in her triumph over me. So I lift her up and embraced her; and said to him—who had sat amazed the while—"*Now*, do you think she loves me? do you think I owe her any love?"[47]

In the French complement to Munby, found in the counternarrative, or "anti-maid's discourse," set up by, among others, Zola, Maupassant, and Mirbeau as an antidote to the saccharine, orthodox model, the indeterminacy of the maid as signifying agent is clearly in evidence. Here the stereotype of the faithful servant qua female cipher is straightforwardly undermined. This change can be historically explained, at least in part, by the transformation of class structure during the nineteenth century. As an arriviste middle class began

---

46. Bruce Robbins, *The Servant's Hand* (New York: Columbia University Press, 1986).

47. Derek Hudson, *Munby, Man of Two Worlds: The Life and Diaries of Arthur J. Munby, 1828–1910* (London: John Murray, 1972), pp. 182–83.

increasingly to hire servants as a way of driving a wedge between itself and the proletariat, the codes and unwritten laws governing service became more and more ambiguous. A new resentment, or perhaps an old hostility more willingly expressed, developed between employer and employee, surfacing in the various bourgeois antipathies that centered on maids. If the "servant of god" fable was no longer possible, neither was the idealized moral epic of a servant's life featuring the dangers to a girl's virtue posed by a lascivious master. Eighteenth-century classics such as Richardson's *Pamela* and Marivaux's *La Vie de Marianne* yielded to the cynical visions of the Goncourts and Maupassant, who described in lurid detail the violent scenes in which servant girls lost their virginity and the promiscuous ways to which years of sexual brutalization forced them to become accustomed.

Le Journal d'une femme de chambre differs substantially from these anterior models insofar as it generates its discourse of the maid in the first-person singular. Mirbeau grafted the upper-class form of the *mémoire intime* onto the lower-class speech patterns and world view of a dispossessed yet self-reliant working woman. By restoring a voice to a silenced part of the population, he succeeded, like few other writers, in releasing the repressed text of servant resentment and inner revolt. To appreciate fully Mirbeau's departure from the norm, we can compare one of Célestine's monologues with a romantic, sentimentalized definition of the faithful servant. Lamartine, with lyrical didacticism, had offered in *Geneviève* a résumé of the old attitudes and values believed to prevail between master and servant:

> J'ai toujours contemplé avec un pieux respect et avec un sourire d'attendrissement ce qu'on appelait l'esclave ou l'affranchi dans l'antiquité, la nourrice en Grèce, ou dans le moyen âge le *domestique*, c'est-à-dire la partie vivante de la maison, *domus* en France, la *famille* en Italie et en Espagne, véritable nom de la domesticité, car le domestique n'est, au fond, que le complément, l'extension de cette chère et tendre unité de l'association humaine qu'on appelle la famille; c'est la famille moins le sang, c'est la famille d'adoption, c'est la famille viagère, temporaire, annuelle, la famille à gages si vous voulez; mais c'est la famille souvent aussi incorporée, aussi aimante, aussi désintéressée, aussi payée par un salaire de sentiments, aussi dévouée à la considération, à l'honneur, à l'intérêt, à la perpétuité de la maison, que la maison même; que dis-je? souvent bien plus.

> I have always contemplated, with pious respect and a tender smile, that which one has called the slave or freedman in antiquity, the nurse in Greece, or domestic during the Middle Ages—that is, the living part of the household, —*domus* in France, *famille* in Italy and Spain; the true name for domesticity, because the domestic, in essence, is nothing but the complement, the extension of this dear and tender unity of that human association which we call the family. It is the family minus the blood ties, it is the family by adoption. It is the rented family, the family for a fee if you like, but often enough it is an incorporated family, as loving and disinterested, as paid by a salary of sentiment, as devoted to the care, honor, perpetuation, and general good of the household as the household itself; what can I say? often even more so than the household itself.[48]

What is interesting about this exegesis of the social and historical origins of servitude is not so much its obvious note of hypocrisy, evident in oxymorons such as "la famille moins le sang" and "un salaire de sentiments" but, rather, the fact that Lamartine uses this very rhetoric of difference as part of a myth of domestic identity ("l'extension de cette...tendre unité"). Just as Rousseau would transform the noble savage into the citizen, so Lamartine would transform the plebian into the noble servitor.

Lamartine's disquisition is refuted virtually point for point by Célestine's counterdiscourse, which accentuates the notions of detachment, marginality, displacement, and anomie so blithely suppressed by Lamartine:

> Un domestique, ce n'est pas un être normal, un être social.... C'est quelqu'un de disparate, fabriqué de pièces et de morceaux qui ne peuvent s'ajuster l'un dans l'autre, se juxtaposer l'un à l'autre.... C'est quelque chose de pire: un monstrueux hybride humain.... Il n'est plus du peuple, d'où il sort; il n'est pas, non plus, de la bourgeoisie où il vit et où il tend.... Du peuple qu'il a renié, il a perdu le sang généreux et la force naïve.... De la bourgeoisie, il a gagné les vices honteux.... L'âme toute salie, il traverse cet honnête monde bourgeois et rien que d'avoir respiré l'odeur mortelle qui monte de ces putrides cloaques, il perd, à jamais, la sécurité de son esprit, et jusqu'à la forme même de son moi.

> The servant, he's not a normal or social being. He's something disparate, fabricated out of spare parts and pieces that can't be made to fit together. He's something even worse: a monstrous human hybrid.... He is no longer of the people from whence he came; nor is he of the

---

48. Alphonse de Lamartine, *Geneviève: Histoire d'une Servante* (1850) (Paris: Nelson, 1925), p. 84.

bourgeoisie where he lives and to which he is drawn.... He has lost the fullbloodedness and simple force of the people he denied.... From the bourgeoisie, he has acquired shameful vices. His soul covered with filth, he travels through this great bourgeois world, and simply by breathing the deadly odors rising up from these putrid cesspools, he loses, forever, not only his peace of mind, but also the very shape of his being. (*JF* 176)

The semiotic of the *tache* ("l'âme toute salie") reemerges, making of the employer's dirty linen an unclean inner lining attached to the domestic self. Congruent neither with herself nor with her superiors or inferiors, the maid is destabilized and dislocated, becoming an omnibus signifier not only of modern defamiliarization but also of that which is monstrous.

And it is specifically this half-concealed monstrous character that can be detected in such stories as Maupassant's "Rosalie Prudent" and "La Mère aux monstres," featuring the maid as denatured mother. Both stories revolve around the crime of infanticide. In the former, Rosalie, seduced by the nephew of her employers, smothers both of the resulting twins rather than choose between them, for she can afford to support only one. In the latter, a similarly victimized maid avails herself of the "corset de force," but instead of dying, her infant is born deformed, and in order to survive expulsion from the village, the mother becomes a "montreur de phénomènes," thereby living off, by showing (*monstrare*), the monster (*monstrum*) she herself has created.[49]

Published in 1886, this singularly horrific tale seems to have its precedent in Barbey d'Aurevilly's *Une Histoire sans nom* (1882) (itself a kind of rewriting of Heinrich von Kleist's *Marquise von O* insofar as it revolves around a miraculous pregnancy), in which the mortified mother tries to stifle her daughter's future progeny with the same sinister method: "Elle laçait elle-même le corset de Lasthénie, et elle ne craignait pas de le serrer trop fort et de lui faire mal.... 'Avez-vous donc si peur que je vous *le* tue?' reprenait Mme de Ferjol avec une sauvage amertume. [She herself laced up Lasthénie's corset, and she never shrank from tightening it so hard that it hurt her.... 'Are you so afraid that I'm going to kill *it*?' Mme de Ferjol rejoined with a savage rancor]."[50] Mirbeau, no doubt following Barbey and Maupassant, also used the image of the corset to

---

49. Maupassant, "La Mère aux monstres," in *Contes et Nouvelles* (1974), 1:845.
50. Barbey d'Aurevilly, *Une Histoire sans nom*, in *Oeuvres romanesques complètes* (1882; Paris: Gallimard, 1966), p. 318.

dramatize infanticide. In one of the vignettes of *Le Journal d'une femme de chambre*, an out-of-work gardener and his pregnant wife are sworn to sterility by a redoubtable countess, herself the tender mother of several children. The poor, she insists, must not encumber the estate with their supplementary charge, and so saying, fixes her exigent gaze on the distended stomach of the guilty woman. Having agreed to her terms, which are themselves the real crime against nature, husband and wife depart:

> La pauvre femme marchait péniblement, tirait la jambe. Comme elle étouffait un peu, elle s'arrêta, posa son sac à terre et délaça son corset.
> —Ouf!... fit-elle en aspirant de larges bouffées d'air....
> Et son ventre, longtemps comprimé, se tendit, s'enfla, accusa la rondeur caractéristique, la tare de la maternité, le crime....
> Le malheur vint. Quatre jours après, la femme eut une fausse couche—une fausse couche?—et mourut en d'affreuses douleurs d'une péritonite.

> The poor woman walked with a painful gait, dragging her leg. Since she had trouble breathing, she stopped, put down her bag and unlaced her corset.
> "Whew!" she said, taking large gulps of air.
> And her stomach, so long confined, relaxed, swelled, and betrayed that characteristic roundness, that taint of maternity, the crime.
> Ill fortune came. Four days later, the woman had a miscarriage—a miscarriage?—and died in terrible pain of peritonitis. (*JF* 332–33)

Despite the evident culpability of society in general, the figure of the servant as potential murderess is nonetheless fed as a popular phantasm, perhaps thereby insinuating itself into the Freudian imaginary as a fetishistic projection of the castrated mother. Such a characterization is fully present even in socially uncritical maids' narratives, as when Geneviève laments, "Parentes sans parenté, familières sans famille, filles sans mères, mères sans enfants, coeurs qui se donnent sans être reçus: voilà le sort des servantes devant vous! [Parents without relatives, intimates without families, daughters without mothers, mothers without children, hearts which offer themselves without ever being received, that is the fate of the servants in your midst!]' and as in Paul Bourget's implausible novella *Une Fille-mère* (1928), in which an unwed mother works as a faithful servant for her son, guarding her identity until her death so that he may conserve his improved class status.[51] Each of these texts confirms the bourgeois distrust of maids as a class of maternally castrated women. They also help to explain why the preferred instrument of infanticide—the corset—might have come to be a fetish, standing in for what was lost to the maid. A punishing phantasm of deadly striations and knots, itself linking fetishism to sadomasochism, the image of the corset (as Karl Abraham, commenting on a patient's fascination with tying up, would observe) places part of the psychic anatomy "in bondage."

In his investigation of how certain "degenerate" practices such as alcoholism or debauchery become "contagious" in large urban areas, the turn-of-the-century sociologist Gabriel de Tarde formulated a set of behavioral laws alleged to govern the interaction between social classes at various hierarchical stations. The influence of his *Les Lois de l'imitation* (1895) is felt throughout *Le Journal d'une femme de chambre*, which at one level can be read as a didactic illustration of its principles.[52] The law of "inside and outside" posits a collaboration between innate and learned behavior that manifests itself in the servant's acquired obedience, as well as his conventionally sanctioned outlets for revolt (group gossip sessions directed against the employer). More pertinent is the law of imitation of superiors by inferiors, which reveals itself as the major motive for Célestine's collusion with her fellow servant, Joseph. Despite her conviction that he is the culprit in the rape and sadistic murder of a village girl, she allows herself to be seduced by his promise to make her the proprietress of a café, so strong is her desire to become a "mistress" in her own right.

The most sardonic exposure of the *bourgeois gentilhomme* phenomenon is directed against Paul Bourget, whose society novels epitomized for Mirbeau the worst kind of literary prostitution. In *Le Journal*, Bourget is portrayed as having so snobbish a fixation on the classes above that he disallows any extension of his famous "psychology" to members of the lower classes (*JF* 118). Taking

---

51. Lamartine, *Geneviève*, p. 301; Paul Bourget, *Une Fille-mère*, in *Les Oeuvres libres* (Paris: Fayard, 1928), p. 7.

52. Gabriel de Tarde, *Les Lois de l'imitation* (Geneva: Slatkine, 1979). Tarde's influence is most discernible in the theory of Emile Durkheim and Roger Callois (see Denis Hollier, *Le Collège de Sociologie, 1937–1939* [Paris: Gallimard, 1979]).

Tarde's theory of imitation to the letter—"It's a recognized fact that we model our characters on that of our masters"—Célestine retaliates by inverting the paradigm of slave copying master. If Bourget refuses to grant a soul to servants, then he will be baptized a "soul drainer" (*videur d'âmes*), and as such, *himself a maid*: "Monsieur Jean vidait les pots de chambre... M. Paul Bourget vidait les âmes [Monsieur Jean emptied chamber pots; M. Paul Bourget emptied souls]". And lest there be any lingering doubts over the analogy, she adds: "Entre l'office et le salon, il n'y a pas toute la distance de servitude que l'on croit! [Between downstairs and upstairs, there's not such a servile distance as you would think!]" (*JF* 368).

Despite her indignation in the face of Bourget's indifference toward his inferiors, Célestine replicates the same attitude. Mimicking the commodity fetishism of her superiors, she creates an altar to kitsch in the bare, insalubrious maid's room to which she is assigned:

> Demain, je tâcherai de m'arranger un peu... Au-dessus de mon lit, je clouerai mon petit crucifix de cuivre doré, et je mettrai sur la cheminée ma bonne vierge de porcelaine peinte, avec mes petites boîtes, mes petits bibelots et les photographies de monsieur Jean, de façon à introduire dans ce galetas un rayon d'intimité et de joie.

> Tomorrow, I'll try to set myself up a little. Above the bed, I'll nail my little brass crucifix, and I'll put my nice painted porcelain virgin on the mantelpiece, with my little boxes, my little knickknacks and the photographs of Monsieur Jean, by way of introducing a ray of intimacy and joy into this garret. (*JF* 56)

Here, the laws of imitation induce an unsettling affinity between proletariat and bourgeois. The modest icons of Célestine's past life project the aura of household gods, just like the hideous bibelots surinvested by her employers, the Lanlaires. Mirbeau seems to insinuate that a universalizing psychology of fetishization overrides the ideological differences of even the most historically divided social castes.

If commodity fetishism is the enemy of class consciousness in Mirbeau's study of the domestic *socius*, so too are the servant's aspirations. As she ascends the social ladder, Célestine conveniently "forgets" her own past, extending the laws of imitation to the mistreatment of the domestics now beneath her. Established with

Joseph in her Cherbourg bistro, she complains: "They're impossible, these maids of Cherbourg, promiscuous and thieving! No, it's simply incredible, disgusting" (*JF* 383). Proust would also capture this sociological law in his portrait of Françoise, who, a loyal *servante d'autrefois*, exhibits no animosity when ordered to go upstairs for nothing (according to an idle whim of Tante Léonie) but displays unmitigated outrage at being told to go downstairs for something, such as the malady of a scullery maid:

· Une de ces nuits qui suivirent l'accouchement de la fille de cuisine, celle-ci fut prise d'atroces coliques: maman l'entendit se plaindre, se leva et réveilla Françoise qui, insensible, déclara que tous ces cris étaient une comédie, qu'elle voulait "faire la maîtresse."

· One night, shortly after her confinement, the kitchen-maid was seized with the most appalling pains; Mamma heard her groans, and rose and awakened Françoise, who, quite unmoved, declared that all the outcry was mere malingering, that the girl wanted to "play the mistress."[53]

Clearly "playing the mistress" herself as she accuses the scullery maid, Françoise, like Célestine, like Paul Bourget, demonstrates the law of imitation from below to above, thus giving a social ascription to the direction of the Freudian gaze.

Mirbeau, again following Tarde, also describes a process that might be called "reverse fetishism" whereby the master, imitating his subordinate, seems impelled downward by some magnetic force. Here, the interchangeability of idealization and humiliation, emphasized by Freud and Karl Abraham in their descriptions of the contradictory impulses of fetishism, becomes most apparent. Jealous of Célestine's good looks and openly avowed weakness for sexual adventure, one of her mistresses becomes a part-time streetwalker, returning from her escapades with her underwear torn and dirty, her corset and garters unlaced, and her hair covered with the feathers of a stranger's pillow. In another instance, a mother anxious to keep her son at home uses Célestine as sexual bait, manipulating her like a madam in a bordello. Lending herself to a game of mimetic rivalry whose object is the ignominious son, Célestine descends to the level of a prostitute, dragging her mistress down with her even further in the course of their altercations:

---

53. Marcel Proust, *Du côté de chez Swann* (Paris: Gallimard, 1954), p. 149. Marcel Proust, *Remembrance of Things Past*, vol. 1, trans. C. K. Scott Moncrieff and Terence Kilmartin (New York: Vintage, 1982), p. 133.

"They descended to the vocabulary level of common hookers" (*JF* 258). A variation of this law of negative imitation can also be found in *Germinie Lacerteux* at the pivotal moment where servant and mistress exchange roles. Having attained "the lower depths," her depravity reigning in the filth and disorder of the household, Germinie terrorizes her lenient mistress, Mademoiselle de Varandeuil, to the point where the latter becomes the "servant of the servant": "Parfois, quand Germinie était sortie, elle se hasardait à donner avec ses mains goutteuses un coup de serviette sur la commode, un coup de plumeau sur un cadre. Elle se dépêchait, craignant d'être grondée, d'avoir une scène, si sa bonne rentrait et la voyait. [Occasionally, when Germinie was out, she risked, with her gout-ridden hands, giving a wipe to the commode, a shake of the featherduster to the picture frame. She hurried, fearing a scolding or a scene, if her maid were to return and see her]."[54] The Goncourts imply an explanation for this reversal in the prehistory of Mlle de Varandeuil's life with Germinie. Faced with adversity during the Revolution, Mademoiselle had been forced by her father to serve both him and the real maid, with whom he has had a child. With this dreadful past behind her, the act of serving Germinie is comparable to the resurgence of an atavism, as if to confirm in the later novel Célestine's conviction that, like hereditary stigmas or diseases, "servitude is in the blood" and can never be wholly extirpated (*JF* 272, 382).

Locked into a carnivalesque ritual of parodic doubling, maid and mistress reproduce the master/slave dialectic as the stuff of high comedy. Which is the real maid, and which is the copy? When does the factotum become less than factitious, something more than ersatz master? The servant's text qualifies as a fetishistic genre in its grotesque simulation of the master's discourse, whereby it becomes a "secondhand" (in the sense of "already used," "handed down") master narrative. Though this genre may be seen as undermining the authority of such canonic works as Flaubert's *Un Coeur simple* or Freud's *Case of the Wolf-man*, it fails, in the end, to empower itself through representational strategies that are themselves free of false consciousness.

•

It is perhaps no surprise that the imbrication of political and psychoanalytical master/slave dialectics that one finds in Mirbeau's

---

54. Edmond and Jules de Goncourt, *Germinie Lacerteux* (Paris: Flammarion, 1930), pp. 130–31.

Le Journal d'une femme de chambre would appeal to a filmmaker such as Luis Buñuel. Though not the first to adapt the book for the screen—Jean Renoir had already done so in 1946 with an American production, *The Diary of a Chambermaid*, starring Paulette Goddard and Burgess Meredith—Buñuel's particular combination of realism and surrealism in *Le Journal d'une femme de chambre* (1963) afforded not just an original interpretation of the novel but also a form of filmic fetishism.

Transposing Célestine's confessional, loosely concatenated narrative into a seamless drama involving proto-Fascist politics (the action is moved up from 1900 to the late 1930s), a sex murder, and the ascendance of a chambermaid to bourgeois respectability as the wife of a provincial seigneur (in the movie, Célestine marries not Joseph but the Lanlaires' neighbor and rival, Captain Mauger), Buñuel plays down the disturbing complicity of Mirbeau's heroine. The foot fetishism episode is collapsed by Buñuel into the central diegesis, itself structured around Célestine's sojourn with the Lanlaires. In this scene, the art of the fetishistic close-up, the hyperrealistic frame that focuses in and concentrates relentlessly on the single image, recalls what Freud implied when he argued, "It seems that when the fetish comes to life, so to speak, some process has been suddenly interrupted." Wiggling and squirming on the screen, as if possessed of a life of their own, defamiliarized and uncannily detached from the leg as in surrealist collages, sculptures, or "picture-objects" (such as Miró's *Poetic Object* of 1936, which features a shoe-clad mannequin leg suspended over a bowler hat and crowned by a stuffed parrot, or Dali's 1931 *Scatological Object Functioning Symbolically*, depicting a large shoe placed beneath its miniaturized photographic replica), Buñuel's boots become obscene, a pair of animated phalluses. Images of perverse desire floating in space, of "suspense" both in the sense of physically suspended and emotionally fascinating, they approximate figures of what John Simon, evoking the myth of Tantalus, would call in a scathing review of Buñuel's later film, *The Discreet Charm of the Bourgeoisie*, "co-eatus interruptus."[55] This expression seems oddly justified when it is remembered that Monsieur Rabour's nemesis is to die, literally, "with his foot in his mouth."

Interruption, one of the techniques of film editing, is instrumentalized as a form of fetishism throughout Buñuel's films. Like the

---

55. John Simon, "*The Discreet Charm of the Bourgeoisie*: Why Is the Co-eatus Always Interruptus?" in *The World of Luis Buñuel: Essays in Criticism*, ed. Joan Mellen (New York: Oxford University Press, 1978), p. 368.

"coupeur de nattes" (pigtail cutter) who races through the case histories of Krafft-Ebing capturing the pigtails of unsuspecting schoolgirls (metonyms for the rest of the female anatomy according to Krafft-Ebing; their odor a source of coprophilic attraction according to Freud), Buñuel refines the art of *découpage* (cutting), deriving a special *jouissance* from the camera's fondling of a visually intransitive fragment. Barthes would query: "Is the tableau then (since it arises from a process of cutting out) a fetish-object?"[56] Extending the discourse of Christian Metz on the role of framing, or *encadrement*, in the fundamentally "erotogenic" experience of film viewing, Barthes privileged the notion of cutting, as when he said of Eisenstein's *Battleship Potemkin*:

> The film is a contiguity of episodes, each one absolutely meaningful, aesthetically perfect, and the result is a cinema by vocation anthological, itself holding out to the fetishist, with dotted lines, the piece for him to cut out and take away to enjoy (isn't it said that in some *cinemathèque* or other a piece of film is missing from the copy of *Battleship Potemkin*—the scene with the baby's pram, of course—it having been cut off and stolen lovingly like a lock of hair, a glove or an item of women's underwear?[57]

By identifying the repertory of objects (on the order of Eisenstein's baby carriage) that are subject to *découpage* and close-up, one might construe Buñuel's personal vocabulary of castrated images, each of which bears the distinctive stamp of a fetish. Drawn from the culture of realist painting and fiction, Buñuel's visual icons point on the one hand to surrealism's parasitical relationship to realism and on the other to the familiar affinities between surrealism and fetishism. Both rely on the psychopathology of childhood memories cluttered with the bric-a-brac of the nursery, articles of clothing worn by the maid, curios of the bourgeois interior or *idées reçues* surrounding these items, as in Flaubert's entry for boots in his "Dictionnaire des idées reçues": "On n'est jamais chaussé qu'avec des bottes [Only with boots is one truly shod]."[58] Both too seem to have a common denominator in the psychoanalytics of vision, specifically a science or theory of "seeing in the dark," which Freud alluded to indirectly with the verb *to scotomize* (*skotos* in Greek means

---

56. Roland Barthes, "Diderot, Brecht, Eisenstein," *Image-Music-Text*, trans. Stephen Heath (New York: Hill and Wang, 1977), p. 71.
57. Ibid., p. 72.
58. Gustave Flaubert, *Bouvard et Pécuchet* (Paris: Garnier-Flammarion, 1966), p. 338.

"darkness"). Finally, both depend on the trope of metonymy as a way of increasing the legibility of desire.

The coupling of metonymy, as brutal montage of intimate artifacts, with magnification—the zoom-lens effect that distorts the miniature by transforming it into the gargantuan—might be seen as one of Buñuel's most distinctive contributions to the definition of filmic fetishism. In a macabre shot of the raped and murdered "little Claire," in *Le Journal d'une femme de chambre*, the camera travels along the spread-eagled legs of the girl (the rest of her body is blocked from view) and focuses obsessively on a viscous, phallic snail perched upon her knee. The snail, like the ants that swarm out of a woman's armpit or appear in the palm of a man's hand in *Un Chien andalou*, designates the fetish as indexical marker of the forbidden, of horror impossible to contemplate. With a splice, obstruction, distraction, substitute image, or any other technique of visual ellipsis or parataxis, Buñuel's camera obscures the "obscure object of desire" while at the same time disclosing its shadowy trace.

Here we are again reminded of that disturbing passage in Freud's essay on fetishism where he takes a painstaking detour in order to contradict an apparently gratuitous term applied by another psychoanalyst to the object or subject that Freud wishes to call repression. This term, *scotomization*, becomes, however, immediately less gratuitous when we realize that it refers to "dizziness, dimness of sight" or, more technically, to "an obscuration of part of the visual field due to lesion of the retina or of the ophthalmic center of the brain."[59] Imputing to the psychoanalyst Laforgue the notion that the fetishist scotomizes the perception of the woman's lack of a penis, Freud then goes on to repudiate the choice of this term: "'Scotomization' seems to me particularly unsuitable, for it suggests that the perception is entirely wiped out, so that the result is the same as when a visual impression falls on the blind spot on the retina. In the situation we are considering, on the contrary, we see that the perception has persisted, and that a very energetic action has been undertaken to maintain the disavowal."[60] Freud's "correction" of Laforgue notwithstanding, his own preferred substitutes—"denial," "denegation" (*Verdrängung, Verneinung*)—carried, as we have seen, no comparable visual denotation. Had he recuperated the term more fully, revising it to include his own emphasis on partial disavowal,

---

59. *Oxford English Dictionary*, s.v. "scotomization."
60. Freud, "Fetishism," *Standard Edition* 21:153–54.

he might have afforded the basis for a definition of filmic fetishism—a "science of skotology"—situated mid-point between the eschatological (regressing to origins or infantile fixations) and the scatological (filthy, perverse, taboo). Within this scheme, the proper instrument of fetishistic vision would no longer be a camera but a *skotoscope* (which we could define as an instrument that enables its user to "see in the dark"), a machine that, by partially obscuring the visual field, literalizes the verbal metaphor of "a fly in the eye."[61] Some such machine was no doubt behind Buñuel's first surrealist film—*Un Chien andalou,* an authentic piece of automatic writing in the dark—where an eye is hideously cut open with a razor, thus joining the motif of castrated vision to the architectural derivation of *skotos* (*skotia*), synonymous with *groove* or *cut*. Appropriately enough, this "cutting of the cut" (or montage) was most directly signaled by Buñuel's own treatment of Mirbeau's text, where an episode seemingly calculated in advance to appeal to a future surrealist is subjected itself to scotomization: Célestine's resigned cutting of the boot out of the mouth of Monsieur Rabour is curiously omitted from Buñuel's footage. Was Buñuel, like Freud, susceptible to suppression of the maid once she appeared fully exposed as maternal castrator?

Mirbeau's maid, Freud's maid, and now Buñuel's maid—each, eventually, seems doomed to negation and visual punishment. The screen "punishes" Célestine, much like the sadistic narrator in Robert Coover's *Spanking the Maid,* as he "cuts" brutally into the narrative of his own fantasies, splicing dissociated frames of the servant entering, exiting, or bending over in submission. The feminist film critic, Laura Mulvey, commenting on the broader issue of the filmic subjection of women, allows us to situate the sadistic treatment of Buñuel's Célestine in relation to the inherently sadistic voyeurism of the male gaze:

> Thus the woman as icon, displayed for the gaze and enjoyment of men, the active controllers of the look, always threatens to evoke the anxiety it originally signified. The male unconscious has two avenues of escape from this castration anxiety: preoccupation with the reenactment of the original trauma (investigating the woman, demystifying her mystery), counterbalanced by the devaluation, punishment, or saving of the guilty

---

61. See Hubert Damisch's explication of the "fly" in Valerio Adami's portrait of Freud as bait (*appât*), spot (*tache*), and signature, in *Fenêtre jaune cadmium* (Paris: Seuil, 1984), pp. 239–64.

object... or else complete disavowal of castration by the substitution of a fetish object.... The first avenue, voyeurism,... has associations with sadism: pleasure lies in ascertaining guilt (immediately associated with castration), asserting control, and subjecting the guilty person through punishment or forgiveness.[62]

Mulvey illuminates the power of the maid as a dual sign: a fetish or cult object on the one hand, an object of visual abuse on the other. More important, by referring us back to the problem of scopic mastery (raised by Cixous, developed by Luce Irigaray), Mulvey enables us to read the maid as a symbolic representation of the potentially threatening female viewer, as a domestic spy who uncovers the insecurities of the master, surprising him in the privacy of unchecked fantasy.[63] Or, as nineteenth-century tradition would have it, the maid, becoming herself the direct agent of fantasy's fulfillment, must be monitored by the phallic look, like the female figure on screen or the feminist film critic, and, if necessary, punished with filmic fustigation.

62. Laura Mulvey, "Visual Pleasure and Narrative Cinema," in *Visual and Other Pleasures* (Bloomington: Indiana University Press, 1989), pp. 21–22.
63. In her important critique of Freudian phallocentrism, Luce Irigaray has challenged the preeminence of (male) scopic perversion, with its obsessive privileging of that phallic place. Summarizing the implications of her argument in *Sexual/Textual Politics: Feminist Literary Theory* (London: Methuen, 1985), Toril Moi notes: "Freud's own texts, particularly 'The uncanny,' theorize the *gaze* as a phallic activity linked to the anal desire for sadistic mastery of the object. The specularizing philosopher is the potent master of his insight; as the example of Oedipus demonstrates, the fear of blindness is the fear of castration. As long as the master's 'scopophilia' (i.e., 'love of looking') remains satisfied, his domination is secure. No wonder then that the little girl's *rien à voir* ('nothing to be seen') is threatening to the male theorist" (p. 134). Subject to a nihilating gaze, covered with "blind spots" that obscure her from view, the maid's body, *as a text*, reveals an anxiety over scopic domination in master and theorist alike.

CHAPTER 9

· *Stigma Indelebile:* Zola, Gide, and the Deviant Detail

· Seventeen years separate two allusions in Freud's oeuvre to the *stigma indelebile*, or indelible trace, a sign that acts as a signature certifying the evidence of fetishistic displacement.

> · Before the child comes under the dominance of the castration-complex—at a time when he still holds women at full value—he begins to display an intense desire to look, as an erotic instinctual activity. He wants to see other people's genitals, at first in all probability to compare them with his own. The erotic attraction that comes from his mother soon culminates in a longing for her genital organ, which he takes to be a penis. With the discovery, which is not made till later, that women do not have a penis, this longing often turns into its opposite and gives place to a feeling of disgust which in the years of puberty *can become the cause of physical impotence, misogyny and permanent homosexuality.* But the fixation on the object that was once strongly desired, the woman's penis, *leaves indelible traces on the mental life of the child.*[1]

> · Aversion from the real female genitals, which is never lacking in any fetishist, also remains as a *stigma indelebile* of the repression that has taken place. One can now see what the fetish achieves and how it is enabled to persist.[2]

Freud's emphasis on the stigma harks back to Krafft-Ebing's *Psychopathia Sexualis*. Commenting on how in fetishistic love a man or woman can become attracted to a single trait, even a physiological defect in the beloved, he noted, "Since the fetish assumes the form of *a*

---

1. Sigmund Freud, "Leonardo da Vinci and a Memory of His Childhood," *Standard Edition* 11:96.
2. Sigmund Freud, "Fetishism," *Standard Edition* 21:154. All further references to this text will be abbreviated "F."

distinctive mark it is clear that its effect can only be of an individual character." For Krafft-Ebing, the indelible stigma as badge or distinguishing mark emerges as that mysterious point at which desire is activated against all the odds posed by appearance: "Thus love exhibits itself now as a mere passion, now as a pronounced psychical anomaly which attains what seemed impossible, renders the ugly beautiful, the profane sublime, and obliterates all consciousness of existing duties toward others."[3] Krafft-Ebing's fetishistic spur approximates what Lacan would designate as the *tychic*—a marker of the place where the scopic drive (the love of looking) "encounters" (from *tuché*) the psychical ("psychique"), thus allowing a repressed desire for the other's ("objet A") other ("objet petit a") to show itself ("faire signe").[4]

If, in his pathography of Leonardo da Vinci, Freud treated the *tychic* stigma qua fetish as the sign of repressed homosexuality, he made this elision even more explicit in "Fetishism": "Probably no male human being is spared the terrifying shock of threatened castration at the sight of the female genitals. We cannot explain why it is that some of them become homosexual in consequence of this experience, others ward it off by creating a fetish," ("F" 201). Homosexuality is presented as an alternative to fetishism though they share specific causes and effects. Both are instigated by castration anxiety, and both imply a turning away from the mother, a visual avoidance or denial of the real female body. As the device that "wards off" homosexuality, fetishism is also implicitly valorized by Freud as a kind of vaccination against a desire of man for man that he is incapable of recognizing in and for itself (that is, as anything other than a defense against the phantom of emasculation). Fetishism emerges then as homosexuality's repressive watchdog, an ensign of homophobia.

But it is not quite so simple. Though Freud does indeed identify the fetish with the suppression of the visible cause of homosexuality, he also allows it to function as a visual incentive, a target for the gaze that loves to look (even as it looks away). It thus becomes an ambivalent site on which the possibility of a homoerotic encounter is held out, *as well as* the mark of society's punishment for any *passage à l'acte*. In what follows, I will be arguing that André Gide's

---

3. Richard von Krafft-Ebing, *Psychopathia Sexualis*, trans. Harry E. Wedeck (New York: Putnam's, 1965), p. 37.

4. Jacques Lacan, *The Four Fundamental Concepts of Pyschoanalysis*, trans. Alan Sheridan, ed. Jacques-Alain Miller (New York: Norton, 1978), p. 80.

treatment of the *tare*, or stigma, reveals just this kind of erotic "coming and going," or "advancing and retreating," within his system of homotextual representation.[5] The tropes of oscillation, uncertainty, displacement, and de-repressed negation that circle around a charged, eroticized object are decipherable as textual expressions of the epistemological affinities and tensions between homosexuality and fetishism.

In tracing this poetics of the "deviant detail," I also want to suggest a contrast between Gide's turn-of-the-century homotextual fetishism and the misogynist realism of the nineteenth-century authors concentrated on thus far. In the writings of the Goncourt brothers, Maupassant, and Mirbeau, misogyny seems bound to realism in its morbid fascination with the feminine detail. Fetishism in these authors is enacted in an array of literary strategies ranging from the use of veiling metaphors, or an *écriture artiste*, to the "masquerade of styles" noted by Walter Benjamin as typical of the century.[6] In virtually all cases, these styles are deployed in order to bolster a fundamental androcentrism in literary and social life. Gide's complicated responses to realist-naturalist detailism are of particular interest not so much because they typify a contrasting gay alternative to this homophobic androcentrism, or because they exemplify an early-twentieth-century refusal of an earlier period's stylistic mannerisms, but rather because they reappropriate the fetishistic detail for homoeroticism. Transposing the detail from its misogynist heritage to new ground, that is, to the domain of the "monstrous" but stirringly attractive "little real," Gide, in a sense, instigated a definitive rupture with a certain kind of nineteenth-century fetishism. Where the avatars of the fin de siècle seemed to want to don fetishistic narrative as a cover for their generalized fear of woman, Gide coded that fetish as young and male, associating it with those "little mysteries" of narrative capable of revivifying worn-out conventions of plot and style.

· J'abandonne la lecture de *L' Oeuvre*, le plus mauvais des livres de Zola dont il me souvienne.... Zola ne semble soupçonner d'autre ennemi du naturalisme, que l'académisme; et encore trouve-t-il le moyen de ramener les angoisses de son Claude à des tares héréditaires.

    5. For a full discussion of what I mean by "homotextuality" in Gide's work, see "Homotextual Counter-codes," in *André Gide and the Codes of Homotextuality* (Stanford: Anma Libri, 1987).
    6. Walter Benjamin, *Das Passagen-Werk, Gesammelte Schriften*, V, ed. Rolf Tiedemann (Frankfurt am Main: Suhrkamp Verlag, 1982), 1:288.

· I give up my reading of *The Masterpiece*, the poorest of Zola's books that I can recall.... Zola does not seem to suspect any other enemy of naturalism than academicism; and even then he manages to relate the anxieties of his Claude to hereditary stigmas.[7]

Written in 1943, Gide's contentious remark encapsulated nearly fifty years of ambivalence toward his realist predecessor. An admirer in his youth of Zola's *La Faute de l'Abbé Mouret*, Gide had pastiched the excesses of idolatrous devotion and its transgressive spirituality in his own post-symbolist *La Tentative amoureuse*. Shortly thereafter, he oscillated toward parody, using Zola's art of "objective" realist description as the target of satire in his *soties*. In *Paludes*, naturalism was mired in its own rhetorical bog of botanical onomastics. In *Le Promethée mal enchaîné*, humorous effect was produced, as in the medieval *sotie*, by submerging a mythic masterplot in a morass of confabulation and period decor (Prometheus in a Parisian café). In *Les Caves du Vatican*, the *fait divers* (tabloid)—a favored genre of the realists—was used to construct the edifice of an elaborate narrative farce. Reassimilated as part of a general espousal of realist ethics in the political climate of the 1930s, and finally to be abandoned with irritation in Gide's turning away from activism, Zola remained a central reference point, positive or negative, in Gide's literary trajectory.

Marked at each moment by entries in the *Journal*, Zola's insistent presence for Gide seems to have taken on the character of a fetish: avowed and disavowed, negated and denegated, displaced, like a prosthesis affixed to Gide's literary anatomy, from one modality of his writing to another. This continual *return* of Zola, in the manner of some uncanny figure or phantasm of a repressed *écriture*, leads us to a reading of Gide's oeuvre that adjusts some of the commonplace generic boundaries used to characterize it and points to a link between fetishism and realism in Gide's own definition of the latter. His clinical fascination with the anomalous, deviant, and perverse became translated, often through the use of realist iconography, into a cipher of psychophysiognomical traces—stigmata, scars, tattoos, and *tares*. His obsessive focus on ironic details—sartorial accoutrements, fragments of the body—approximated the fixated

7. André Gide, *Journal*, 2 vols., *1899–1939* and *1939–1949* (Paris: Gallimard, 1951–54), 2:161; trans. Justin O'Brien as *The Journals of André Gide*, 4 vols. (New York: Knopf, 1947–55), 4:1951. Further references to the French edition will be abbreviated *Jour*; those to the English will be abbreviated *JAG*. Undesignated translations are my own.

gaze of the Freudian fetishist on the disembodied maternal phallus, an object of both attraction and repulsion.[8] But perhaps most significant was the way in which Zola and the realist text itself became implicated in the coded language deployed by Gide, unwittingly or not, to communicate his own private psychopathologies. When in 1924, placing himself in the role of Freudian doctor-analyst, he queried, "Quelles vengeances secrètes peut alors se préparer la part de l'être qui n'a pas trouvé place au festin? [What secret forms of revenge are then prepared by that part which had no share in the feast?]" it was as if he espied, in his own texts, the resentful trace of a suppressed part of his own Being, or the compromising evidence of his own irrepressible "weaknesses" (*JAG* 1:786).[9]

Any post-Freudian reader of the detail, sensitive to the referential fallacies of Barthes's "effet du réel," is struck by the number of banal objects apparently gratuitously introduced in *Les Caves du Vatican*; a repertory including ties, collars, cuff links, spectacles, and hats. The same aura of superfluity surrounds the description, rendered with exaggerated "exactitude and rigor," of a giant wen

---

8. In her important book *Reading in Detail: Aesthetics and the Feminine* (New York: Methuen, 1987), Naomi Schor concludes with an assessment of the "reality effect" or "detailism" within the realist canon: "To say that realism, in particular French nineteenth-century realism, is a 'detailism' (to recall again Lewes's term), is to rehearse a topos which runs through all of the critical discourses on realism from Brunetière to Barthes, from Lewes to Lukács. Whether the association is positively or negatively valorized, whether the detail is said to be in the service of a conservative or a revolutionary aesthetics, producing its mimetic effect by means of a referential emptiness or plenitude, the detail occupies—despite or perhaps because of its insignificance—a privileged position in the theory of realism" (p. 141).

9. This remark comes at the end of a long passage in Gide's *Journal* in which he speculated on "Freudianism," specifically the displacement theory of sexual desire: "The point on which my assiduous investigations (if I were a doctor) would bear is this: what happens when, for social, moral, etc. reasons, the sexual function is forced, in order to find satisfaction, to leave the object of its desire; when the satisfaction of the flesh involves no assent, no participation of the rest of the person, when it is divided with a part of itself remaining behind?...What remains subsequently from that division? What traces? What secret forms of revenge are then prepared by that part which had no share in the feast?" (*JAG* 2:351). Gide referred to Freud relatively little in his writings though there is no doubt that he was greatly impressed by Freud's theories. Elisabeth Roudinesco has recently suggested that Gide's portrait of a woman psychoanalyst in *Les Faux-Monnayeurs* was modeled on the "Doctoresse" Eugénie Sokolnicka, whose salon attracted noted literati (among them Gide's friends Jacques Rivière, Roger Martin du Gard, Gaston Gallimard, and Jean Schlumberger). See Roudinesco's *Histoire de la psychanalyse en France*, vol. 2: *1925–1985* (Paris: Seuil, 1986), p. 107.

whose unchecked growth on the neck of the behavioral psychologist Anthime Armand-Dubois proportionally measures the progression of his heretical "free-thinking":

> Ici, malgré tout mon désir de ne relater que l'essentiel, je ne puis passer sous silence la loupe d'Anthime Armand-Dubois. Car, tant que je n'aurai pas plus sûrement appris à démêler l'accidentel du nécessaire, qu'exigerais-je de ma plume sinon exactitude et rigueur?...
>
> Ça lui était venu il ne savait comment, peu de temps après son mariage; et d'abord il n'y avait eu, au sud-est de son oreille gauche, où le cuir devient chevelu, qu'un cicer sans autre importance; longtemps, sous l'abondant cheveu qu'il ramenait en boucle par-dessus, il put dissimuler l'excroissance; Véronique, elle-même, ne l'avait pas encore remarquée, lorsque, dans une caresse nocturne, sa main soudain la rencontrant:
> "Tiens! qu'est-ce que tu as là?" s'était-elle écriée.
> Et comme si, démasquée, la grosseur n'avait plus à garder de retenue, elle prit en peu de mois les dimensions d'un oeuf de perdrix, puis de pintade, puis de poule et s'en tint là, tandis que le cheveu plus rare se partageait à l'entour d'elle et l'exposait. A quarante-six ans, Anthime Armand-Dubois n'avait plus à songer à plaire; il coupa ras ses cheveux et adopta cette forme de faux cols demi-hauts dans lesquels une sorte d'alvéole réservée cachait la loupe et la révélait à la fois. Suffit pour la loupe d'Anthime.

> And now, notwithstanding my desire to relate nothing but what is essential, I cannot pass over in silence Anthime Armand-Dubois's wen. For until I have learned to distinguish more surely between the accidental and the necessary, what can I demand from my pen but the most rigorous fidelity?...
>
> It had made its appearance, without his knowing how, shortly after his marriage; and at first it had been merely an inconsiderable wart, southeast of his left ear, just where the hair begins to grow; for a long time he was able to conceal this excrescence in the thickness of his hair, which he combed over it with a curl; Veronica herself had not noticed it, till once, in the course of a nocturnal caress, her hand had suddenly encountered it.
> "Dear me!" she had exclaimed. "What have you got there?"
> And, as though the swelling, once discovered, had no other reason for discretion, it grew in a few months to the size of an egg—a partridge's—a guinea-fowl's—and then a hen's. There it stopped, while his hair, as it grew scantier, exposed it more and more to view between its meager

strands. At forty-six years of age, Anthime Armand-Dubois could have no further pretensions to good looks; he cut his hair close and adopted a style of collar of medium height, with a kind of recess in it, which hid and at the same time revealed the wen. But enough of Anthime's wen![10]

With his final "But enough of Anthime's wen!" the narrator calls all the more attention to its protracted amplification, in turn identifiable as a signature technique of the realists. Zola's depiction of medically accurate hysterical seizures (*Une Page d'amour*) and careful recording of the degrading permutations of syphilis (*Nana*), Flaubert's staging of Emma Bovary's demise, the Goncourts' portrayals of the hospital (*Soeur Philomène*, *Germinie Lacerteux*), and Maupassant's charting of madness (*Le Horla*) were just several of many celebrated moments in the literary history of realism in which the extended representation of horror was perfected by the masters of Medan. By substituting a risible skin disorder for a tragic decline, Gide not only inverted the order of the sublime and the ridiculous (as conventionalized in romantic and realist fiction), and not only played on the phallic transfer from below to above typical since medieval times of the mock mystery and carnival travesty, but also gave realist description itself the status of a castrated phallus or fetish, transferable from the socially serious to the sexually profane. As the wen flourishes, increasingly tumescent, adumbrated by ovarian metaphors each more insupportable than the last, the impression of naturalist fecundity gone awry is accordingly reinforced.

The second displacement of the wen occurs in connection with the famous Gidean *acte gratuit* (gratuitous act), an unmotivated murder posited as the precise antithesis of the realist crime, which, like the *fait divers* that invariably serves as a model, valorizes its psychological causality. Here, the false collar used by Anthime to conceal his cyst reappears on the neck of the gullible Fleurissoire en route to save the pope. Lafcadio (Gide's quintessential perverse adolescent), contemplating his future victim in their shared train compartment as he fumbles with his collar, infers, "Il doit souffrir d'une fistule, ou de quelque affection cachée [He must be suffering from a fistula or some unpleasant complaint of that kind]" (*CV*

10. André Gide, *Les Caves du Vatican*, in *Romans, récits et sôties* (Paris: Gallimard, 1958), pp. 685–86; trans. Dorothy Bussy under the title *Lafcadio's Adventures* (New York: Vintage, 1925), pp. 10–11. Further references to the French edition will be abbreviated *CV*; those to the English will be abbreviated *LA*.

828; *LA* 185). What looks like an innocent appeal for help in sartorial adjustments is converted by an evil law of reversal into the final provocation to assault. As Lafcadio pushes Fleurissoire from the train, however, he acquires the fatal stamp of disgrace on his neck.

In his chapter on Gide in *Legacies of Anti-Semitism in France,* Jeffrey Mehlman offers a provocative reading of the cluster of "dermatological" permutations deriving from the wen: from Fleurissoire's neck wound; to the blemishes ("boutons") on his face; to the cuff links that he wears on the day of the murder ("boutons de manchette"); to Gide's explanation of the critical neglect of *Les Caves* with the phrase "Je n'ai pressé aucun bouton," that is, "I made no effort to stir publicity." Mehlman concludes, by way of a reference to Proust and a metonymical beaver hat lost at the scene of the crime, that these signs function as the indexes of a circumcision ritual: "Recall now that Gide's dreamily phallic ephebe is projected into the cycle of familial (heterosexual) desire by an act that leaves him with the family mark on his neck, while removing violently his beaver hat. With the foreskin removed from the phallus, initiation, alas, has been achieved."[11] Though one may be hard-pressed to follow the link to anti-Semitism, Mehlman elucidates a striking chain of physical disfigurations—a virtual writing on the body inscribed as sciatica, insect bites, scars, and contusions—that easily doubles as a language of fetishism, a nexus of partially scotomized images denoting some inflamed area of psychosexual shame.[12] As Zola was the writer most clearly associated with the figuration of the hereditary *tare,* it seems plausible to interpret Gide's ironic use of such imagery in *Les Caves* as, on one level, part of a larger scheme of realist travesty and, on another level, proof that for Gide, Zola was the surrogate, scapegoat, and symbol of some inner moral chagrin.

Before exploring these psychohistorical subtexts, however, one might first establish some of the primary intertexts that annex Gide's *Caves* to works by Zola. His early novel *Thérèse Raquin* provides the strongest example. Based, as is well known, on a *fait divers,* the novel reworks the Agamemnon tragedy: a husband (Camille) betrayed and finally murdered by his adulterous wife

---

11. Jeffrey Mehlman, *Legacies of Anti-Semitism in France* (Minneapolis: University of Minnesota Press, 1983), pp. 66–67.
12. See Sigmund Freud, "Fetishism."

(Thérèse) and her lover (Laurent). The scene of the murder anticipates with uncanny exactitude that of Fleurissoire's downfall. Where Fleurissoire scratches his assailant's neck as he is hurled from the train, Camille bites the neck of his rival as the latter throws him from a boat. The coincidence of particulars in these parallel scenes is also reproduced in the description of the neck wound. Lafcadio, in a description akin in its attention to morbid detail to the *blazon* of the wen, appraises the damage as follows:

> Son cou, à deux endroits, était vilainement balafre; une étroite traînée rouge partait de derrière la nuque et, tournant vers la gauche, venait mourir au-dessus de l'oreille; une autre, plus courte, franche écorchure celle-là, deux centimètres au-dessus de la première, montant droit vers l'oreille dont elle avait atteint et un peu décollé le lobe.

> There were two ugly furrows on his neck; one, a thin red streak, starting from the back of his neck, turned leftwards and came to an end just below the ear; the other and shorter one, was a deep scratch just above the first; it went straight up towards the ear, the lobe of which it had reached and slightly torn. (*CV* 831; *LA* 189)

Laurent, in *Thérèse*, undertakes the same inspection:

> Il rabattit le col de sa chemise et regarda la plaie dans un méchant miroir de quinze sous accroché au mur. Cette plaie faisait un trou rouge, large comme une pièce de deux sous; la peau avait été arrachée, la chair se montrait, rosâtre, avec des taches noires; des filets de sang avaient coulés jusqu'à l'épaule, en minces traînées qui s'écaillaient. Sur le cou blanc, la morsure paraissait d'un brun sourd et puissant; elle se trouvait à droite au-dessous de l'oreille.

> He pulled down his shirt collar and looked at the wound in the nasty, cheap mirror on the wall. It was a red hole as wide as a two-sou piece, where the skin had been torn away and the flesh showed pinkish with dark spots. Thin trickles of blood had run down to his shoulder and congealed. Against the whiteness of his neck the bite looked a deep, dull brown; it was on the right side, below the ear.[13]

---

13. Emile Zola, *Thérèse Raquin* (Paris: Fasquelle, 1965), p. 95; trans. Leonard Tancock under the same title (New York: Viking Penguin, 1987), p. 106. Further references to the French edition will be abbreviated *TR*; those to the English will be abbreviated *LT*.

Each of these descriptions offers a kind of physical mapping of the wound's contours: the blood of Laurent's gash flows down to the shoulder in "minces traînées," or "thin trails," then travels toward "the right" and up until it attains a patch of neck just "below the ear." A precise mirror image, Lafcadio's scar consists of "une étroite traînée," or "narrow trail," that winds from behind the neck toward "the left" and comes to rest just "above the ear." Completing the effect of similitude, both characters will continue to be afflicted by their wounds: Lafcadio's begins to bleed again profusely as he is chasing the thief of his travel case, and Laurent's scar, instead of healing, festers as a throbbing reminder of the murder victim. So close are these twin depictions that one is tempted to interpret Gide's version as a trope on the trope of the detail. The scar, no longer in possession of a convincing signified (the *crime passionel*), now points only to what it used to represent; designating the absence of motive (the *acte gratuit*) and the ironic superfluity of its trace.

In *L' Oeuvre*, Zola's much later work, the motif of the scar is reutilized, inflated into a global metaphor not only of artistic self-destruction but also of the realist text itself with its stylistic fissures and mutilations. In an outburst of fury against his recalcitrant tableau, Claude Lantier attacks the canvas, causing a hideous tear that appears to him like a mortal wound. Piecing together the remnants ("lambeaux") with the help of his wife, Claude manages to reconstitute the picture but remains unable to eradicate the thin scar ("mince cicatrice") whose location renders the vital organ of the feminine model (his wife) a glaring synecdoche of the sacred heart, and by extension, the martyred text. This very gesture of reassembling torn fragments, in addition to finding its echo in the opening of Gide's *La Porte étroite* (where the narrator, Jérôme, proposes to "piece together" the "remnants" of his tragic story), also anticipates a scene of private ritual in *Les Caves*. Lafcadio, having stabbed himself for disobeying his own inner (Nietzschean) moral code, consummates the punishment by tearing the only existing photograph of his mother into pieces, ripping off the silk handkerchief which he wears as a tie, and then symbolically repairing the damage by outfitting himself as a proper bourgeois: cravat, hat, and all. This finale, which substitutes the restoration of a work of art with the restitution of a wardrobe, maliciously undercuts the pathos of Zola's aesthetic allegory (*CV* 720).

If the congruence between Claude's bleeding canvas and Lafcadio's secret stigmata implies a firm connection between *L'Oeuvre* and *Les Caves* (all the more "textual" since Lafcadio treats his thigh like a canvas or parchment that records the cipher of his own diabolical inspiration) this is only reinforced by their common and continued recourse to the motif of the *tare*. In *L'Oeuvre*, the painter's son Jacques, his head preternaturally large, his brain stricken by a disease of permanent somnolence that resembles encephalitis, bears witness to the stigma of madness that travels through successive generations of Lantiers. Puny, his giant head nodding from the neck, Jacques's *tare* is homonymically transmitted through the verb *taire*, enunciated in his mother's repeated injunctions to keep silent: "Jacques, tais-toi." Subdued to the point of aphasia, neglected by his obsessive parents, Jacques dies, and just as Claude's scarred portrait of his wife had become "all heart," a dripping symbol of the stigmata, so the rendering of the dead child becomes "all head," a concentrated sign of familial disgrace: "Ah! *L'Enfant mort*, le misérable petit cadavre n'était plus, à cette distance, qu'une confusion de chairs, la carcasse échouée de quelque bête informe! Etait-ce un crâne, était-ce un ventre, cette tête phénoménale, enflée et blanchie? [So that was the 'Dead Child,' pour little thing! Hanging where it did it was just a confused mass, like the carcass of some shapeless creature cast up by the tide, while the abnormally large head might have been any white, swollen object, a skull or even a bloated belly]."[14]

Gide evinced his distaste for this mode of figuration, confiding to his *Journal* that he found Zola's psychology "thin" when "his theories of heredity came to the rescue" (*JAG* 3:246, August 1932). His pejorative comment, together with his isolation of the *tare* as object worthy of derision, supports a reading of his own semiotic tattoos as so many pricks of the satirical knife but still leaves the question of the deeper significance of such a pastiche. Perhaps, as we have already implied, Zola's social realism was threatening to Gide and his post-symbolist contemporaries.

Zola, despite his own bourgeois politics, was perceived as the moral conscience of Gide's generation. Léon Blum, a co-contributor to *La*

---

14. Emile Zola, *L'Oeuvre* (Paris: Fasquelle, 1980, p. 404; trans. Thomas Walton under the title *The Masterpiece* (London: Elek Books, 1957), p. 297.

Revue Blanche, acknowledged Zola as the symbolic father of his own political commitment, but where Blum in the teens and twenties ratified his commitment by entering politics, Gide and many of his friends remained aloof. He was conspicuously silent during the Dreyfus affair, and when he finally declared himself a Dreyfusard he specified that it was primarily because the army had conducted the case dishonorably.[15] For a generation of aestheticized writers Zola's "J'accuse" was a monument of political morality that cast a guilty shadow over its profile of profound disengagement. In this context, Gide's wen emerges as depoliticized realism that, once stripped bare of historical referentiality, becomes a naked aesthetic of the ugly or purely comic. This may have been Gide's way of exposing Zola's moral pretenses and scientific pretexts for using sensational detail as a sham, an excuse for the prurient focalization of the fetishist. This imputation of perverse interest is easily played back on Gide, however. By revealing the ungainly poetics of Zola's realism Gide may have been endeavoring to distract the reader, whether consciously or not, from his own ethical relativism. Perhaps it was the very capriciousness of his own political conscience that hovered somewhere around the dreadful blight of the wen.

Gide's *Journal* attests to the ambivalence of both his political convictions and his critical reflexes toward a realist *écriture*. In the early 1930s he professed to enjoying Zola's "excessive" depictions of low-life scenes, savoring an episode in *Pot-Bouille* in which bourgeois adulterers, while "slumming it" in the sullied lodgings of their domestics, duly acquire the taint of their moral inferiors:

· Je viens de relire *Pot-Bouille* avec admiration.... C'est l'outrance même de *Pot-Bouille* qui me plaît, et la persévérance dans l'immonde. Le rendez-vous d'Octave et de Berthe dans la chambre de bonne et la salissure de leur misérable amour sous le flot ordurier des propos de la valetaille; ...sont tracés de main magistrale et ne se peuvent oublier.

· I have just reread *Pot-Bouille* (*Piping Hot*) with admiration.... It is the very excess of *Pot-Bouille* that I like and its perseverance in the filthy. The rendez-vous between Octave and Berthe in the maid's room and the soiling of their miserable love under the foul flow of the menials'

---

15. For further discussion of Gide and the Dreyfus affair, see Georges I. Brachfeld, *André Gide and the Communist Temptation* (Geneva: Droz, 1959), and Jean-Denis Bredin, *L'Affaire* (Paris: Julliard, 1983).

language...are done with a masterly hand and cannot be forgotten. (*Jour* 1:1137; *JAG* 3:241 [July 17, 1932])

Interestingly, Gide would extend the metaphor of Zola's descriptive "filth" to the effects of reading his works. Though he knew that there was a "fundamentally *moral*" purpose behind Zola's sordid "reality effects," he remained ultimately unable to digest his style. Zola's documentary techniques clung to Gide's literary temperament like a film or layer of scum that had to be expunged by high literature:

· J'achève *Au Bonheur des Dames*. Le dernier chapitre beaucoup moins bon; infériorité d'autant plus sensible que le précédent était un des meilleurs... L'exposition de blanc est d'une apothéose un peu facile, avec de lassantes insistances et redites dans les énumérations.
 Par besoin de me ressuyer, je rouvre Whitman avant d'aller dormir. (*By Blue Ontario's Shore*)

· I finished *Au Bonheur des Dames* (*At the Sign of Ladies' Delight*). The last chapter much less good; a more noticeable inferiority since the preceding one was one of the best.... The linen exhibit forms a rather too easy apotheosis, with tiresome insistences and repetitions in the enumerations.
 Through a need to bathe myself clean, I open Whitman before going to sleep. (*By Blue Ontario's Shore*) (*Jour* 1:1141; *JAG* 3:244 [July 22, 1932]; my emphasis)

If, in this exemplary instance, Walt Whitman's poetry came to the rescue, relieving Gide of the unpleasant detritus of the "real," the vexed question of "politically correct" realism plagued him throughout his literary career. In 1948, defensively positioning himself against Sartre and his demand for authorial *engagement*, he characterized as journalistic everything that would fail to stand the test of time, even referring to his own engaged works from *Souvenirs de la cour d'assises* to *Retour de l'U.R.S.S.* as having no relationship to literature (*Jour* 2:322). Such a purist contempt for "journalism" (by which Gide implies a genre of engaged writing, a writing of the real and ephemeral), as opposed to what he calls "literature," was, however, belied by his own practice. In what could almost be seen as the realist underbelly of his contributions to high literature, Gide was continuously preoccupied with his own form of documentary reportage. Thus in 1912, while working on *Les Caves du Vatican*, Gide served as a member of the jury in the assizes court of Rouen. The experience appears to stand at the center of an oscillation between a moral enthusiasm for the real and the particular, and a literary lassitude that prompted him to seek refuge in problems of a purely aestheticist order. During the month of June 1912, some eight days after a jury session, he admits to having "perdu l'élan que je rapportais de là-bas. A Cuverville depuis quatre jours, l'esprit flasque et la phrase complètement retombée [lost the impetus I had brought back with me. At Cuverville for the last four days, my mind flabby and my style utterly flat]" (*Jour* 1:379, *JAG* 1:330). But if here engagement seems to drain off literary energy, one year later a reciprocal pattern emerges whereby the perusal of decadent literature—Keats, Pater's *Marius the Epicurean*, and the works of Oscar Wilde (on whom Gide was then composing a short book)—spurs him in his work on *Souvenirs de la cour d'assises*, which he qualifies, using a militant expression, as "a very good exercise (*un très bon exercice*]" *Jour* 1:389).

Unlike his aesthetic manifestos, his classical récits, and his *soties*, all of which he painstakingly "writes," *Souvenirs* is rapidly "dictated," produced according to an astonishing rhythm of literary discipline: "Since 3 November a secretary has been coming every morning. I work with her from nine to eleven thirty.... I cannot find a minute for the piano, alas! Go almost every day to swim for an hour at rue de Chazelles—which makes me feel very good" (*JAG* 1:342), Gide notes, stressing temporal precisions and the substitution of cultural leisure with the rigors of sport. "Dictation," accompanied as it is by a refusal of escapism and a renewed taste for the actuality of case studies, finally encroaches on the hallowed terrain of "literature." Shortly before commencing *Souvenirs*, Gide reads a portion of the *Caves* manuscript to Paul Laurens, after which he self-deprecatingly comments in his *Journal*: "Il me semble que, dans tout ce que j'ai écrit jusqu'à présent, j'ai fait la parade, avant que le *vrai* spectacle ne commence, et que c'est maintenant seulement qu'on va entrer dans la boutique [It seems to me that everything I have written up to now has been nothing but barking and outside show before the *real* show begins and that it is only now that the public is going to enter the booth" (*Jour* 1:392; *JAG* 1:342; Gide's emphasis).

This stated resolve to "enter the shop" may be read as a figure for Gide's deep-seated longing to infuse his overly intellectualized modern fables with a dose of real life, but it was a desire that for the most part he suppressed or displaced into parodies. Gide the stylist would find it virtually impossible to play the role of "shopkeeper" cum "reporter." He denigrated Léon Blum's qualities as a writer by praising him as an "excellent rapporteur" (perhaps confirming Mehlman's anti-Semitism hypothesis, Jews do not make good writers).[16] When, in the 1930s, he set himself the task of writing up the most nefarious cases encountered in courts of the period—those of the Redureau murders and the celebrated "incarcerated girl of Poitiers"—he prefaced their publication with a warning to the reader against confusing such documentary material with literature: "Notre désir n'est pas de l'amuser, mais de *l'instruire*. Nous nous plaçerons en face des faits, non en peintre ou en romancier, mais en naturaliste [Our desire is not to amuse the reader, but *to instruct him*. We plant ourselves firmly before the facts, not as painter or novelist, but as naturalist]."[17] Extending the opposition "writer-reporter" to that of "novelist-naturalist," Gide not only revealed yet again his prejudice against those authors who allowed themselves to be contaminated by "facts" but also demonstrated his fear of becoming associated with their ranks in the mind of the reader. *La Séquestrée*, Gide's caveats and disclaimers notwithstanding, is perilously close to a novel in its form, and though it too was "dictated," the collaged citations, descriptive details, and lurid footnotes comprise a totality that demands to be read, grotesquely perhaps, as a repressed realist narrative.

The story concerned a woman named Blanche Monnier, who, for reasons never made clear (madness, pregnancy out of wedlock,

---

16. In 1907 Gide wrote in his *Journal* (1:228): "The artist in him hasn't any great value, and his sentence, like Stendhal's, does not need to go out of its way to achieve anything more than the mere movement of his thought, which flows from his mouth or his pen at once abundant and clear—clearer, to be sure, than abundant, without any noticeable *Schaudern* [dread]—but, as a consequence, easily and completely expressible; having a beginning and an end and always properly clothed. You cannot imagine a more exact, clearer, more elegant, easier summary than Léon Blum can give, on the spur of the moment, of an event or a book or a play. What an excellent committee chairman he must be in the Conseil d'Etat! (*JAG* 1:197). This mildly derogatory comment on Blum's literary sensibility was strengthened in 1914 when Gide avowed that Blum made him feel intellectually inferior and inhibited (*impuisssant*). He endeavored to recover his own self-esteem by treating Blum's acuity as a sign of his inadequacy as poet. (See *Jour* 1:397 and 2:320, for a slip in this critique to what could legitimately be interpreted as anti-Semitism.)

17. Gide, "L' Affaire Redureau," in *Ne jugez pas* (Paris: Gallimard, 1930), p. 98; Gide's emphasis. Further references to this book will be abbreviated *NJP*.

her defenselessness as victim?), was imprisoned by her sadistic mother (widow of a respected dean) in a room of the house for twenty-five years. Forced to live amid her own excrement, deprived of light, human contact, food, and clothes, infested with vermin, her hair matted, her body encrusted with filth, Blanche Monnier was the living incarnation of the grotesque. As if to make matters worse, she seemed to have grown attached to her ignoble "taudis" (hovel), referring to it after her liberation with macabre terms of endearment: "mon cher grand fond Malampia" and "Oh! comme ce serait beau si l'on avait deux bouquets pareils avec une grotte au milieu et une petite Vierge dans la grotte [My dear old home Malampia. Oh! how nice it would be if I could have two such bouquets with a grotto in the middle and a little virgin in the grotto].[18] This fecal Vestal, a Rabelaisian muse of squalor, accedes to the status of saintly martyr by virtue of her mystical communion with the "worms of darkness"—the "ténébréons"—which proliferate in her bed covers.[19] Gide, unwilling to exploit such an obvious allegoreme of the biblical Serpent, reserved his scientific observations on this repugnant detail for a footnote. This gesture of discretion, however, like the narrator's excuses in speaking of the wen in *Les Caves*, attracts all the more attention to the repellent object in question. Not only do these "ténébréons" recall the infamous "mille-pattes" of *Les Caves*—the army of bedbugs with which Amédée does battle in his Marseilles hotel room, the fleas of Toulon, the mosquitoes of Gênes—but they also conjure up the urban arcades with their hideous "boutiques pleines de ténèbres [shadow-filled shops]" in *Thérèse Raquin*, described as "autant de trous lugubres dans lesquels s'agitent des formes bizarres [so many lugubrious vacuums in which bizarre shapes would dance]" (*TR* 16). Like Blanche Monnier, Thérèse is virtually imprisoned in this dark hovel "où la nuit habite pendant le jour [where night lived during the day]" and like "la séquestrée de Poitiers," Thérèse becomes insidiously commingled with her surroundings; her pale, shadowy profile "sortait vaguement des ténèbres [stood out dimly from the shadows]" (*TR* 17–18).

La Séquestrée de Poitiers was the first volume to appear in a

18. Gide, "La Séquestrée de Poitiers," in *NJP*, pp. 225-27.
19. Philippe Roger's *Roland Barthes, roman* (Paris: Seuil, 1986) contains an interesting interpretation of Barthes's quasi-suppressed mysticism in relation to his reading (*Fragments d'un discours amoureux*) of Gide's *Séquestrée*.

collection of legal case histories the publication of which Gide inaugurated at the *Nouvelle Revue Française* in 1930 under the general heading "Ne jugez pas." His ostensible aim was to bring to public attention those borderline areas between psychopathology and criminal behavior that render justice particularly difficult to administer. Certainly, as far as his revived interest in jurisprudence is concerned, his encounter with colonial oppression in the Congo (1925–26) played a crucial role, but his social conscience was also resensitized by an interest in the Soviet Union, which in turn provoked a *mise-en-question* of his former assessment of realism. In his journal entry of September 1, 1934, he began by challenging his previous radical ahistoricism:

> Ce sentiment de la durée, qui me manquait à peu près complètement (sans que je susse qu'il me manquait; et du reste l'influence de Mallarmé et de la philosophie allemande achevait de me précipiter dans ce sens où me portait naturellement déjà ma nature anti-historique; on prétendait oeuvrer dans l'absolu; il y avait là également une réaction contre les théories de Taine, etc.). Fernandez acheva de m'ouvrir les yeux là-dessus. De sorte que, depuis deux ans à peu près, en réaction contre moi-même, j'ai souci de situer et d'asseoir dans le temps mes pensées. Révision de toutes les valeurs littéraires.

> The feeling of historical duration which I lacked almost completely (without knowing that I lacked it; and moreover Mallarmé's influence and that of German philosophy finished pushing me in that direction to which my antihistorical nature already inclined me; we claimed to work in the absolute; there was also in this a reaction against Taine's theories, etc.). Fernandez eventually opened my eyes on this subject. So that, for about two years now, reacting against myself, I take care to situate and anchor my thoughts in time. Review of all literary values. (*Jour* 1:1218; *JAG* 3:313)

A mere month later, this "review of all literary values" culminated in a contrite revalorization of Zola, reminiscent of the sort of statement that would accompany the rehabilitation of a fallen party leader or renegade saint:

> Je voudrais écrire un article sur Zola, où protester (mais doucement) contre la méconnaissance actuelle de sa valeur. J'y voudrais préciser que mon admiration pour Zola ne date pas d'hier et n'est nullement inspirée par mes "opinions" actuelles (simplement ces opinions me permettent de mieux jauger aujourd'hui son importance)....

Depuis quelques années, je relis chaque été quelques volumes des *Rougon-Macquart*, pour me convaincre à neuf que Zola mérite d'être placé très haut—en tant qu'artiste et sans aucun souci de "tendance."

I should like to write an article on Zola, in which to protest (but gently) against the present lack of appreciation of his value. I should like to bring out in it that my admiration for Zola is not recent and is in no wise inspired by my recent "opinions" (simply that those opinions allow me to gauge his importance better today)....

For several years I have reread each summer several volumes of *Les Rougon-Macquart* in order to convince myself anew that Zola deserves to be placed very high—as an artist and without any concern for "tendency." (*Jour* 1:1220; *JAG* 3:314)

The "recent 'opinions'" refer of course to Gide's conversion to communism during the early thirties. Though the "idyll," as it is often called, was brief (his voyage in 1936 to the Soviet Union culminated in disillusionment), 1934 was a year of high enthusiasm for fellow traveling. It was also a year of crisis in Gide's literary career. As an aging author of sixty-five, vulnerable to fears of literary and sexual impotence, he looked to Zola's earthy positivism for rejuvenation as a writer just as he looked to the intellectual left for a young and supportive fraternity.

Gide's overdrawn assertion of his early reverence for Zola may be construed as a means of redressing his former sins against realism, a realism that in 1934 he was trying to appropriate in certain respects for his little-known Communist play entitled *Robert ou l'intérêt général*.[20] Stylistically brittle, this *pièce à thèse* revolves around the conflict provoked in a bourgeois family when the son of an industrialist (Robert) decides to sympathize with the general strike in the plant. The son (Michel) complicates matters further by falling in love with the daughter of his father's illegitimate brother (himself a Marxist). The play ends lugubriously with the death of Michel on the picket line, a break-up of the strike, the restoration of the old corrupt order, and Robert's hypocritical efforts to rationalize the tragedy in the name of the general good of family, church, and state. To his political hatchetman he confides: "Eliminer les éléments tarés, c'est le premier devoir de l'Etat et de la famille

20. See *Les Cahiers de la petite dame*, vol. 6: *Cahiers André Gide* (Paris: Gallimard, 1974) for accounts of Gide's embarrassing readings of *Robert* to his friends, as well as Mme Van Rysselberghe's conjectures as to why he became committed to the USSR and the writing of such a play.

[Eliminate the degenerate elements, that is the first duty of the State and the family]."[21]

Where in *Les Caves* the *tare*, or fatal mark, was simply an ironic sign of a depoliticized realism, in *Robert* these *éléments tarés* denote the weak, socially marginal, and politically oppressed, a stigmatized population that, in addition to bearing a remarkable family resemblance to Zola's urban underclass, proves compatible with other partis pris. As Walter Benjamin noted in relation to a passage from *Les Nouvelles Nourritures* that struck him as an "apology for poverty," Gide's appeals on behalf of the proletariat were inextricable from his interest in the widest range of human "weaknesses": "If Gide, throughout his work, was naturally attracted to multiple forms of weakness, and if, in his study of Dostoievsky (in many respects a portrait of the artist by himself), he reserved a central place for weakness as 'insatisfaction of the flesh,' 'anxiety,' 'anomaly,' and so on, the only weakness to which he continually returned and which merits particular interest is the weakness he described of man for man."[22] Benjamin states straightforwardly what other critics would hesitate to affirm—namely, that Gide's political engagement could ultimately be traced to his overriding commitment to the cause of homosexual rights. His injunction—"Ne jugez pas!"—could be read as a covert plea for tolerance, freedom from prejudice, and indulgence for all, but most especially for "inverts," who, like his hero Oscar Wilde, had learned the severity of society's judgment of their "crimes." Gide himself insinuated that he was an effective jury member of the assizes court not because of his superior capacity to determine guilt or innocence but, rather, because of his special understanding of adolescent delinquency.

Whether or not Gide wanted to "normalize" Marcel Redureau's monstrous crime in the same way that he might have wanted to "depathologize" homosexuality remains a matter of debate. Less uncertain is the similarity between the conflictual attitude he evinced toward his own sexual preferences and the ambivalence he addressed to the accused. On the one hand, his instinctive identification with the defendant might be read as a displaced form of "Ne (me) jugez

---

21. André Gide, *Robert ou l'intérêt général*, in *Littérature engagée* (Paris: Gallimard, 1950), p. 304.
22. Walter Benjamin, "André Gide et ses nouveaux adversaires," in *Walter Benjamin*, vol. 2: *Poésie et Révolution*, trans. Maurice de Gandillac (Paris: Denoël, 1971), p. 213.

pas" and, on the other, as a masked demand for public exposure and indictment (as if to say, "Punish me, for as a moralist, I am a fraud"). This practice of simultaneous disclosure and concealment, the duplicitous "incognito" that Benjamin recognized, emerged most often under the sign of the tempting *ténébréon*. In *L'Immoraliste* we might identify the code word of Gide's homosexuality in the vermin with which Michel becomes infested after spending the night with a group of Arab boys. Pierre Herbart observed a similar fetishism of vermin in Gide himself.

It was Herbart who also noticed a strange growth on Gide's own hand:

· A un moment il posa la main sur le bras de mon fauteuil. Je baissai les yeux et vis que cette main, à la base du pouce, était abîmée par une assez laide excroissance de chair.... Je me sentais si démonté que j'interrogeai plusieurs de ses amis: Non; aucun ne se souvenait que la main de Gide eût été pareillement déformée. Ainsi je m'étais trompé. J'en conçus un grand trouble, et, vingt ans plus tard, il m'arrivait encore de jeter un regard soupçonneux sur la solide main paysanne de Gide—cette main que je tenais, déjà inerte dans la mienne, la nuit qui précéda sa mort.

Une telle 'erreur' peut-elle déterminer le cours de toute une amitié? Ne vais-je pas la renouveler à chaque page de cette étude sur Gide?

· At one point he placed his hand on the arm of my chair. I lowered my eyes and saw that this hand, at the base of the thumb, was marred by a rather horrible fleshy growth.... I was so disconcerted by this sight that I asked a number of his friends about it: No, not a single one recalled that Gide's hand was deformed in this fashion. So, I must have been mistaken. A great uneasiness resulted, and twenty years later I would find myself shooting a suspicious glance over to Gide's solid, peasant hand—the very hand that I held, already inert in mine, the night before his death.

Could such an "error" determine the course of an entire friendship? Do I not come back to it on every page of this study of Gide?[23]

A note accompanying this account dispels Herbart's doubts about the growth's existence. "La petite dame" (Madame Théo van Rysselberghe), on reading this description, reassured Herbart: "Vous ne vous êtes pas du tout trompé. Gide a bien eu un kyste à l'endroit

23. Pierre Herbart, *A la recherche d'André Gide* (Paris: Gallimard, 1952), pp. 10–11.

que vous dites, et qu'il a fait réduire [You were not at all mistaken. Gide certainly did have a cyst on the spot that you indicated, and had it removed]." For Herbart, this wenlike growth clearly symbolized Gide's ambiguous character, his peculiar ability to dissimulate and reveal his inner shame at the same time. Whether wen or cyst, the *stigma indelebile* identified by Freud as the sign of fetishistic displacement, might be seen as that hypothetical "vengeance secrète" undermining Gide's pose as (in the elegant phrase of Michel Tournier) "un personnage en plein jour."[24]

Gide's adaptation in 1946 of Kafka's *The Trial* (in collaboration with Jean-Louis Barrault) returned him to a repertory of juridical allusions deriving from his experience both as a jury member in the Rouen assizes court and as a collector of tabloid stories focusing on anomalies and sensational or seemingly gratuitous crimes. Though allegorical play and lowbrow *fait divers* seem hardly to fit into a common theoretical frame, both belong in the context of Gide's long-term meditation on the metaphysics of justice. As I have suggested, Christ's words "Ne jugez point" served, at some profound level, as the motto for Gide's own personal allegory, an allegory of moral anxiety induced by his stubborn and courageous decision to live a life of sexual infraction. Despite the puritanical strictures of his Protestant family and the efforts of friends (Paul Claudel, Charles de Bos, Jacques Maritain) to pry his soul loose from the clutches of the Tempter, Gide resisted the authority of his judges, even as he put himself on trial before the reader over and over again.

Though it is easy to dismiss Gide's conceits of literary self-prosecution as so many tropes of authorial manipulation, ultimately designed to acquit the writer of all blame or implicate the reader in an epistemology of guilt, his allegories of judgment significantly parallel allegories of reading. They elucidate the inevitable slips and lapses of intersubjective evaluation; they articulate the way in which the language of moral value deconstructs (rotating truth and error in a continual and often irritating whirligig), and most important, they reveal how a life intersects deceptively with the hermeneutics of interpretation. Read today, Gide's documentary

---

24. Michel Tournier, "Cinq clefs pour André Gide," in *Le Vol du vampire* (Paris: Gallimard, 1981), p. 222.

writings raise the question of how one judges criminal acts in an age that radically questions the legitimacy or referential possibility of ethical foundational principles.[25]

The collection of case histories published under the rubric *Ne jugez pas* allowed Gide both to recuperate realism (a genre which, as I attempted to show in the previous section, he tended to dismiss as unliterary, deserving of pastiche rather than emulation) and to explore its opposite—the genres of allegory, both theological and jurisprudential. Today these *faits divers* merit critical attention not only because up until now their influence on Gide's oeuvre has been relatively neglected but also because as hermeneutical conundrums that defy moral resolution they check the impulse to resurrect reassuring legal and metaphysical certainties in an age where such certainties are suspect. Gide's writings on the *fait divers*, or what he often referred to as the "curiosité," describe the uncanny, unsettling workings of epistemological aporia, those dense quantities of the "unknown" or inexplicably perverse which give shape to fiction and judicial process alike. I would argue that his reading of life's "little mysteries" as so many allegories of unfathomable justice yields a definition of narratological perversity that in turn prefigures our own poststructuralist "trials of psychoanalysis."

As far as the conventional iconography of justice is concerned, it was neither the blindfold nor the scales that assumed special significance for Gide. In his stage version of Kafka's *Le Procès*, he highlighted a judge's vain insistence on being painted for posterity seated in a giant chair: "c'est un tout petit juge [he's only a very little judge]," the portraitist Titorelli exclaims, "mais il tient à ce que je le représente assis sur un trône, un grand trône [but he insists I show him on a throne, a great big throne]."[26] The same

---

25. In an article entitled "Justice ou Charité," originally published in *Le Figaro*, February 25, 1945, and republished in *Feuillets d'automne* (Paris: Mercure de France, 1949), Gide wrote of his skepticism toward justice: "Pour avoir été juré aux Assises, je ne crois plus beaucoup à la Justice" (p. 232). ["Having been sworn in at the Assize court, I no longer believe very much in justice": André Gide, *Autumn Leaves*, trans. Elsie Pell (New York: Philosophical Library, 1950), p. 241.] In the same essay, he appears to go against the very title that he had earlier chosen for his collection of *faits divers*. Intimating that the divine injunction "Ne jugez point" [never judge] promotes a Christian ideal of individual suffering at the expense of the masses who labor under adverse working conditions, Gide seems to discard his earlier position that no one should happily sit in judgment on another and to argue *in favor* of passing (negative) judgment on cases of social injustice (pp. 233–34).

26. André Gide and Jean-Louis Barrault, *Le Procès* (Paris: Gallimard, 1947), p. 164; trans. Leon Katz under the title *The Trial* (New York: Schocken Books, 1963), p. 104.

portrait intrudes voyeuristically into a scene in which K endeavors surreptitiously to fondle the body of a young woman. In the opening paragraphs of his *Souvenirs de la cour d'assises,* the literal function of "sitting" in court had already been given full symbolic weight. "De tout temps les tribunaux ont exercé sur moi une fascination irrésistible [Tribunals have always exercised an irresistible fascination on me]," Gide wrote; "mais à présent je sais par expérience que c'est une tout autre chose d'écouter rendre la justice, ou d'aider à la rendre lui-même. Quand on est parmi le public on peut y croire encore. Assis sur le banc des jurés, on se redit la parole du Christ: *Ne jugez point* [But at present, I know from experience that it is quite another matter to listen to justice being rendered, or to help in the process of rendering it. When one is part of the audience one can still believe in it. Seated in the jury box, one repeats the words of Christ: 'Judge not']" *(NJP* 9; Gide's emphasis). Once he was "seated on the bench," the solemnity of Christ's caveat returned; it was as if the bench with its stern figures in upright, expectant postures was alone sufficient to convey the sense of awe and ritual terror surrounding the administration of justice. As Gide would note when a young rape victim took the stand, it was the apparatus of justice, rather than her testimony, that impressed him:

- A présent c'est le tour de l'enfant. Elle est propre et gentille; mais on voit que l'appareil de la justice, ces bancs, cette solennité, l'espèce de trône où sont assis ces trois vieux messieurs bizarrement vêtus, que tout cela la terrifie.

- Now it is the child's turn. She is clean and well-behaved; but one sees that the apparatus of justice, these benches, this solemnity, this species of throne on which three bizarrely clothed gentlemen are seated, that all this terrifies her. *(NJP* 22–23)

The elevated position of the chairs of the judges—"like a throne"—accentuated the meekness of the subject, seated, so to speak, at the "knee" of the law. As Derrida wrote of Blanchot's récit *La Folie du jour,* in which the "scenography" of justice, according to his interpretation, is rendered in terms of "un drame du debout/assis [a drama of standing up/sitting down]," man approaches the tabernacle of the law with the inclined posture of the penitent ("en se baissant").[27] The guardian of the law grows larger than life in the

27. Jacques Derrida, "Préjugés," in *La Faculté de juger* (Paris: Minuit, 1985), p. 125.

face of his interlocutor, only to shrink in turn before the immensely overscaled persona of the law herself. For Derrida, conceived in this way, "l'histoire de la loi marque le surgissement du *sur* ou de la différence de la taille (*Grössenunterschied*) [The history of the law charts the mastery of the prefix 'above,' of a difference in size]."[28]

If Gide, seated in the Rouen courtroom, was perturbed by the diminutive size of the girl, it was perhaps because the image bore an allegorical affinity to another kind of spectacle, witnessed in a brothel in Algiers at the turn of the century. It was precisely the *sur*plus in *taille* that Gide remarked as he sat, passing judgment, on the tyrannical spectacle of his friend Daniel lording over the prostrated body of a compliant Arab boy:

- Puis, tandis que je restais assis près des verres à demi vidés, Daniel saisit Mohammed dans ses bras et le porta sur le lit qui occupait le fond de la pièce. Il le coucha sur le dos, tout au bord du lit, en travers; et je ne vis bientôt plus que, de chaque côté de Daniel ahanant, deux fines jambes pendantes. Daniel n'avait même pas enlevé son manteau. Très grand, debout contre le lit, mal éclairé, vu de dos, le visage caché par les boucles de ses longs cheveux noirs, dans ce manteau qui lui tombait aux pieds, Daniel paraissait gigantesque, et penché sur ce petit corps qu'il couvrait, on eût dit un immense vampire se repaître sur un cadavre. J'aurais crié d'horreur.

- Then, while I remained sitting beside the half-empty glasses, Daniel seized Mohammed in his arms and carried him to the bed which was at the other end of the room. He laid him on his back on the edge of the bed, cross-wise, and soon I saw nothing but two slim legs dangling on either side of Daniel, who was labouring and panting. Daniel had not even taken his cloak off. Standing there in the dim light beside the bed, with his back turned, his face hidden by the curls of his long black hair, his cloak falling to his feet, he looked gigantic. As he bent over the little body he was covering, he was like a huge vampire feasting on a corpse. I could have screamed with horror.[29]

Despite his expressed moral outrage at this scene of colonial conquest (the boy's name, Mohammed, is of obvious significance here) and sexual exploitation ("For myself, who can only take my pleasure face to face and without violence, and who am often, like Walt Whitman, satisfied with the most furtive contact, I was horri-

28. Ibid., p. 125.
29. Gide, *Si le grain ne meurt* (1924; Paris: Gallimard, 1955), p. 345; trans. Dorothy Bussy under the title *If it die...* (New York: Random House, 1938), p. 310.

fied both by Daniel's behaviour and by Mohammed's complacent submission to it"),[30] Gide nonetheless shared in the guilt insofar as he used the episode to great literary effect in his autobiographical *Si le grain ne meurt* and showed himself, on other occasions (*Ainsi soit-il, Carnets d'Egypte*), equally susceptible to the attractions of the "view from behind."[31] Seated in the jury box—a symbolic filling of the paternal chair, for it must be remembered that Gide's father was a doctor of law and his grandfather the president of the Uzès tribunal—Gide surely sat in judgment on his own projected transgressions. For him, the motto *testis esto*, employed in a series of allegorically entitled essays ("Justice ou Charité," "Courage," and "Vérité") intended to temper the fury of postwar *épuration*, superimposed an erotic connotation on the juridical meaning, so that the sense of "bearing witness" (*testis*, testimony) was subverted by the sexual subtext (testicle).[32]

Gidean allegories of justice, I seem to be implying rather heavy-handedly, deconstruct into self-implicating erotic *mise-en-scènes*. Whether it is in the image of sitting itself, suggestive of prurient spectatorship and mastery, or in the titillating prospect of seeing one's own transgressive inclinations mirrored in the attitude of a disempowered plaintiff, Eros insinuates its way into the courtroom and perverts the protocol of judicial process. Gide, in a word, seemed intent on equating the monstrous and morally suspect nature of judgment itself with the criminal monstrosity the jury was charged to condemn.

Not that Gide was against the monstrous. On the contrary, monsters belonged to that very cluster of concepts—curiosity, anomaly, deviation, deformity, stigma, gratuitous crime—to which Gide was obsessively drawn and which guided his selection of newspaper *canards* deemed worthy of republication in the *Nouvelle Revue Française*. Gide's personal archive of tabloid literature, still in the possession of his daughter, Catherine, and as yet neither collated nor classified, is grouped in dusty paper envelopes marked, for example, "vols," "Dreyfus," "Eglise," "séquestrés," "parricides,"

30. Gide, *If it die...*, p. 311.
31. Ibid., p. 346.
32. Gide, "Justice ou Charité," "Courage," and "Vérité," in *Feuillets d'automne*, pp. 232–44. In "Courage" Gide evokes the Latin motto "Testis esto" in the context of a discussion of martyrdom and the power of conviction over actual testimony (p. 238).

"évasions," "exécutions," "curiosités" (thefts, Dreyfus, Church, the incarcerated, parricides, escapes, executions, curiosities). A rapid perusal of these *cahiers* (which also contain letters and manuscript copy) suffices to ascertain their importance as source material for Gide's novels (*Les Caves du Vatican* in particular) as well as his nonfictional writings.

Taken together, these human interest stories resemble a Barthesian *mythologie*—the kind of media fodder designed to quell the mass-market appetite for freakish exhibitions or displays of human misfortune. But Gide eschews the ironic distantiation typical of the *mythologie*, preferring instead a didactic tone in his presentation of this Grub Street literature. Arguing against Remy de Gourmont (whose *La Physique de l'amour* had appeared in 1907) that human mating patterns far surpassed those of insects and animals when it came to sexual anomaly, Gide prepared the ground for a column that would instruct his readers in the art of deciphering life's "curiosities": "La curiosité est un des ressorts de notre activité qui me paraît avoir été le plus méconnu et le moins bien étudié" [Curiosity is one of those spurs to our actions that seems to be the most misunderstood and the least well studied]," he wrote in his "Seconde lettre sur les faits divers" (*NJP* 147–48). Introducing zoological analogies, his criticism of Gourmont notwithstanding, he noted a *ménage à trois* among chaffinches and pondered such "little mysteries" as the spectacle of "a wild gazelle who overcame her timidity to approach an open suitcase" (*NJP* 149).

Gide's *faits divers*, both published and unpublished, illustrate the cliché that life imitates and even outstrips art in its configurations of the grotesque and bizarre. In this respect they form a perfect counterpart to novels such as *Les Caves du Vatican* and *Les Faux-monnayeurs*, the plots of which are stamped with the imprint of deviant narrative strategies typically found in the *fait divers*. Gide's irony, consisting of an endlessly spiraling pastiche of tabloid imitating *sotie* and *sotie* imitating tabloid, resonates in the titles of his chosen newspaper clippings, most of which fall neatly into the categories of classic literary genres—romantic melodrama: "Le Don Juan des abattoirs" (Don Juan of the slaughterhouse); tragedy: "L'Enfant martyr" (The martyred child); horror: "Une Femme enterrée vivante accouche dans son cerceuil!" (A woman buried alive gives birth in coffin!); comedy: "L'ennui d'être trop riche" (The boredom of being too rich); and, most relevant to *Les Caves*, religious miracles. "La Vierge qui pleure," concerning a talking virgin who confides to a concierge her woe over the envisioned "malheurs qui vont atteindre la France impie [misfortunes due to befall an impious France]" belongs to the same genus from which Anthime Armand-Dubois's garrulous Madonna sprang. In an article published in *Le Matin* on Monday October 9, 1905, entitled "Les Emmurés de Lourdes" (The walled-in people of Lourdes), the topos of papal sequestration is announced, some nine years prior to the publication of *Les Caves*. In this story of an evil bishop who walls in and starves out an undesired hotel proprietor, the figure of the ecclesiastical charlatan, so prevalent in *Les Caves*, is likewise prefigured. Finally, Gide's hand-picked archive contains a wealth of accounts pertaining to the 1907 scandal reported as "Les Ecumeurs d'Eglises" (The church robbers). This band of swindlers masquerading as a respectable furniture company would replace church relics and icons with copies and then sell the originals, in London, to art collectors. The similarity of this story to *Les Caves*, with its ersatz religious statuary, rumors of Masonic conspiracy, and corruptible priests, points yet again to the abrogation of boundaries between the fabulistic *sotie* and the *fait divers* and underscores the role of fetishized simulacra as catalysts within both genres.

If one were to try to glean one principle of selection from these *faits divers*, it would be the fact that they almost unilaterally bear the character of a riddle or test that proves unsolvable. We see this same criterion in evidence in the texts singled out for republication in *Ne jugez pas*. The apparently gratuitous massacre of the Mabit family by their servant, Marcel Redureau, obdurately remained, for the defendant's lawyer as well as for Gide, a "psychological mystery." The same inscrutable quality prevailed in the terrible case of "la séquestrée de Poitiers":

- Nous tacherons de comprendre un peu mieux ce que furent ces "criminels": cette mère et ce frère que, d'autre part, l'on nous présentera comme de si honnêtes gens; quel furent les motifs de leur crime?... Ce qui me paraît si particulièrement intéressant dans cette affaire, c'est que le mystère,... s'approfondit, quitte les faits, se blottit dans les caractères, aussi bien du reste dans le caractère de la victime que dans le caractère des accusés.

- We will try to understand a little better just who these "criminals" were: this mother and this brother who, elsewhere, were presented to us as upright citizens; what were the motives of their crime? What strikes me as particularly interesting in this case, is that the mystery... goes deeper and deeper, escapes the facts, crouches inside the personalities, as much, for that matter, inside the personality of the victim as in the personality of the accused. (*NJP* 233-34)

For Gide, the beautiful crime ("le beau crime"), like the "beautiful *fait divers*," was distinguished by the fact that it embodied a kind of "blindness and insight" mechanism, that is, it disclosed less the more it was scrutinized. The arsonist who set his family's house on fire for no ostensible reason; the son who committed parricide as a means of avoiding the mortal sin of his own suicide; and the Nietzschean "superman" who stabbed his girlfriend to death on the occasion of a capricious dare, all exemplified in their crimes a supreme irrationality and absence of motive, a surfeit of what Gide called "disinterest." Analogous in his view to madness, illness, or sexual perversion, the disinterested crime occupied that shaded region where psychopathology merged with the exceptional, whether diabolical or genial.

A variant of the "blindness and insight" effect could already be descried in Gide's analysis of Dostoevsky in 1923. Initially delivered as a series of lectures, this pioneering psychobiographical case study, foreshadowing Freud's *Dostoevsky and Parricide* of 1928, emphasized the decisive impact of epilepsy on Dostoevsky's literary masochism. Referring to the disease as "a little physiological mystery [*un petit mystère physiologique*]," on a par with "insatiable lust," "anguish," "anomaly" and the *tare*, he pointed to the preponderance of such stigmas in the characters of "great men." "Mahomet était épileptique, épileptique les prophètes d'Israël, et Luther, et Dostoïevski. Socrate avait son démon, saint Paul la mystérieuse 'écharde dans la chair,' Pascal son gouffre, Nietzsche et Rousseau leur folie [Mohammed was epileptic, so too the prophets of Israel, and Luther, and Dostoevsky. Socrates had his daemon, Saint Paul his mysterious 'splinter in the flesh,' Pascal his abyss, Nietzsche and Rousseau their madness]."[33] Epilepsy, compared by Gide to a thorn or saintly wound, resurfaced in Freud's interpretation linked to an equally abrasive metaphor—"a knife that cuts both ways," or "stick with two ends." This was how Freud characterized the irony of Dostoevsky's autoaccusation of parricide (convertible, he affirmed, into a confession of epilepsy), and it was also the figure he used to

33. Gide, *Dostoïevski* (Paris: Gallimard, 1923), pp. 216–17.

describe the mutual vulnerability of psychology and justice, the trap set by each for the other. Writing of *The Brothers Karamazov* he argued:

> In the speech for the defence at the trial, there is the famous joke at the expense of psychology—it is a "knife that cuts both ways": a splendid piece of disguise, for we have only to reverse it in order to discover the deepest meaning of Dostoevsky's view of things. It is not psychology that deserves to be laughed at, but the procedure of judicial enquiry. It is a matter of indifference who actually committed the crime; psychology is only concerned to know who desired it emotionally and who welcomed it when it was done.[34]

In this complex interpretation of the "trial of psychoanalysis," the "little mystery" is subsumed in the larger mystery of analytic procedures, themselves constructed on unstable foundations, or, in practice, mutually exclusive. In the same way it was as a paradigm of heuristic "double binds" that Lacan evoked the words of Christine Papin, who, in an act that inspired Genet's *Les Bonnes*, performed the ritual murder of her mistress with the assistance of her sister Léa:

> On that fateful evening, in the anxious anticipation of an imminent punishment, the sisters welded the image of their mistresses to the mirage of their own pain. It is their own distress that they detest in the couple that they drag into their terrible quadrille. Like the avenging Bacchae, they would tear out the eyes. The sacrilegious curiosity which has constituted man's anguish through the ages is what fuels them when they desire their victims, when they stalk them in their gaping wounds, and which Christine would later, before the judge, call in all innocence, the "mystery of life."[35]

For Lacan the *folie à deux* of the Papin sisters derived its "mystery" from a secret motive that floated somewhere among inadequate explanatory structures: "social tensions" (master/slave), paranoia, and (feminine) castration anxiety. A crime situated outside the circumference of legal understanding, confounding even the most sophisticated expertise within clinical knowledge, the case of the

---

34. Freud, *Dostoevsky and Parricide*, trans. James Strachey, in *Sigmund Freud: Collected Papers* (1888–1938), vol. 5 (New York: Basic Books, 1959), p. 236.
35. Jacques Lacan, *De la psychose paranoïaque dans ses rapports avec la personnalité suivi de Premiers écrits sur la paranoïa* (Paris: Seuil, 1975), p. 398.

Papin sisters was given a Gidean reading by Lacan. Like Lafcadio's *acte gratuit*, the sisters' mimetic murder of their employer and her daughter could be seen, ultimately, as governed by elusive laws of chance and obsession.

If Lacan, sidestepping orthodox Freudian interpretation, represented psychological enigmas with the help of knots and anamorphoses, Gide explored a parallel narrative technique, using plot structures imbricated with coincidence, trompe l'oeil illusionism, fetishism, and paranoia. In the representation of the *acte gratuit*, for example, there emerges a narrative and thematic fetishism of chance. Lafcadio, savoring in advance the embarrassment to the police of an unmotivated crime, yet hesitating at the thought of possible dangers, resolves to commit the murder on the basis of its value as a *game of risk*. The murder accomplished, he deliberates once again whether to disembark from the train and retrieve his beaver hat:

> Mais par-dessus tout il avait l'indécision en horreur, et gardait depuis nombre d'années, *comme un fétiche,* le dé d'un jeu de tric trac que dans le temps lui avait donné Baldi; il le portait toujours sur lui; il l'avait là, dans le gousset de son gilet.
> "Si j'amène six, se dit-il en sortant le dé, je descends!"
> Il amena cinq.
> "Je descends quand même."

> More than all, he hated indecision, and for ten years he had kept on him, *like a fetish,* one of a pair of cribbage dice, which Baldi had given him in days gone by; he never parted from it; it was there in his waistcoat pocket.
> "If I throw six," he said to himself as he took it out, "I'll get down."
> He threw five.
> "I shall get down all the same." (*CV* 831; *LA* 189; my emphasis)

Lafcadio's infatuation with the throw of the dice (no doubt a satirical reference to Mallarmé's "Un coup de Dés") produces an alternate code of morality, a "lawlessness" binding him to Protos, who himself impersonates a myopic lawyer named Defouqueblize. The grand master of the dice, Protos prevents Lafcadio from leaving the train by absconding with his case ("Well! Good-by to my portmanteau! It can't be helped! The throw said I wasn't to get out here. It was right," Lafcadio affirms to himself superstitiously [*LA* 190]). Moreover, by manipulating Lafcadio's insurmountable attraction to small, fetishistic objects Protos further ensnares him in his traps.

Like the Dahomeyan fetish, Legba, characterized by the French ethnologist Marc Augé as a "personal god" endowed with the contradictory properties of chaos and order, the chain of random objects encountered by Lafcadio forms a narrative noose around his apparently undetermined destiny.[36] Starting with the religious figurines manufactured by Fleurissoire and his associates ("Le Carton-Romain-Plastique") through to the virtual conspiracy of vestimentary accessories (pince-nez, cuff links, stockings, hat labels) deployed by Protos as a means of unnerving his prey, the realist detail qua fetish object is used to induce a paranoia bordering on psychosis in the unrepentant assassin.

The most curious object, the most perturbing "little mystery," which like a lure or fly is flung away from its proprietor only miraculously to return, is a pair of cuff links—kitsch jewelry boasting four totemic cats' heads fashioned out of moonstone:

> Ils présentèrent—reliés deux à deux par une agrafe d'or et taillés dans un quartz étrange, sorte d'agate embrouillardée, qui ne laissait rien voir au travers d'elle, bien qu'elle parût transparente—quatre têtes de chat encerclées. Comme Venitequa portait—avec cette forme de corsage masculin qu'on appelle costume tailleur, ainsi que je l'ai déjà dit—des manchettes et comme elle avait le goût saugrenu, elle convoitait ces boutons.
>
> Ils n'étaient point tant amusants que bizarres; Lafcadio les trouvait affreux; il se fût irrité de les voir sur sa maîtresse; mais du moment qu'il la quittait...

> They were joined together two and two by a little gilt chain and were cut out of a peculiar kind of quartz—a sort of smoky agate, which was not transparent, though it looked as if it were—and made to represent four cats' heads. Venitequa, as I have already said, was in the habit of wearing a tailormade coat and skirt and a man's shirt with stiff cuffs, and as she had a taste for oddities, she coveted these sleeve-links.
>
> They were more queer than attractive; Lafcadio thought them hideous;

---

36. Marc Augé, "Le Fétiche et son objet," in *L'Objet en psychanalyse: Le Fétiche, le corps, l'enfant, la science*, ed. Maud Mannoni (Paris: Denoël, 1986), p. 56.

it would have irritated him to see his mistress wearing them; but now that he was going to leave her... (*CV* 731; *LA* 66)

Similar to the shaman's grigri or witch's talisman, the cuff links exert an ambivalent fascination, both repulsive and compelling. In their cloudy transparency they foreshadow Protos's heavy spectacles (used as a decoy, when dropped in the train corridor, so as to obstruct Lafcadio's escape). As opaque mirrors they symbolize leitmotifs developed throughout the *sotie*: dupery, the blindness of faith, the *faux* authenticity of simulacra (as in Anthime Armand-Dubois's conversion by the plaster cast Virgin or Protos's believability when disguised as a lawyer or priest). As masculine adornments on a female body they signal the danger of gender indeterminacy. Most important, as "links" or agents of connectibility, they signify the tendency of diegetic transitivity to undo the effects of narrative serendipity. Though temporarily repressed, an implacable sense of inevitability comes back to haunt the adolescent protagonist seeking freedom in an irrational game.

The journey of the cuff links describes a circular narrative movement. They begin their providential trajectory as Lafcadio's ritual offering to his abandoned mistress, Carola Venitequa, who bestows them in turn on Fleurissoire. After his disappearance, one of them comes mysteriously into the possession of Protos, who delivers it back to Lafcadio. Like one of Diderot's *bijoux indiscrets*, a jewel that tells a compromising story, the missing cuff link that had rolled away from Fleurissoire at the moment of his death creates a scandal as it clatters into Lafcadio's plate:

· Là, devant lui, à découvert, au milieu de l'assiette tombé l'on ne sait d'où, hideux et reconnaissable entre mille... n'en doute pas, Lafcadio: c'est le bouton de Carola! Celui des deux boutons qui manquait à la seconde manchette de Fleurissoire. Voici qui tourne au cauchemar... Mais le garçon se penche vers le plat. D'un coup de main, Lafcadio nettoie l'assiette, faisant glisser le vilain bijou sur la nappe....

Non, ce n'était pas une hallucination: il entend le bouton crisser sous l'assiette; il soulève l'assiette, s'empare du bouton; le glisse à côté de sa montre dans le gousset de son gilet; tâte encore, s'assure: le bouton est là, bien en sûreté... Mais qui dira comment il est venu dans l'assiette? Qui l'y a mis?

· There, right in front of him, plain to his sight, in the very middle of his plate, fallen from God knows where, frightful and unmistakable among a thousand—don't doubt it for an instant, Lafcadio—there lies Carola's sleeve-link! The sleeve-link which had been missing from Fleurissoire's second cuff! The whole thing was becoming a nightmare. But the waiter is bending over him with the dish. With a sweep of his hand, Lafcadio wipes his plate and brushes the horrid trinket on to the table-cloth....

But no! it was not an hallucination; he hears the squeak of the link against his plate; he raises his plate, seizes the link, slips it into his waistcoat pocket beside his watch, feels it again, makes certain—yes! there it is, safe and sound! But who shall say how it came on his plate? Who put it there? (*CV* 851; *LA* 214)

As the cuff link joins the die in Lafcadio's jacket it too becomes an unreliable fetish, a sign of pure chance masquerading as fate. Here Gide ironically employs a technique of trompe l'oeil coincidence: events that appear to be devoid of intentionality are revealed to be motivated *only* in the eyes of the very planner and architect of their gratuitousness! The murderer, in this case, becomes a victim of the devious "fault lines" of a master plot.

A similar paradigm of diegetic deviance (in which characters, having pitched their intellects against the global wit of plot structure, lose out) is repeated as a kind of coda or parable at the end of *Les Caves*. Reading the account of his crime over the shoulder of Count Julius, Lafcadio is dismayed to learn that fate has again tampered with his murder of Fleurissoire, tidied it up (*retouché*), so to speak, with an array of possible motives. Though the *fait divers*' reporter had omitted theft as a possible cause, thereby leaving an inexplicable gap in the story, Julius intervenes to fill it by giving credence to Fleurissoire's far-fetched account of an anti-Vatican plot. To Lafcadio's immense frustration, his crime is deprived of its gratuitousness in the eyes of the outside world, as if there were a conspiracy to judge him innocent no matter how flagrantly he manifests his guilt. Not only can this ironic inversion of truth and falsity be read as a lesson in the perversity of justice (a lesson inculcated repeatedly in the assizes courtroom), but it also may be seen as a parody of psychoanalytic logic, so riveted on resolving the riddles of motive that it "touches up" the facts in order to render them psychoanalytically legible.

Reversing Freud's "crime from a sense of guilt," Gide's protagonist offers the paradigm of a recursive "innocence from a sense of crime." No doubt this formula suited Gide just fine, the Gide, that is, who put himself on trial before the reader with compulsive frequency, soliciting exoneration for sexual preferences deemed criminal by a homophobic society. But whether Gide himself was to be acquitted or convicted (by himself, the public, or the reader) is hardly the point. Rather, what I wish to emphasize is the ingenious, mischievous way in which Gide, with the help of a "low" genre that focused on human weaknesses and anomalies, wrested a ludic, outlaw eroticism from the repressive balance scales of justice. Desublimating and exposing the perverse "little mysteries" that undercut legal, psychoanalytical, and literary explanations alike, Gide used the *fait divers* to ensconce the deviant in fiction and to befuddle the would-be interpreter bent too sanctimoniously on reassigning a moral function to literature with the help of resurrected absolutes of truth and error. As Jean Paulhan, concluding his *Entretien sur des faits divers* (Interview on human interest stories) with his imaginary interlocutor, would maintain: in the allegorical "Palace of Reason" in which Justice is housed, the place of "mysteries" embedded in the *fait divers* must always, without fail, be secured.[37]

37. Jean Paulhan, *Entretien sur des faits divers* (Paris: Gallimard, 1945), p. 156.

· Conclusion

· By focusing on late-nineteenth-century authors such as Zola, the Goncourt brothers, Maupassant, Mirbeau, and Uzanne, I have sought to uncover ways in which male writers created a kind of fetishistic fiction pegged on simulations of a woman's consciousness. Exploring epiphenomena distilled from a fin-de-siècle culture of femininity—bibelot-collecting, sartorial narcissism, religious self-stigmatization, maternal melancholia, and the sadomasochistic phantasms surrounding maid service—I examined the ways in which forms of female fetishism unrecognized as such by psychoanalysis intersected with male fetishizations of femininity. In this way, a lost chapter of psychoanalytical history (female perversion) was, in a sense, filled in by a chapter of literary history (replete with late naturalist chronicles by men of female passions, manias, and attachments).

There were, of course, important women novelists in this period who wrote comparably fetishistic fictions combining the sexological-sociological memoir with realist-naturalist stylistics. Zulma Carraud, Gyp, Séverine, Rachilde, and Colette all engaged to some extent in this literary project. Their contribution merits a separate study concentrating, for example, on the role of the female authorial voice in turn-of-the-century representations of sexual obsession and perversion. My concern here has been primarily with the question of why male authors at this time devoted themselves so consistently to writing about feminine clothing, feminine eccentricities, feminine interior visions. The answer is no doubt traceable in part to that European fin-de-siècle crisis in masculinity which, according to Elaine Showalter, spawned self-servingly masculinist versions of sexual difference.[1] Fetishism was particularly amenable to being used to this end, for perhaps more than any other "perversion," it emphasized the phallus and provided through its language of substitution, artifice, and displacement a unique psychological and aesthetic means of disguising Victorian-era castration anxiety.

By emphasizing the degree to which male authors of this period *depended* on fetishistic fictions of femininity I have tried to feminize the fetish itself, de-monumentalizing the fiction of castration anxiety predominant even today, locating a kind of female phallus in the sartorial superego, and dislodging (if ever so slightly) gendered canon alignments.

This said, I should hasten to add that it would be delusionary to think that revisionist readings of misogynist texts on the decorated, fetishized female body (as in the bejeweled nudity of Salammbô and Salomé) suffice to redeem them for a "new" canon. An irredentist gynophobia comes to the fore even when one tries to salvage historic "feminine perspectives" from literary characterizations of women by men. Mirbeau, for example, forged a connection between the love of looking at cruelty (fetishistic *Schaulust*) and female erotomania in *Le Jardin des supplices* that can only be described as profoundly misogynistic. In his Oriental torture garden, spectacles of pain are presented as "what a woman wants," while the male narrator, looking on, disculpates himself of his own scopic desire by fetishizing it in the gaze of a femme fatale. Turn-of-the-century writers, one could argue, seem to have been terrified of discovering what was behind a woman's gaze. Their punishment of the female observer who dares to look (Pandora) emerges as a recurrent misogynist tactic. Ultimately, one might say, it was necessary to perpetrate a myth of feminine scopophilia to safeguard the right to fetishize women: if woman was "in fact" castratory (both on the symbolic level and the real), then the male subject was fully justified in making parts of her body the object of displacement.

Rarely in the male-authored fin-de-siècle novel is the reader allowed to see what a woman sees without layers of misogynist mediation in itself complicitous with psychoanalytical orthodoxies

1. Elaine Showalter, *Sexual Anarchy: Gender and Culture at the Fin de Siècle* (New York: Viking Penguin, 1990), pp. 8–18.

and commonplaces. The woman's gaze is invariably "hysterical," barred by the law (*lex talionis*), "veiled" in tears, or maniacally, preoedipally affixed to a partial object at the expense of a totalizing picture. Though one could perhaps argue that this impaired vision of partial objects "adds up" to seeing what one wants to see, more often than not it appears in the works of male authors to be a symptom or scar marking the site of organs that have been removed or made to disappear.

Though throughout this study I have tried to thwart these scotomizations of the female body by restoring a face to the prostitute, mystic, or maid, it has been difficult to constitute a "mistress" gaze. Nor is looking to woman writers of the period necessarily helpful. When Mirbeau launched *Marie-Claire* (1910)—the working-class novel by an autodidactic seamstress named Marguerite Audoux—with a preface lauding her rendering of "the spectacle of the everyday," he gave his relentless misogyny a temporary rest.[2] But *Marie-Claire* is an example of humble, submissive *écriture féminine*—of prose that is timid, regional, circumspect, and myopic in its field of vision. More subversive was a work written by his own wife, Alice Regnault, rumored to have been a prostitute skilled in specialty vices before becoming Mirbeau's spouse. *Mademoiselle Pomme*, published in 1886 some thirteen years prior to *The Torture Garden* and now fallen into obscurity, is the intimately told biography of a well-to-do courtesan's daughter stigmatized in society by her mother's profession. Full of informative glimpses of the daily life of kept women in the *belle époque*, the novel contains one particular scene that, read in tandem with equivalent scenes in Mirbeau's *Torture Garden*, shows the "difference" of a woman's scopic fix:

> C'était une femme, une de ses malheureuses qui, tous les soirs, moyennant trois francs, servent de décor vivant, d'enseigne en vrai, à ces établissements spéciaux, qui venait d'avoir une attaque de nerfs.
> On se rassura.
> —Ohé! ohé...criiii!...fit une voix qui imitait le cri de douleur parti de la scène.
> Quelques applaudissements ironiques éclatèrent. Des miaulements,

---

2. Octave Mirbeau, preface to *Marie-Claire* (Paris: Charpentier, 1910), p. viii. Audoux's novel is a largely autobiographical, sentimental, pastoral, deeply Christian account of an orphan's life, first in a "pension," and then as a shepherdess gradually acclimated to brute poverty. Though its sickly sweetness makes it almost unreadable today, Mirbeau praised the work for its "taste, depth,...and force of interior action" (p. vii).

des aboiements, des gloussements, des cocoricos se répondirent d'un bout à l'autre du jardin.
—Ohé! ohé...criiii! répéta la même voix.
C'était très gai. On rit, on chanta, on accompagna, en frappant avec les cannes les tables, les verres et les carafes, la malheureuse dont les cris devenaient à chaque instant plus déchirants, plus douleureux, et donnaient la sensation d'une chose horrible, d'un corps tordu par la souffrance et qui se roulait et se débattait, comme en une effroyable agonie.
—Ohé! ohé...criiii.
Et le rideau se releva.
En effet, une place était vide; un mouchoir, un éventail brisé, une fleur froissée, jonchaient encore le tapis rouge. Un monsieur s'avança, et l'orchestre attaqua un air chahutant de quadrille. Le monsieur s'égosilla, la grosse caisse, les cymbales, les pistons firent rage, essayant de couvrir le cri sous leurs hurlements déchaînés, mais ce cri de la femme dominant tous les bruits, s'éleva plus strident, courut, plus rapide, sur tout ce tâpage.
Et rien n'était poignant dans ce bastringue, en cette luminère fausse, sous ces arbres déverdis, parmi tous ces gens hébétés, comme ce cri de douleur, ce râle de suppliciée qui rythmait cet air enragé de cancan.
—Rentrons, dit Lina toute pâle.

It was a woman who had just had a nervous attack, one of those unfortunates who, for an average of three francs a night, served as live décor, a kind of human sign, in these special establishments.
Everyone was reassured.
"Ahh! ahh! criiii!" screamed a voice, imitating the cry of pain that came out from the stage.
Several bursts of ironic applause erupted. Meowing, barking, clucking, crowing, filled the garden from end to end.
"Ahh! ahh! criiii!" the same voice repeated.
It was very festive. People laughed, sang, and pounded tables, glasses, and pitchers with their canes accompanying the unfortunate woman, whose cries became at each moment more searing and painful, giving the sensation of a horrible thing, of a body, contracted by suffering, struggling, rolling around in frightful agony.
"Ahh! ahh! criiii!"
And the curtain came up again.
In effect, there was an empty spot; nothing but a handkerchief, a broken fan, a pressed flower, remained strewn over the red carpet. A gentleman came forward and the orchestra kicked up a raucous dance tune. The gentleman began to shout, the kettle drum, cymbals, and percussion raged on, trying to bury the woman's cry beneath their uncontrollable bellows. But the cry of this woman dominated the racket,

rising ever more stridently, running ever more rapidly over all the din.

And there was nothing poignant in this dive, in this false light, under the leafless trees, among all these dazed people, save for this cry of pain, this death-rattle of the tortured one, in step with the enraged rhythm of the cancan.

"Let's go home," said Lina, very pale.[3]

Where Mirbeau's Clara rejoices at seeing male and female bodies in pain, Regnault's Lina balks at the sight of theatricalized cruelty, illustrating how male conventions for representing feminine scopophilia break down when the author is a woman. Here the contrast between male and female constructions of the woman's gaze can be resumed as follows: Mirbeau, allowing Clara *to see too much*, capitalizes on her sadism to make his humanist case, whereas Regnault generates a psychic space of identification out of what is *not seen* by her female viewer. Lina, in listening, must look away, and one might conclude that Regnault achieves a more subtle critique of specular cruelty by denying visual access to the scene of transgression. Representing the poor actress as a lack registered only faintly by a broken fan, a handkerchief, and a flower; posing a public "eargasm" over and against misogynist *Schaulust* (as in Mirbeau's novel), she refuses to gratify the reader's voyeurism. Displacing the affective charge from the eye to the ear, she performs an operation that is fundamentally fetishistic, but fetishistic in the service of human sympathy rather than in the service of an illusion of sexual mastery. By compelling the reader to focus on the "blue angel" atmospherics of collective barbarism rather than on the erotically splayed body of a torture victim, she forces us to *listen* to the "real" sound of human suffering instead of leaving us "dazzled" by the blinding images of pornographic violence. Sympathetic to her prostitute-heroine, just as her prostitute-heroine is sympathetic to the unfortunate creature screaming offstage, Regnault implicitly refutes vampiric models of fin-de-siècle femininity.

Though one would not want to overdetermine essentialist expectations regarding vision, voice, and gender difference, this passage from *Mademoiselle Pomme* provides nonetheless an emblematic example of how closely associated authors of opposing genders distributed the burden of visual punishment in an era of oculocentric naturalist poetics. In contrast to her husband, Alice Regnault not only refuses the popular fin-de-siècle topos of Medusa's gaze, she

---

3. Alice Regnault, *Mademoiselle Pomme* (Paris: Paul Ollendorff, 1886), pp. 50–52.

also forgoes that quintessential naturalist icon—the clinical death scene—in which the body of the fallen woman, disintegrating into a mess of putrefaction, is transformed into a kind of carrion feast for the eye.

Though Mirbeau and his contemporaries exploited naturalism's phobic visualizations of the female body to the extreme, they also, as I have argued throughout this book, distinguished themselves as experts on the detailism of feminine culture. Perhaps they could be said to have fetishized femininity for homeopathic purposes: fixating on how women masked their *manque à être* (lack in being), focusing on a woman's distancing of manliness through an impostor's show of womanliness, misogynist authors distracted themselves all the more effectively from any reminder of phallic deficiency. It is in this context that the supreme attention paid to "femme-ness" becomes more readily decipherable. The secret details of an elegant feminine toilette, microsociologies of flirtation and seduction, careful notations of the totemic perfume bottles and Meissen figurines that composed and particularized a woman's surroundings at the century's end, these recurrent descriptive obsessions can be read as so many managements of lack, involving the exchange of one kind of phallic prosthetics (the classic fetish) for another (the masquerade of femininity), more susceptible to mastery. As Daniel Sibony has recently argued, "perversion is not the transgression of limits, but rather the establishment within limits of fetishes that one can master."[4]

Another way of looking at this exchange of missing referents might be in terms of a double fetishism whereby male writers are seen to be pretending to be women pretending to be men. By recuperating the errant masculinity of the "woman with a masculinity complex," they garner, second hand, a means of successfully masquerading as men! The paradox, of course, is that this very move to impersonate maleness via the femininity masquerade transformed antifeminist male authors into the guardians and avatars of cultural feminization.

4. Daniel Sibony, "Des liens pervers et toxicos," in *Libération*, July 17, 1990, p. 5.

. SELECTED BIBLIOGRAPHY:

* *Medical and Psychoanalytical Discourse*

Abraham, Karl. "Remarks on the Psycho-Analysis of a Case of Foot and Corset Fetishism." [1910]. In *Selected Papers of Karl Abraham*. Translated by Douglas Bryan and Alix Strachey. New York: Basic Books, 1953.
Abraham, Nicolas, and Maria Torok. *Cryptomanie: Le Verbier de l'Homme aux Loups*. Paris: Aubier Flammarion, 1976.
Aubry, Paul. *La Contagion du meurtre*. Paris: Alcan, 1894.
Augé, Marc. "Le fétiche et son objet." In *L'Objet en psychanalyse: Le Fétiche, le corps, l'enfant, la science*, edited by Maud Mannoni. Paris: Denoël, 1986.
Avalon, J., and Albert Charpentier. "Restif de la Bretonne fétichiste." *Aesculape* (April 1912): 89–93.
Ball, Benjamin. "De l'érotomanie ou folie érotique." *L'Encéphale* (1883): 129–39.
———. "La folie érotique." *L'Encéphale* (1887): 188–97, 257–415.
Barthes, Roland. "Sémiologie et médecine." In *L'Aventure sémiologique*. Paris: Seuil, 1985.
Bellemin-Noël, Jean. *Gradiva au pied de la lettre*. Paris: Presses Universitaires de France, 1983.
Bersani, Leo. *The Freudian Body: Psychoanalysis and Art*. New York: Columbia University Press, 1986.
Bertrand, Louis. "Les Origines morbides de la sensibilité de Flaubert." *Aesculape* 13 (1923): 265–70; 14 (1924): 18–23.
Binet, Alfred. "Le Fétichisme dans l'amour." *Revue Philosophique* 24 (1887): 142–67, 252–74.
———. "La Vision mentale." *Revue Philosophique* 27 (1889): 337–73.
Binet, Léon, and Pierre Vallery-Radot. *Médecine et littérature: Prestige de la médecine*. Paris: Expansion Scientifique Française, 1965.
Binswanger, Ludwig. *Analyse existentielle et psychanalyse freudienne*. Translated by Roger Lewinter. Paris: Gallimard, 1970.
Blin, Georges. *Le Sadisme de Baudelaire*. Paris: J. Corti, 1948.

Bonnet, Gérard. "Fétichisme et exhibitionnisme chez un sujet féminin." In *Voir, être vu: Etudes cliniques sur l'exhibitionnisme*, vol. 1. Paris: Presses Universitaires de France, 1981.
———. *Les Perversions sexuelles*. Paris: Presses Universitaires Françaises, 1983.
Borch-Jacobsen, Mikkel. *The Freudian Subject*. Translated by Catherine Porter. Stanford: Stanford University Press, 1990.
Bourget, Paul. *Essais de psychologie contemporaine*. 2 vols. Paris: Librairie Plon, 1895.
———. *Physiologie de l'amour moderne*. Paris: L'Intelligence, 1906.
Cabanès, Augustin, *Le Cabinet secret de l'histoire*. Paris: A. Maloire, 1900. Translated by W. C. Costello under the title *The Secret Cabinet of History*. Paris: Charles Carrington, 1897.
———. *La Flagellation dans l'histoire et la littérature*. Clermont, Oise: Daix Frères, 1899.
———. *Grands névropathes*. 2 vols. Paris: A. Michel, 1930–31.
Charcot, Jean-Martin. *La Foi qui guérit*. Paris: Progrès médical, 1897.
———. *Leçons du mardi à la Salpêtrière: Policlinique, 1887–1888, 1888–1889*. 2 vols. Paris: Progrès médical, 1889.
Charcot, Jean-Martin, and Valentin Magnan. "Inversion du sens génital et autres perversions sexuelles." *Archives de Neurologie* 3 (Jan.–Feb. 1882): 53–60, and 4 (July 1882): 296–322.
Charcot, Jean-Martin, and Paul Richer. *Les Démoniaques dans l'art*. [1887]. Introduction by Pierre Fédida. Postface by Georges Didi-Huberman. Paris: Editions Macula, 1984.
Chasseguet-Smirgel, Janine. *Ethique et esthétique de la perversion*. Seyssel: Champ Vallon, 1984.
Clavreul, Jean. "The Perverse Couple." In *Returning to Freud: Clinical Psychoanalysis in the School of Lacan*, translated and edited by Stuart Schneiderman. New Haven: Yale University Press, 1980.
Clérambault, Gatian de Gaeton de. *Oeuvre psychiatrique*. Edited by Jean Fretet. Paris: Presses Universitaires de France, 1942.
———. *La Passion des étoffes chez un neuro-psychiatre*. Edited by Yolande Papetti et al. Paris: Solin, 1981.
Coulont-Henderson, Francoise. "Sang, mort et morbidité dans *Madame Gervaisais* d'Edmond et Jules de Goncourt." *Nineteenth-Century French Studies* 14 (Spring–Summer 1986): 295-302.
Daudet, Léon. *L'Hérédo: essai sur le drame intérieur*. Paris: Nouvelle Librairie Nationale, 1916.
Deleuze, Gilles. *Masochism: An Interpretation of Coldness and Cruelty*. Translated by Jean McNeil. New York: George Braziller, 1971.
Delpierre, Guillaume. *Etude psycho-pathologique sur Guy de Maupassant*. Montrouge: V. Hello, 1939.
Didi-Huberman, Georges. *Invention de l'hystérie: Charcot et l'Iconographie photographique de la Salpêtrière*. Paris: Editions Macula, 1982.
Dumesnil, René. *Flaubert et la médecine*. Paris: Société Française d'Imprimerie, 1905.

Ellis, Havelock. *From Rousseau to Proust*. London: Constable, 1936.
———. *Studies on the Psychology of Sex*. 2 vols. New York: Modern Library, 1905–42.
Esquirol, Jean-Etienne-Dominique. *Des maladies mentales considérées sous le rapport médical, hygiénique et médicolégal*. 2 vols. Paris: J.-B. Baillière, 1838.
Feldstein, Richard, and Henry Sussman, *Psychoanalysis and...* New York: Routledge, 1990.
Féré, Charles. *Dégénérescence et criminalité, essai psychologique*. Paris: Bibliothèque de Philosophie Contemporaine, 1888.
———. *L'Instinct sexuel*. Paris: Alcan, 1899.
Forel, Auguste. *The Sexual Question: A Scientific, Psychological, Hygienic, and Sociological Study*. Translated by C. F. Marshall. New York: Rebman, 1908.
Foucault, Michel. *The Birth of the Clinic: An Archaeology of Medical Perception*. Translated by A. M. Sheridan-Smith. New York: Random House, 1975.
———. *The History of Sexuality*. Vol. 1: *An Introduction*. Translated by Robert Hurley. New York: Vintage, 1980.
Fournier, Alfred-Jean. *L'Hérédité syphilitique*. Paris: G. Masson, 1882.
Freud, Sigmund. *The Complete Letters of Sigmund Freud to Wilhelm Fliess (1887–1904)*. Translated and edited by Jeffrey Moussaieff Masson. Cambridge: Harvard University Press, 1985.
———. *The Standard Edition of the Complete Psychological Works of Sigmund Freud*. Translated by James Strachey et al. 24 vols. London: Hogarth Press, 1953–74.

"Character and Anal Eroticism." [1908]. 9:168–75.
"Charcot." [1893]. 3:11–23.
"'A Child Is Being Beaten.': A Contribution to the Study of the Origin of Sexual Perversions." [1919]. 17:179–204.
"Constructions in Analysis." [1937]. 23:255–69.
"Delusions and Dreams in Jensen's *Gradiva*. [1907 (1906)]. 9:7–95.
"Dostoevsky and Parricide." [1928 (1927)]. 21:177–94.
"The Economic Problem of Masochism." [1924]. 19:159–70.
"Female Sexuality." [1931]. 21:225–43.
"Femininity." [1933]. 22:112–35.
"Fetishism." [1927]. 21:152–57.
"Heredity and the Etiology of the Neuroses." [1896]. 3:141–56.
"Hysteria." [1888]. 1:39–59.
The Interpretation of Dreams. [1899]. 4 and 5.
"Leonardo da Vinci and a Memory of His Childhood." [1910]. 11:63–137.
"Mourning and Melancholia." [1917 (1915)]. 14:243–58.
"Negation." [1925]. 19:235–39.
"Notes upon a Case of Obsessional Neurosis." [1909]. 10:153–318.
"Obsessions and Phobias: Their Physical Mechanism and Their Aetiology." [1895]. 3:74–84.
"Obsessive Actions and Religious Practices." [1907]. 9:117–27.
"Preface to the Translation of Charcot's *Lectures on the Diseases of the Nervous System*. [1886] 1:21–22.

"The Psycho-Analytic View of Psychogenic Disturbance of Vision."
[1910]. 11:211–18.
The Psychopathology of Everyday Life. [1901]. 6:1–279.
"Repression." [1915]. 14:146–58.
"Splitting of the Ego in the Process of Defence." [1940 (1938)]. 23:275–78.
"Studies on Hysteria." [1893–95] 2:1–312.
Three Essays on the Theory of Sexuality. [1905]. 7:135–243.
Freud, Sigmund, and René Laforgue. "Correspondence (1923-1937)." *Nouvelle Revue de Psychanalyse* 15 (Spring 1977): 251-311.
Gardiner, Muriel. *The Wolf-man by the Wolf-man.* New York: Basic Books, 1971.
Garnier, Paul. *Les Fétichistes pervertis et invertis sexuels: Observations médico-légales.* Paris: Baillière et Fils, 1896.
Gay, Peter. *The Bourgeois Experience: Victoria to Freud.* Vol. 2: *The Tender Passion.* New York: Oxford University Press, 1986.
Gilman, Sander. *Difference and Pathology: Stereotypes of Sexuality, Race, and Madness.* Ithaca: Cornell University Press, 1985.
Goldstein, Jan. *Console and Classify: The French Psychiatric Profession in the Nineteenth Century.* Cambridge: Cambridge University Press, 1987.
Gould, Stephen Jay. *The Mismeasure of Man.* New York: Norton, 1981.
Gourmont, Remy de. *Physique de l'amour: Essai sur l'instinct sexual.* Paris: Les Editions 1900, 1989.
Granoff, Wladimir, and François Perrier, eds. *Le Désir et le féminin.* Paris: Aubier-Montaigne, 1979.
Greenacre, Phyllis. "Fetishism." In *Sexual Deviations,* edited by I. Rosen. London: Oxford University Press, 1979.
Grellet, Isabelle, and Caroline Kruse. *Histoires de la tuberculose: Les Fièvres de l'âme, 1800–1940.* Paris: Ramsay, 1983.
Haan, P. *Nos ancêtres les pervers.* Paris: Obvier Orban, 1979.
Harris, Ruth. *Murders and Madness: Medicine, Law, and Society in the Fin de Siècle.* Oxford: Oxford University Press, 1989.
Heine, Maurice. "Note sur un classement psycho-biologique des paresthésies sexuelles." *Minotaure* 3-4 (December 1933).
Hirschfeld, Magnus. *Anomalies et perversions sexuelles.* Translated by Anne-Catherine Stier. Paris: Corréa and Guy Leprat, 1957.
———. *Le Corps et l'amour.* Paris: Gallimard, 1937.
Horney, Karen. *Feminine Psychology.* New York: Norton, 1967.
Jacob, P. L. *Curiosités de l'histoire de France.* Paris, 1858.
Jones, Ernest. *The Life and Work of Sigmund Freud.* Vol. 2: *1901–1919.* New York: Basic Books, 1955.
Kaplan, Louise. *Female Perversions: The Temptations of Emma Bovary.* New York: Doubleday, 1991.
Krafft-Ebing, Richard von. *Psychopathia Sexualis.* [1886]. Translated by Harry E. Wedeck. New York: Putnam's, 1965.
Kristeva, Julia. *Soleil noir: Dépression et mélancholie.* Paris: Gallimard, 1987.

Lacan, Jacques. *De la psychose paranoïaque dans ses rapports avec la personnalité suivi de Premiers écrits sur la paranoïa*. Paris: Seuil, 1975.
——. "Du Baroque." In *Le Séminaire de Jacques Lacan, Livre XX: Encore*. Text established by Jacques-Alain Miller. Paris: Seuil, 1975.
——. "Guiding Remarks for a Congress on Feminine Sexuality." In *Feminine Sexuality: Jacques Lacan and the école freudienne*, edited by Juliet Mitchell and Jacqueline Rose, translated by Jacqueline Rose. New York: Norton, 1985.
——. *Le Séminaire de Jacques Lacan, Livre XI: Les Quatre Concepts fondamentaux de la psychanalyse*. Paris: Seuil, 1973. Translated by Alan Sheridan and edited by Jacques-Alain Miller under the title *The Four Fundamental Concepts of Psycho-analysis*. New York: Norton, 1978.
——. "La signification du phallus." In *Ecrits*, vol. 2. Paris: Seuil, 1971. Translated by Jacqueline Rose under the title "The Meaning of the Phallus," in *Feminine Sexuality*, edited by Mitchell and Rose.
Lacan, Jacques, and Wladimir Granoff. "Fetishism: The Symbolic, the Imaginary, and the Real." In *Perversions, Psychodynamics, and Therapy*. London: Tavistock, 1956.
Lacassagne, Zacharie. *La Folie de Maupassant*. Toulouse: Gimet-Pisseau, 1907.
Laforgue, René. *L'Echec de Baudelaire: Essai psychologique sur la névrose de Charles Baudelaire*. Paris: Denoël, 1931.
——. *L'Evolution psychiatrique: Psychanalyse—psychologie clinique*. Paris: Payot, 1925.
——. *Relativité de la réalité: Réflexions sur la genèse du besoin de causalité et sur le conditionnement de l'intelligence*. Genève: Mont-Blanc, 1963.
——. "Verdrängung and Skotomisation." *Internationale Zeitschrift für die Psychoanalyse* 12 (1926): 54–65.
Lanteri Laura, Georges. *Lectures des perversions: Histoire de leur appropriation médicale*. Paris: Masson, 1979.
Laplanche, Jean. *Life and Death in Psychoanalysis*. Translated by Jeffrey Mehlman. Baltimore: Johns Hopkins University Press, 1985.
Laqueur, Thomas. *Making Sex: Body and Gender from the Greeks to Freud*. Cambridge: Harvard University Press, 1990.
La Tourette, Gilles de. *Traité clinique et thérapeutique de l'hystérie*, vol. 2. Paris: Plon, 1895.
Laurent, Paul. *Fétichistes et érotomanes*. Paris: Vigot Frères, 1905.
Lemoine-Luccioni, Eugénie. *La Robe: Essai psychanalytique sur le vêtement*. Paris: Seuil, 1983.
Le Rider, Jacques. *Modernité viennoise et crises de l'identité*. Paris: Presses Universitaires de France, 1990.
Littré, Emile. *Pathologie verbale ou lésions de certains mots dans la cours de l'usage*. Paris: Société des Amis de la Bibliothèque Nationale, 1986.
Lombroso, Cesare, and Gina Lombroso Ferrero. *La Femme criminelle et la prostituée*. Paris: Alcan, 1896.
Macé, Gustave. *La Police parisienne: Un joli monde*. Paris: Charpentier, 1887.

McGrath, William J. *Freud's Discovery of Psychoanalysis: The Politics of Hysteria.* Ithaca: Cornell University Press, 1986.
Mannoni, Octave. *Clefs pour l'Imaginaire ou l'Autre Scène.* Paris: Seuil, 1969.
Marcus, Steven. *Freud and the Culture of Psychoanalysis: Studies in the Transition from Victorian Humanism to Modernity.* New York: Norton, 1984.
Masson, Jeffrey Moussaieff. *A Dark Science: Women, Sexuality, and Psychiatry in the Nineteenth Century.* New York: Farrar, Straus and Giroux, 1986.
Meige, Henri. *Charcot artiste.* Paris: Masson, 1925.
Miller, Gérard. *Lacan.* Paris: Borda, 1987.
Mitchell, Juliet, ed. *The Selected Melanie Klein.* New York: Free Press, 1986.
Moll, A. *Les Perversions de l'instinct génital.* Paris: Georges Carré, 1893.
Moreau de Tours, Paul. *Des Aberrations du sens génésique.* Paris: Asselin, 1880.
Morel, Bénédict-Augustin. *Traité des dégénérescences physiques, intellectuelles et morales de l'espèce humaine.* Paris: Baillière, 1857.
Nordau, Max. *Degeneration.* New York: Howard Fertig, 1968.
Nunberg, Herman, and Ernst Federn, eds. *Minutes of the Vienna Psychoanalytic Society.* Translated by M. Nunberg. 3 vols. New York: International Press, 1962–75.
Nye, Robert. *Crime, Madness, and Politics in Modern France.* Princeton: Princeton University Press, 1984.
Objets du fétichisme. Special issue of *Nouvelle Revue de Psychanalyse* 2 (Autumn 1970).
Ribot, Théodule. *L'Hérédité psychologique.* Paris: Librairie Germer Baillière, 1882.
Richer, Paul. *L'Art et la médecine.* Paris: Goultier, Magnier, 1902.
Roger, Alain. *Hérésies du désir: Freud, Dracula, Dali.* Seyssel: Champ Vallon, 1985.
Rose, Jacqueline. *Sexuality in the Field of Vision.* London: Verso, 1986.
Rose, Louis. "The Psychoanalytic Movement in Vienna: Toward a Science of Culture." Ph.D diss., Princeton University, 1986
Roudinesco, Elisabeth. *Histoire de la psychanalyse en France.* 2 vols. Paris: Seuil, 1986.
Ryckère, Raymond de. *La Servante criminelle: Étude de criminologie professionelle.* Paris: A Maloine, 1908.
Sollier, Paul. *Les Phénomènes d'autoscopie.* Paris: Alcan, 1903.
Stekel, Wilhelm. *Sexual Aberrations: The Phenomena of Fetishism in Relation to Sex*, vol. 1. Translated by Samuel Parker. New York: Liveright, 1971.
Tarde, Gabriel de. *Les Lois de l'imitation.* Geneva: Slatkine, 1979.
Taxil, Léo. *La Prostitution contemporaine: Etude d'une question sociale.* Paris: Librairie Populaire, 1884.
Taxil, Léo, and Karl Milo. *Les Débauches d'un confesseur.* Paris: Librairie Anticlérical, 1885.
Torok, Maria. "Maladie du deuil et fantasme du cadavre exquis." *Revue Française de Psychanalyse* 4 (1968): 715–33.
Weininger, Otto. *Sexe et caractère.* [1904]. Translated from the German by Daniel Renaud. Lausanne: Editions l'Age d'Homme, 1975.

Yeazell, Ruth Bernard. *Sex, Politics, and Science in the Nineteenth-Century Novel.* Baltimore: Johns Hopkins University Press, 1990.

Gender Critique

Abel, Elizabeth, ed. *Writing and Sexual Difference.* Chicago: University of Chicago Press, 1982.

Adams, Parveen. "Per Os(cillation)." *Camera Obscura* 17 (May 1988): 7–29.

Adams, Parveen, and Elizabeth Cowie, eds. *The Woman in Question.* Cambridge: MIT Press, 1990.

Apter, Emily. *André Gide and the Codes of Homotextuality.* Stanford French and Italian Studies. Saratoga, Calif.: Anma Libri, 1987.

———. "Fore-skin and After-image: Photographic Fetishism in Tournier's Fiction." *L'Espirit créateur* 29 (Spring 1989): 72–82.

Aulagnier-Spairani, Piera. "Remarques sur la féminité et ses avatars." In *Le Désir et la perversion.* Paris: Seuil, 1967.

Benhabib, Seyla, and Drucilla Cornell, eds. *Feminism as Critique.* Minneapolis: University of Minnesota Press, 1988.

Bonaparte, Marie. *Female Sexuality.* New York: International Universities Press, 1953.

Brennan, Teresa. *Between Feminism and Psychoanalysis.* London: Routledge, 1989.

Burgin, Victor, James Donald, and Cora Kaplan, eds. *Formations of Fantasy.* London: Methuen, 1986.

Butler, Judith. *Gender Trouble: Feminism and the Subversion of Identity.* New York: Routledge, 1990.

Carpenter, Edward. *Selected Writings.* London: GMP, 1984.

Cixous, Hélène. "Le Rire de la Méduse." *L'Arc* 61 (1975): 39–54.

Cixous, Hélène, and Catherine Clément. *The Newly Born Woman.* Translated by Betsy Wing. Minneapolis: University of Minnesota Press, 1986.

Copjec, Joan. "Flavit et Dissipati Sunt." *October* 18 (Fall 1981): 20–40.

———. "The Sartorial Superego." *October* 50 (Fall 1989): 56–95.

Coward, Rosalind. *Female Desires: How They Are Sought, Bought, and Packaged.* New York: Grove Press, 1985.

———. "Sexual Violence and Sexuality." In *Sexuality: A Reader,* edited by Feminist Review. London: Virago Press, 1987.

Dellamora, Richard. *Masculine Desire: The Sexual Politics of Victorian Aestheticism.* Chapel Hill: University of North Carolina Press, 1990.

Doane, Mary Anne. "Film and the Masquarade: Theorizing the Female Spectator." *Screen* 23, no. 3–4 (1982): 74-88.

———. "Veiling over Desire: Close-ups of the Woman." In *Feminism and Psychoanalysis,* edited by Richard Feldstein and Judith Roof. Ithaca: Cornell University Press, 1989.

———. "Woman's Stake: Filming the Female Body." *October* 17 (Summer 1981): 22–36.

Evans, Martha Noel. *Masks of Tradition: Women and the Politics of Writing in Twentieth-Century France.* Ithaca: Cornell University Press, 1988.

Feldstein, Richard, and Judith Roof, eds. *Feminism and Psychoanalysis.* Ithaca: Cornell University Press, 1989.
Fraser, Nancy. *Unruly Practices: Power, Discourse, and Gender in Contemporary Social Theory.* Minneapolis: University of Minnesota Press, 1989.
Gaines, Jane, and Charlotte Herzog. *Fabrications: Costume and the Female Body.* New York: Routledge, 1990.
Gallop, Jane. *Thinking through the Body.* New York: Columbia University Press, 1988.
Garber, Marjorie. "Fetish Envy." *October* 53 (Fall 1990): 45–56.
Gilbert, Sandra M., and Susan Gubar. *The Madwoman in the Attic.* New Haven: Yale University Press, 1979.
Grosz, Elizabeth. *Sexual Subversions: Three French Feminists.* Sydney: Allen and Unwin, 1989.
Grunberger, Bela. "Jalons pour l'étude du narcissisme dans la sexualité féminine." In *La Sexualité féminine,* edited by Janine Chasseguet-Smirgel. Paris: Payot, 1964.
Heath, Stephen. "Joan Riviere and the Masquerade." In *Formations of Fantasy,* edited by Victor Burgin, James Donald, and Cora Kaplan. London: Methuen, 1986.
Hirsch, Marianne, and Evelyn Fox Keller, eds. *Conflicts in Feminism.* New York: Routledge, 1990.
Hunt, Lynn, ed. *Eroticism and the Body Politic.* Baltimore: Johns Hopkins University Press, 1990.
———. *The New Cultural History.* Berkeley: University of California Press, 1989.
Irigaray, Luce. *Ce sexe qui n'en est pas un.* Paris: Minuit, 1977.
———. *Ethique de la différence sexuelle.* Paris: Minuit, 1984.
———. *Passions élémentaires.* Paris: Minuit, 1982.
———. *Sexes et parentés.* Paris: Minuit, 1987.
———. *Speculum of the Other Woman.* Translated by Gillian Gill. Ithaca: Cornell University Press, 1985.
Jacobus, Mary. *Reading Woman: Essays in Feminist Criticism.* New York: Columbia University Press, 1986.
Jardine, Alice A. *Gynesis: Configurations of Women and Modernity.* Ithaca: Cornell University Press, 1985.
Kaplan, E. Ann. *Women and Film: Both Sides of the Camera.* New York: Methuen, 1983.
Kelly, Mary. *Post-Partum Document.* London: Routledge and Kegan Paul, 1985.
Kendrick, Walter. *The Secret Museum: Pornography in Modern Culture.* New York: Viking, 1987.
Koestenbaum, Wayne. *Double Talk: The Erotics of Male Literary Collaboration.* New York: Routledge, 1989.
Kofman, Sarah. "Baubô: Theological Perversion and Fetishism." Translated by Tracy B. Strong in *Nietzsche's New Seas: Explorations in Philosophy, Aesthetics, and Politics,* edited by Michael Allen Gillespie and Tracy B. Strong. Chicago: University of Chicago Press, 1988.

———. "Ça cloche." In *Les Fins de l'homme: A partir du travail de Jacques Derrida*. Paris: Galilée, 1981.
Krauss, Rosalind, Jane Livingston, and Dawn Addes. *L'Amour Fou: Photography and Surrealism*. New York: Abbeville Press, 1985.
Kristeva, Julia. *Histoires d'amour*. Paris: Gallimard, 1983.
Kroker, Arthur, and Marilouise Kroker. *Body Invaders: Panic Sex in America*. New York: St. Martin's Press, 1987.
Kunzle, David. *Fashion and Fetishism*. Totowa, N.J.: Rowman and Littlefield, 1982.
La Belle, Jenijoy. *Herself Beheld: The Literature of the Looking Glass*. Ithaca: Cornell University Press, 1989.
Le Doeuff, Michèle. *The Philosophical Imaginary*. Translated by Colin Gordon. Stanford: Stanford University Press, 1990.
Marcus, Jane. "The Asylums of Antaeus: Women, Ware, and Madness—Is There a Feminist Fetishism?" In *The New Historicism*, edited by H. Aram Veeser. New York: Routledge, 1989.
Martin-Fugier, Anne. *La Bourgeoise: Femme au temps de Paul Bourget*. Paris: Grasset, 1983.
———. *La Place des bonnes: La Domesticité féminine à Paris en 1900*. Paris: Grasset, 1979.
Mayne, Judith. *The Woman at the Keyhole: Feminism and Women's Cinema*. Bloomington: Indiana University Press, 1990.
Miller, Nancy K. *Subject to Change: Reading Feminist Writing*. New York: Columbia University Press, 1988.
Millot, Catherine. *Nobodaddy: L'Hystérie dans le siècle*. Cahors: Points Hors Ligne, 1988.
Mitchell, Juliet, and Jacqueline Rose, eds. *Feminine Sexuality: Jacques Lacan and the école freudienne*. New York: Norton, 1985.
Modleski, Tania. *Loving with a Vengeance: Mass-produced Fantasies for Women*. New York: Routledge, 1982.
———. *The Women Who Knew Too Much: Hitchcock and Feminist Theory*. New York: Methuen, 1988.
Moi, Toril. *Sexual/Textual Politics: Feminist Literary Theory*. London: Methuen, 1985.
Montrelay, Michèle. *L'Ombre et le nom: Sur la féminité*. Paris: Minuit, 1977.
Morris, Meaghan. *The Pirate's Fianceé: Feminism, Reading, Postmodernism*. London: Verso, 1988.
Mulvey, Laura. *Visual and Other Pleasures*. Bloomington: Indiana University Press, 1989.
Nochlin, Linda. *The Politics of Vision: Essays on Nineteenth-Century Art and Society*. New York: Harper and Row, 1988.
Parker, Rosika, and Griselda Pollock. *Old Mistresses: Women, Art, and Ideology*. New York: Pantheon Books, 1981.
Pollock, Griselda. *Vision and Difference: Femininity, Feminism, and the Histories of Art*. London: Routledge, 1988.

Richards, Arlene Kramer. "Female Fetishes and Female Perversions: Hermine Hun-Hellmuth's 'A Case of Female Foot or More Properly Boot Fetishism' Reconsidered." *Psychoanalytic Review* 77 (Spring 1990): 11–23.
Riviere, Joan. "Womanliness as Masquerade." In *Formations of Fantasy*, edited by Victor Burgin, James Donald, and Cora Kaplan. London: Methuen, 1986.
SAMOIS, ed. *Coming to Power: Writings and Graphics on Lesbian S/M*. Boston: Alyson Publications, 1981.
Schneiderman, Stuart. *An Angel Passes: How the Sexes Became Undivided*. New York: New York University Press, 1988.
——, ed. *Returning to Freud: Clinical Psychoanalysis in the School of Lacan*. New Haven: Yale University Press, 1980.
Schor, Naomi. *Breaking the Chain: Women, Theory, and French Realist Fiction*. New York: Columbia University Press, 1985.
——. "Female Fetishism: The Case of George Sand." In *The Female Body in Western Culture*, edited by Susan Suleiman. Cambridge: Harvard University Press, 1986.
——. *Reading in Detail: Aesthetics and the Feminine*. New York: Methuen, 1987.
Schor, Naomi, and Henry F. Majewski, eds. *Flaubert and Postmodernism*. Lincoln: University of Nebraska Press, 1984.
Sedgwick, Eve Kosofsky. *The Epistemology of the Closet*. Berkeley: University of California Press, 1990.
Showalter, Elaine. *Sexual Anarchy: Gender and Culture at the Fin de Siècle*. New York: Viking, 1990.
Silverman, Debora. *Art Nouveau in Fin-de-Siècle France: Politics, Psychology, and Style*. Berkeley: University of California Press, 1989.
Silverman, Kaja. *The Acoustic Mirror: The Female Voice in Psychoanalysis and Cinema*. Bloomington: Indiana University Press, 1988.
——. "Fragments of a Fashionable Discourse." In *Studies in Entertainment: Critical Approaches to Mass Culture*, edited by Tania Modleski. Bloomington: Indiana University Press, 1986.
Simmel, Georg. *Georg Simmel: On Women, Sexuality, and Love*. Translated and with an introduction by Guy Oakes. New Haven: Yale University Press, 1984.
Soloman-Godeau, Abigail. "The Legs of the Countess." *October* 39 (Winter 1986): 65–108.
Spackman, Barbara. *Decadent Genealogies: The Rhetoric of Sickness from Baudelaire to D'Annunzio*. Ithaca: Cornell University Press, 1989.
Spivak, Gayatri Chakravorty. "Displacement and the Discourse of Woman." In *Displacement: Derrida and After*, edited by Mark Krupnick. Bloomington: Indiana University Press, 1983.
Sprengnether, Madelon. *The Spectral Mother: Freud, Feminism, and Psychoanalysis*. Ithaca: Cornell University Press, 1989.
Stallybrass, Peter, and Allon White. *The Politics and Poetics of Transgression*. Ithaca: Cornell University Press, 1986.

Stambolian, George, and Elaine Marks, eds. *Homosexualities and French Literature: Cultural Contexts/Critical Texts*. Ithaca: Cornell University Press, 1990.
Suleiman, Susan Rubin. *Subversive Intent: Gender, Politics, and the Avant-garde*. Cambridge: Harvard University Press, 1990.
Thomas, Chantal. *La Reine scélérate*. Paris: Seuil, 1989.
Todd, Jane Marie. "The Philosopher as Transvestite: Textual Revision in *Glas*." In *Literature as Philosophy/Philosophy as Literature*, edited by Donald Marshall. Iowa City: University of Iowa Press, 1987.
Vance, Carol S., ed. *Pleasure and Danger: Exploring Female Sexuality*. Boston: Routledge and Kegan Paul, 1984.
Waelti-Walters, Jennifer. *Feminist Novelists of the Belle Epoque*. Bloomington: Indiana University Press, 1990.
Weed, Elizabeth, ed. *Coming to Terms: Feminism, Theory, Politics*. New York: Routledge, 1989.
Williams, Linda. "Fetishism and Hard Core: Marx, Freud, and the 'Money Shot.'" In *The Dilemma of Violent Pornography*, edited by Susan Gubar and Joan Hoff. Bloomington: Indiana University Press, 1989.

Literary Sources

Adler, Laure. *Secrets d'alcôve: Histoire du couple de 1830 à 1930*. Paris: Hachette, 1983.
———. *La Vie quotidienne dans les maisons closes, 1830–1930*. Paris: Hachette, 1990.
Artinian, Artine. *Guy de Maupassant: Correspondence inédite*. Paris: Belles Lettres, 1954.
Asselineau, Charles. *L'Enfer du Bibliophile*. Paris, 1860.
Auerbach, Eric. *Mimesis: The Representation of Reality in Western Literature*. Translated by Willard R. Trask. Princeton: Princeton University Press, 1973.
Beizer, Janet. "The Body in Question: Anatomy, Textuality, and Fetishism in Zola." *L'Espirit créateur* 29 (Spring 1989): 50–60.
Belot, Adolphe. *La Bouche de Mme X....* Paris: Dentu, Librairie de la Société de Gens de Lettres, 1882.
Berman, Jeffrey. *The Talking Cure: Literary Representations of Psychoanalysis*. New York: New York University Press, 1987.
Bernheimer, Charles. *Figures of Ill-Repute: Representing Prostitution in Nineteenth-Century France*. Cambridge: Harvard University Press, 1989.
Bersani, Leo. *The Culture of Redemption*. Cambridge: Harvard University Press, 1990.
Bersani, Leo, and Ulysse Dutoit. *The Forms of Violence*. New York: Schocken, 1985.
Bertrand, Jean-Pierre. "Fragments d'une rhétorique fétichiste." *Lendemains* 13, no. 49 (1988): 70-76.

Blanc, Charles. *Art in Adornment and Dress*. Translated from the French. London: Chapman and Hall, 1877.
Bonnaffé, Edmond. *Causeries sur l'art et la curiosité*. Paris: Quantin, 1878.
Borel, Pierre. *Le Destin tragique de Guy de Maupassant*. Paris: Editions de France, 1927.
Bosc, Ernest. *Dictionnaire de l'art, de la curiosité et du bibelot*. Paris, 1883.
Bossard, Abbé Eugène. *Gilles de Rais, maréchal de France, dit Barbe-Bleue*. Paris, 1885.
Bourget, Paul. "Une Fille-mère." In *Les oeuvres libres*. Paris: Fayard, 1928.
Bowlby, Rachel. *Just Looking: Consumer Culture in Dreiser, Gissing and Zola*. New York and London: Methuen, 1985.
Bowman, Frank Paul. *French Romanticism: Intertextual and Interdisciplinary Readings*. Baltimore and London: The Johns Hopkins University Press, 1990.
Bredin, Jean-Denis. *L'Affaire*. Paris: Julliard, 1983.
Bretonne, Restif de la. *Le Pied de Fanchette*. [1769]. Paris: A. Quantin, 1881.
Briggs, Asa. *Victorian Things*. Chicago: University of Chicago Press, 1989.
Buisine, Alain. "L'Impossible Couleur: L'Impressionisme et la critique d'art." *Word and Image: A Journal of Verbal/Visual Enquiry* 4 (1) (Jan.–Mar. 1988): 131–38.
Buraud, Georges. *Les Masques*. Paris: Seuil, 1948.
Carraud, Zulma. *Une Servante d'autrefois*. Paris: Hachette, 1866.
Castex, Pierre-Georges. *Le Conte fantastique en France*. Paris: Corti, 1951.
Cazalis, Henri. *Pensées douleureuses* and *Le Livre du néant*. Paris: Alphonse Lemerre, 1872.
Chambers, Ross. *Story and Situation: Narrative Seduction and the Power of Fiction*. Minneapolis: University of Minnesota Press, 1984.
Clarétie, Jules. *L'Obsession: Moi et l'autre*. Paris, 1908.
Cogny, Pierre. *Maupassant: L'Homme sans dieu*. Paris: La Renaissance du Livre, 1968.
Coppée, François. "Fétichisme." *Le Journal*, Dec. 15, 1894.
Corbin, Alain. *Les Filles de noce*. Paris: Flammarion, 1978.
———. "La Relation intime ou les plaisirs de l'échange." In *Histoire de la vie privée*, vol. 4. Edited by Michelle Perrot. Paris: Seuil, 1987. Translated by Arthur Goldhammer under the titles "Backstage," *A History of Private Life*. vol. 4: *From the Fires of Revolution to the Great War*. Cambridge: Harvard University Press, 1990.
Coward, David. "The Sublimations of a Fetishist: Restif de la Bretonne." *Eighteenth-Century Life* 9 (May 1985): 98–108.
Daudet, Léon. *Devant la douleur: Souvenirs des milieux littéraires, artistiques et médicaux, de 1880 à 1905*. Paris: Nouvelle Librairie Nationale, 1915.
———. *Mélancholia*. Paris: B. Grasset, 1928.
———. *Les Morticoles*. Paris: Charpentier, 1894.
Derrida, Jacques. *Glas*. Paris: Galilée, 1974.
———. *La Vérité en peinture*. Paris: Flammarion, 1978.
———, ed. *Mimesis des articulations*. Paris: Flammarion, 1975.

Dijkstra, Bram. *Idols of Perversity.* New York: Oxford University Press, 1986.
Dolan, Thérèse. "Musée Goncourt: Manette Salomon and the Nude." *Nineteenth-Century French Studies* 18, no. 1–2 (1989–90): 173–85.
Droz, Gustave, *La Femme gênante.* Paris: Ollendorff, 1900.
Festa-McCormick, Diana. *Proustian Optics of Clothes: Mirrors, Masks, Mores.* Saratoga, Calif.: Anma Libri, 1984.
Gallé, Emile. *Ecrits pour l'art.* [1908]. Marseille: Lafitte Reprints, 1980.
Genette, Gérard. *Mimologiques: Voyage en Cratylie.* Paris: Seuil, 1976.
———. *Nouveau discours du récit.* Paris: Seuil, 1983. Translated by Jane E. Lewin under the title *Narrative Discourse Revisited.* Ithaca: Cornell University Press, 1990.
Gide, André. *Dostoïevski.* Paris: Gallimard, 1923.
———. *Littérature engagée.* Paris: Gallimard, 1950.
———. *Ne jugez pas.* Paris: Gallimard, 1930.
———. *Si le grain ne meurt.* Paris: Gallimard, 1955.
Ginisty, Paul. *Le Dieu Bibelot.* Paris: A. Dupret, 1888.
Goncourt, Edmond de. *La Maison d'un artiste.* Paris: Charpentier, 1881.
Goncourt, Edmond de, and Jules de Goncourt. *La Femme au dix-huitième siècle.* Paris: E. Dentu, 1875.
———. *Journal: Mémoires de la vie littéraire, 1851–1896.* 3 vols. Paris: Robert Laffont, 1989.
———. *Madame Gervaisais.* [1869]. Paris: Gallimard, 1982.
Grunfeld, Frederic V. *Rodin: A Biography.* New York: Henry Holt, 1987.
Hamon, Philippe. *Expositions.* Paris: Joseph Corti, 1989.
Harari, Josué V. *Scenarios of the Imaginary: Theorizing the French Enlightenment.* Ithaca: Cornell University Press, 1987.
Huysmans, J. K. *Marthe.* Paris: Union Générale d'Editions, 1975.
Lainovoic, Risto. "La Signification des objets-fétiches dans l'oeuvre de Pierre Loti." *Revue Pierre Loti* 9 (Jan.–Mar. 1988): 17–19.
Leiris, Michel. *L'Afrique fantôme.* Paris: Gallimard, 1981.
———. "Alberto Giacometti." *Documents* 1, no. 4 (1929): 209. Translated by James Clifford in *Sulfer* 15 (1986): 38–40.
Lejeune, Philippe. "Maupassant et le fétichisme." In *Maupassant, miroir de la nouvelle,* edited by Jacques Lecarme and Bruno Vercier. Paris: Presses Universitaires de Vincennes, 1988.
Marivaux. *La Vie de Marianne, ou les aventures de Madame la Comtesse de ***.* Paris: Garnier-Flammarion, 1978.
Maupassant, Guy de. "Bibelots." In *Chroniques.* Vol. 2. Paris: Union Générale d'Editions, 1980.
———. *Fort comme la mort.* Paris: Gallimard, 1983.
Mehlman, Jeffrey. *Legacies of Anti-Semitism in France.* Minneapolis: University of Minnesota Press, 1983.
Meige, Henri. *Charcot artiste.* Paris: Masson, 1925.
Miller, Christopher. *Blank Darkness: Africanist Discourse in French.* Chicago: University of Chicago Press, 1988.
Mirbeau, Octave. *Des artistes.* Paris: Union Générale d'Editions, 1986.

———. *Le Jardin des supplices.* [1899]. Paris: Gallimard, 1988.
———. *Le Journal d'une femme de chambre.* [1900]. Paris: Garnier-Flammarion, 1983.
———. *La Pipe de cidre: Oeuvres inédites.* Paris: Flammarion, 1919.
———. *La 628-E-8.* [1907]. Paris: Union Générale d'Editions, 1977.
Munthe, Axel. *The Story of San Michele.* New York: Carroll and Graf, 1984.
Nivet, Jean-Francois. "Octave Mirbeau entre espoirs et cauchemars." *Les Cahiers Naturalistes* 61 (1987): 218–27.
Paulhan, Jean. *Entretien sur des faits divers.* Paris: Gallimard, 1945.
Porter, Laurence. *The Crisis of French Symbolism.* Ithaca: Cornell University Press, 1990.
Quiguer, Claude. *Femmes et machines de 1900: Lectures d'une obsession moderne style.* Paris: Klincksieck, 1979.
Reik, Theodor. *The Secret Self: Psychoanalytic Experiences in Life and Literature.* New York: Farrar, Straus and Young, 1952.
Reinach, Salomon. *Cultes, mythes, et religions.* Paris: Ernest Leroux, 1912.
Ricatte, Robert. *La Création romanesque chez les Goncourt (1851–1870).* Paris: Armand Colin, 1953.
———. *La Genèse de "La fille Elisa."* Paris: Presses Universitaires de France, 1960.
Robbins, Bruce. *The Servant's Hand.* New York: Columbia University Press, 1986.
Rodenbach, Georges. *Bruges-la-morte.* [1892]. Paris: Flammarion, 1987.
Schneider, Michel. *Blessures de mémoire.* Paris: Gallimard, 1980.
Segalen, Victor. *Les Cliniciens ès lettres.* Montpellier: Fata Morgana, 1980.
Spitz, Ellen Handler. *Art and Psyche: A Study in Psychoanalysis and Aesthetics.* New Haven: Yale University Press, 1985.
Stols, Alexandre Alphonse Marius, ed. *Les Livrets du bibliophile.* Maestricht: A. A. M. Stols, 1926.
Taine, Hippolyte Adolphe. *Histoire de la littérature anglaise.* 2 vols. Paris: Hachette, 1863.
Tanner, Tony. *Adultery in the Novel: Contract and Transgression.* Baltimore: Johns Hopkins University Press, 1980.
Terdiman, Richard. *Discourse/Counter-Discourse: The Theory and Practice of Symbolic Resistance in Nineteenth-Century France.* Ithaca: Cornell University Press, 1989.
Tournier, Michel. "Le Fétichiste." In *Le Coq de bruyère.* Paris: Gallimard, 1978.
Uzanne, Octave. *L'Art et les artifices de la beauté.* Paris: Juven, 1902.
———. *Le Bric-à-brac de l'amour.* Paris: Edouard Rouveyre, 1879.
———. *Caprices d'un bibliophile.* Paris: Edouard Rouveyre, 1878.
———. *Etudes de sociologie féminine: Parisiennes de ce temps.* Paris: Mercure de France, 1910.
———. *L'Eventail.* Paris: A. Quantin, 1882.
———. *Féminies.* Paris: Académie des beaux livres, 1896.
———. *Les Ornements de la femme.* Paris: Librairies Imprimeries Réunies, 1892.

———. *Le Paroissien du célibataire: Observations physiologiques et morales sur l'état du célibat.* Paris: Maison Quantin, 1890.
———. *La Parure excentrique époque Louis XVI: Coiffures de style.* Paris: Edouard Rouveyre, 1895.
———. *Son Altesse la femme.* Paris: Quantin, 1885.
———. *Les Zigzags d'un curieux: Causeries sur l'art des livres et la littérature d'art.* Paris: Maison Quantin, 1888.
Vial, André. *La Genèse d' "Une Vie."* Paris: Belles Lettres, 1954.
Weber, Eugen. *France, Fin de Siècle.* Cambridge: Harvard University Press, 1986.
Williams, Roger L. *The Horror of Life.* Chicago: University of Chicago Press, 1980.

Cultural Theory

Adorno, Theodor. *Aesthetics and Politics.* London: Verso, 1977.
———. "Fetish Character in Music and Regression of Listening." In *The Essential Frankfurt School Reader,* edited by Andrew Arato and Eike Gebhardt. New York: Continuum, 1988.
Agamben, Giorgio. *Stanze.* Translated into French by Yves Hersant. Paris: Christian Bourgois, 1981.
Ariès, Philippe. *L'Homme devant la mort.* Paris: Seuil, 1977.
Barker, Francis. *The Tremulous Private Body: Essays on Subjection.* London: Methuen, 1985.
Barry, Judith. "Dissenting Spaces." In *Damaged Goods: Desire and the Economy of the Object.* New York: New Museum of Contemporary Art, 1986.
Barthes, Roland. "Diderot, Brecht, Eisenstein." In *L'Obvie et l'obtus.* Paris: Seuil, 1982.
———. *Fragments d'un discours amoureux.* Paris: Seuil, 1977.
———. *Image-Music-Text.* Translated and edited by Stephen Heath. Glasgow: Collins, 1977.
———. *Le Plaisir du texte.* Paris: Seuil, 1973.
———. *Roland Barthes: Le Texte et l'image.* Exhibition Catalog. Paris: Pavillon des Arts, 1986.
Baudrillard, Jean. *De la séduction.* Paris: Editions Galilée, Denoël, 1979.
———. *For a Critique of the Political Economy of the Sign.* Translated by Charles Levin. St. Louis, Mo.: Telos Press, 1981.
Benjamin, Walter. *Charles Baudelaire: A Lyric Poet in the Era of High Capitalism.* Translated by Harry Zohn. London: New Left Books, 1973.
———. *Paris: Capitale du XIXe siècle: Le Livre des passages.* Translated into French by Jean Lacoste. Paris: Les Editions du Cerf, 1989.
Berger, John. *About Looking.* New York: Pantheon Books, 1980.
Brosses, Charles de. *Du Culte des dieux fétiches, ou parallèle de l'ancienne religion de l'Egypte avec la religion actuelle de Nigritie.* Paris, 1760.

Browne, Ray B. *Objects of Special Devotion: Fetishism in Popular Culture.* Bowling Green: Popular, 1982.
Calinescu, Matei. *Five Faces of Modernity: Modernism, Avant-garde, Decadence, Kitsch, Postmodernism.* Durham: Duke University Press, 1987.
Certeau, Michel de. *The Practice of Everyday Life.* Translated by Steven Rendell. Berkeley: University of California Press, 1988.
Clark, T. J. *The Painting of Modern Life: Paris in the Art of Manet and His Followers.* New York: Knopf, 1984.
Clifford, James. *The Predicament of Culture.* Cambridge: Harvard University Press, 1988.
Dessoir, Max. *Aesthetics and Theory of Art.* Translated by Stephen A. Emery. Detroit: Wayne State University Press, 1970.
Dulaure, Jacques. *Des cultes qui ont précédé et amené l'idolâtrie ou l'adoration des figures humaines.* Paris: Fournier Frères, 1805.
Eagleton, Terry, Fredric Jameson, and Edward W. Said, eds. *Nationalism, Colonialism, and Literature.* Minneapolis: University of Minnesota Press, 1990.
Eleb-Vidal, Monique. *Architectures de la vie privée: Maisons et mentalités XVII–XIX siècles.* Brussels: Archives d'Architecture Moderne, 1989.
Flandrin, Jean-Louis. *Le Sexe et l'Occident.* Paris: Seuil, 1981.
Flugel, J. C. *The Psychology of Clothes.* London: Hogarth Press, 1930.
Foster, Hal. *Recodings: Art, Spectacle, Cultural Politics.* Port Townsend, Wash.: Bay Press, 1985.
———, ed. *The Anti-Aesthetic: Essays on Postmodern Culture.* Port Townsend, Wash.: Bay Press, 1983.
Freedberg, David. *The Power of Images: Studies in the History and Theory of Response.* Chicago: University of Chicago Press, 1989.
Geras, Norman. "Fetishism in Marx's 'Capital.'" *New Left Review* 65 (Jan.–Feb. 1971): 69–86.
Goux, Jean-Joseph. *Symbolic Economies: After Marx and Freud.* Translated by Jennifer Curtiss Gage. Ithaca: Cornell University Press, 1989.
Grossberg, Lawrence. *Marxism and the Interpretation of Culture.* Urbana: University of Illinois Press, 1988.
Haraway, Donna. *Primate Visions: Gender, Race, and Nature in the World of Modern Science.* New York: Routledge, 1990.
Jameson, Fredric. *Postmodernism, or, The Cultural Logic of Late Capitalism.* Durham: Duke University Press, 1990.
Krauss, Rosalind. *The Originality of the Avant-garde and Other Modernist Myths.* Cambridge: MIT Press, 1985.
Kuhn, Annette. *The Power of the Image: Essays on Representation and Sexuality.* London: Routledge, 1985.
Kuhn, Roland. *Phénoménologie du masque: A travers le test de Rorschach.* Zurich: Desclée de Brouwer, 1957.
Malinowski, Bronislaw. *The Sexual Life of Savages in North-Western Melanesia.* New York: Halcyon House, 1929.
Marx, Karl. *Capital: A Critique of Political Economy.* [1867]. Translated by

Samuel Moore and Edward Aveling, edited by Frederick Engels. New York: Modern Library, 1906.
Mitchell, W. J. Thomas. *Iconology: Image, Text, Ideology*. Chicago: University of Chicago Press, 1986.
Mudimbe, V. Y. *The Invention of Africa: Gnosis, Philosophy, and the Order of Knowledge*. Bloomington: Indiana University Press, 1988.
Perrot, Philippe. *Les Dessus et les dessous de la bourgeoisie*. Paris: Fayard, 1981.
Pietz, William. "The problem of the fetish, I." *Res* 9 (Spring 1985): 5–17.
———. "The problem of the fetish, II." *Res* 13 (Spring 1987): 23–45.
———. "The problem of the fetish, III a: Bosman's guinea and the enlightenment theory of fetishism." *Res* 16 (Autumn 1988): 105–23.
Pomian, Krzysztof. *Collectionneurs, amateurs et curieux: Paris, Venise, XVI–XVIII siècle*. Paris: Gallimard, 1987.
Saisselin, Rémy. *The Bourgeois and the Bibelot*. New Brunswick: Rutgers University Press, 1984.
Squiers, Carol, ed. *The Critical Image: Essays on Contemporary Photography*. Seattle: Bay Press, 1990.
Stewart, Susan. *On Longing: Narratives of the Miniature, the Gigantic, the Souvenir, the Collection*. Baltimore: Johns Hopkins University Press, 1984.
Stocking, George W., Jr., ed. *Observers Observed: Essays on Ethnographic Fieldwork*. Madison: University of Wisconsin Press, 1983.
Taussig, Michael. *The Devil and Commodity Fetishism*. Chapel Hill: University of North Carolina Press, 1980.
Torgovnick, Marianne. *Gone Primitive: Savage Intellects, Modern Lives*. Chicago: University of Chicago Press, 1990.
Tylor, Edward. *Primitive Culture*. 2 vols. New York: Brentano's, 1924.
Ulmer, Gregory. *Applied Grammatology: Post(e)-Pedagogy from Jacques Derrida to Joseph Beuys*. Baltimore: Johns Hopkins University Press, 1985.
Verrier, E. *Du Tatouage en Afrique*. Paris: Joseph André, 1895.
Wallis, Brian, ed. *Art after Modernism: Rethinking Representation*. New York: New Museum of Contemporary Art; and Boston: David R. Godine, 1984.
Zizek, Slavoj. *The Sublime Object of Ideology*. London: Verso, 1989.

Index

abasement, 48, 126, 189, 193
aberration, xi, xiv, 41, 52
abjection, 22, 193
Abraham, Karl, 181n
Adam, Juliette, 68
Adams, Parveen, 128, 129n, 137n
Adler, Laure, 42
Adorno, Theodor, 8
Agamben, Giorgio, 4
Alexander the Great, 38
allegory, x, 62, 77, 87, 114, 152, 163, 175, 219, 231–34
anal eroticism, 52, 102
androcentrism, 212
Annales school, xvi
anomaly, xiv, xv, 18, 24, 35, 153–58, 178, 211–13, 228, 234–37
anorexia, 37, 128
anti-Semitism, 157, 160, 217, 224
aphasia, 151, 220
Apollinaire, Guillaume, 4
Apter, Emily, 212n
Aragon, Louis, 181
art nouveau, 62, 74, 167, 171
Asselineau, Charles, 57n
Aubry, Paul, 157, 158n
Audoux, Marguerite, 246
Auerbach, Erich, 195
Augé, Marc, 240
Aulagnier-Spairani, Piera, 103–4
Avalon, J. 18, 71n

Bachelard, Gaston, 70n

Bacon, Francis, 3
Badinter, Elisabeth, 67, 68n
Ball, Benjamin, 18n, 56–57
Balzac, Honoré de, 25, 40, 57, 64, 194
Barbey d'Aurevilly, 24, 199
Barnes, Julian, 10
Barras, Louis, 18n
Barrault, Jean-Louis, 230, 231n
Barré, M. L., 41n
Barrère, Didier, 57n
Barry, Judith, 8, 68, 76
Barthes, Roland, 70n, 80, 144–46, 183n, 195n, 206n, 214
Bataille, Gorges, 10
Bathory, Elizabeth, Countess, 38
Baudelaire, Charles, 40, 75, 82, 100, 109, 169–70
Baudrillard, Jean, 1–3
Bellemin-Noël, Jean, 29n, 180n
Belot, Adolphe, 23, 29–30, 32n
Benjamin, Walter, 7–8, 44, 45n, 62, 63n, 72–73, 212, 228–29
Bernheim, Hippolyte, 157, 158n
Bernheimer, Charles, 47n, 80
Bertillon, Alphonse, 19, 157
bibelot, 58–61, 244
bibliomania, 57–59
Binet, Alfred, 18–30, 37, 133, 149–50, 183
bisexuality, 127
Blanc, Charles, 74n, 218, 222
Blanchot, Maurice, 232
Blum, Léon, 152, 220–24

Bonaparte, Napoleon, 32, 66
bondage, 143–45, 201
Bonnet, Gérard, 73, 122–23, 183
bordello, xiv, xv, 45–59, 172, 203
Borges, Jorge Luis, 57
born prostitute, 56, 63, 158
Bossard, Abbé Eugène, 126
Boucher, François, 70, 85
Boulanger, Georges Ernest Jean Marie, General, 32
Bourget, Paul, 25, 53n, 60, 82, 190, 200–203
Bowman, Frank, 127–28, 145n
Brachfeld, Georges, 221n
Bredin, Jean-Denis, 221n
bric-a-bracomania, x, 17, 39–41, 58
Briggs, Asa, 58n, 101
Brooks, Peter, xiv
Brunswick, Ruth Mack, 66
Buñuel, Luis, 205–8
Buraud, Georges, 70n
Butler, Judith, 65, 75n, 94n

Cabanès, Augustin, 18, 22, 34, 40
Caran d'Ache, 156
carnival, xiv, 111, 216
Carraud, Zulma, 190–93, 194n, 195, 244
case history, xi, 29–36, 100, 129, 155, 178–83
castration, x, xv, 3, 20–21, 29, 32, 43, 55, 65, 80, 81, 92, 102–5, 109, 114, 121–22, 130, 140, 182–84, 187–90, 208–11, 238
castration anxiety, x, 3, 20, 55, 65, 81, 102–5, 114, 121–22, 183, 190, 208, 211, 238
Cazalis, Henri, xi, 27
Cézanne, Paul, 153, 166n, 167
Charcot, Jean-Martin, 17, 18n, 28–30, 56, 62–63, 100, 124–26, 147–49, 155–57, 163–65, 172–73, 183
Charpentier, Albert, 18, 71n
Chasseguet-Smirgel, Janine, 182
Chatwin, Bruce, 10
Christ neurosis, 133
Cixous, Hélène, 189–90, 209
Claudel, Camille, 149
Claudel, Paul, 57n, 149, 230
Clavreul, Jean, 51
Clément, Catherine, 163, 189–90
Clérambault, Gaëtan Gatian de, 56–57, 83, 106–7, 122–23
Clifford, James, 7–10
clinical realism, xii, 23, 25

collecting, x, 17, 41–44, 53, 57–62, 99–101, 115, 123, 244
collectomania, xv, 54, 57–61, 105
colonialism, 9, 12, 129, 160–61, 226
commodity fetishism, 1, 5, 109, 202
consumerism, x, 8, 62–65
Copjec, Joan, 65, 80n, 81, 106n, 156n
corprophilia, 52, 102–5, 108, 182, 206
Corbin, Alain, 42, 59n
Coste, Didier, 59n
Courbet, Gustave, 33
Cowie, Elizabeth, 113n
Crébillon fils, 41, 86
criminology, x, xi, xvi, 25, 178
crossdressing, 145
curiosity, xii, xiii, xiv, 40, 49, 53, 99, 101, 152, 160, 231–38
cut, x, xii, 6, 10, 21, 31, 33, 42, 108, 111, 139, 145, 147, 183, 206–8, 216, 240

Dali, Salvador, 205
Dallemagne, Jules, 27
Damisch, Hubert, 39, 208n
Daudet, Léon, 27
de Brosses, Charles, 4, 19
de Tarde, Gabriel, 201–3
deconstruction, xvi, 230–32
Degas, Edgar, 85
degenerate, 16, 155, 201, 228
Delacroix, Eugène, 167
Deleuze, Gilles, 139n, 143n, 152N
délire érotique, 125
Delteil, Joseph, 126
dénégation, xii, 107, 111
denial, xii, xiii, 95, 111, 148, 207, 211
Denon, Vivant, 39, 40
Derrida, Jacques, 11n, 62, 70n, 71n, 110–11, 114, 119, 179n, 232–33
Descartes, René, 106
desire, xi, xiii, 1–4, 11, 20, 31, 36, 42–57, 69, 80, 83, 94–95, 100–106, 109, 118–21, 132, 138, 145–50, 159, 175–82, 192, 201–17, 224, 238, 245
Dessoir, Max, 27
detail, xi, 23, 29, 31–36, 50, 56, 66, 183, 197, 210–12, 214, 218–19, 221, 225, 240
detailism, 33, 212, 249
Deutsch, Helen, 66, 137
deviance, xi, 16, 21, 41, 102, 210, 212–13, 235, 242–43
Dickens, Charles, 101

Index • 269

Diderot, Denis, 39, 41, 130, 241
Didi-Huberman, Georges, 148n
disease, xii, 28, 56, 61, 68, 115, 153, 192, 194–95, 220, 237
disgust, 29, 52, 102, 131, 183, 210
dismembered body, x, 33, 183
Doane, Mary Ann, 42n, 65, 70n, 88n, 90–96
domesticity, x, xi, xiv, xv, 39–44, 61–63, 101–5, 125, 160, 177–78, 183, 198–209
Dostoevsky, Fyodor, 36, 237–38
Douglas, Ann, 93n
Dreyfus, Alfred, 127, 150–60, 174, 221, 234–35
Droz, Gustave, 24, 58n
Dudley, G. A., 103
Duhamel, Georges, 57n
Dumas fils, 24

Eleb-Vidal, Monique, 39n
Eliot, T. S., 170
Ellis, Havelock, 18, 34
Enlightenment, 3, 5, 19
eroticism, x, xiii–xvi, 10–11, 20–23, 29, 40–47, 52–56, 61–63, 66, 71–73, 86–87, 95, 100–108, 120–27, 129, 131, 137, 141–46, 152–54, 159, 170–80, 185–90, 210–12, 234, 243
erotomania, 17, 20, 41–43, 54–59, 185, 245
Esquirol, Jean-Etienne-Dominique, 44
essentialism, 26, 67–70, 90–93, 106, 132, 145, 245–48
ethnography, xvi, 7–8
exhibitionism, xv, 15, 30, 102, 128, 185

fait divers, 25, 213–17, 230–37, 242–43
fashion, x, xv, 23, 53, 58–60, 65–83, 87, 98, 109, 127, 184, 229
Fédida, Pierre, 113n
female domestic, xv, 178, 183
femininity, xv, 16, 65–66, 70–98, 104–6, 111, 125, 244, 248–49
feminism, ix, xiii, xv–xvi, 43, 65–66, 72, 96–97, 100–103, 109, 113, 142, 145–46, 189, 208–9, 245
femme fatale, 156, 245
Féré, Charles, 27
Ferenczi, Sandor, 118n
Ferrero, Gina, 157
Festa-McCormick, Diana, 80n
fetishism, fetishes:
  bonnet de nuit, 183

boot, 28–29, 177–85, 208
bra, 10, 11
charm, 4, 53, 68, 70, 77, 89, 205
commodity, 1–12, 43, 55, 62, 87, 109, 198, 202
corset, 201
disavowal, 13, 57, 104, 148, 178, 207, 209
displacement, x, 20, 84, 108, 187, 190, 198, 210, 216, 230, 245
female, ix, 47, 80, 97–106, 110–14, 118–23, 244–45
fetisso, 3, 5, 19
foot, 72, 111, 184
fur, x, 13, 84
gloves, x
hair, x, 99–100, 108–112, 118n, 119–21
handkerchief, 10, 48, 219, 247–48
hat, 32, 73, 145, 205, 217, 219, 239–40
shoe, x, 13, 20–21, 71, 85
value, xiii, 1–12, 43, 62, 87–89, 94
veil, 31–34, 70, 88, 98
velvet, x, 13, 14, 16, 31
fetishistic fiction, xi, 29
Flaccus, Louis, 97
Flaubert, Gustave, 10, 44, 57n, 82, 176, 190, 193, 204–6, 216
Flugel, J. C., 81n, 97
focalization, xiii, 23, 28, 111, 221
forepleasure, xiv
Forster, E. M., 36
Foster, Hal, 9–10
Foucault, Michel, 16, 52, 70n, 178
Fragonard, Jean-Honoré, 70, 85
frame, xiv, 6, 16, 32–34, 47, 75, 99, 130, 170, 185, 204–6, 230
France, Anatole, 57n, 152
Freud, Sigmund, 1, 2, 4, 10, 11–14, 17–23, 30, 34–37, 43–44, 52, 57, 64–66, 70, 80–84, 91–97, 101–8, 111–15, 118, 121–22, 128, 130–32, 147–48, 155, 161, 173–214, 217N, 230, 237–39, 242
Fumaroli, Marc, 130

Gaines, Jane, 90n
Gallé, Emile, 168n, 171
Gallop, Jane, 145n, 187, 190
Gambetta, Léon, 40, 41n
Gardiner, Muriel, 188n
Garnier, Paul, 127n
Gauguin, Paul, 167

270 • Index

Gautier, Théophile, 27, 82
Geffroy, Gustave, 164n
gender, x–xi, xv–xvi, 11, 16, 26, 31, 67, 72–76, 90–92, 98, 101, 107–16, 119, 134, 190, 241, 248
Genet, Jean, 190–91, 238
Giacometti, Alberto, 9, 10n
Gide, André, 17, 146, 171n, 210–43
Gilles de Rais, 38, 40, 126–27
Gilman, Sander, 34
Ginisty, Paul, 58
Giradin, Delphine de, 82
Giverny, 165–67, 170
Goethe, Johann Wolfgang von, 64
Gogol, Nicolas, 36
Goldstein, Jan, 25n, 101n
Goncourt, Edmond and Jules de, 22–23, 43, 60, 65–77, 80–84, 89–90, 93, 98, 124–31, 134–46, 163, 190, 197, 204, 212–16, 244
Goncourt, Edmond de, 28, 45, 54, 60, 61n, 66–67
Gould, Stephen Jay, 19n
Gourmont, Remy de, 25–26, 28, 82, 171, 235
Graf, Max, 37
Grand-Carteret, John, 18n
Grellet, Isabelle, 190n
Grigg, Kenneth, 187n
Grosz, Elizabeth, 104–5
grotesque realism, xv, 33
Grunberger, Bela, 97
Grunfeld, Frederic, 167
Gyp, 156, 244

Hall, Radclyffe, 36
Harris, Ruth, 25n
Hauptmann, Gérard, 27
Heath, Stephen, 91n, 92n
Hegel, G. W. F., 5
Heidegger, Martin, 5
Heine, Maurice, 15, 18
Hennique, Léon, 37
Herbart, Pierre, 229n
heredito-degenerescence, 19, 27
hermeneutic, 18, 113, 230–31
heterosexuality, 94, 217
Hirschfeld, Magnus, 20n, 35, 131n, 132
homophobia, xii, 211–12, 243
homosexuality, 15, 75, 102, 105, 127–28, 210–12, 228–29
Horney, Karen, 66
Hoschedé, Alice, 170
Huchet, Jean-Charles, 107n

Huidobro, Vincente, 127n
Huysmans, Joris-Karl, 43–45, 54–55, 57, 126–28, 164–65, 170–71
hysteria, xii, xv, 27–29, 56, 68, 100, 124–26, 147–52, 162–65, 173–75, 188, 216, 244–46

idealization, 21–24, 32–35, 68, 86, 126–33, 140, 179, 185, 197, 203
Irigaray, Luce, 65, 95–98, 105n, 121, 135, 142–46, 155, 209n
Jack the Ripper, 38
Jacob, P. L., 34, 40
James, Henry, 7, 57
Jardine, Alice, 96n
Jaurès, Jean, 156
Jones, Ernest, 91
jouissance, 23, 48, 106, 122–25, 130, 141, 162, 206
Joyes, Claire, 166n

Kafka, Franz, 230–31
Kamuf, Peggy, 62n
Kant, Immanuel, 5, 10, 33, 132
Keitel, Evelyne, 37–38
Kelly, Mary, 105, 113n, 114–16, 122–23
Kendrick, Walter, 41n
kitsch, 32, 117, 202, 240
Klein, Melanie, 91
Kleist, Heinrich von, 37, 199
Kofman, Sarah, 109–10, 113–14, 119, 123
Kracauer, Siegfried, 63, 64
Krafft-Ebing, Richard von, 17, 19, 27, 30, 34, 41, 50, 102n, 180n, 181, 183, 206, 210–21
Kraus, Karl, 28, 29n
Krauss, Rosalind, 152n
Kristeva, Julia, 138n
Kruse, Caroline, 190n
Kuhn, Roland, 70n

Lacan, Jacques, 33–34, 56, 70n, 93–96, 103–6, 140–42, 148–49, 159, 163, 211, 238–39
lack, xii–xiii, 13, 50, 56–57, 93–98, 122, 137, 149, 167, 183, 207–10, 227, 248–49
Lacordaire, J. B. H., 127–28
Lafayette, Madame de, 146
Laforgue, René 148, 207
Lamartine, Alphonse de, 115, 190, 193, 195, 197–98, 201n
Lammenais, Félicité de, 127

Lampl-de-Groot, Jeanne, 66
Lanteri Laura, Georges, 30n
Laplanche, Jean, 119n
Larbaud, Valéry, 57n
Latour de Lorde, André, 19n
Laurens, Paul, 223
Laurent, Méry, 170
Laurent, Paul, 17n, 18n, 19n, 27
Leiris, Michel, 2n, 4n, 10
Lejeune, Philippe, 100n, 108n
Leonardo da Vinci, 35, 36
lesbianism, 104–5, 145
Lévy-Bruhl, Lucien, 7
libertinage, 16, 18, 41, 66, 68, 87
Littré, Emile, 25, 67
Lombroso, Cesare, 19, 37, 56, 157–58
Lorrain, Jean, 37
Loti, Pierre, 6–7, 27
love, xi–xii, 10, 20–22, 24–27, 40–41, 52, 56, 60, 67, 70, 75, 78, 87, 94–99, 115–16, 122, 131, 141–42, 147, 159, 165–66, 171–74, 183–87, 192–93, 210–11, 221, 227, 245
Loyola, Ignatius, 127
Lucas, Prosper, 26

Macé, Gustave, 16n
Maeterlinck, Maurice, 109, 171n
Magnan, Valentin, 17, 30, 56
maid, 60, 122, 176–209, 221, 244–45
Mallarmé, Stéphane, 4, 57n, 82, 153, 170–71, 226, 239
Manet, Edouard, 46, 85, 164
mania, 17, 40–44, 58, 60, 83, 116, 171
Mannoni, Octave, 14, 113n
Maire Antoinette 38, 74, 89n
Maritain, Jacques, 230
marivaudage, 70
Marivaux, Pierre, 69–71, 86, 197
Martin du Gard, Roger, 152
Martin-Fugier, Anne, xiv, 58n, 190n
Marx, Karl, 1–4, 10, 12n, 19, 43
masculinity, 16, 75–78, 89–96, 104–5, 245–49
mask, 9, 26, 70–75, 90–95, 111, 167
masochism, xv, 15–18, 21–22, 30, 47, 93, 102, 127–29, 132–36, 143–46, 201, 237
masquerade, ix, 3, 14, 55, 65–66, 70–71, 75, 80–83, 90–98
master, xv, 3–4, 9, 13, 25, 43–45, 60–64, 91, 110, 135, 145, 160–62, 176–79, 181, 187
maternal phallus, 2, 13

Maupassant, Guy de, 23–29, 37, 58, 85, 99–110, 111n, 113–23, 190, 196–99, 212, 216, 244
Maza, Sarah, 77n
McGrath, William, 187n
Mehlman, Jeffrey, 217, 224
Meige, Henri, 62, 63n, 99, 115, 244
melancholia, 88
Mercier, Sebastien, 40
Metz, Christian, 206
Michelet, Jules, 125
Miller, Nancy K., 57n
mimesis, xi, 5, 14, 73, 92, 95, 130, 203, 239
Mirbeau, Octave, 29, 33–34, 122–26, 147–82, 193–212, 244–49
Miró, Joan, 205
misogyny, 167, 210–12, 246
Mitchell, William J., 3
Modleski, Tania, 91n
Mohammed, 38, 233, 237
Moi, Toril, 209n
Molière (Jean-Baptiste Poquelin), 28, 195
Moll, A., 18
Monet, Claude, 147, 153, 164–71
Montesquiou, Robert de, 59
Montrelay, Michèle, 65, 95–96
Moreau de Tours, Paul, 29n, 56n
Morel, Bénédict-Augustin, 26
mourning, 61, 99–100, 114, 117, 122, 170
Mudimbe, V. Y., 6–7
Müller, Max, 20
Mulvey, Laura, 208–9
Munby, A. N., 196
Munthe, Axel, 41
museum, x, xiv, 7, 9, 35, 39, 53, 60–63, 114–16, 155
mysticism, 25, 63, 125, 135–37, 141–45, 150–52, 246

narcissism, 10, 15, 67, 78–83, 97, 104–5, 114–20, 244
naturalism, ix, xv, 25–28, 36, 68, 153, 157, 212–16, 224, 244, 248–49
necrophilia, 15, 112–18
negation, 208, 212
Nietzsche, Friedrich, 70, 88n, 237
Nodier, Charles, 44, 57n, 58n
Nordau, Max, 27
nosological realism, 25, 29, 34
Nye, Robert, 25n

object fixation, 16, 22

oculocentrism, xii–xiv, 55, 248
ornament, 64–67, 74–78, 85–89, 98, 130
Otway, Thomas, 47, 48n

Panizza, Oskar, 34, 35n
Papin sisters, 238–39
partial object, x, 246
Pascal, Blaise, 27, 193, 237
Pater, Walter, 145, 223
pathography, xi–xii, xv, 15, 34–40, 124–29, 135, 211
pathology, xi, 15, 24–25, 102, 152, 158, 164, 178, 188
Paulhan, Jean, 146n, 243
Péguy, Charles, 152
Peignot, Colette, 146n
perversion, ix, xiv–xv, 5, 10, 12, 15–16, 19–24, 35, 38–43, 51–52, 102–7, 122–28, 152, 168, 171, 178–84, 237, 244–49
pessimism, 25–26
physiognomy, 35, 78, 154–57, 195
Pietz, William, 5, 110n
Pilon, Edouard, 166n
Pissarro, Camille, 166n, 167
pleasure, 16, 21–22, 31, 42, 46, 50, 78, 83, 87–91, 115, 127–29, 141–46, 152–54, 172–75, 181, 209, 233
Poe, Edgar Allan, 44–45, 169–70, 173
Pollock, Griselda, 45n
Pomian, Krzysztof, 39n
Pontalis, J. B., 119n
pornography, 41, 59, 110–14, 152–54, 160, 193, 248
positivism, 25, 227
primitivism, 4–9, 16, 25–28, 129, 158–60, 181
prosthesis, 55, 65, 71, 95, 111, 129, 140, 213
prostitute, xvi, 43, 45, 56–63, 143, 158, 203, 246–48
prostitution, 30–31, 39–43, 46–49, 55–59, 73, 201
Proust, Marcel, 26, 43, 48, 49n, 51n, 52–54, 64, 78, 79n, 80, 151–52, 170–71, 190, 202n, 203, 217
psychoanalysis, ix–xii, xv–xvi, 3, 16, 30, 34–38, 43–44, 51, 62–66, 80, 90–91, 97, 102–3, 110–13, 122–23, 131, 148, 186, 190, 231, 238, 242
psychopathology, 24, 68, 178, 206, 226, 237

race, 26, 258, 191
Rachilde (Marguerite Valette), 26, 244
racism, 6–7, 25, 91, 156–60
Rank, Otto, 21, 37, 81
Réage, Pauline (Dominique Aubry), 143, 144n, 146
realism, ix–xv, 8, 23–34, 50, 67, 82–85, 155, 205–6, 212–16, 220–31, 240, 244
Redelsperger, R., 90n
Regnault, Alice, 246–48
reification, 97, 104, 119
Reik, Theodor, 37
Reinach, Salomon, 127n
representation, xiii, 4, 7, 24, 43, 63, 80, 87, 92–93, 101–10, 114, 119, 123, 147, 159, 163, 195–96, 209, 212, 216, 239
Rétif de la Bretonne, 18, 71
Ribot, Théodule, 26, 27
Richard, Jean-Pierre, 163n
Rilke, Rainer Maria, 36
Riviere, Joan, 65–66, 90–96
Robbins, Bruce, 196
Rodenbach, Georges, 24, 111, 112n
Rodin, Auguste, 153, 166n, 167
Roger, Alain, 185n
Roger, Philippe, 225n
Rolland, Romain, 152
Rose, Jacqueline, 70n, 106
Rose, Louis, 37n, 80n
Rosolato, Guy, 104n
Roudinesco, Elisabeth, 19n, 25n, 100n, 106n, 214n
Rousseau, Jean-Jacques, 18, 20–22, 69, 71n, 198, 237
Ryckère, Raymond de, 178
Rysselberghe, Madame Théo van, 229

Sacher-Masoch, Leopold, 143, 152
Sade, Donatien Alphonse François, 15, 18, 154, 175
Sadger, Isador, 37
sadism, xv, 17, 30, 86, 111, 125–28, 136, 149, 153–56, 162, 187, 201, 208–9, 225, 248
sadomasochism, 145
Saint-Amand, Pierre, 76n, 89n
sartorial superego, xv, 65, 81, 89, 97
Sartre, Jean-Paul, 149, 222
scapegoating, 158–60
schaulust, 148, 172–75, 245–48
Schnitzler, Arthur, 36

Schopenhauer, Arthur, 25–27
Schor, Naomi, 80, 101–9, 214n
scopic, the, xiii–xv, 10, 32–33, 45, 106, 140, 149, 152, 160, 168, 195, 209, 211, 245–46
scopophilia, ix, xiii, 52, 147, 172–75, 245, 248
scotomization, xii–xiii, 31–32, 149–50, 162, 165, 174, 178, 207–8, 217
secret, 1, 2, 31, 34, 36, 40–43, 47–54, 61, 67, 83, 88, 100, 120, 190, 196, 214, 220, 238, 249
Segalen, Victor, xi, 4, 27
sentimentality, xvi, 67, 99–101, 115, 119, 195–97
servant, xv, 111–12, 176–78, 183–98, 200–4, 208, 236
Séverine, 156, 244
sexism, 107, 110
sexology, 18, 25, 26, 42, 47, 129, 244
sexual difference, 16, 26, 78, 97–98, 110, 140, 245
sexual ethnography, 25
Shaw, Bernard, 126
Showalter, Elaine, 245n
Sibony, Daniel, 249
Sieburth, Richard, 158n
Silverman, Debora, 62, 74, 75n
Silverman, Kaja, 79n, 139–40
Simmel, Georg, 88–89, 98
Simon, John, 205n
simulacrum, 4, 9, 13, 14, 100, 104, 120, 162, 204
spectacle, xiv, 31, 43–45, 53, 76, 87, 95–96, 136, 149, 158–60, 162, 172, 182, 223, 233, 235, 246
specularity, ix, 3, 13–14, 48, 106, 120–21, 140, 152, 163, 248
speculum, 121, 143, 155
Spencer, Herbert, 26
Spivak, Gayatri Chakravorty, 70n, 71n, 88n
splitting, 29, 111, 121, 130–31, 178
Stallybrass, Peter, 189n
Stekel, Wilhelm, 37, 105, 106n, 116–17, 132–34
Stendhal (Henri Beyle), 20, 24
stereoscopy, xiv, 47, 64
Stifter, Adalbert, 101
stigma, xv, 17, 25, 28, 157–58, 171, 210–13, 220, 228–34, 246

subjection, 144, 208
substitution, x, 11, 20–22
Süsskind, Patrick, 10
Swan, Jim, 187n
symbolism, ix–x, 4, 27, 32, 64, 72, 88, 153–54, 165–70, 185, 213, 220
synecdoche, 21, 24, 29, 31–33, 71

tabloid, 38, 230–35
Taine, Hippolyte, 7, 27, 47, 226
Tarde, Gabriel de, 201n
tattoos, xi, 157–58, 213, 220
Taxil, Léo, 45–46, 125, 126n
taxonomy, 9, 35, 155
Torok, Maria, 101n, 118n, 187n
Tourette, Gilles de la, 28
Tournier, Michel, 10–12, 127n, 230n
Tylor, Edward, 4, 127, 230

Uzanne, Octave, 18n, 46, 59–60, 65–67, 81–90, 244

Valéry, Paul, 4
Van Gogh, Vincent, 167
veiling, 70, 65, 70n, 83, 88–90, 93, 106, 212
Vial, André, 32, 37n
Vigny, Alfred de, 106
voice, xv–xvii, 27, 46, 50, 58, 69, 84, 100, 130–32, 138–46, 174, 195–97, 244, 247
Voltaire, (François-Marie Arouet), 4
voyeur, xiii–xv, 7, 31, 42–52, 59, 144–47

Watteau, Antoine, 70, 85
Weininger, Otto, 27
West, Paul, 10
White, Allon, 189n
Whitman, Walt, 222, 233
Wilde, Oscar, 223, 228
Williams, Roger, 25n
Wolff, Albert, 164
Wundt, Wilhelm, 150

Zavitzianos, George, 103
Zola, Emile, 23, 26–28, 40–47, 48n, 64, 156, 171, 190, 196, 210–22, 226–28, 244
Zweig, Stefan, 36